PR
**Strategy and
Application**

W. TIMOTHY COOMBS AND SHERRY J. HOLLADAY

PR
Strategy and Application
MANAGING INFLUENCE

WILEY-BLACKWELL

A John Wiley & Sons, Ltd., Publication

This edition first published 2010
© 2010 W. Timothy Coombs and Sherry J. Holladay

Blackwell Publishing was acquired by John Wiley & Sons in February 2007. Blackwell's publishing program has been merged with Wiley's global Scientific, Technical, and Medical business to form Wiley-Blackwell.

Registered Office
John Wiley & Sons Ltd, The Atrium, Southern Gate, Chichester, West Sussex, PO19 8SQ, United Kingdom

Editorial Offices
350 Main Street, Malden, MA 02148–5020, USA
9600 Garsington Road, Oxford, OX4 2DQ, UK
The Atrium, Southern Gate, Chichester, West Sussex, PO19 8SQ, UK

For details of our global editorial offices, for customer services, and for information about how to apply for permission to reuse the copyright material in this book please see our website at www.wiley.com/wiley-blackwell.

The right of W. Timothy Coombs and Sherry J. Holladay to be identified as the authors of this work has been asserted in accordance with the Copyright, Designs and Patents Act 1988.

Library of Congress Cataloging-in-Publication Data

Coombs, W. Timothy.
  PR strategy and application : managing influence / W. Timothy Coombs and Sherry J. Holladay.
    p. cm.
  Includes bibliographical references and index.
  ISBN 978-1-4051-4408-7 (pbk. : alk. paper) 1. Public relations. I. Holladay, Sherry J. II. Title. III. Title: Public relations strategy and application.
  HD59.C6213 2009
  659.2—dc22

                                                              2009021974

A catalogue record for this book is available from the British Library.

Set in 10/12.5pt Century by SPi Publisher Services, Pondicherry, India
Printed in Singapore

01   2010

Contents

Preface

For a very long time this book was known simply as "book two." We knew this book should expand on ideas presented in our book *It's Not Just PR: Public Relations in Society* (2007). And we knew "book two" would need to incorporate some of the more standard functions of public relations such as media relations, online communication, and issues management. But we also wanted to move beyond those traditional treatments of public relations and continue to challenge readers' thinking about public relations by exploring functions such as social marketing, reputation management, and crisis communication. We also were committed to emphasizing critiques of the practice and introducing the concept of public relations literacy. We had an exciting vision for the new book, but no name.

Through brainstorming with the patient staff at Wiley-Blackwell, we arrived at the title *PR Strategy and Application: Managing Influence*. The title captures three key elements in this book: a strategic focus, application of theories and principles, and managing influence. Because strategy is what makes public relations effective, it was a logical fit with our title. Public relations should be deliberate and goal-oriented. We should not think of public relations without the word strategy. Public relations also is an applied field. Public relations theories and principles are designed with an eye toward how they can be used in practice. Strategy and application are inextricably linked. Strategies are developed by applying theories and principles to public relations actions. Chapters 6 through 14 discuss various theories and principles and how they can be applied to the strategic practice of public relations.

That leaves managing influence. We are indebted to Elizabeth Swayze for this defining element of the title. This book reflects our belief that influence underlies all strategic efforts in public relations. Influence is the meta-goal shared by all public relations actions. Public relations is often equated with informing people or sharing information. However, because we believe public relations involves the strategic use of information, it is much more than simply informing people. What information people are told – or not told – shapes their interpretations of situations. Public relations is about influence, attempts to alter how people think and ultimately how they act. Although some public relations actions are more explicit in their use of influence than others, all involve strategic efforts to shape behaviors in some way. Realistically, it is influence management that defines and shapes the public relations practice.

With the discussion of influence comes the concern with self-interests. As much as public relations seeks to take constituents into account, we must be aware there is a self-interest motive present as well. Yes, insurance companies promote safe teen driving initiatives and legislation. Fewer people are killed or injured in accidents (constituent interest) and insurance companies save money (self-interest). Claiming self-interest in public relations messages is not a condemnation of the field or of organizations engaged in the practice. Rather, we must realize self-interest is inherent in the public relations process. The problems associated with public relations, especially ethical question marks, occur when self-interests are hidden. Public relations' ethics is improved when we acknowledge self-interests and make them explicit. This is an essential element of transparency, a topic addressed in chapter 3.

Concerns over self-interests and influence give rise to the notion of public relations literacy. Public relations literacy emphasizes people critically evaluating the public relations messages they consume. Chapters 1 and 15 present a further discussion of what we mean by public relations literacy. People may not be cognizant of the influence and self-interests embedded in public relations actions. In some cases people may not even realize the messages are public relations. Critics of public relations often mention a fear of how stealthy public relations can be. Watchdog groups, such as PR Watch, aim to expose self-interests and influence, although they are frequently overzealous and hypercritical. Though we may not appreciate their methods and conclusions, we can applaud their concern with transparency. Consumers of public relations need to know a message is public relations and the source attached to a message if they are to properly evaluate that message. Ethical communication involves clearly identifying sources and their connection to messages. Moreover, public relations literacy helps people to identify public relations actions and provides some rudimentary tools for evaluating those efforts.

When Microsoft launched Vista, the company sent expensive new laptops to influential bloggers. The idea was that the bloggers could test these Vista-loaded computers and report their experience to others. Microsoft was hoping to seed the Internet with positive word-of-mouth. Most of the bloggers failed to disclose the gift from Microsoft. Other bloggers were critical of this lack of transparency and the failure to disclose this possible biasing factor. Might not an expensive laptop sway your views of Vista? The concern about transparency and acknowledging both influence and self-interest are recurring themes in this book. The repetition of this idea is strategic because we must understand how transparency, or lack thereof, impacts the field of public relations and the ability of consumers to properly assess public relations actions. While chapters 5 through 14 discuss how various disciplines of public relations are practices, they also provide critiques of the field and a foundation for the critical evaluation of public relations efforts. In other words, the chapters describe both the practice of public relations and ideas that are useful for developing public relations literacy.

When most people think of public relations they think of how corporations use public relations to further their economic interests. Consistent with our first book, this book seeks to counter that corporate-centric bias by discussing how the roots of public relations can be traced to early activists' efforts. We explore how public relations is being practiced today by activist groups seeking to counter the power of big corporations and improve the human condition by giving voice to those whose concerns have been marginalized.

We see public relations as valuable to society. It helps to knit the social fabric that binds us all together. However, we would be remiss to overlook the problems public relations can create. The writing reflects the critical evaluation of public relations we feel all consumers should bring to the field. Proper public relations can survive and thrive in a public relations literate society while abuses are unmasked and punished. We are proud of the public relations field, but all fields benefit from careful self-reflection on what it is doing. Blindness to faults stunts a field's development. In the end, we hope people will find the book useful and insightful whether they are involved in the practice or the consumption of public relations. Bear in mind that even public relations practitioners are consumers of the public relations actions executed by others.

Acknowledgments

We would like to thank the people at Wiley-Blackwell for all their support for this book and its forerunner, *It's Not Just PR: Public Relations in Society*. We are grateful to Elizabeth Swayze, our editor for the project, for her enthusiasm and all the work from Margot Morse. Jayne Fargnoli oversaw the project while Elizabeth was on leave and Jana Pollack had responsibility for the blurb, an important but tricky piece of writing. We also thank those involved in the production process, including Dave Nash for his relentless efforts in securing permissions and images, along with Jack Messenger who took the project through copy-editing and proofing. Finally, we would like to thank the reviewers for their time, effort, and useful comments that were invaluable to the final product.

Upton Sinclair.

1

Introduction and Overview

Let us consider a day in the life of a person named Pat. In the morning, Pat reads the nutritional information on her cereal box because she is concerned about eating too much salt. When Pat gets into her car, she buckles her seatbelt. For lunch, Pat chooses a place to eat that does not have trans fats in their food because she read a story online that said how bad trans fats were for your heart. For dinner, Pat and her friends go to a new restaurant she read about in the paper last week. After dinner, Pat stops by a jewelry store to look for a gift. Pat selects a jewelry store that supports "No Dirty Gold," an effort to reduce pollution and other harmful effects from gold mining.

As an average person, Pat may be unaware of how much public relations may have shaped her actions that day. The nutritional label on the cereal box was a result of years of issues management by corporations and activist groups. For decades, public relations has been part of the social marketing efforts to promote seat belt usage. The concern about trans fats and health are a result of various activists creating awareness of the problem and pressuring companies to change their use of trans fats in foods. The news story about the restaurant was a result of media relations efforts by the restaurant's public relations staff. Pat learned about "No Dirty Gold" when directed to their website that decried the dangers of gold mining by an advertisement or link on another website.

Public relations does seek to persuade people. It can influence what you buy, how you use a product, and what you do to improve your health. Yet the average person may have no real idea of how omnipresent public relations is in their lives. In fact, most people do not know what public relations really is. Critics warn us that the hidden public relations industry is a danger and that stealth is a strategic choice. Public relations is unseen largely because people choose not to see it. News outlets do not announce a story was the result of a news release or pitch letter. However, if you look closely at the news you can determine which stories are likely to have public relations origins. Do some research and you will quickly learn about nutrition labels and the efforts to shape their content, the groups pushing for bans on trans fats and companies changing their products, and what efforts are underway to promote "No Dirty Gold" and who is doing the promoting.

Public relations is just below the surface in our daily lives. We can realize its existence and potential influence on our lives if we critically examine the messages generated by public relations. We want readers to think about their consumption of public relations as they learn how to construct those messages. Later in this chapter we discuss the notion of *public relations literacy*, the application of critical thinking skills to the examination of public relations techniques and the effects of those techniques on individuals and society. Public relations should be able to survive thoughtful interrogation. Those who would abuse and misuse public relations should fear public relations literacy. The tricks of these charlatans could and should be exposed. We think it is good for people to critically examine public relations messages and to understand how public relations might be shaping their lives and society. This opening example highlights a relationship between persuasion and public relations.

Periodically in the public relations literature there are defenses of the use of persuasion. For those of us from a communication studies background, such defenses appear to be an unusual and needless exercise. Of course a communication-based activity such as public relations would involve persuasion. Most, if not all, communication has a persuasive dimension. However, some in the field of public relations try to divorce the field from persuasion and claim public relations is objective and neutral. They contend public relations, like the news media, just presents the facts to people. They see public relations as a mechanism for carrying information from organizations to publics.

The objectivity of the news media has always been a myth. Journalists select what to report and how to report it. These selections involve subjectivity. The same holds true for public relations. Trying to argue there is no persuasion in public relations denies the fact that public relations does promote self-interests. That is not inherently a bad thing. Moreover, public relations as a field looks naive and even deceptive to people outside the field when it claims to be objective and simply a conduit for the facts. In this book we embrace rather than deny the self-interest that motivates public relations and believe persuasion lies at the core of public relations. Public relations is about influencing behaviors, knowledge, and attitudes. The practice must accept the implications that accompany the use of influence including issues of power and its abuse. This chapter begins by explaining our definition and conceptualization of public relations, considers how public relations' own history has mis-served it, and ends with an outline of the book.

The Quest to Define Public Relations

In *It's Not Just PR: Public Relations in Society*, we defined public relations as "the management of mutually influential relationships within a web of stakeholder and organizational relationships" (Coombs & Holladay, 2007b, p. 26). We choose the term *stakeholder* because it captures the idea that entities have some connection to one another for some reason. They are interdependent. These connections are why actors are enmeshed in a web of relationships. In addition, stakeholder theory does denote some consideration of power. Stakeholders are people, groups, organizations, or systems that can affect or can be affected by an organization. Managers look beyond shareholders and financial stakes to a broader range of stakes or connections to an organization. Stakeholder theory, rooted in the work of R. Edward Freeman (1984), seeks to identify and to understand the various stakeholders in an organization. By better understanding stakeholders, managers can decide who deserves their attention and time. Managers then work with the more important stakeholders with a hope of advancing organizational interests (Mitchell, Agle, & Wood, 1997). Stakeholders can shape organizational practices through their giving or retracting of stakes (support). If it is important for stakeholders to grant an organization a license to operate, they do have some power. However, critical scholars have expressed some concerns over using the term stakeholder.

The concern is that the term stakeholder has been co-opted by corporations and reflects the continuing corporate-centric bias in public relations. A corporate-centric view of public relations emphasizes how corporations use public relations to achieve economic success. True, Freeman's (1984) work does place the organization at the center of his explanation of stakeholders. Originally, stakeholders were conceptualized as groups whose support was essential to the survival of the organization. Later, stakeholders were seen as those who were affected by or could affect the organization. Ultimately, the term stakeholder today can legitimately be viewed as a way that organizations, especially corporations, evaluate groups jockeying for their attention. There is compelling evidence to support the critical claim that "stakeholder" is tainted by its corporate use and an emphasis on the centrality of the organization.

Alternatively, some have argued for the use of the term *public*. However, the corporate-centric taint also plagues "public." A public forms "when stakeholders recognize one or more of the consequences as a problem and organize to do something about it or them" (Grunig & Repper, 1992, p. 124). The consequences center on the connection between the organization and stakeholders. Hence, publics form in reaction to organizational actions. Publics develop when they realize they share a concern over an organization's action and join forces to address that "issue." Publics are aware they are connected to one another and choose to take action. Stakeholders may realize others share their stake but are not an active entity. "Publics ... organize around issues and seek out organizations that create those issues" (Grunig & Repper, 1992, p. 128).

Grunig's (1989a, 1989c) situational theory of publics tells public relations practitioners to engage those publics most likely to communicate on an issue. The situational theory of publics uses surveys to determine which people are aware of a problem and interested in doing something about it. The surveys assess public interest by determining the extent to which people perceive a problem (problem recognition), the amount of concern they have for the problem (level of involvement), and extent to which they perceive factors limiting their ability to address the problem (constraint recognition) (Grunig, 1989a). Situational theory makes value judgments and is used to prioritize publics – who will receive an organization's attentions. Clearly, the organization is still at the center of how public relations theorists have conceptualized "public." The terms stakeholder and public both use organizations as a reference point in their conceptualizations. Hence, we see no reason to favor the use of the term public over stakeholder in an effort to be more neutral in our definition.

Perhaps the term *constituencies* is a better choice than stakeholders and organizations. Constituencies can be defined as groups of people in a similar situation. By this definition stakeholders are constituencies and organizations are constituencies. Stakeholders share a stake while people in organizations share an affiliation with that organization. We are not saying that organizations have not used the term constituencies and that the term is perfectly neutral. However, the conceptualization of constituencies was not developed using organizations as a reference point. We could revise our definition: *public relations is the management of mutually influential relationships within a web of constituency relationships.*

Definitions are a point of view. They tell people what is important and, by implication, what is unimportant. The ideas that are important for us are mutual influence, web of relationships, and management. Let's start with mutual influence. Contrary to some views, we feel public relations is far from a neutral activity. As Moloney (2005) rightly notes, people engage in public relations largely from self-interest and self-advantage. Even those entities engaged in social marketing – the application of traditional marketing principles to solving societal problems and benefiting the recipients of the message (Weinreich, n.d.) – have an interest that drives their public relations effort. We feel public relations is about advocacy and power. Too often, those who write about public relations use the guise of informational efforts to hide intent but should acknowledge they are engaged in persuasion. Moreover, we do not pretend that the influence is equal among constituents. Influence is a type of power when one constituency can alter the behavior of another. Rarely do two parties in a relationship have equal influence/power. In most instances, corporations and government agencies are the constituencies with the most power in the web of relationships. Still, any constituency has some power when it can remove itself from the web of relationships. Moloney (2005) considers public relations a "struggle for communicative advantage" (p. 553) and we concur. Constituencies use public relations to compete with one another in efforts to influence the other players in the web of relationships.

Frequently, public relations textbooks treat each relationship between two constituencies in isolation from the others. Generally, the textbooks are

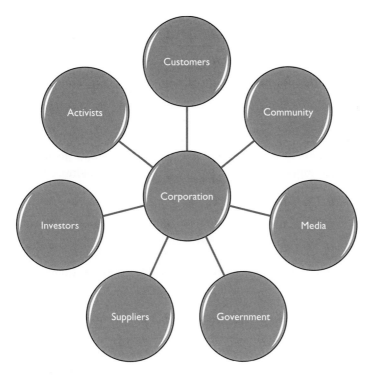

Figure 1.1   Corporate-centric view of public relations

corporate-centric, as illustrated in figure 1.1. So students learn about media relations or community relations as distinct units and processes. This creates the impression that the relationships are independent rather than interdependent. When constituencies take action (communicate with others), it has the potential to affect more than one relationship. Therefore, it is important to remember the web of relationships.

Another important feature of the web of relationships is the connection to social capital. *Social capital* is "The aggregate of the actual or potential resources which are linked to possession of a durable network of more or less institutionalized relationships of mutual acquaintance or recognition" (Bourdieu, 1985, p. 248). Constituencies want to manage the web of relationships because of the social capital generated by that web. Social capital makes it easier for constituencies to achieve their goals. This can include advocacy efforts to improve the health of a community, reduce greenhouse gases, or reduce impediments to corporate profitability.

Modern public relations has attempted to re-energize the term *relationship*. This reclamation includes an emphasis on building strong relationships with constituencies and ways to measure the strength of those relationships. The relationship-oriented public relations research reflects the corporate-centric view. Organizations are said to derive benefits from close relationships with constituencies. The rationale for the relationships clearly is grounded in the benefits the constituents provide the organization. Customers are a prime illustration.

Corporations want customers that have close ties to the corporation and perhaps even become advocates or evangelists for the brand.

Consider an alternative view based on Simon's Empty World Hypothesis. The Empty World Hypothesis holds that most things are weakly connected to one another, what Weick (1979) terms *loose coupling*. People or entities often benefit more from their weak ties than from their strong ties. The typical example is that weak ties are the most common route to finding employment. Weak ties extend a person or entity's reach and supply them with unique information they are unlikely to find in their close relationships. Research across a variety of fields supports the value of weak connections/loose coupling/weak relationships.

More recently, activists have begun to recognize the value of weak connections/relationships. Instead of creating large organizations that have a strong central structure, some experts argue that activists should be netcentric. *Netcentric activists* are collections of weakly linked activist groups that form a loosely connected coalition (Kearns, n.d.). When action is needed, the activist groups are mobilized through tighter/stronger links, but then return to their loosely connected structure once the action is completed. Weak links create communication channels that are used to reach and to mobilize the various activist groups and form a tightly connected coalition for short periods of time. Moreover, the weak ties help to build social capital that can be spent on activist efforts.

As figure 1.2 illustrates, constituencies can be heavily interconnected. Are all these links regularly active? Probably not. Figure 1.2 shows the potential reach of a relationship web, not the strength of the relationships. The web of relationships is rather fluid. The links that are active and relationships that are close will vary over time and situations. In addition, no one constituency is monolithic. Each constituency can be subdivided into smaller units. For instance, figure 1.2 illustrates the links that might be active when a community group seeks to block the building of a facility it deems harmful to the community and potential subgroups that may emerge within the constituencies. Coalitions shift in the relational web as different constituencies and subgroups form temporary strong ties and may even conflict with other constituencies in the web.

Perhaps corporations should take a lesson from the activists. It could be unrealistic to expect most or even a larger percentage of a corporation's constituencies to have close relationships with an organization. Weak links/relationships may be sufficient. Weick's (1979) idea of partial inclusion is helpful here. *Partial inclusion* holds that people have connections and affiliations with a wide range of groups, not just one. As a result, people have divided loyalties. People are invested in a variety of constituencies, not just one – they are partially included in the various constituencies. It forces people to choose between the conflicting groups. So which constituency is favored when issues are contested? A person typically selects the group in which she or he has invested the most or rejects those in which they have minimal investments. The investment is a type of social capital. However, investment is not a perfect predictor of which constituency

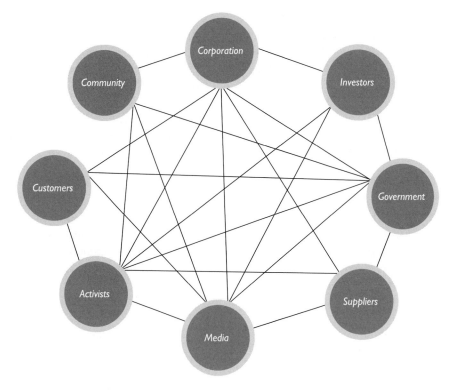

Figure 1.2 Interconnectedness of constituents

a person will select when there are conflicts. If the investments in conflicting constituencies are small, the outcome is difficult to predict.

The weak ties provide avenues for staying connected and building social capital, but do not have to be overused. The role of public relations may be to build and maintain links, not to obsess over the relationship quality. Those links need to be two-way. All constituents need to be open and responsive to communication from others in the relationship web. Responsiveness could be the hallmark of an effective link. I do not need to talk with you all the time, but I do need to know that when I contact you, you will respond. Ties need to be strengthened when a constituency is seeking support. Again, the issue of partial inclusion is a factor. Different entities may vie for the support of the same constituencies. When entities vie for support, they are targeting the undecided or uncommitted constituencies. The entities should have already rallied their supporters (those with close connections) to their sides. Links are used to send messages designed to build support. When there is true competition for support, constituents are more likely to choose the entity that can craft the most appealing message. The point here is that corporations and other entities should not think all ties must be strong ties with all constituencies all the time. A more likely scenario is that most constituencies have weak ties to entities. It is the maintenance and utilization of those weak ties that will make the greatest difference when self-interests collide in the web of relationships.

In our definition of public relations, "management of relationships" may seem to have a negative connotation because management is often equated with efforts to control or manipulate. We are using management not as control but as attempts to shape relationships. Those attempts to shape relationships can easily fail. Public relations utilizes various communication tools in its efforts to influence constituencies and to shape the web of relationships. Public relations is one mechanism for attracting and retaining constituencies in the web of relationships and those efforts are an exercise in influence.

Consider the following example. A corporation tries to convince an environmental activist group to partner with them in an effort to reduce its carbon footprint. The partnership results in changes to corporate policies and reductions in emissions. A campaign is undertaken to make various constituencies aware of the partnership and changes in the organization's practices. Communities benefit from cleaner air, employees have a source of pride, customers have another reason to buy the corporation's products, investors have another reason to purchase the corporation's stock, the activist groups have switched from protesting against to counseling and testifying for the corporation, and the news media can present stories about the "green" corporation. The web of relationships is enhanced and the organization benefits from a friendlier operating environment. But activists can reject the partnership bid or other constituencies may view the campaign as "greenwashing." Greenwashing refers to corporations enacting only superficial changes in behaviors, but relying on public communication to convey the impression they are concerned about environmental issues and taking actions to limit negative impacts on the environment. When activist groups counsel corporations, the groups run the risk of being viewed as "selling out" to corporate interests. The partnership effort may fail because it creates a reason to not be a part of the web of relationships with either the corporation or the activist group.

An "Alternate Reality" for Public Relations

The term *public relations* does not always bring out the most favorable reaction when it is used. Too often, the media and people in general use the term as a derogatory comment, such as "It's a public relations move." The insult involves the belief that public relations is all about style and not substance. Clearly, people who have been through a public relations course know – or should know – differently. Public relations must be rooted in actions to be effective. Yes, a great deal of public relations is symbolic; but any field that trades in communication is largely symbolic. Symbols are great. They make society possible. It is the misuse of symbols and communication that is problematic.

Public relations often is equated with spin and publicity. Spin doctors make sure only the positive information about an organization or individual is communicated to others and reported in the news media, or they reinterpret information to cast it in a more favorable light. Public relations practitioners are roadblocks to people being truly informed. The public assumes public relations is a mechanism corporations use to polish their images by hiding their true selves. Again, an introductory public relations course should correct that perception. The problem is that the vast majority of people who encounter the term public relations never had and will never have had a public relations course. Instead, the term public relations is victimized by its own past that leads many to treat it as a pariah in society. As we have argued in *It's Not Just PR: Public Relations in Society*, we see public relations as a necessary component of society (Coombs & Holladay, 2007b).

In science fiction, writers often talk of alternate timelines or realities. These realities are similar but have variations due to different choices that have been made in the parallel worlds. Perhaps there is an alternate reality where public relations is embraced and widely recognized for its contributions to society. We posit that such a reality would not be that different from the one we currently experience. All that needs to be changed is one critical choice the field of public relations seems to have made. Obviously, people in a field really made the choices that place public relations where it is today, or could be, in our alternate reality.

The critical choice is to designate the beginning of the twentieth century as the birth of public relations. Many writers, especially public relations historians, claim that public relations was born from corporate reactions to the muckrakers and reformers of that time. This choice gives rise to two of the common criticisms of public relations. Journalists left newspapers to become public relations practitioners for corporations. First problem, public relations is a tool of corporations. Second problem, public relations is just a simplistic form of media relations (attempts to place information into the news media) or spin.

Corporations are not inherently evil; some just choose to act that way. However, for many social critics, being a "corporate tool" is a scathing indictment. From their perspective, public relations has been used to oppress workers, exploit consumers, harm society, and ravage the environment. During the course of this book we will examine examples of how public relations has been part of these and other acts against humanity. We also will consider how public relations has been used to improve the human condition. Furthermore, if journalists created public relations, then at its heart it is just media relations. Moreover, the practice was born to protect corporations by promoting the corporation's view of reality through the presentation of selective facts under the guise of objectivity borrowed from journalism. To say it another way, the need for spin ushered public relations into this world. People do not have to be social critics to adopt this view of public relations. The news media frequently tell people that public relations is spin.

In our alternate reality, public relations historians trace its roots to reformers of the 1800s. Public relations becomes an important device in civil society. Civil society is composed neither of business nor government, but is essential to the operation of a democracy. Non-governmental organizations (NGOs) and private voluntary organizations (PVOs) are part of civil society. Civil society allows people to come together and to debate issues of the day and petition the government for change. Those seeking to end slavery, support women's rights, and fight the evils of alcohol are the founders of public relations in our alternate reality. Public relations was a tool for social reform. It was born from activists desiring to improve the human condition and was a tool of public advocacy. Public relations was persuasion designed to convince people of the need to make changes to society. What if the term public relations had been used to describe what those First Reform Era activists were doing? These activists would be the founders of public relations. Public relations would be rooted neither in the corporate realm nor journalism/media relations. It would be a valued tool in social reform. When corporations and their journalist cronies began using public relations in the 1900s, it would be treated as the spread of public relations to the corporate sector, not its birth. The roots of public relations would be firmly planted within reform and civil society rather than corporations and the news media.

Our alternate reality is not that far fetched. The key difference is that the term public relations was not used until around 1900. What the First Reform Era activists did was indeed public relations. They sought to use various communication tactics to influence public opinion. How different is that from the claims of what corporations were doing later? Moreover, the corporate response itself was to the public relations efforts of the muckrakers and other activists. There was a battle to shape public opinion that had at least two sides.

Because we have no way to visit this alternative reality, public relations is where it is today, saddled with the corporate and media baggage it packed long ago. Nor will any revisionist history of public relations radically alter how most people view the field. What can be done is to recognize all that public relations is. This means examining the good and the bad, the activist as well as the corporate use of public relations, and embracing rather than denying the advocacy and self-interests associated with public relations.

Howard Zinn (2005) wrote a controversial but influential history text titled *A People's History of the United States*. Zinn sought to give voice to those history had forgotten, the oppressed and the marginalized. So his text includes the genocide of Native Americans, the details of slavery, and the oppression of American workers. Critics of the book saw it as overly critical and overly pessimistic about the US, and as having a pronounced political edge. There is some truth to all these charges. However, there is a bigger picture to be appreciated through Zinn's work. That bigger picture is the value of hearing multiple voices, the very cornerstone of democracy. One of the objectives of this book is to continue our work from *It's Not Just PR* and give voice to the activist contributions to public relations and to view the field, warts and all. We believe this is to some degree an alternate vision of public relations. Historically and contemporaneously, what have the marginalized voices given and continue to give to public relations? How has public relations helped to shape people's lives for the better and for the worse? Why does society need public relations?

The concept of public relations literacy, the ability to identify, analyze, and evaluate public relations messages, can help us to wrestle with these larger issues. Public relations literacy is inspired by and derived from media literacy. In general, media literacy helps people develop a critical understanding of the media, the techniques used by the media, and the effects of those techniques (Media Literacy, 1997).

The Aspen Media Literacy Leadership Institute defines media literacy as "the ability to access, analyze, evaluate and create media in a variety of forms" (Aspen Institute, 1992). It is useful to move beyond the definition to specific elements of media literacy. To be media literate, a person should understand how the mass media industries operate, be aware of how mass media can affect society and individuals, apply critical thinking skills to the evaluation of media content, and have frameworks for analyzing media messages (Silverblatt, 2001).

Public relations is primarily a mediated enterprise and does have effects on individuals and society. Therefore, media literacy is relevant. In fact, some public relations issues do appear in discussions of media literacy (Baran, 2008). We feel public relations literacy is more specific and warrants consideration in its own right although it is informed by media literacy. In addition, public relations literacy is not a criticism nor a condemnation of public relations. The point is to create critical consumers of public relations actions who understand the effects of those actions. The point is not to create people who will simply bash public relations as a profession. We need critical consumers because public relations trades in influence and people must be critical when evaluating influence attempts.

Public relations literacy is the application of critical thinking skills to the examination of public relations techniques and the effects of those techniques on individuals and society. Public relations literacy skills include the ability and willingness to understand public relations messages, an understanding and respect for the power of public relations messages, and the ability to critically evaluate a public relations message regardless of its source. Public relations literacy demands an understanding and interrogation of the public relations process. Just as the media have various genres or forms, public relations has various disciplines. To be critical, a person needs a working understanding of the various disciplines of public relations. Chapters 5 through 14 present common disciplines in public relations. The theories and principles discussed in those chapters provide insight into the disciplines. Furthermore, the reflections in each of the chapters suggest key points to consider when interpreting and evaluating public relations actions for each discipline.

The critical evaluation of public relations would be built around a series of questions:

- Who is creating the public relations action/message?
- Why did they create the public relations action/message?
- Who will gain or lose from the public relations action/message?
- Who is the intended audience for the public relations action/message?
- Whose voices are heard and absent from the public relations action/message?

Answering these questions helps to reveal the self-interests and influence goals in the public relations actions. Self-interests are critical when evaluating ideas and choices. We start by understanding who is actually sending the message and what they have to gain – their motivation for engaging in public relations. As some people win, others may lose as a result of the public relations action. We must look deeper into the public relations action to determine if there are specific losers if we are to consider the full ramifications of a public relations action.

Understanding the target for the public relations action is insightful because it reminds us who is considered relevant and irrelevant. Will the target for the public relations action benefit, lose, or simply facilitate the process? Why were other constituents not targeted? We can learn whose interests are being advanced and whose are being ignored. Finally, public relations should be about the free exchange of ideas that permits people to select the ideas that best fit with their views, what is often called the marketplace of ideas. Chapter 3 provides additional details on the marketplace of ideas. The marketplace of ideas is reflected by the voices appearing in public relations actions. Who is being heard, who is silent, and who might be being drowned out by the voices of others? It is instructive to learn who is being excluded and who seems to have no voice in public relations matters. Is the marketplace of ideas inclusive or restrictive? Ideally, the goal is to increase the number of voices in the marketplace, but this is not always the case.

The five questions for public relations literacy push people to look below the surface of public relations actions to unpack their effects on individuals and society. We try to address many of these questions in the reflection sections of chapters 5 through 14. Chapter 15 returns to public relations literacy and reviews key ideas from these ten chapters that could be used to build public relations literacy. We also recognize additional questions can be useful as well. Public relations literacy is in its infancy and will evolve as more people consider what other ideas will improve this nascent concept.

The Future of Public Relations

If public relations' past is constraining and problematic, what of its future? It is difficult to predict the exact future of public relations. However, we can identify trends and issues that will be salient in the field's future. Two central trends are technology and globalization. Two relevant issues are ethics and transparency.

As with most fields, the future of public relations is bound to technology and globalization. Today, technology refers to online communication. Constituencies have many more and improved options for communicating with one another than they did ten or even three years ago. Consider the availability of interactive video, instant messaging, blogs, vlogs (video weblogs), and other communication tools. You can use all of these from a mobile phone such as the I-phone. Chapter 7 will consider the role of online media in public relations in detail.

The academic and practitioner literatures have rushed to embrace and to promote the use of online communication. However, the embrace has been too enthusiastic at times. We are not neo-Luddites advocating a rejection of technology. But we do recognize the original Luddites and neo-Luddites do have a point in their contention that technology can dehumanize people and its effects may not be completely positive. Think of the "cyborgs" you see walking around linked to work through the blue tooth technology in their ears or the PDAs in their hands. We caution against a rush to online communication at the expense of other communication channels and the use of overly aggressive online tactics that seem to violate the spirit of the Internet. We must always remember a mix of channels is usually best. Each situation should be examined carefully to determine which channels will prove most effective for a public relations effort. A blog is not the cure-all to every public relations concern. Public relations people must learn how best to integrate the online environment into their efforts. Almost every chapter in this book will include a discussion of online communication and its impact on public relations.

The public relations move to the online world is viewed as rather aggressive by some critics. Public relations is corrupting the independent exchange of information spirit of the Internet. Public relations practitioners now pitch or even buy bloggers to write favorable comments about an organization. Under the banner of public relations, actions have been taken to suppress fair comment and free speech to comment on corporations. The word *flog* (fake blog) was created to cover public relations practitioners posing as "independent" bloggers. Granted, these are isolated examples for the most part and do not reflect all public relations activities on the web. Still, these abuses by those claiming to practice public relations serve to pollute the online environment and cast additional criticisms on the field.

There are favorable trends developing from the online application of public relations as well. Activist groups can use various online technologies that are comparatively inexpensive ways to reach potential constituents and build their power. Online resources are used to recruit and mobilize supporters, pressure decision makers, generate media coverage, and raise money for other public relations efforts (Coombs & Holladay, 2007a). But some activist groups have abused that power by trying to silence the voices of others. Chapters 5 and 7 provide a further discussion of activists and online public relations. Public relations will continue its quest to understand the online environment and how best to integrate online public relations with traditional public relations.

More and quicker communication has made the world smaller. By smaller we mean easier to communicate and to connect with one another. Webs of relationships are global rather than local or national. Although chapter 14 concentrates on global public relations, each chapter discusses how public relations is now global because constituent networks are global. Public relations efforts still can involve just more than local members of a relationship web. Consider local citizens seeking to change the policy of how utility companies trim trees. There is no need for this issue to go global. But it does not take much to move a public relations effort from the local to the global level when such a move is desirable for one or more of the constituencies involved. Consider how a band of rebels in the poorest area of Mexico, the Zapatistas, used laptops and the Internet to make the world aware of their struggles to preserve a way of life in a remote area of Mexico few had even heard of before their postings.

The Zapatistas, or the Zapatista Army of National Liberation (EZLN), is composed mostly of indigenous peoples from the state of Chiapas in southeastern Mexico. They are fighting for control over their lands and resources as well as opposing globalization. The Zapatistas fear that the cattle ranchers and oil companies will continue to take their land, resources, and eventually their way of life. The Internet is one way that the Zapatistas have brought their plight to the notice of the rest of the world and continue to garner global support for their efforts (Holloway & Pelaez, 1998). Today, constituencies need to think of the global implications of their words and actions.

Ethics always will remain a concern because of public relations' role in influencing others. Consider how the professional associations have and continue to wrestle with ethics. Visit any popular public relations blog and you will read postings about ethics. Public relations is influence and influence is dangerous when abused. Concerns for ethics remind practitioners to honor their responsibilities to society. Discussions of ethics are as old as the written word. Ethics never should go out of style.

Transparency is becoming a partner with ethics. Transparency is about being open and honest with constituents and constituents seeking to make organizations transparent. Transparency relates directly to ethics. Transparency can reveal unethical practices and the threat of exposure can keep the unethically inclined in check. People are less likely to violate the trust of constituents if they fear that indiscretion will be exposed and punished. The vast majority of public relations practitioners are ethical and welcome transparency. Unfortunately, the field continues to be plagued by the small minority of unethical practitioners. The various chapters in this book discuss the unethical practices to reinforce the "right" way to engage in public relations. Ideally, greater transparency should reduce unethical behavior, but only time will tell if that ideal is realized.

Structure of the Book

This book is divided into three sections: orientation, functions, and conclusion. The orientation section is composed of the first five chapters. These chapters orient the readers to how we are conceptualizing and operationalizing public relations. Chapter 1 has presented our definition and view of public relations. Chapter 2 considers ethical concerns with public relations and why that topic is so germane to the field. Chapter 3 discusses the concepts of transparency and the marketplace of ideas along with public relations' role in those debates. Chapter 4 emphasizes how public relations is strategic. Chapter 5 elaborates on the role of activists and activism in public relations.

The functions section examines the primary functions of public relations and how these functions interconnect various constituencies in the web of relationships. Chapter 6 examines media relations, a basic public relations function. Chapter 7 addresses the new online media and the way in which public relations has both adopted and at times abused online communication. Chapter 8 ties public relations to social marketing and use of communication to shape people's lives and health. Chapter 9 develops the process of reputation management, what many now view as a central function in corporate public relations. Chapter 10 explores the dynamics of issues management and how it is utilized by a variety of constituencies. Chapter 11 discusses risk management and how it serves as a common concern for constituencies. Chapter 12 is dedicated to crisis management and considers how the tension between financial and social concerns impacts how constituencies are treated in a crisis. As with chapter 9, it reflects the strong corporate focus of some public relations functions.

Chapters 13 and 14 move to a more global level with corporate social responsibility and public diplomacy. Chapter 13 explores the concept of corporate social responsibility, including its global nature and how it may serve to bind constituencies into a web of relationships. Chapter 14 focuses on international public relations, focusing on globalization, terrorism as a form of public relations, and public diplomacy and how it is used to shape international perceptions of various constituencies. The final section is chapter 15, the conclusion. Chapter 15 presents a review of key elements of the book with an emphasis on answering the question "Does society need public relations?" It also includes a return to the discussion of public relations literacy.

Discussion Questions

1 In this chapter we presented this definition of public relations: "Public relations is the management of mutually influential relationships within a web of constituency relationships." Explain key concepts in this definition.

2 Describe the distinctions among the terms *stakeholder*, *public*, and *constituency*.

3 What are the benefits of "weak ties"?

4 How does a corporate-centric view of public relations limit our understanding of the practice of public relations?

5 What is public relations literacy? Why is this concept important in contemporary society?

Image of balanced scales.
PHOTO SEBASTIAN KAULITZKI / SHUTTERSTOCK

2

Public Relations Contested and Ethically Challenged

Consider these brief scenarios:

Gene's supervisor instructs him to leak information about a possible merger to the press to boost stock prices. Gene is aware that a merger had been discussed. However, he had heard through the office grapevine that the merger probably was not going to occur. He is unsure about what to do.

Rosa knows that a philanthropic campaign that her organization sponsors donates 5 percent of the profits from purchases of a particular product to a charitable cause. However, she learned that one third of the donation actually goes for administrative and advertising costs related to the campaign and not to the cause itself. Rosa feels uncomfortable about writing press releases touting the success of the campaign.

Jason works in the new media division of a public relations agency. His supervisor announces a plan to build word-of-mouth for a client's new soft drink. The plan is to pay people who blog about beverages to write favorable blog entries for the client. Jason has been given a list of potential bloggers to contact. He thinks the bloggers should have to disclose the payment, but his manager does not. Jason is less than enthusiastic about contacting the bloggers.

These scenarios provide a sampling of the types of ethical dilemmas that may confront public relations professionals. Some ethical violations may seem more egregious to you than others. Indeed, it is unlikely that all people would arrive at unanimous agreement regarding the extent to which these represent ethical controversies, let alone how they should be managed. You may say the evaluation of any ethical dilemma may depend on one's position. Are you a community member affected by the decision who believes an organization is withholding all the facts? Are you a public relations practitioner instructed by your supervisor to communicate the information to stakeholders? Are you a shareholder? Are you an employee of the organization? If your answer differs depending on your position in the scenario, does this reveal anything about the challenges of identifying and resolving ethical dilemmas in general?

Some may see ethical violations as akin to pornography: "I know it when I see it." The obvious problem with this stance is it suggests we can best identify ethical violations *after* they have occurred, when we have the benefit of observing the actual outcomes of our choices and others' reactions to our choices. While it is important to be able to discern "right" decisions from "wrong" decisions in retrospect, it would be much more productive to identify the *potential* for ethical dilemmas before selecting and enacting communication strategies. This would help guarantee we are not merely relying on the consequences or outcomes of our decisions to judge their ethical implications. If we determine some action must have been unethical only because we got "caught," then it probably was not an ethical act to begin with!

There is a need for greater consistency in the assessment of the ethics of communication choices in public relations. So while we may believe we have the ability to identify ethical violations when we see them, the better approach is to understand ethical concerns at a more fundamental level. This would empower us to anticipate potential problems with our choices of means and ends and make well-reasoned assessments of alternative actions *before* taking action.

A useful starting point for thinking about ethics is Parsons' (2004, p. 21) *five pillars of ethical decision making* in public relations. The issues are:

1   *Veracity:* tell the truth.
2   *Non-maleficence:* do no harm, including demonstrating respect for others.
3   *Beneficence:* do good; when choosing between alternatives, select the one that will do the most good for the public, not just the one that would enhance your image.
4   *Confidentiality:* respect privacy.
5   *Fairness:* be fair and socially responsible; try to respect all parties involved in an issue.

These five provide important foundational elements that most people would see as central to ethical practices. We introduce these early in this chapter to stimulate your thinking about ethics. Do these pillars seem ethical to you? Might these apply to other professions as well?

Although we devote an entire chapter to a consideration of ethics, ethical implications of public relations are woven into every chapter. This raises an interesting point. In what other professions are discussions of ethics seen as so central to the profession? A primary reason public relations is concerned with ethics is that the practice is viewed as a form of strategic communication that typically involves persuasion (Pfau & Wan, 2006). The public is naturally cautious when it comes to persuasion. Marconi (2004) observed: "A public relations person's role is to present a person, company, or subject in the best possible light, a function which is often regarded with suspicion, as if that objective could only be achieved by lying or misrepresentation" (p. 15). This skepticism reinforces the importance of adhering to commonly accepted ethical practices in order to counter these negative images. Public relations professionals are public communicators who have access to the media and therefore have special responsibilities to be ethical in their influence attempts. Critics of public relations may argue that large corporations, because of their access to tremendous monetary resources, have an unfair advantage in situations involving persuasion (e.g., Dinar & Miller, 2007; Grunig & Grunig, 1992; Stauber & Rampton, 1995). This criticism may be more an indictment of the power of "big business" than of the power of public relations. However, the potential for abuses of power associated with public communication necessitates a closer examination of ethical concerns.

This chapter has several goals related to helping you understand the ethical implications associated with the practice of public relations. Our overarching goal is to clarify why ethical concerns are associated with public relations functions and how the practice itself has addressed ethics. This chapter is designed to stimulate your thinking about ethics by exploring how media depictions of public relations often portray the profession as ethically challenged, discussing why public relations often is seen as having special obligations to act in ethical ways, presenting ethical perspectives that can be used to evaluate decisions, discussing the role of codes of ethics, and concluding with a basic model for ethical decision making.

Media Portrayals of Public Relations

To better understand why people may view public relations with suspicion and as ethically challenged, we can refer to studies that examine the way "public relations" is used in the media. These kinds of studies are important because they reveal how common understandings develop among the population and how the media can convey particular attitudes toward public relations that can, in turn, shape readers' attitudes. In general, research suggests public relations has a "reputation problem." For example, Spicer (1993) examined connotations of public relations in print news and magazine stories and found about 80 percent of the references to public relations used the term in a negative way. He identified seven common themes or definitions of public relations in these news stories. Public relations was portrayed as (1) a distraction, where public relations is seen as a quick fix or as a way to distract from the truth of the situation; (2) a disaster, where an action was taken that was a mistake or was damaging to the organization; (3) a challenge, where public relations might be used to present another side to the story or to honestly deal with difficulties; (4) hype, where actions were taken to artificially generate excitement or to act as a publicity gimmick or stunt; (5) merely public relations, where no substantive action was taken; (6) public relations war or battle, where there was an ongoing battle to gain positive public opinion; and (7) schmoozing, where public relations was depicted as smooth talking or as using a charming spokesperson to achieve ends.

Clearly, these negative connotations of public relations may influence how people interpret the role of public relations in society. Rather than portraying public relations as a means for facilitating communication and managing mutually influential relationships, the analysis suggests the popular press portrays public relations as a practice used to hide or manipulate the truth. Public relations practices often are framed as less than honest and ethically questionable. While we are not saying that public relations professionals never engage in unethical practices, we are saying that negative media images may outweigh positive portrayals. Positive public relations actions garner little publicity, while egregious violations of the public trust naturally attract attention. Given negative characterizations of public relations, it is no wonder that the general public may view the practice with some distrust and skepticism.

In addition to identifying how general media coverage has depicted the term public relations in negative ways, we also can point to well-known specific cases of unethical public relations actions and abuses of the public trust that have deservedly attracted negative media coverage. For example, Hill and Knowlton, one of the world's best-known public relations firms, created a front group called "Citizens for a Free Kuwait" to encourage US involvement in the first Gulf War in 1992. Stauber and Rampton (1995) report this front group was developed to conceal the connection between the Kuwaiti government and the George H. W. Bush administration as it moved the US toward involvement in the Gulf War. The front group made it appear that Kuwaiti citizens were lobbying desperately for an intervention to stop Saddam Hussein from invading and exploiting their country. The "Citizens for a Free Kuwait" case is presented in more detail at the end of chapter 3 on transparency.

Front groups are designed to look like grassroots movements among ordinary, concerned citizens who organize to express their views. Politicians and other decision makers do pay attention to (legitimate) grassroots organizations. However, front groups create the false impression that there is active support among citizens for or against a particular issue, decision, or problem. These front groups are created by organizations or corporations to serve corporate interests. Front groups misrepresent "the will of the people," conceal corporate interests in the issue, and knowingly fabricate information to support their interests. Their lack of concern for the truth and their attempts to undermine democratic processes make them an easy target for critics of public relations.

Another example of a front group is AFACT, the American Farmers for the Advancement and Conservation of Technology. Sourcewatch, a media watchdog group associated with the Center for Media and Democracy, reported that Monsanto, a manufacturer of rBST, a synthetic growth hormone that can be injected into dairy cows to make them produce more milk, hired an agricultural marketing company to help defend farmers' use of the growth hormone. Monsanto wanted the front group to oppose laws that ban or restrict labeling of milk products as "rBST free." Monsanto argues that labeling will lead consumers to believe the milk from cows that have been treated with rBST is inferior (American Farmers, 2008). In this case the front group was designed to foster the impression that the organization was comprised of farmers who need to use rBST and that rBST-treated milk poses no health concerns to humans. However, the group's connection to Monsanto, the manufacturer of the chemical, was concealed and this failure to disclose corporate ties is problematic.

In other cases, what appear to be genuinely pro-social motives on the part of corporations can be exposed to reveal a darker side. Organizations may be shown to be less altruistic or socially responsible than what was originally portrayed in reputation-building ads, promotional materials, or media representations of their efforts. Being exposed as a corporation that misrepresents its "good works" can be an embarrassment and seriously damage reputations.

For example, PR Watch reported a campaign they felt misrepresented the amount of charitable contributions going to programs designed to help provide children in Africa with clean drinking water (A 'humanitarian campaign', 2008). Starbucks' Ethos Water Fund was designed to raise money for charitable causes that benefit Africans who lack drinking water. Starbucks' brand of bottled water, Ethos, sells for $1.80 per bottle. Promotional materials indicate Ethos purchases will benefit this worthy cause. However, critics claim the 5 cents of each purchase that actually goes to the fund is underwhelming, misleading, and not a sign of a socially responsible company. Starbucks has been accused of making a profit while claiming to support a humanitarian effort.

Along the same lines, other companies such as Gap, Apple, and Dell are part of the Red Campaign. The Red Campaign is a cause marketing effort designed to provide medicines for AIDS patients in Africa. In a cause marketing effort, companies promise to donate a percentage of their profits from particular items to specific causes. Chapter 8 provides additional information on cause marketing. Cause marketing items have been quite popular with consumers, who can feel good by supporting a cause by purchasing a product. Involvement in cause marketing can benefit corporate reputations. However, the percentages actually donated by corporations often do little to help the cause. For instance, Dell "Red" computers retail at over $1,000, but only $5–80 are donated per computer purchased. At one point, the advertising cost for the Red Campaign was at $100 million while the charity had raised only $18 million.

Journalists may have "love-hate" relationships with the public relations profession due to their reliance on corporate public relations functions. Due to budget cutbacks, the ranks of journalists have been downsized. That means there are fewer people to gather and report the news. However, corporations may assist journalists with background research about their organizations, products and services, and issues. Public relations professionals often produce video news releases (VNRs) about organizations and their operations. The VNRs are broadcast-quality video that is ready to be aired. Using corporate-produced VNRs may be cost effective for journalists because they provide high quality visuals that can be incorporated into broadcasts. Journalists can elect to use entire VNRs or only portions of VNRs. The controversy stems from the fact that VNRs produced by an organization often are not identified by journalists as having been supplied by the organization. While some might fault corporations for having too much influence in the coverage of supposedly objective news when journalists use VNRs, it also is the case that journalists could choose to disclose their sources of information when they rely on VNRs. Journalists might be seen as acting unethically when they fail to engage in full disclosure. So, although journalists seem uncomfortable with the arrangement with public relations professionals, they do indeed rely on these relationships in order to perform their jobs.

Overall, media coverage of public relations practices often focuses on actions that are ethically suspect. Exposés may uncover front groups as tools of the powerful or cause marketing efforts as empty gestures designed to generate positive publicity. Undoubtedly, these abuses of the public trust deserve critique and are newsworthy. Spicer's (1993) work demonstrated the term public relations typically is associated with negative connotations, as reflected in colloquialisms like "it's just PR," "PR maneuvers," or "PR ploy," suggesting the practice represents all style with no substance. But the great majority of public relations actions do not attract negative media attention because they do not represent ethical transgressions. Most practitioners follow Parsons' (2004) five pillars of ethical decision making in their practice of public relations: veracity, non-maleficence, beneficence, confidentiality, and fairness.

Ethical Issues in the Practice of Public Relations

Attention to the potential for unethical behavior is warranted because public relations professionals could confront ethical challenges that are inherent to the practice. The profession probably has been much more intensely scrutinized than most other professions! An important reason for this attention stems from perceptions that the profession has the ability to exercise a great deal of influence and often does so on behalf of large, powerful corporations. Anti-corporate sentiments may reflect a growing cynicism toward big business in general and a desire to evaluate more critically the messages emanating from corporate interests. A common belief is that "deep pockets" buys influence that may benefit a few (e.g., stockholders, executives) but may not be in the best interests of society as a whole.

We now consider several issues that confront the practice of public relations. We examine public relations professionals as public communicators, the role of persuasion in public relations, and how public relations professionals may be disconnected from decision making processes in organizations. Exploring these topics will help us understand why ethical considerations are implicated in the practice and why the public may be suspicious of public relations practices.

Public communication and public relations

In addition to often being the focus of negative depictions and linked to all that is perceived to be wrong with big business, the practice of public relations has come under close scrutiny because of its role in public communication. As public communicators, public relations professionals have the kind of access to the media that makes it possible for them to influence public opinion. The belief is that public communicators have special responsibilities to balance the needs of society with the needs of clients. This concern can be traced back to the "rhetorical tradition" of Greek and Roman orators that emphasized the practice of ethical communication within the public arena. They believed speakers and their speech content should be carefully scrutinized. Communicators should be critically examined based on their personal character (credibility, goodwill, morality) and the quality of their communication, including the accuracy of their claims, quality of their arguments, and the ethics of what was said to persuade others in a public forum. They believed vigilant examination of public communication was necessary to a democratic society (Coombs & Holladay, 2007b).

More recent writers also have emphasized the importance of the public arena, often referred to as the *public sphere* (Habermas, 1989). Similar to ancient thinking about public communication, the idea is that we should maintain this public forum through the creation of an ideal speech situation where conflicts can be publicly debated and rationally resolved. Within the public sphere we see the potential for genuine dialogue and emancipation. Speakers will be able to engage in discourse with others that will question basic assumptions and commitments of those involved. Speakers will present arguments and the force of better arguments will prevail. To create this ideal speech situation, speakers should engage in a particular type of discourse practice called *communicative action*. Communicative action is a form of speech that will move us toward truth (reflecting what is rational and in the best interests of society), a necessary component for a democratic society.

Public relations can be seen as a form of communication in the public sphere that can be used to manage mutually influential relationships and contribute to this process of dialogue. However, as public communication professionals with access to this public sphere, practitioners are obligated to evaluate the ways in which they participate as well as the goals they pursue. Bowen's statement, "The power to influence society means that public relations holds enormous responsibility to be ethical" (2005a, p. 294) reflects this concern for their roles as public communicators. During this public communication process public relations professionals act as *boundary spanners*, connecting the organization with the public, and engage in both speaking and listening in order to practice ethical communication. As advocated by the ancient Greeks and Romans and more contemporary thinkers like Habermas, they must be concerned with both the means and ends of their participation in the public sphere.

Understandably, evidence of power abuses increases skepticism of public relations' ability to truly participate in this type of communicative action. After all, it is only logical that public relations practitioners have divided loyalties. While they are concerned for what is best for society, they must also balance that with loyalties to employers or clients, the profession, and themselves (Parsons, 2004). Trusting public relations professionals to be committed to balancing the needs of society with the needs of clients may be requesting a leap of faith that not all members of the public are willing to make.

A further complication arises from the fact that it may be difficult to determine what constitutes "the public interest" in a complex society (Coombs & Holladay, 2007b). Society is comprised of many constituencies representing diverse and often conflicting points of view and interests. Trying to consider all possible perspectives and engaging in dialogue with all interests may be an impossible task.

Persuasion and public relations

Although most people view persuasion as an essential feature of public relations (Fitzpatrick & Bronstein, 2006; Pfau & Wan, 2006), some scholars have protested the centrality of persuasion to public relations (Grunig & Grunig, 1992) by arguing that all forms of persuasion are unethical and manipulative. Some writers suggest the ubiquity of public relations, as a form of weak propaganda that is available to the powerful, poses threats to democracy (Ewen, 1996; Grunig & Grunig, 1992; Moloney, 2006; Stauber & Rampton, 1995). Fears surrounding propaganda and persuasion may intensify when we question the intentions of large corporations that are perceived to exercise a great deal of power in comparison to other groups in society.

It is important to realize that not all scholars view persuasion as inherently unethical. Some contend persuasion, as a form of strategic communication, can be done in an open, authentic way. The Public Relations Society of America (PRSA) positions *advocacy* first in its list of professional values. Advocacy can be broadly defined as speaking or writing in support of something, an act that certainly implicates persuasion. The PRSA states: "We serve the public interest by acting as responsible advocates for those we represent. We provide a choice in the marketplace of ideas, facts, and viewpoints to aid informed public debate" (PRSA 2000, p. 1). To be "responsible advocates," practitioners should consider the ethical appropriateness of particular means to persuade as well as the ends or goals of their persuasive efforts (Pfau and Wan, 2006). In addition to benefiting organizations by selling their products and services and enhancing their reputations, persuasion also can serve the public good by encouraging people to engage in healthy behaviors (e.g., stop smoking, monitor caloric intakes) or pro-social actions (volunteer for community programs, donate blood). Sometimes strategic communication to constituents involves information sharing (e.g., providing information in annual reports, updating community members on building projects, asking for employee input on modifications to benefits packages). Other times strategic communication clearly involves persuasion (lobbying, marketing, influencing reputations). In many cases, strategic communication involves a mix of information-giving and persuasion. These information sharing and persuasive functions are not in and of themselves unethical. Parsons (2004) echoes this idea in her distinction between persuasion and propaganda. She acknowledges that while both try to change people's opinions and attitudes, propaganda does this to satisfy the needs of the propagandist while persuasion takes into consideration the mutual benefit of the persuader and those being persuaded (p. 107). Persuasive communication persuades without resorting to falsifications, specious reasoning, or using overly emotional appeals to circumvent critical thinking.

Decision making and public relations

The extent to which public relations practitioners are involved in the larger strategic decision making within the organization varies greatly. While the media image of the public relations function in general may lead people to believe that these professionals wield a great deal of power in corporations, often times this is not the case. In fact, they may not be involved in the dominant coalition responsible for developing the overall business strategy. Many public relations professionals occupy lower-ranking positions that obligate them to follow the instructions of their superiors. Often, they simply create specific messages in line with those directives. For this reason they may not be in a position to fully understand or critically evaluate the decision making and the ethical implications of decisions made within the organization (Moloney, 2006).

Although they often do not play a central role in strategic decision making, public relations professionals do collect information that could be valuable to those formulating macro business strategies. They act as boundary spanners when they connect the client/organization with society as a whole. In this way they act as an information conduit. Public relations practitioners are uniquely positioned to represent the concerns of stakeholders to the organization and vice versa. Ideally, the role enables them to engage in listening and information-sharing to create mutual understanding as well as mutual influence, what is often referred to as two-way symmetrical communication (Grunig & Hunt, 1984). However, this boundary-spanning role may create tensions as they attempt to balance an organization's needs with society's needs within a context where they ultimately have little knowledge of the organization's strategy and little power to influence that strategy (Coombs & Holladay, 2007b). Interestingly, this picture of the public relations professional as a boundary spanner representing the public interest(s) to the organization is not the picture the public sees. Instead, as discussed earlier, media portrayals tend to depict public relations as one-way influence involving deception, publicity, or "spin."

To better understand the role of ethical considerations in the practice of public relations, we turn to a discussion of ethics, including factors influencing the development of one's ethics and how general ethical perspectives can be applied to more systematically assess decision making and courses of action.

Defining Ethics

At its core, *ethics* concerns value judgments of good and bad, right or wrong. These judgments naturally are complicated by the fact that people do not uniformly embrace similar values, nor do people generally agree unanimously on evaluations of good or bad. Ethical principles reflect judgments and should not be confused with legal requirements. However, it is important to acknowledge that our laws and the legal system itself are based upon particular values. As Fitzpatrick (2006, p. 2) notes, "Law is about what people *must* do, while ethics is about what people *should* do, they advise. Ethics begins where the law ends. Law is about compliance with set rules and procedures, while ethics involves more discretionary decision making.... Law is not an appropriate guide for determining parameters of ethical behavior." So while our laws offer relatively clear guidelines for behaviors, ethics does not. While the "letter of the law" may seem black and white, ethics may be more aptly represented by shades of gray. It is this gray area of ethics that complicates our actions and that we explore here.

What are the sources of values?

We have described values as foundational to ethics. But where do our values come from? What influences their development and how do they figure into decision making?

To return to our basic definition of ethics, we see that values are central to ethics and judgments of good and bad. *Values* reflect what is desirable in terms of practices (behaviors or processes we should engage in) and end-states of existence (goals we should seek) (Rokeach, 1968). In this way values influence people's decisions because they tell us what goals are important and how we should pursue those goals. Values undergird ethics and one's values presumably reflect personal, organizational, and societal standards (Treadwell & Treadwell, 2005). These three standards point to the potential for conflicting perspectives when considering ethics. Let's explore these three in more detail.

At a *personal level*, people bring their own values into the organization. Personal values can be traced back to early socialization experiences in families, educational institutions, communities, religious institutions, and so forth. During their formative years people develop fundamental orientations and beliefs about what is good and bad, right and wrong. These early orientations may be modified throughout life as people's range of experiences and possible influences expands.

This can help to explain why members of the same family may embrace different value systems and make different decisions based upon those values.

At the *organizational level*, we can examine how organizations develop unique cultures that encompass that culture's accepted methods of doing things, ways of thinking, assumptions, and preferred goals. At a fundamental level, organizational culture can be understood as "the way we do things around here." We think of organizations *as* cultures. What we do, how we think of what we do, and how we communicate about these issues creates the culture and influences subsequent practices by members of the organization. Practices, values, and communication both comprise and reflect the culture in this reflexive relationship. While decision makers in the organization bring their own personal values into their actions, they also are likely to be influenced by the specific organizational culture in which they are embedded. However, what is viewed as a desirable practice in one organizational culture may be viewed as ethically suspect in another. Some organizations such as Enron, Arthur Andersen LLP, WorldCom, Halliburton, and Tyco became (in)famous for their cultures that rewarded unethical behavior. People may feel uncomfortable when their own values clash with those of their organizations. Moreover, these value conflicts carry over into the evaluation of ethical courses of action.

At the *societal level*, we recognize that our judgments of good and bad are shaped by societal expectations. Societal values are likely to be internalized within the individual. These societal values are promulgated by significant documents, the society's interpretation of its own history and of other societies' histories, etc. For example, the US Constitution guides the general population's thinking about issues like "life, liberty, and the pursuit of happiness," voting rights, and free speech. The ideas that seem foundational to US society may seem strange to those outside the society.

Ethics can be influenced by the values associated with national culture and the norms for conducting business in particular countries. We think of certain cultures as reflecting particular values, and these values are echoed in their business practices. Geerte Hofstede (1980) systematically explored cultural differences in his oft-cited study of 40 countries and the four dimensions that can be used to compare national cultures. He identified *power distance*, the extent to which people accept inequality in organizations and political systems; *uncertainty avoidance*, comfort with risk taking, conflict, and ambiguity; *individualism*, how individuals view themselves in their relationships with larger collectivities including families, organizations, and society; and *masculinity*, the extent to which achievement, recognition, and independence are viewed as important, as representing important value differences between cultures. Because cultures and countries vary along these dimensions, what might be seen as a normal legitimate practice in one culture may be seen as inappropriate bribery in another. One example of the cultural variability of ethics is paying for news stories about your organization. In some countries, such as Turkey, the practice is acceptable, while most countries consider it unethical.

Clearly, these cultural differences complicate ethical decision making when the values of two cultures come into conflict. An ethical dilemma may arise when the expectations for doing business differ. Should you follow the ethical business practices of your own country or adapt to the business practices of the other country? Sometimes there is no simple answer to this question. However, to ensure employees behave in line with organizational values and conform to US laws governing business transactions, some corporations have developed specific policy statements about what may and may not be done to facilitate the development and maintenance of global business alliances.

Yet another important concern in ethical considerations is *historical context* and *shifting values*. Historical time periods reflect different ideas about acceptable behaviors, value orientations, and ethical standards. So values within a society or organization can change over time. A good example relates to our use of technology. Social networking sites like Facebook, MySpace, and Friendster make it possible to share personal information with anyone who has access to the Internet. The practice of sharing with others what once was considered private information represents a shift in values among younger generations. While older generations may not value this kind of online openness, "digital natives," those who have always known access to the Internet, may see personal information sharing as appropriate and highly desirable. Similarly, fifty years ago not many people were as concerned with environmental pollution, animal rights, and sustainable development as we see today. Today, manufacturers, cosmetics companies, and fast food restaurants are under closer scrutiny in part because at least some people's values have shifted away from environmental exploitation to greater concern for environmental stewardship. We must remember at another point in time in US history it was considered ethical and lawful to deny restaurant service to African-American patrons, to prohibit women and African-Americans from voting, to dismiss pregnant women from their jobs, and to hold public hangings. However, times and values change.

So, given all of the possibilities for value differences, who gets to decide what is ethical? In many cases there would be consistent agreement on the evaluation. However, when conflicting views exist, who or what should function as the final arbitrator? Clearly, the lack of consensus on what counts as ethical behavior complicates the public relations landscape. Fortunately, beginning with the early Greek and Roman periods and continuing through to the present day, scholars and philosophers have provided guidance on ethical decision making. The unfortunate part is that the ethical perspectives they pose do not always lead to similar evaluations of the most ethical courses of action.

Are business ethics different from ethics?

A common perspective may be to think of business practices, including the practice of public relations, as amoral – that business decisions are "just business" and really have no ethical imperative beyond the profit motive. It is as if people believe you can "excuse" a business for acting unethically because it is in its nature to do so. Perhaps we expect businesses to do whatever is necessary to make a profit. The implication is that ethics will not be the primary driving force when a business chooses between courses of action. If a business decision is ethical, that's great, but it is not expected. Rather, businesses might be assumed to act in self-interested ways.

This perspective suggests that business has its own rationale, the profit motive, and that value takes precedence over all else. After all, if an organization fails to make a profit, then it is no longer in business. This sentiment was reflected in Milton Friedman's (1970) oft-cited piece, "The Social Responsibility of Business is to Increase Its Profits." This article emphasized the importance of business returning value to shareholders. Friedman acknowledged limitations to this perspective when he argued that business must not violate laws in order to do so. However, his comments are often interpreted to mean that organizations should do what they can "get away with" while not breaking any laws and they will try to be ethical when they can. From this perspective ethics might be perceived as secondary to profits. This perspective may be what guides people's thinking when they focus on public relations as a business function. However, businesses that engage in unethical actions are not likely to be successful for long. So most people believe that all business decisions should be examined for their ethical implications. Business decisions should not be immune from evaluation because they are not value neutral.

Ethical Perspectives

Different ethical perspectives emphasize different criteria for determining the morality of an action or decision. For this reason, the same action may be judged as ethical or unethical, depending on the values underpinning the assessment and the ethical perspective that is applied.

Thus far we have discussed ethics in general. How do we determine if a specific course of action or decision is ethical? Philosophers and scholars have long debated questions about ethics and various ethical perspectives have been proposed as foundations for making judgments. Evaluating ethics would be simple if there were just one, universal ethical perspective that should be applied in all situations. However, this is not the case. Judging the ethics of a decision or act necessitates the selection of an ethical perspective to guide decision making. An exploration of major ethical perspectives will illustrate how ethical decision making is not conveniently straightforward. Adhering to different ethical perspectives can lead to judging different courses of action as the most ethical. Although we think we know an ethical act – or unethical act – when we see it, alternative ethical frameworks can be applied, resulting in different determinations of the most ethical course of action.

Egoist perspective

Critics of public relations often assume that practitioners operate from an egoist perspective. *Egoist ethics* focuses on the consequences or outcomes of an action. The egoist framework acknowledges that actions should be limited to those permissible by law; but it endorses the idea that individuals or groups/organizations should evaluate behavior in terms of what will bring the most good to themselves. It assumes behavior reflects a *self-interest*. The perspective suggests public relations practitioners should do whatever is possible (within legal limits) to benefit their organizations.

An obvious problem arises from this perspective. What happens when all parties pursue their own self-interests and their actions conflict with each other's pursuits? The solution may lie in *cooperation* so that all parties can pursue their self-interests without interfering with others. A name commonly associated with the egoist ethics framework is Milton Friedman, whom we mentioned earlier. This well-known Nobel laureate and conservative economist focused on the economic outcomes of business decision making. In his famous *New York Times* (1970) essay referred to above, he argued that organizations have an obligation to maximize profits (increase shareholder value) because this is the primary purpose of business. They exist to increase shareholder value and to do this by creating jobs and producing high-quality, low-cost products. Of course, this should be done within the parameters of the law. So, from this perspective, ethical decisions would be ones that maximize shareholder value, a form of self-interest.

Teleological perspective

A *teleological approach* to ethics, often referred to as a *consequentialist approach* to ethics, suggests one should consider the *consequences* or outcomes of an action to determine its ethical merit. Although egoist ethics is considered a type of consequentialist ethic because it focuses on the outcome reflecting self-interest, the teleological perspective more often is associated with the idea that ethical actions bring about the "greatest good for the greatest number" who are affected by the decision. It also is associated with the idea that the "ends justify the means." The underlying assumption is that actors should examine the overall benefits or advantages as well as the costs or disadvantages of the outcomes expected to follow from the decision. The most ethical decision is the one that results in the *most positive consequences* and the *least negative consequences* for those affected by the action (Bowen, 2005c).

Within the teleological framework two types of *utilitarianism* can be used to evaluate actions: act utilitarianism and rule utilitarianism. Both suggest you consider the consequences of actions. *Act utilitarianism* suggests ethical actions are contingent on the nature of the situation. It recommends you look at the specific situation, and select the act that *maximizes the greatest balance of good* for all affected. In contrast, *rule utilitarianism*, associated with John Stuart

Mill, emphasizes the importance of *general rules of conduct* that emphasize the greatest universal utility. It reflects concern with the public good or the public interest, a concern for the rights of all members of society. People are obligated to select a course of action that brings about the greatest good to the public. *Professional codes of conduct* that specify guidelines for behavior provide these kinds of rules of conduct that may be established and modified over time to reflect the knowledge gained from the profession's experience (Stoker, 2005).

A problem associated with the teleological approach is that it assumes we can *predict* accurately the possible consequences or outcomes of decision alternatives and then select the superior one (Bowen, 2005c). Admittedly this type of clairvoyance is problematic! Another problem is associated with the difficulty of balancing the interests of all groups potentially affected by a decision. Recall, organizations have numerous constituencies. It may be necessary to focus on those who are most directly affected rather than those more indirectly affected by a decision when determining the most ethical course of action.

Deontological perspective

The *deontological* ethical perspective emphasizes "rule following," stressing rights, moral principles, obligations, and duties. The American Bill of Rights provides an example of rights that are guaranteed to all US citizens. Decision making should be guided by moral principles that apply equally to all people (Bowen, 2005a). The assumption is that if you follow the "contract" (contractarianism), you will be making an ethical decision. Two lines of thought are delineated within the deontological perspective: the *ethics of duty* and the *ethics of rights*. Although both stress rule following, they differ in their locus.

An *ethics of duty* emphasizes obligation to *moral rules* (duties) based on universal, self-evident requirements. Engaging in moral action fulfills duty. The emphasis is on the *duty itself*, not the consequences of the act. Using a professional code of ethics that says members of the profession must always be truthful in their communication provides an example of duty. Perhaps the best example of the ethics of duty perspective is Immanuel Kant's *categorical imperative*. Kant, a German philosopher, believed that people had absolute moral duties (categorical duties) to never lie, steal, or murder; people also have a duty to improve themselves and help others. The *motive* for an action, or *the worth of the act itself* – not its consequences – should be considered in evaluating its ethics. Kant's categorical imperative would be used to judge the worth of the act itself. Should this behavior become universal law? Should we be expected to act in this way under all circumstances? Kant believed that following moral principles that transcend situations and cultures should eliminate self-interested behavior. According to advocates of the deontological perspective, when the potential consequences of a decision are considered, as in teleological approaches, there is a greater potential for bias and self-interest to enter the picture (Stoker, 2005). Because the deontological perspective considers the act itself, not the outcome of the act, it is possible that acts can produce undesirable consequences. However, the categorical imperative suggests we must discharge these categorical duties because of their inherent morality.

The second type of deontological decision making, the *ethics of rights*, often is associated with the British political philosopher John Locke and his social contract theory. The ethics of rights argues that people have certain rights and entitlements that should be respected. However, a person's actions may not impinge upon the rights of another. For example, the US Constitution guarantees the right to privacy, freedom of conscience, the right of free speech, and the right to due process. The assumption is these rights should apply equally to all people and that the government should not interfere with these rights.

Locke's approach focuses on the obligation of the community or government to the individual. He argued that government is designed to police conflicts so that people are free to pursue those rights to life, liberty, and property, for example. Laws should preserve and enlarge individual freedoms. The assumption is that the authority of the government derives from a voluntary agreement among people to form a political community and obey the laws they have created. The social contract between the community and individuals must not be broken. When the system violates the rights of a group of people and no longer benefits them, it will collapse. For example, Locke would contend that if the US government (or court system) failed to uphold citizens' rights to free speech or due process, the government should be dismantled by the people.

The ethic of care

An *ethic of care* represents an additional ethical perspective that could guide public relations practitioners. An ethic of care emphasizes "maintaining connections and nurturing the web of relationships in which they were embedded" (Simola 2003, p. 354). This perspective fits well with the boundary-spanning role of public relations and is consistent with our view of public relations as managing mutually influential relationships within a web of constituency relationships. As Heath and Coombs (2006) suggest, a useful metric for assessing ethics is the extent to which the organization builds, maintains, and strengthens relationships in mutually beneficial ways and meets public standards of ethical behavior.

Simola (2003, 2005; see also Coombs & Holladay, 2007b; Heath & Coombs, 2006) draws upon Carol Gilligan's (1977, 1982) work that advocates for the value of the ethic of care and its emphasis on interdependence, authentic relationships, mutual understanding, and responsiveness to the needs of others. It reflects a concern for trying to meet conflicting responsibilities to different people, a challenge commonly experienced by public relations professionals. Simola acknowledges this involves a particular kind of *process*, not outcome, where we experience genuine engagement with others to understand and evaluate their concerns. This ethical perspective would value giving voice to stakeholders as well as voicing organizational perspectives and engaging in dialogue and open conflict to negotiate relationships in the public sphere (see also Hirschman, 1970).

The ethic of care is consistent with a growing interest in the public relations literature with the idea of *dialogue*. As Kent (2005) notes, dialogue often is described as a form of interpersonal conversation based on trust and mutual respect. The idea is that using dialogue as a guiding framework for communication will result in a more ethical process and produce beneficial outcomes. Because this approach advocates listening to and responding to the diverse voices of different relational partners, a weakness of this approach is it can produce decisions that seem to privilege some relationships over others. It is unlikely that all competing voices will feel their relational partners made a decision in their best interests. However, the process itself – of listening, authentic engagement, etc. – may be valued by the participants, as well as the public as a whole, even when their perspectives do not win out. The products of the dialogic process include trust, satisfaction, and sympathy (Kent & Taylor, 2002). Participants may feel satisfied that their concerns were heard even when decisions do not go their way.

Professional Associations and Ethics

The ideas associated with these ethical perspectives often are reflected in the codes of ethics developed by professional associations. Public relations practitioners may choose to join one or more professional organizations that endorse ethical communication practices. However, the public relations profession does not have a certifying body like medical professionals (AMA), accountants (CPA), or attorneys (the Bar Association) do. While some professional associations in other fields can remove or penalize members for engaging in unethical practices, this is not the case for public relations practitioners. Because virtually anyone could claim to possess the expertise to practice relations, this complicates the "policing" of the professional landscape. Public relations practitioners may elect to join professional organizations including the Public Relations Society of America (PRSA), the International Association of Business Communicators (IABC), the Chartered Institute of Public Relations (CIPR), and Global Alliance.

The PRSA is a professional organization specifically geared toward PR professionals in the US. The preamble to its Code of Ethics (2000) describes the code as a "useful guide for PRSA members as they carry out their ethical responsibilities" (p. 1). It contains statements of professional values, principles of conduct, and explanations of commitment and compliance. The document also provides brief examples of actual cases of misconduct that can be used to demonstrate unethical practices that violate the code provisions.

The PRSA's list of "professional values" that underlie the Code of Ethics includes advocacy (providing a voice), honesty (accuracy and truth), expertise (applying specialized knowledge), independence (objective counsel and accountability for actions), loyalty (to clients and the public interest), and fairness (in deal-ing with clients, competitors, the media, and the general public; demonstrating respect for all opinions and supporting the right of free expression) (PRSA, 2000, pp. 1–2). These are fairly "predictable," non-controversial values that also appear in the codes of the other professional public relations organizations. These pro-fessional values are consistent with Parsons' (2004) pillars of ethical decision making. It is worth noting that all of these organizations stress honesty as well as advocacy, suggesting that ethical communication requires truthfulness and accuracy in the pursuit of strategic, persuasive communication. Similar to eth-ics codes in other professions, the codes focus on the means, not the ends or outcomes, of communication. Moreover, there are no mechanisms for enforcing these codes of ethics. For instance, while the PRSA notes it does not enforce the code, it does mention that the PRSA board of directors reserves the right to expel members or bar membership.

Overall, the codes of ethics developed by professional associations for public relations practitioners are sensitive to their roles as public communicators and their obligations to society. However, these codes also acknowledge practitio-ners' obligations to their clients. Discussions of persuasion or advocacy stress the importance of honesty and accuracy in dealing with others. While the codes have no teeth for enforcement, the underlying assumption seems to be that mem-bers understand they may be putting their employment opportunities at risk if they engage in unethical behaviors.

A Model for Ethical Decision Making

Based upon our discussion of the responsibilities of public relations profes-sionals and ethical perspectives, we propose a basic model to guide our quest for ethical decision making. These items represent factors to consider when evaluating courses of action. The model considers both the means and the ends of communication choices. However, as we discussed earlier, sometimes these may conflict with each other. While the model may not be exhaustive, it should stimulate thinking about a wide range of concerns implicated in ethi-cal decision making. As you read through these, consider how personal level, organizational level, and social level values may be implicated in the decision making:

1   *Identify that an ethical dilemma may exist.* This involves recognizing the salient dimensions of the situation, any relevant parties, and potential chal-lenges associated with the specific communication situation (e.g., potential conflicts of interest between the organization and constituencies, potential conflicts of interest between constituencies, relational histories with the groups, threats to important values, previous patterns or routes of decision making in the organization, public standards of ethical behavior, etc.).

2   *Examine potential courses of action by applying ethical perspectives.* This would require assessment of issues such as: What actions are being considered? What are the goals? Which ethical perspective(s) underlie the possible courses of actions? Do any ethical perspectives suggest this course of action would be unwise? Weigh competing interests. Who might be affected? Will the process of communication be open? Will the process demonstrate interdependence between parties by using both listening and speaking? Consider potential consequences of the actions. To what extent are the decision making and the actions transparent? What would a third party think of these? Do these actions honor relationships with constituencies? Would these actions contribute positively to relationships with stakeholders? Which constituencies might benefit? Which constituencies might be disadvantaged by this action?

3   *Assess possible short-term and long-term consequences of pursuing the course of action.* What does the organization gain (or lose) in the short term and long term? What do various constituencies gain or lose in the short term and long term? How will the public likely view the consequences of pursuing the course of action?

4   *Determine and enact the most appropriate course of action.* Select specific tactics (message contents) that are consistent with the goal(s) and the idea of mutual influence and respect in relationships. Are these tactics enacted with a critical eye toward the process used? Do the tactics reflect respect for social responsibility? Do the selected tactics meet basic guidelines for truthfulness, accuracy, and transparency?

5   *Assess the extent to which desired goals were achieved.* Where did they fall short in terms of process and outcomes? Were goals pursued and achieved in a way that honored relationships with stakeholders? Did the public perceive these actions to be transparent? To what extent were these seen as acceptable by salient constituencies and society at large?

Reflection

We have reviewed several common ethical perspectives that can be applied to decision making dilemmas. The communication choices (including whether to communicate at all) made by public relations practitioners are ethical choices and it behooves practitioners to understand these ethical perspectives. As public communicators, the activities of public relations professionals should be open to scrutiny. Increasing calls for transparency in decision making (also discussed in chapter 3) reflect this concern with ethics. We acknowledged how national cultural values, societal values, and the values of the organizational culture may influence the ethical perspectives used to evaluate decisions. These value systems are important not only to the decision maker but also to the public judging the ethical merits of the decision. We also discussed how personal values underlie ethical deliberations. The professional codes of ethics include personal values that practitioners should consider. Ultimately, people are responsible for their own actions. They can choose to obey or disobey a directive from a superior that conflicts with their own values. So, at the most basic, personal level, adhering to ethical standards is a personal choice. However, what might matter most is the "court of public opinion." It can be difficult to hide ethical violations. Although the organization and the practitioner may believe they acted ethically, constituencies may decide otherwise and question the actions. As a part of the larger society, organizations are legitimately subject to public evaluations of their actions.

Discussion Questions

1 Consider the three scenarios presented at the beginning of this chapter. What are the bases of the ethical dilemmas faced by Gene, Rosa, and Jason? What advice would you give to each? Which ethical perspective(s) inform your advice?

2 What is your reaction to Parsons' (2004) five pillars of ethical decision making in public relations? What parallels do you see with the ethical perspectives described later in the chapter? Would you add any pillars to her list?

3 Identify examples of how the term public relations is used in media reports. What connotations are associated with the term? Do you believe these represent accurate depictions of the practice of public relations?

4 Visit PR Watch's website (www.prwatch.org) to view examples of their reports on the questionable practices of various corporations. Identify which ethical perspective(s) guide their critiques of the corporate activities.

5 Identify examples of the use of VNRs (video news releases) in local or national news broadcasts. How were the sources of the VNRs identified (if at all)?

6 What do we mean when we describe public relations practitioners as boundary spanners? Explain why this role may be associated with ethical dilemmas.

7 Describe the major ethical perspectives that can be used to evaluate decision making. Develop hypothetical scenarios to illustrate how applying different ethical perspectives could lead to different evaluations of the most ethical courses of action. How should we make decisions in these cases?

8 Visit the websites of these professional organizations and consult examples of their professional codes of ethics: PRSA (www.prsa.org), CIPR (www.cipr.co.uk), Global Alliance (www.globalpr.org), and IABC (www.iabc.com). What similarities and differences do you observe?

UN Global Compact logo.

3

Public Relations
and Transparency

The word transparency seems to be everywhere you look these days. The news media, corporations, the government, and activists all talk about the need for and the benefits of transparency. Transparency centers on the availability of information to constituents. Naturally, public relations should be linked in some way to transparency because it involves the flow and exchange of information between constituencies. This chapter seeks to explore the concept of transparency in some detail and to unpack public relations' place within the realm of transparency. The chapter begins by placing transparency in society, then moves to an elaboration of the concept as a precursor to discussing public relations' role in transparency.

Transparency's Place in Society: The Public Sphere and the Marketplace of Ideas

Cox (2006), working from Habermas (1974), defines the *public sphere* as "a realm of influence that is created when individuals engage others in communication – through conversation, argument, debate, or questioning – about subjects of shared concern or topics that affect a wider community" (p. 30). A public sphere develops when constituents talk about issues in a public forum. An issue moves from private to public when people openly discuss the issue. For example, Cox (2006) discusses an environmental public sphere that has developed in the US through public hearings, editorials, rallies, and any other mechanism for people to say and do things about the issue. Cox notes that influence does occur within the public sphere and spheres themselves can influence policy decisions, such as environmental policy making.

The marketplace of ideas is akin to a public sphere. Recall, the marketplace of ideas refers to how multiple ideas and voices should be available to listeners.

First amendment concerns are often justified based upon the concept of the marketplace of ideas. However, the public sphere introduces influence to the process. It is not just that the best idea wins in the marketplace. Rather, it is the notion that people are influenced to believe it is the best or simply influenced to accept the idea as the most viable alternative. People rarely thoroughly consider all of the available options when making decisions. We are victims of "bounded rationality." Bounded rationality refers to the idea that there are limits on our human abilities to systematically process all the information available to us, and we often must make decisions in a limited amount of time. People select a viable or adequate solution, but not one that necessarily maximizes returns, what Hebert Simon (1959) calls *satisficing*. Satisficing was created by combining the words "satisfy" and "suffice." So where do these concepts lead us? People are unlikely to sort through all the ideas in the marketplace and may be subject to the influence efforts of those presenting the ideas. Public relations is a crucial mechanism through which groups attempt to exert influence in the marketplace of ideas. As we posit, public relations is a matter of *mutual but not necessarily equal* influence.

Ideally, transparency adds "products" to the marketplace of ideas and facilitates the development of a public sphere. Generally speaking, transparency is about information availability for constituents. Corporations release information to constituents or constituents find information and share it with others. Ideally, the information allows constituents to "see" the inner workings of an organization by detailing policies and even offering insights into how decisions are made. An example is the immense amount of information US tobacco companies were required to make public during the congressional hearings into the negative effects of tobacco and the tobacco industry's role in misrepresenting and concealing information about nicotine and addiction. The Legacy Tobacco Documents Library is a searchable and retrievable digital archive of tobacco industry documents made possible by the American Legacy Foundation. The companies in the library include Brown & Williamson, American Tobacco, Lorillard, Liggett & Myers, Phillip Morris, RJ Reynolds, and the Tobacco Institute. The library can be found at www.legacy.library.ucsf.edu/. If you are inclined, visit the site and search for "public relations" to catch a glimpse of how the tobacco industry was using the term. Constituents are learning all kinds of new and often sordid details about those tobacco companies. Public relations is an integral part of transparency and is involved in the dissemination of information by corporations and the facilitation of the demands of constituents for corporate information. Ultimately, transparency should help constituents make informed decisions about public issues and their involvement with specific corporations.

Transparency: Elaborating on an Enigmatic Concept

The term transparency is used and perhaps abused widely as it has become a business buzzword (Best, 2005). The solution to any problem these days seems to be transparency, including public relations. Transparency is not a panacea that can be applied to every problem. Moreover, the concept of transparency is problematic as we have little idea of what it really means or how it should look in practice. In reality, transparency means many things and different things to different people. In this section we examine why transparency has emerged as a critical issue in public relations, how we can define/conceptualize transparency, and its implications for public relations.

The rise of transparency

Transparency exploded into the international lexicon following the financial meltdown in Asian markets and the US corporate scandal parade led by Enron at the beginning of the twenty-first century. In finance, transparency means the full, accurate, and timely disclosure of information (Transparency, n.d.). Regulations such as the Sarbanes-Oxley Act of 2002 were designed to increase financial transparency and prevent market crises by allowing "problems" to emerge quickly rather than to fester and build into "crises." For example, the act stipulates that the governance of the organizations must be transparent. Additionally, Sarbanes-Oxley holds executive officers personally accountable for organizational actions. Executives are required to certify the accuracy of financial statements and provide that financial information in real time, when possible.

Transparency is also applied to international politics as a means of combating corruption. For example, Transparency International tries to strip away the shields that prevent people from seeing the corrupt practices of governments such as bribe taking. The Bribe Payers Index (BPI), sponsored by Transparency International, is one method for revealing international corruption. The index focuses on what governments are taking bribes from business entities. The UN is actively seeking to curb corruption as part of its UN Global Compact. The UN Global Compact is the world's largest global citizenship initiative and anti-corruption practices are one of its four major areas of concern. The Global Compact is also discussed later in this chapter in conjunction with social reporting mechanisms. The UN Global Compact seeks to make globalization a positive force by ensuring that it benefits societies and economies everywhere. Businesses are asked to align their operations with the ten universally accepted principles of the UN Global Compact that cover the four areas of human rights, labour, environment, and anti-corruption. For a complete list of the ten principles, see box 3.1.

Corporations are reporting information about corporate social responsibility (CSR) to appease and to attract constituents interested in CSR-related issues such as sustainability. In summary, a number of different interests have promoted the use of the term transparency in the business world and that concern is reflected in the growing interest public relations is showing in transparency (Gower, 2006).

In public relations, one use of transparency is full disclosure of sources. Transparency is often tied to ethics through VNRs, blog postings, spokesperson identification, and front groups. The common thread is identifying who is the owner of the true voice. This is sometimes referred to as *authenticity of a voice.*

Box 3.1   UN Global Compact

Human rights
Principle 1   Businesses should support and respect the protection of internation-
ally proclaimed human rights;
Principle 2   make sure that they are not complicit in human rights abuses.

Labour standards
Principle 3   Businesses should uphold the freedom of association and the effec-
tive recognition of the right to collective bargaining;
Principle 4   the elimination of all forms of forced and compulsory labor;
Principle 5   the effective abolition of child labor;
Principle 6   the elimination of discrimination in respect of employment and
occupation.

Environment
Principle 7   Businesses should support a precautionary approach to environmen-
tal challenges;
Principle 8   undertake initiatives to promote greater environmental responsibility;
Principle 9   encourage the development and diffusion of environmentally friendly
technologies.

Anti-corruption
Principle 10   Businesses should work against corruption in all its forms, including
extortion and bribery.

As described in chapter 2's discussion of ethical concerns, VNRs are frequently aired as news stories with no attribution to the public relations people who created them. Edelman posted blogs for Wal-Mart that appeared to be written by Wal-Mart employees and customers but were actually written by Edelman employees or people paid by Edelman. The Edelman-Walmart case is discussed in chapter 7 that covers online communication.

In another case, there was an issue over the misidentification of a source from SBC. SBC was originally known as Southwest Bell Corporation. The name was changed to SBC Communications Inc. to demonstrate the company was now national, not just a regional provider of telecommunications services and equipment. Their core business was wireless and land-based telephone services. SBC is now part of AT&T. While still SBC, a person was quoted in a news story and self-identified himself as an employee of SBC. In reality, the man was not an employee of SBC, but an employee of their public relations firm. The journalist covering the story was none too happy about being duped and turned what was a simple story into an exposé. Along the same lines, front groups, as discussed in chapters 2 and 10, purposefully hide who is funding and running a supposed citizens' group. We can look at these examples and identify the ethical concerns and the methods by which transparency can prevent ethical dilemmas about disclosing sources. However, transparency and its application to public relations extend far beyond attributing messages to the proper sources. The next section explores what transparency is, followed by its application to public relations.

Defining transparency

The phrase "full, accurate, and timely disclosure" is both vague and, to a degree, naive. Transparency is often taken as a *quality* that an organization possesses. The assumption can be that organizations will practice full disclosure because we believe it is required by law to disclose all financial information. We must remember there is more information than just financial information that is of interest to stakeholders. Moreover, businesses do not reveal everything, even when it involves financial information. Consider the term *proprietary information*. This is the information that provides a competitive edge and is not to be disclosed. In addition, we have the realms of competitive intelligence and counter-intelligence. Competitive intelligence is the legal collection and analysis of information about competitors and markets. Competitive intelligence provides timely, relevant, accurate, and unbiased intelligence on potential threats to an organization's competitive position. Competitive intelligence is a rapidly growing professional field because it helps a company gain an edge over its rivals.

Organizations purposely release information in ways to prevent competitive intelligence gathering. This is known as *defensive competitive intelligence*. It attempts to make it more difficult for competitors to find useful information about your company. That means information is often released in ways meant to disguise its true value or make analysis of the information difficult. *Cloaking* is an important part of defensive competitive intelligence. Cloaking involves efforts to screen your organization's information from the eyes of competitors or any other constituents. Clearly, there is no way to make information about an organization completely invisible, but there are means to mask and to hide information that is supposed to be in plain sight (Coombs, 2008; McGongale & Vella, 2007). So we should delve deeper than full disclosure to explore the meaning of transparency.

Transparency can mean the quality of being transparent. So we must consider what transparent means. According to Merriam-Webster, transparent can mean: sheer enough to see through, having the property to transmit light so that objects lying beyond are clearly seen, free of pretense or deceit (Transparent, n.d.). From these base definitional molecules we can construct more complex meanings for transparency in business.

The earlier discussion of transparency as full disclosure reflects the sheerness notion of transparent. Organizations can vary in how sheer they are – how easy it is for stakeholders to collect specific types of information about organizations. Ideally, the information we see is free of deceit. However, defensive competitive intelligence is but one among many factors that can preclude "deceit-less" information. Consider the terms greenwashing and bluewashing. *Greenwashing* involves a corporation promoting its environmental friendliness while continuing to commit many environmental abuses. A corporation talks publicly about its environmental commitment and/or promotes one area in which it has changed its practices while it is still fundamentally an environmental threat. Similarly, *bluewashing* occurs when a corporation signs on to support the United Nations Global Compact but does not make substantial changes relative to the document. It is called bluewashing because blue is the official color of the United Nations. Whatever the hue, pretending to support a social or environmental cause to boost reputation and avoid interference by stakeholders is antithetical to transparency but does occur frequently.

Transparency as a quality is problematic because control and power still rest largely with corporations. Granted, there are some laws and regulations that require exposure of select corporate information. As noted earlier, most of the required transparency is in the area of finance. What about the effects operations and products have on the environment? How do they treat their workers? How do corporations define and categorize their customers? What progress has been made toward reducing poverty and protecting human rights? We find no Sarbanes-Oxley legislation or similar requirements for social and environmental concerns. Corporations are not suddenly providing access to all their information and communications to constituencies. There is still strategic self-censorship of information by corporations when the information is not legally required.

Gower (2006) argues that true transparency occurs "when a corporation respects the integrity of all its stakeholders and does not seek to manipulate them by controlling access to information" (p. 92). While that is a nice sentiment, it can be considered both naive and impractical. Corporations are free to decide their level of transparency on most social and environmental concerns. It should be clear that transparency is at its roots communicative – what information does the corporation provide constituencies. A group has power when it can control the communication process (Mumby, 1988). Corporations have a power advantage because management can control the transparency communication process for social and environmental issues. Organizations cannot reveal all their information; it would be overwhelming and impractical to do so. Moreover, information is not value neutral. Management strategically selects what it presents to constituents and how it frames it in part to help craft its reputation. This selection process by its very nature is a matter of interpretation and reputation/impression management that some could call manipulation. The interpretation involves both the selection and presentation (framing) of the information. There needs to be some "motivation" for corporations to allow access to social and environmental information. Adding the notion of motivation for transparency takes us in the direction of transparency as *process*.

The implied value of transparency is that it can be a deterrent to illegal and unethical behavior. People are less likely to engage in questionable behavior if they are caught and hopefully punished in some way for that behavior (Gower, 2006). The idea of strategically revealing information to influence behavior is not new in public relations. I can remember being told years ago that public relations counselors often tell management not to do anything they would not mind seeing in the newspaper the next day. Today, that advice would be not to do anything they would not mind seeing on the Internet that day. Transparency serves as a control mechanism. An example is useful at this point.

Consider an organization that mines gold. A large quantity of waste is created in the gold mining process. If constituents learn a company mines in a legal but environmentally destructive way, constituents might revoke their support for the company and perhaps even oppose the company. As a result, the company utilizes environmentally friendly practices for fear of reprisals if their environmentally destructive practices were known. This hypothetical gold mining company chooses its mining practices based on how information about those practices might influence constituents. The company seeks to avoid punishment and to gain rewards from constituents. Rewards come from continued support and lack of opposition from constituents. However, this assumes that the mining information will be disclosed and that constituents will care about it.

We should pay more attention to the idea of transparency as the ability to allow objects lying beyond to be clearly seen. This definition moves us from *transparency as a quality* to *transparency as a process*. Transparency is more than something an organization has; it is a tool constituents use to inspect the organization and to "regulate" the organization. Transparency is not just the sheerness of corporations but the efforts of constituents to examine what rests beyond. A simple metaphor will help illustrate the process notion. Imagine that corporations place their information in a box. Transparency as quality simply asks how easy is it to see into the box. We never ask what is in the box. Constituencies use their binoculars to peer into the box. They then evaluate the information they find and search for information they think should be in the box. If important information is missing, constituents try to look beyond the box (other sources inside and outside of the organization) while pressuring management to place more information in the box.

Resources and power are in play when constituents find insufficient information in the box. Resources include other sources that can supply information. One resource would be governmental databases. In the US the Environmental Protection Agency (EPA) maintains a variety of databases that supply information about hazardous material safety and accidents. Many of the databases can be downloaded and examined free of charge. For example, anyone with computer access and a statistical analysis program can examine data about chemical releases, including the types of chemicals and the need to evacuate or shelter-in-place. Another resource would be insiders who leak information about organizational practices to the Internet or news media. For example, Wal-Mart was embarrassed by a PowerPoint presentation on their categorization of consumers that was leaked to the Consumerist website. Wal-Mart was so upset that their lawyers forced the Consumerist website to remove the PowerPoint presentation, but bootleg copies still exist in the hinterlands of the Internet. Also consider how the release of a Clorox Corporation crisis management plan to Greenpeace in 1991 created problems for the corporation. The leaked information made Clorox Corporation look like a bully and exposed some unethical public relations practices. The plan referred to environmental critics as "terrorists" and detailed how the company was combating negative media coverage about chlorine by sending supposedly "independent scientists" on media tours. Clorox was opaque rather than transparent with its efforts to conceal the affiliations of "their" scientists.

We can use the phrase *constituent intelligence* to describe peering into an organization. Constituent intelligence reflects a process view of transparency. First, the desired information must be found. Second, the desired information has to be analyzed – someone must interpret the information. Third, the results must be relayed to others. We can return to the idea of competitive intelligence. Cloaking attempts to hide information that is in plain sight. Information is disguised, presented in ways that are difficult to analyze, and placed in obscure locations. Constituent intelligence demands that constituents be able to locate and to analyze the desired information. Even in a transparent world where certain information must be disclosed, constituent intelligence can be a complex game of hide and seek. Moreover, constituents must be motivated enough to engage in intelligence seeking. The "Free Kuwait" case at the end of this chapter provides an excellent illustration of information hiding in plain sight.

Power becomes an issue when the desired information is nowhere to be found. What happens when a corporation is not required by law to disclose the information and there are no leaks? Constituents must be able to induce the corporations into disclosing the information. Corporations may not reveal the information because of the negative consequences of the disclosure. Managers can fall into the trap of not wanting to disclose negative information for fear it will damage their reputations. Public relations would counsel against not releasing any negative information. However, we must disclose the good and the bad information or become the "spin doctors" that many critics use to label public relations. Constituents can use that same fear in leveraging the disclosure of the information. Public pressure from constituents for the release of information can attract negative attention and harm corporate reputations. In fact, evidence suggests that organizations are harmed less by negative information when they are the first to disclose the information (Arpan & Roskos-Ewoldsen, 2005).

The notion of the Hegelian dialectic emerges here. Georg Wilhelm Friedrich Hegel was a German philosopher writing in the early 1800s during a period of philosophy known as German idealism. Among his many contributions to philosophy is the Hegelian dialectic, a system for explaining change across a wide range of disciplines (Redding, 2006). A Hegelian dialectic is a system of inquiry that can be used to explain historical developments. The central notion is that progress is a function of conflict. The Hegelian dialectic begins with an idea or thesis. A conflicting idea or antithesis is presented as a counter to the thesis. Synthesis is used to reconcile the common truth in the two ideas and to create progress. The corporation's initial information is the thesis, the pressure from the constituents for more information is the antithesis, and the resulting information disclosure (transparency) is the synthesis.

Constituents must leverage their power to pressure corporations to release information. Chapter 5 provides an additional discussion of this subject under the topic of the activist-corporation conflict and the Excellence dialectic. In the end, constituent power and/or corporate goodwill result in the information being released. Either way, the constituents change the transparency habits of the corporations to meet the informational demands of the constituents. The number of social reports released by corporations is an excellent example of changes in transparency habits. These social reports parallel financial annual reports and document social efforts such as composition of workforce, leadership by women and minorities, community involvement, energy consumption, and pollution emissions.

The Global Reporting Initiative (GRI) is the closest framework there is to a standardized system for reporting social issues. GRI uses the term *sustainability reports*. However, their reporting system includes a variety of social factors as well. The primary categories for reporting include economics, environment, human rights, labor, product responsibility, and society. Box 3.2 provides examples of what is reported under each of these categories. Still, there is no required standard to be met for reporting social and environmental concerns. When corporations produce their CSR reports they are free to report what they want and exclude information they would rather not discuss. Rawlins, Paine, and Kowalsi (2008) found that sustainability reports do not provide much negative information at all. This is similar to how annual reports always sound positive for a corporation.

Organizations that participate in the UN Global Compact have a prescribed format for reporting their progress on the ten points of the UN Global Compact. As discussed earlier, the UN Global Compact is the largest global citizenship initiative. The goal is to prevent many of the negative consequences associated

---

Box 3.2   GRI Sustainability Reports

GRI provides extensive information on how to construct sustainability reports. However, there are no internationally accepted rules for exactly what must go into a sustainability report. The GRI system is based around six categories with each category having a number of sub-points organizations are expected to address. This box provides the sub-categories to illustrate examples of what is reported in each of the six categories. Keep in mind many of the sub-points do have multiple points, but the box uses one representative point for each sub-point. The points illustrate the complexity and scope of sustainability reporting.

Economic
Economic performance: direct economic effect of an organization's activities.
Market presence: interactions in specific markets.
Indirect economic impacts: additional effects of an organization's economic activities.

Box 3.2   (*cont'd*)

Environment
Transportation: impact from transporting goods.
Products and services: actions to mitigate impacts of goods and services.
Compliance: any fines for non-compliance with regulations.
Emissions, effluence, and waste: amount of various emissions, effluence, and waste.
Water: total water withdrawal.
Energy: energy consumption.
Materials: materials used by weight.
Biodiversity: location and size of land owned and leased.

Human rights
Investment and procurement practices: percent and total number of agreements that include human rights clauses.
Security practices: percent of security forces trained in company's human rights policies.
Indigenous rights: number of incidents violating rights of indigenous people.
Non-discrimination: total number of discrimination incidents and resolution.
Freedom of association and bargaining: actions taken to support these rights.
Child labor: efforts to eliminate child labor and locations where it is a risk.

Labor
Employment: total workforce by employment type.
Training and education: average number of hours of training per employee.
Labor-management relations: percent of employees covered by collective bargaining.
Diversity and equal opportunity: composition of governance body and workforce.
Occupational health and safety: percent of workforce represented by management-worker health and safety committees.

Product responsibility
Compliance: fines for non-compliance with regulations.
Customer privacy: number of complaints about breach of privacy from customers.
Product and service labeling: percent of products and services covered by such regulations.
Marketing communications: programs for adhering to regulations and voluntary codes for advertising, promotion, and sponsorship.
Customer health and safety: percent of products and services assessed for health and safety effects on consumers.

Society
Community: nature and effectiveness of programs designed to help the community.
Corruption: number of business units at risk for corruption.
Public policy: participation and positions on public policy issues.
Anti-competitive behavior: total number of anti-competitive charges and outcomes.
Compliance: total fines for non-compliance.

Source: Sustainability reporting framework (n.d.)

with globalization. (For a more detailed discussion of globalization, see chapter 14.) The belief is that if the principles of the UN Global Compact are followed, markets and commerce will develop in a way that benefits societies and economies everywhere. There are ten universally accepted principles based on four areas. The four main categories are human rights, labor, environment, and anti-corruption. Human rights covers protection and complicity in abuse. Labor includes freedom of association and collective bargaining, forced and compulsory labor, child labor, and discrimination. Environment includes the precautionary approach, environmental responsibility, and environmentally friendly technology. Anti-corruption includes efforts to curb corruption. Note that the UN system would require reporting some negative information such as contributing to human rights abuses. But these guidelines only hold for organizations involved in the UN Global Compact and how they communicate their progress on the goals. Hence, many corporations would never issue such reports.

One final set of CSR reporting guidelines can be found in Socrates, the corporate social ratings monitor. Socrates is a database that rates and describes 600 companies in terms of their CSR records. Socrates provides four broad ratings indicators: environmental ratings (e.g., climate change, pollution, and recycling), social ratings, governance ratings, and controversial business involvements (e.g., alcohol or adult entertainment). The social rating includes five areas: (1) community support such as housing initiatives or support for the arts; (2) diversity, including race, gender, disability, and sexual orientation; (3) employee support, such as safety and union relations; (4) human rights, including labor rights and treatment of indigenous people; and (5) products, including quality and benefits to the economically disadvantaged (Bhattacharya & Sen, 2004). However, Socrates is not prescriptive and does not require corporations to include specific information in their reports. It simply describes what information does exist in CSR reports.

Transparency as process moves us from a passive to an active view of the subject. Constituents do not wait to see what a corporation might show. Constituents seek information and demand important information that is not released. Obviously, not all constituents will be active in transparency. The burden will fall to the deeply involved, activist element of constituents. James Grunig developed the situational theory of publics to identify people (publics) who want to communicate with your organization – they will actively seek information (active communication behavior). Grunig's situational theory of publics is based on people's involvement with a problem and willingness to communicate about it with others. Three variables are used to assess how likely publics are to be actively involved with a problem:

1   *Problem recognition:* people realize a situation is problematic and feel something should be done about it.
2   *Constraint recognition:* people perceive obstacles that prevent solving the problem.
3   *Level of involvement:* the extent to which people feel connected to the problem/situation.

The situational theory research has consistently identified four types of publics:

1 *Apathetic:* inattentive on most issues.
2 *Hot-issue:* active on issues that involve almost everyone/are widely discussed in the mainstream media.
3 *Single-issue:* active on one or a small set of issues.
4 *All-issue:* active on all issues. (Grunig, 1989c, 2005)

The activist constituents are likely to be single-issue and all-issue publics. They are motivated to find the information, demand missing information, interpret the information, and share it with other constituents. For instance, only highly involved customers (single-issue and all-issue publics) will seek and demand information about trans fats in foods. The involved consumers can then relay their results to others who are interested but less involved (hot-issue publics).

Transparency as a process emphasizes multiple channels for transparency information. The corporation is not the only channel for the release of information. Other constituents are sources for revealing information as well. The Internet intensifies the threat of disclosure of information from other constituencies (Coombs, 1998; Gower, 2006; Heath, 1998). The Internet allows for potentially widespread dissemination of what constituents find when they carefully examine an organization.

Transparency is an active process that ideally is driven by constituents. Constituents drive transparency by identifying the types of information they need and want from corporations. For instance, research indicates that constituents in the US favor CSR information about the treatment of workers over other CSR issues (Bhattacharya & Sen, 2004). All corporations must consider the information demands of their constituents to understand what it is they need to be transparent about.

Transparency as process is consistent with our view of public relations as mutually influential relationships. Most times we think little about the influence in these webs of relationships. Constituents are mostly quiescent, providing at least tacit support for an organization. When constituents see a problem in the relationship, they can become aroused and exercise their influence by trying to alter the organization or by detaching themselves from the organization's web of relationships. The fear of constituents becoming agitated and the need for quiescence is a motivator for transparency. We must believe that constituents will seek information they feel is essential to their needs. It behooves organizations to be transparent and to provide that information. Failure to provide the information can result in constituents seeking the information from other sources, efforts to force the disclosure of the information, or severing ties with the organization. To avoid these problems, an organization engages in more ethical behavior so that it can disclose the desired information without creating agitation. The earlier gold mining example illustrates this point. If an organization knows it will be held publicly accountable for an action, the organization will want to make sure that it is behaving in a way that does not create opposition from constituents.

Transparency is a process involving the disclosure of information, accountability for actions, and consequences for those actions. Information disclosure is the lynchpin of transparency. Again, it is unrealistic to assume full disclosure of all information in an organization is possible or even desirable. In reality, the key is relevant information. Constituents must have access to and be aware of the information they deem important to them. Consider a corporation's sustainability report. Is the information constituents desire in the document? Do they know how to access that document? Not only must the information be accessible, it must circulate among constituents as well. That is the Internet's strength, creating easy access to and distribution of information.

While necessary, relevant information is not sufficient for transparency to establish accountability. Constituents must be motivated and/or care enough to act on the information. Those actions might be praise or quiescence when the information is favorable or punishment when the information is unfavorable. Let us return to the gold mining example. If constituents do not seem to care about pollution from gold mining, waste production is not an issue. A few committed constituents may complain about the waste, but if no one else echoes or seems likely to echo the message, there is little pressure for the mine operators to change. In fact, the need for concern is what leads some experts to speculate that constituents cannot be counted on to drive real change for sustainability. The problem is that not enough constituents will care enough to establish an accountability system for corporations (Collins, Kearns, & Roper, 2005). No amount of transparency (openness of information) will matter if a critical mass of constituents is not sufficiently motivated to respond to the information.

Is it pessimistic to assume corporations will not simply see the light and will fail to make the necessary reforms without any pressure or fear of retribution from constituents? Yes, but it is also realistic. What in the long history of corporations would suggest otherwise? The struggle of the labor unions and confrontations with activists are evidence corporations are not naturally evolving toward self-enlightenment. Granted, there are those shining beacons of enlightened corporations such as the Body Shop, Patagonia, and Stoneybrook Farm. But these are the exceptions, not the norm. Improvements are more likely to be driven by accountability to constituents. Managers will make changes when they see a tipping point on the horizon – a significant mass of constituents are or can become aroused. For constituent-driven accountability to function, there needs to be a fair degree of transparency on relevant information and a significant amount of constituents that actively care or potentially could be activated.

The Role of Public Relations

We can define enlightened corporations as those that anticipate potential constituent concerns and take action before efforts to force that action occur. Research consistently finds that voluntary changes in corporate behaviors are viewed more positively by constituents than involuntary changes (Husted & Salazar, 2006). Hart and Sharma (2004) argue that corporations can gain significant competitive advantages by listening to marginalized and remote constituents instead of routinely listening to the more powerful constituents. Public relations is one of the means for hearing these distant constituents. A basic tenet preached in public relations courses is that public relations serves both organizational and societal interests. Postmodernists expand on this idea by suggesting that public relations should advocate for constituents when management is making decisions (Holtzhausen & Voto, 2002). Whatever the label, public relations can and should be a voice *for* constituents as well as a messenger *to* constituents.

Public relations personnel ideally should be in contact with their constituents. This contact should include efforts to understand the needs and wants of constituents. In turn, public relations can use that information to shape organizational decisions. Public relations can represent the various constituency concerns to other managers, thereby entering those concerns into the decision making equation. One reason some constituents are marginalized is that they have difficulty being heard by management. Public relations, as their advocates, can help constituents to be heard. Of course, for this system to work, managers must accept the belief that listening to the marginalized is constructive (Hart & Sharma, 2004).

To end this discussion of transparency and public relations we should revisit the notion of spin. Although spin is often used as a synonym for public relations, the two are different. *Spin* involves simply presenting only the positive information. For instance, an organization never seems to report any bad news, implying it never does anything wrong. Read an annual report and you would think no organization ever had a bad financial year and they all anticipate bright futures. If something does go wrong, some positive aspect is located and featured prominently. It was not a bad year economically; the organization simply was changing strategy and it will take a while for the numbers to respond.

Public relations must be willing to address the good and the bad news. At times things do go wrong and problems do occur. We believe that ultimately public relations must be based on real actions and that entails both the good and bad. Transparency as a process attempts to defeat spin by looking behind the words to see alternative realities. Constituents can utilize public relations to help make that transparency process function. Part of public relations requires collecting information as well as disseminating that information to others. Transparency can help to keep public relations honest and public relations can be utilized to help the transparency work properly. It is an odd but potentially fruitful union when public relations works in tandem with transparency.

Case Study: Citizens for a Free Kuwait

If you have read many public relations books, the odds are you are familiar with Hill & Knowlton's role in selling the US people on the need to liberate Kuwait from the 1990 invasion by Saddam Hussein. Although this is an older case, it helps illustrate important ideas covered in this chapter. We would like to revisit this case from the viewpoint of transparency. Actions in the effort to "free Kuwait" raise a number of issues with hiding information both in plain sight and covertly.

Hiding information in plain sight

The Citizens for a Free Kuwait was the organization that hired Hill & Knowlton, the prominent public relations firm, to win public and political support in the US for liberating Kuwait. The Citizens for a Free Kuwait were foreign agents, non-US citizens who were engaging in public relations in the US through Hill & Knowlton. As such, everything Hill & Knowlton did for the Citizens for a Free Kuwait was subject to the Foreign Agents and Registration Act (FARA). According to the US Department of Justice, which oversees the process, FARA is

a disclosure statute that requires persons acting as agents of foreign principals in a political or quasi-political capacity to make periodic public disclosure of their relationship with the foreign principal, as well as activities, receipts and disbursements in support of those activities. Disclosure of the required information facilitates evaluation by the government and the American people of the statements and activities of such persons in light of their function as foreign agents. (FARA, n.d.)

A translation of this bureaucratic text is in order here. In the US, public relations firms that represent foreign agents must register with the Justice Department and provide documentation about their clients, including samples of the public relations messages that are created. Anyone can request copies of this information from the Justice Department. There is a fee of 50 cents per page for copies. The Justice Department offers a search of FARA documents at its website. A person then requests the specific documents, pays for copies, and receives the materials. FARA provides for transparency in public relations for foreign agents.

When Hill & Knowlton was hired by the Citizens for a Free Kuwait, the evidence that the Kuwait government was behind the effort was in plain sight. An examination of the FARA documents would have revealed that $11.8 million was paid by the Kuwait government while 78 other people in the US and Canada contributed some money as well (Carlisle, 1993). Citizens for a Free Kuwait was a front group for the Kuwait government. But no one bothered to look at the time; the information was "found" by later investigative reports. Although the system was transparent, no one bothered to look inside for the information. The information was hidden in plain sight. The Kuwait government, through Hill & Knowlton, were executing an extensive plan to build and to garner support for US intervention in Kuwait. The speculation is that the US would have been less supportive had the truth been known about the Citizens for a Free Kuwait and their sponsorship of the propaganda effort.

Covert actions

Not every action by Hill & Knowlton and the Citizens for a Free Kuwait was transparent. A highly publicized and later highly criticized public relations tactic was the October 10, 1990 testimony of 15-year-old Nayirah before Congress's Human Rights Caucus. Her testimony described Iraqi troops murdering babies by throwing them from their incubators. This horrific account was parroted frequently by those looking to build support for US intervention, including then President George Bush and members of Congress. The story also became a video news release that aired on over 700 news broadcasts. It was reported that Nayirah's real identity was hidden for safety reasons.

John MacArthur, author of the *Second Front: Censorship and Propaganda in the Gulf War*, was among the few to question this compelling testimony. With a few phone calls, he discovered Nayirah was really the daughter of Sheikh Saud Nasir al-Sabah, Kuwait's ambassador to the US (Rowse, 1992). Later, efforts by Amnesty International were unable to confirm Nayirah's testimony. Interviews of staff members working at the hospital at the center of the testimony did not remember Iraqis killing babies by removing them from incubators (Carlisle, 1993). By the time the revelations surfaced, the US was already involved in liberating Kuwait – the Kuwait government had achieved its public relations objective. However, the field of public relations suffered additional reputation damage and Hill & Knowlton was criticized for questionable judgment and unethical behavior in employing a front group. Did public relations alone make the difference in US efforts to liberate Kuwait? We cannot know for sure, but we can speculate that at the very least it made the task easier and more palatable for the US people.

Transparency lessons

The case reinforces the notion that transparency is a *process* rather than a quality. FARA does provide a transparent quality to public relations work for foreign agents. However, if no one looks, does the transparent quality matter? We would answer no. If no one looks for the information, it is still unknown. We also see that organizations will attempt to hide critical information from constituents or even manufacture information that would benefit an organization's cause. Without a process that seeks to examine and to vet information, such deception is likely to succeed, at least long enough to win a tarnished victory. Use of deception does not build long-term trust but, in some cases, such as the Kuwait government, a single victory was enough, regardless of the cost to trust and reputation. When constituents regularly apply transparency as a process, organizations are less likely to engage in deceptive behavior, or at least be more likely to be exposed early on in the process. Society benefits when constituents attempt to make public relations efforts transparent.

Case questions

1 How do we distinguish between overt actions and covert actions in this case?
2 How does FARA seek to aid transparency?
3 What risks do public relations firms run when they fail to be transparent?
4 Who, or what agencies, should be responsible for evaluating the ethics of public relations efforts? A frequently quoted adage in advertising is "Let the buyer beware." Should this be applied to public relations efforts as well?

Discussion Questions

1 Distinguish between the concepts of the public sphere and the marketplace of ideas. How are they associated with the practice of public relations?
2 What do we mean by "transparency"? Why are constituents concerned with transparency? How can transparency be seen as related to ethical and legal considerations?
3 How can transparency be seen as both a quality and a process? What is the role of public relations in transparency? What are the limits to transparency?
4 Visit the website of the Legacy Tobacco Documents (www.legacy.library.ucsf.edu) and search for "public relations" to learn how the tobacco industry was using the term. Based

on what you learned in this chapter, how concerned was the tobacco industry with transparency?

5 Visit the website of Transparency International to view the Bribe Payers Index (BPI) (www. transparency.org/policy_research/surveys_indices/bpi). Under what circumstances, if any, is it permissible to use bribes to facilitate business transactions?

6 Visit the website of the Global Reporting Initiative (www.globalreporting.org/Home) to view how they conceptualize economic, environmental, and social performance reporting as being as significant as financial reporting. What dimensions are emphasized in their reports?

7 Visit the website of KLD, the firm that uses the Corporate Social Ratings Monitor (Socrates) to describe organizational performance (www.kld. com/research/socrates/index.html). How should public relations practitioners be involved in publicizing organizational performance?

8 Visit the website explaining the UN's Global Compact (www.unglobalcompact.org/AboutThe GC/index.html). What elements comprise the compact? How are these associated with concerns for transparency?

9 In this chapter we discussed transparency. For public relations practitioners, what are the advantages and disadvantages of transparency? What challenges do constituent demands for transparency create for the profession?

Bert the Salmon.

4

Public Relations as Strategic Communication

A story appears in the *New York Times* about a new product a company is about to release. The story explains how the product was developed and how it will benefit consumers. A clever reader can surmise that the news story is the result of public relations efforts because it is a form of positive publicity for the company. Publicity is still the most visible aspect of public relations. However, a repeated theme in this and other writings on public relations is that public relations is more than publicity. The phrase "more than publicity" has two meanings. First, public relations practitioners use a variety of channels when communicating with stakeholders, not just the media. As Grunig (1989b) noted many years ago, publicity is a rather limited channel of communication. Later, this chapter will detail the various communication channels used in public relations.

Second, publicity is a means to an end in public relations. It is wrong to think that the news story (publicity) is the end. Effective public relations is *strategic* – it is purposeful. Publicity also must be strategic to be of value. Ask yourself, "What might this story help management to achieve?" Some answers include: stimulate sales, reassure investors, and help build a favorable reputation. Publicity is not the mindless generation of news stories. Rather, publicity is the mindful use of news stories to achieve larger organizational goals and objectives. This chapter explores the strategic aspect of public relations by examining key concepts, reviewing the basic practice of public relations, detailing the basic model of public relations, and considering the role of return on investment in the process.

Key Terms

To say public relations is "strategic" implicates the use of a number of terms. This section defines key terms to prevent us from simply writing in jargon. Among the key terms are strategy, goal, objective, and tactics.

Strategy itself is a very broad concept. A strategy guides action. It is both a plan and the enactment of that plan (Moss, 2005). To say public relations is strategic means that the practice is purposeful. Simply put, there are reasons for the public relations actions. Part of management is formulating strategy to provide direction for action. *Tactics* are the tools that are used to enact strategies. Public relations tactics, then, are the wide range of tools practitioners have at their disposal (Merkl & Heath, 2005). Public relations tactics include news releases, brochures, websites, blogs, advocacy advertisements, town hall meetings, newsletters, and lobbying. Tactics make strategy a reality. The strategy helps to provide the purpose for public relations. The practitioners are trying to achieve specific goals and objectives – the markers of direction.

Though related, goals and objectives should be separated conceptually. A *goal* is "a general statement of what you hope to achieve with your public relations effort" (Coombs, 2005, p. 364). Goals are vague statements of where a practitioner wants to go. A goal might be "to improve perceptions of corporate social responsibility." Notice how the goal is vague. There is a general direction (improve perceptions) and focus (corporate social responsibility). However, more detail is needed for this goal to be more effective.

Objectives are the specific versions of goals. An objective seeks to detail exactly what is expected from the public relations effort. An effective objective must be quantifiable – it must be measurable. Objectives can be divided into two broad categories: (1) process and (2) outcome. A process objective checks to see that certain steps were taken in the preparation and execution of a public relations action. Process objectives would include writing a news release, getting approval of stories for a newsletter, or securing a permit for a fun run. Each of these actions can be translated into an objective: "To send out a news release to twelve media outlets by June 27," "To receive management approval of all newsletter stories by October 13," and "To secure the permit for the fun run by February 17." All three of these objectives can be measured. You either have completed the action or not, and each establishes a specific time frame for when the action should be completed. Process objectives answer the question, "Did we do what we were supposed to do?" Your public relations action may have failed because a certain step was not taken. Think of process objectives as a checklist for steps that must be taken in your public relations action. You develop this list of actions in the planning and execution stage.

Objectives are not just something educators preach to their students in class. The Public Relations Society of America (PRSA), a professional organization for public relations professionals, is dedicated to spreading the word about objectives as well. Each year the PRSA presents the Silver Anvil Awards for exemplary public relations practices. (The anvil represents the forging of public opinion.) Each entry must provide specific objectives for the public relations actions, along with other pieces of information we have discussed in this chapter. The PRSA reinforces the importance of objectives to the profession by making it a component of one of its most prestigious awards.

Outcome objectives determine whether or not the public relations action was a success. They specify what you hoped to achieve with the public relations action. A proper outcome objective specifies the target audience. Because a public relations action is focused on a specific target audience, that audience should be included in any discussion of the outcome objectives to ensure you assess the right people when collecting evaluation data.

An outcome objective is composed of an action verb preceded by "to," specifies the amount of desired change or target behavior stated as a percentage or number, and describes the target for the public relations effort (Coombs, 2005; Stacks, 2002). Here are some examples of outcome objectives: "To increase blood donation from first-time donors by 10 percent" and "To win shareholder approval of resolution five at the annual meeting." Each of the sample outcome objectives specifies the target for the action and the desired outcome in a measurable fashion.

Let us return to our earlier goal and convert it into an effective outcome objective. One possible revision is "to increase by 8 percent the number of customers who rate our company 'very strong' for contributing to local charities." The goal becomes more specific as a target is provided (customers), an amount of change is specified (8 percent), and the change is measurable (people can be asked to rate the organization's contributions to local charities).

But why the concern over specificity? Specificity relates to how objectives help to facilitate strategic public relations actions. Specificity helps to provide direction. Which is a better direction for action: go north or follow Interstate 55 north for 25 miles? Goals and objectives are based upon a careful understanding of the situation. Practitioners use research to understand the situation, a point we shall address in greater detail shortly. Actions are taken in reaction to problems and opportunities. Problems are situations that can threaten an organization. Loss of customer trust, conflict with a community group, or regulations that could hamper operations are all examples of threats. If a problem is not resolved, the organization will suffer some form of loss. Opportunities are situations that can benefit an organization. Collaborating with an activist group, reaching new customers, and building a positive reputation are all benefits. An opportunity is a chance for an organization to create some gain by utilizing the situation to its advantage. At this point, it is helpful to place these terms in the context of the public relations process. Box 4.1 provides a summary of objectives.

Box 4.1   Objectives

Objectives, more specifically outcome objectives, are the standards used to evaluate the success or failure of a campaign. Outcome objectives can involve knowledge, attitude, or behavior. Knowledge means constituents know something after a public relations action they did not know before the effort. In this book we talk about attitude and behavior throughout. As McGuire's (1981) work indicates, the three types of objectives are related. Knowledge can be used to shape attitudes and attitudes can influence behavior. We use the word *can* because the connections are not automatic between the objectives. Constituents can form attitudes without knowledge and behaviors can be independent of attitudes. Behavior change is the most challenging objective, followed by attitude change and then knowledge gain. Constituents offer less resistance to efforts to educate them than to efforts to change their minds or behaviors.

An outcome objective should be measurable and specific (Coombs, 2005). If you cannot measure something, it should not be part of an objective. If we are to use outcome objectives to assess success or failure, they must be measurable. A specific objective has the desired amount of change and the target constituent. The target amount of change is critical to accessing success or failure. If you just said "increase donations," then any increase is success. If you say "increase donations by 9 percent," you must hit or exceed 9 percent to be a success.

Specifying the target constituency clarifies who is to receive the message and who should be evaluated when judging the effectiveness of the public relations effort. Specifying the target constituency is a matter of segmentation. A specific segment will be homogenous, allowing for targeted messages. The messages are designed to resonate with the values, attitudes, and/or behaviors of the segment. Also, the channels that best reach that segment are utilized to deliver the message. You also know who to sample when evaluating the public relations effort. Including non-target constituents for your evaluation is a recipe for failure. Why should people outside of your target have been exposed to the message or have found it interesting? The message was not designed to resonate with them. For instance, a health message targeted to men over forty should not include women or men under forty in the evaluation effort.

An example that converts a general objective to a specific objective will illustrate the characteristics of a proper outcome objective. The general objective says "to increase participation in the annual river clean-up." The objective has no specific amount or target constituency. A more specific objective could be "to increase by 12 percent participation of local youth organizations in the annual river clean-up." There is now a specific amount, 12 percent. You have youth organizations as the target constituency. Messages should be designed for youth organizations and distributed through channels that will reach them. For instance, posters at local schools or sending speakers to youth organization meetings could be employed. Evaluation would involve comparing the number of participants from youth organizations this year to those from last year to determine if there was a 12 percent increase.

The public relations process

Although writers have given it different names, many agree that public relations actions unfold in a four-step sequence:

1   Formative research
2   Planning
3   Message design and execution
4   Evaluation

The four-step process works fine for routine public relations actions. *Routine* refers to public relations actions a department or agency executes regularly, such as an annual silent auction or investor reception. The routine helps you to understand when formative research is needed. There is a problem with the four steps when we move beyond the routine: how do we know we need formative research? We posit that there are *five steps* in public relations actions, starting with *environmental scanning*.

The five steps build upon one another as information from a previous step is used as a foundation for the next step. For example, a practitioner has nothing to evaluate until a message is communicated. A message cannot be communicated until it is planned. A practitioner should not plan until the formative research is completed and the situation is understood. A practitioner does not know what formative research is needed without scanning the environment for problems and opportunities. Figure 4.1 illustrates the five-step process. Exploring the five-step public relations process will help to clarify the strategic nature of public relations.

Step 1: Environmental scanning

Environmental scanning is a common practice in issues management (discussed in chapter 10) but is used less in discussions of the basic public relations process. We contend that environmental scanning is the essential first step in the public relations process. Environmental scanning is a form of radar. Public relations practitioners actively look for pieces of information in the environment, such as events or trends, that indicate a change may be occurring in the environment in which their organization is embedded. Practitioners are trying to identify changes that are likely to affect the organization in the future. Such changes can be problems or opportunities. Recall that a problem is a situation that *could* be harmful to your organization, while an opportunity is a situation that *could* be beneficial to your organization. Although organizations can simply stumble into a problem or opportunity, this is a relatively ineffective method of research. The earlier a problem or opportunity is identified, the easier it is to address.

Information is scanned from a variety of sources to understand emerging situations that may stem from social, health, political, regulatory, technological, or economic factors. An important aspect of environmental scanning is *listening to*

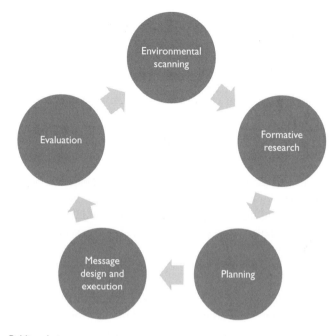

Figure 4.1   Public relations process

constituents. What are their concerns and values? What do constituents expect in general and from your organization more specifically? Practitioners will scan traditional news media, online sources, government documents, and messages from stakeholders, including employees. Later chapters will further illustrate the scanning process. It should be noted that the Internet keeps increasing as an important realm to scan. Organizations must be cognizant of what is being said about them on relevant blogs, discussion boards, websites, and Internet news sources. Companies such as Visible Technologies and Cision provide online monitoring services that include social media. Refer to chapter 7 for information about public relations and the online environment.

The information collected from environmental scanning is interpreted to determine how it might be relevant to the organization. Information is analyzed and management plots future organizational actions based upon that information and assessments of how it may impact the organization. Someone analyzes the information, thereby converting it into knowledge. Information by itself is not helpful. Information must be processed into knowledge before it is usable and helpful. Public relations practitioners use environmental scanning to identify the situation they plan to address through their actions. Once a potential situation is identified, it is monitored. Monitoring requires a focused research effort. Monitoring can involve collecting feedback or tracking a situation's development. Formative research is a form of monitoring that can be used to generate the information to start the public relations process.

In September 2001, Edelman, a prominent public relations firm, was scanning its environment and located a potential problem. A Harris/Impulse Research poll found Edelman was ranked ninth in quality reputation by its non-clients, a significant drop from its fourth ranking in 2000. Edelman decided this piece of information warranted closer examination and launched an extensive formative research effort to better understand the situation (problem).

Step 2: Formative research

Research, or more precisely *formative research*, involves the systematic collection and analysis of information about a situation identified through environmental scanning. Formative research answers the question, "What is going on?" The public relations practitioner seeks to understand the nature of the problem or the opportunity. Research provides the situational analysis and is the foundation for strategic action.

The need for a public relations action comes from the situation. The situation may be a problem or opportunity the organization faces. To correct a problem or utilize an opportunity, a public relations practitioner must have an in-depth understanding of the situation. That means the practitioner must engage in background or formative research. Formative research is applied research; you use it when a decision must be made about a specific, real-life problem or opportunity. Formative research in public relations represents a systematic effort to generate information for making decisions in public relations. In any new situation there are gaps in what you know about the situation. Those information gaps create uncertainty; you feel unsure as to what to do because you lack a clear picture of what is happening. Formative research involves collecting information that clarifies the situation by reducing uncertainty – it fills in the information gaps. Formative research is like sonar on a submarine. It tells the public relations practitioner what lies ahead.

There are three critical gaps public relations practitioners face: (1) who is involved, (2) why each group or individual is involved, and (3) the cause of the problem or reason for the opportunity. In any situation practitioners want to know the key players. Practitioners must know the people or groups involved because they are the ones the practitioners will be communicating with as they become involved in the situation. Once they have identified who is the starting point, practitioners then need to find out why they are involved. Practitioners want to know the goals of these key players: what do they want out of the situation? Each person or group will have some connection to the situation and something they hope to achieve from the situation. Practitioners gain insight into the key players when they know why each of these groups is playing. The better the practitioners understand those involved, the more effectively they can communicate and work with these groups in the future.

Practitioners also need to realize what makes a situation a problem or opportunity. For a problem, practitioners will need to know its cause(s). A public relations action will involve some solution and effective solutions begin with a detailed understanding of the problem. Similarly, practitioners must dissect the opportunity. Practitioners will need to understand why this is an opportunity if they are to effectively utilize the opportunity. What harms and/or benefits might the organization face? Practitioners are creating situational awareness. Situational awareness indicates enough is known about the situation to make an informed decision – plot a course of action.

Notice the collection of information also requires its analysis. Information simply places facts in context while knowledge analyzes the information so that it is useable by people in the organization. By understanding if a situation is a problem or opportunity and further detailing that problem or opportunity, a practitioner is converting information into the knowledge necessary to enact an effective public relations action.

Some of the information practitioners want to collect includes: the attitudes and behaviors of key constituents, possible constraints, the factors (history) which led up to the current situation, possible allies, possible enemies, potential causes of a problem, and potential benefits of opportunities. Various research tools are used to collect the necessary information to create situational awareness. But at its heart, formative research is a form of listening. Management listens to input from various constituencies to help craft a picture of the current situation. Although the input usually is solicited through active research, constituents may provide unsolicited information as well. Unsolicited information would include blog postings, letters to the editor, and comments on discussion boards. Public relations practitioners need to listen carefully and collect and analyze as much information as reasonably possible.

Research can be divided into informal/qualitative and formal/quantitative. *Informal research* is subjective. Subjective means that how people interpret the information can vary greatly. Common techniques for informal research include in-depth interviews, focus groups, databases, case studies, and content analysis. In-depth interviews are semi-structured. The interviewer has a starting point and rough outline of questions or issues, but allows the interviewee (the person who is asked the questions) to control the process. Open-ended questions are asked and the interviewer uses follow-up questions to discover more detailed information. A focus group is much like an in-depth interview except that 3–20 people are asked questions and respond to those questions in a group setting. The multiple ideas of the group members are likely to generate additional discussion and raise additional questions that are addressed by the group. A facilitator will lead the discussion with a rough guide, but the responses of the focus group dictate much of the process.

The focus group moderator facilitates the discussion. Moderators keep the group on topic, ask follow-up probes when necessary, and try to prevent participants from either dominating or not contributing to the group discussion. The moderator's job is difficult and a good moderator is often the difference between useable and useless focus group information. Focus group research also involves a number of issues about recruiting and rewarding participants, selecting the appropriate location, and making sure the room for the focus group is conducive to discussion.

In-depth interviews and focus groups are an excellent way to understand why constituencies hold certain attitudes or engage in certain behavior. For instance, constituencies can be asked why they feel positively or negatively about an organization. Follow-up questions can be used to understand why they hold these views of the organization's reputation. No two in-depth interviews or focus groups will be exactly alike because interviewees differ and the research process will differ. Researchers create transcripts of the interviews or focus groups. The transcripts are then examined to discover themes or patterns in the responses. Locating themes is subjective, as different people can look at the same transcripts and "see" different themes.

Databases are collections of information, typically documents, that can be accessed and searched via computers. Students regularly search databases when conducting library research using LEXIS/NEXIS or InfoTrak. These same databases are still valuable outside of the academic setting. A case study is a detailed examination of an event, organization, or constituents. Case studies can be found in databases or constructed from databases and other sources (Stacks, 2002). Practitioners potentially can gain valuable insight from cases when a case is similar to situations they face. Similar cases may suggest fruitful and fruitless courses of actions. Practitioners use cases to learn from the successes and failures of others.

Database research is sometimes called archival research. All of these database/archival sources can be used to illuminate the situation. They can help you understand how your organizations and key constituencies have become involved in the situation and why they are involved in the situation. Practitioners have illuminated the situation when they have detailed the problem or opportunity, identified the constituencies involved in or likely to become involved in the situation, and understood why each constituency is involved. This information provides a map of the public relations situation that will guide later actions.

Content analysis "is the systematic, objective and quantitative method for researching messages" (Stacks, 2002, p. 107). Though systematic, content is still considered informal. Content analysis is used to analyze news stories, blogs, websites, videotapes, and media releases. Any careful analysis of printed materials, including Internet or traditional media coverage, is a form of content analysis. True content analysis requires developing careful and thorough rules for how people should code the data. Coders must be able to agree on how material should be coded or there is no consistency in the coding. If the coding is inconsistent and lacks reliability, people cannot make comparisons between the coded materials. This would be a problem, for instance, if an organization wanted to track its news media coverage over time. The organization could not be sure if changes in the news coverage were a function of the news media coverage or the coders.

Formal/quantitative research is objective and rigidly structured. The information is collected in the form of numbers. This numerical information is then examined using a statistical program. Statistical tests are considered objective because they will provide the same results regardless of who performs the test. If the information shows a correlation of .53 between customer satisfaction and use of the organization's website, any researcher conducting the correlation

Table 4.1   Sample survey items for the Coombs and Holladay Organizational Reputation Scale

		Strongly agree				Strongly disagree
1	The organization is basically honest	1	2	3	4	5
2	The organization is concerned with the well-being of its publics	1	2	3	4	5
3	I trust the organization to tell the truth about the incident	1	2	3	4	5
4	I would prefer to have nothing to do with this organization	1	2	3	4	5
5	Under most circumstances, I *would not* be likely to believe what the organization says	1	2	3	4	5

Source: Coombs & Holladay (2002); items are modified from McCroskey's (1966) credibility scale

test will reach the same conclusion. There are conventions for how to interpret various statistical tests, but the details of those processes are beyond the scope of this book. The use of common statistical tests and accepted ways of interpreting the significance of those tests is what makes formal research objective.

Surveys are the most common formal research technique used in public relations. A survey is a collection of items or questions. The items are predominantly close-ended questions. Survey respondents are given options from which to choose. Those response options might be presented in a yes/no format or arranged in a continuum to reflect intensity of feeling. For the latter, respondents may indicate how strongly they agree or disagree with a statement. Table 4.1 provides some sample items from surveys. Respondents may take a survey in a variety of ways. Surveys can be completed in person, over the phone, online, or through postal mail. The responses to the items are assigned numerical values that are used for later analysis. For the survey in table 4.1, the scores are added together to form a reputation score for the organization. The scores could be used to assess current reputations or collected over time to track any changes in an organization's reputation.

The discussion of surveys raises the issue of samples. A sample is a subset of the total population to be studied. Suppose a practitioner wants to understand how investors feel about an organization's efforts to "go green." Instead of asking all the investors to answer a survey, a sample of the investors is asked to complete the survey. If the sample is representative, it will accurately reflect the views of all investors. There are different scientific ways to select a sample to ensure it is representative (Stacks, 2002). It is important to note that an unscientific sample is not representative and may provide biased results because it may not accurately reflect the attitudes or behaviors of the target stakeholder group. Non-probability samples are not representative. That means a practitioner would only know how the people surveyed felt about the topic and could not draw conclusions about the larger population. A short trip through the world of sampling is warranted at this point.

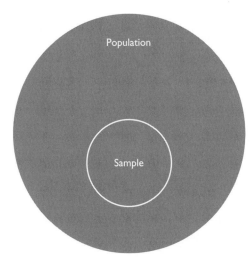

Figure 4.2   Illustration of sampling

A census is the complete population. Countries frequently conduct a census to find out how many citizens they have. Samples are a subset of the census/complete population. Figure 4.2 illustrates the idea of a sample. A probability sample is when every possible member of a population (person or message) has an equal chance of being chosen for the sample. Specific sampling strategies are used to randomly select members of the population for the sample, including simple random samples, simple systematic sampling, and cluster sampling. In a simple random sample, the entire population is entered into a database, then a specified number are selected randomly. A simple systematic sample commonly has a list of the population. A random starting point is chosen, then a skip interval system applied. A skip interval means you select every "nth" item from the list. It might be every 10th, 22nd, or 113th, it just depends on the size of your population and the size of the sample. Cluster sampling divides the population into easily identifiable clusters. A practitioner would randomly select the clusters then select all or some of the units in that cluster (Stacks, 2002). Practitioners might create clusters of investors or customers then sample those clusters.

Non-probability samples are sometimes used because a practitioner does not have access to representative sampling techniques or may not know the entire population. Non-probability samples include convenience, purposive, and volunteer. Convenience sampling means just that, the unit area easy to access. Purposive sampling is when only certain units are desired and placed in the sample. An example would be selecting community members that live within a 2-mile radius of an organization. Volunteer sampling is of those people who agree to be surveyed. A practitioner may stand outside a store and ask shoppers to complete a survey. Even if every tenth shopper is picked, the sample is non-probability. Only the shoppers at the store that day can be in the sample, meaning the entire sample does not have an equal chance of being in the survey. This is not an exhaustive discussion of sampling, but gives the reader a feel for the process.

The amount of formative research a practitioner conducts depends on the number and size of the information gaps. The more and the bigger the information gaps, the more research a practitioner will need to conduct before initiating a public relations action. Seasoned practitioners will need little research for routine tasks. Practitioners use their past experience as a resource for the simple and routine public relations actions. A news release will serve as an example. Suppose a manager has received an award from the local chapter of the Red Cross. The award is an opportunity to reinforce the view that the organization contributes to local charities. A skilled practitioner will have the required information to complete the public relations actions. Experience tells the practitioner which media outlets will be interested in this type of story, who should receive the news release, the requisite contact information, and the format the reporter prefers for receiving news releases.

Research should and often does shape public relations actions. In 2000, for instance, management at ConAgra decided the company should become involved in world hunger because its core business is agriculture. But the issue of world hunger is vast and management was unsure how it should get involved. A public relations agency was hired to conduct research that would guide ConAgra's entry into the world hunger issue. A total of fifty hunger experts were interviewed for the project. The information suggested a focus on children because they were disproportionately affected by hunger. ConAgra management used the research to develop a program that raised awareness of the plight of children in hunger and to sponsor a program to help alleviate child hunger. ConAgra illustrates that once the formative research is examined, the next step is to develop a plan.

The discussion of formative research demands that we answer one additional question: "How did we find the problems and opportunities?" Of course, organizations can simply stumble into a problem or opportunity, but that is an ineffective method. Management should be scanning the environment for signs of problems and opportunities. Scanning involves collecting and analyzing information from the environment. The analysis seeks to understand how the information might affect the organization. In other words, analysis tells you if you have a problem, an opportunity, or nothing. The earlier a problem or opportunity is identified, the easier it is to address. Hence, managers must actively scan the environment for information that could be relevant to the organization. Elements of the environment that are examined for information include social, regulatory, market, political, technology, and economic factors. When a potential problem or opportunity is identified, managers monitor (focus attention on) the situation by collecting additional information – engage in formative research.

Step 3: Planning

Planning, the third step, aids strategy by mapping what needs to be done. That sounds simple but it is actually a complex process. Planning centers around an objective, details how to reach the objective, and identifies how much money that effort will cost. A public relations effort is a type of project, an organized attempt to create a unique product or service (Hallahan, 2005; Martin & Tate, 1997). A project has a specified time frame for completion and is comprised of a series of tasks necessary to reach the objective (Davidson, 2000). Managers should create program management documents for the public relations action. These documents will identify the tasks to be completed, the person or persons responsible for each task, and the time required to complete each task. Public relations, like other occupations, engages in project management. Refer to box 4.2 for more information on this topic.

Box 4.2   Project Management

Project management is a systematic approach to planning and organizing a task from start to finish. Project management is routinely used in construction, architecture, and computer software development. Many, but not all, public relations actions qualify as projects. The principles of project management apply where a building is being constructed, software developed, or a public relations action executed. This chapter strongly reflects core elements of project management such as planning, monitoring, and execution.

The concept of project management is raised because of its emphasis on the interrelatedness of four key factors: scope, cost, schedule, and quality. Project management maintains that changing one of these factors significantly affects the others. New practitioners must appreciate this dynamic from the start. Scope is what must be done to accomplish the project's objectives. Cost is the budget or amount of money allocated to the project. Schedule is the amount of time available to complete the project. Quality is the grade of the project's outcome.

We should assume that every organization or client wants a project that is done on time, within budget, fits the desired scope, and is of the desired quality. Decisions about the project that alter scope, cost, schedule, or quality could jeopardize the project by changing the other factors. Let's use a proposed project to have a local clean-up the river day. The project scope is to clean-up a 1.5 mile stretch of the river by removing debris and planting some flowers. The budget is $5,000, there are 20 days before the event, and quality will be assessed by the lack of visible trash debris and visibility of the flowers. Equipment has been rented for a specific day and changing the date will increase the cost. If the schedule is pushed back, the budget for flowers will decrease. If the budget for flowers decreases, quality will suffer as there will be less flowers. If the scope is increased to 2.5 miles, quality will suffer as volunteers will have to clean more in the same time frame and the flowers will be spread over a wider space. If quality is changed to include natural debris such as tree branches, it will result in the need for additional equipment rental and pay for qualified operators. The point is that changes to any one of the four core elements of a project has a significant effect on the project by altering the requirements for other elements.

At this point it is useful to elaborate on objectives before addressing the planning process. We have focused on outcome objectives because they are the standard by which success and failure are judged. *Outcome objectives* can be one of three types: knowledge, attitude, and behavior. *Knowledge objectives* seek learning. The target stakeholder should know something after the public relations action that they did not know before. Knowledge objectives include simple exposure to the message, comprehension of the message, and retention of the message (constituencies remember the message).

Attitude objectives seek to change or to reinforce how constituencies think about an issue or an organization. A reputation is a form of attitude. An attitude is an evaluation of some object. "I love track and field" or "I dislike processed corn" are examples of attitudes. In each case an evaluation ("love" and "dislike") is made of some object ("track and field" and "processed corn"). In an outcome objective, a practitioner is looking for changes in the attitudes of the target audience. We want the target stakeholders to alter their evaluations of a particular object. People should hold different attitudes after the public relations effort than before it. A common attitude addressed in public relations is reputation, people's evaluation of an organization. Chapter 10 provides an in-depth examination of reputation. In baseball, the San Francisco Giants now play in Pacific Bell Park. Their old home was 3Com Park. Pacific Bell, a telecommunications company, wanted to promote the shift in homes with the Giant Pacific Bell Park Pitch. Pacific Bell had paid millions of dollars for the rights to the name of the park and wanted fans to know about the change. More importantly, they wanted fans to have a more favorable attitude toward Pacific Bell. Specifically, they wanted to increase positive fan perceptions of Pacific Bell by 10 percent. The baseball from the last ceremonial pitch thrown at 3Com Park was saved and toured Northern California and Nevada. Over 25,000 fans threw the ball on its 3,000 mile journey. That ball was then used for the ceremonial first pitch ever pitched at new Pacific Bell Park. Fans' positive perception of Pacific Bell as a company increased 18 percent after the public relations effort. Fans developed a more positive attitude toward Pacific Bell, the attitude objective.

Behavior objectives seek to change or to reinforce how people act. Buying a product, using a service, adopting a healthier lifestyle, or investing in a company are behaviors of interest to public relations. Behavior change is the toughest of all outcome objectives. It is fairly easy to create knowledge gain, difficult to change attitudes, and extremely difficult to change behaviors. People are "creatures of habit" and generally hate to change those habits – their behaviors. In an outcome objective, a practitioner is hoping to change how people behave. People should act differently after the public relations effort than before it. Seattle Public Utilities initiated a public relations effort designed to conserve water by having homeowners decrease watering their lawns. They wanted to increase the number of homeowners not watering their lawns by over 5 percent. A series of radio promotions, "Habit Change Kits," and television advertisements were used. At the end of the public relations effort, the percent of homeowners who did not water lawns increased from 18.4 percent to 29 percent. The homeowners did change their lawn watering behaviors with a 10 percent increase in the desired behavior.

Knowledge, attitude, and behavior objectives are often viewed as building on one another. A reputation will be used to illustrate the interdependence of these objectives. You need to know about an organization before you form a strong reputation (attitude). A strong, favorable reputation (attitude) should result in support behavior toward the organization (e.g., buy products, seek employment, or say good things about the organization to others). While this progression makes sense, the reality is that people often skip steps. The main point is that outcome objectives may seek to address knowledge, attitudes, or behaviors.

We would argue that any one of these three objectives is useful to the management of mutually influential relationships – what we see as the core of public relations. It is clear that behavior-change efforts are influence. The purpose is to change how people act. Attitude change has elements of influence as well when attempts are made to alter evaluations of attitude objectives. Moreover, the hope is that the changed attitude will stimulate behavior change. For instance, cultivating a more favorable reputation can lead to purchasing or investment actions. Chapter 10 provides more information on how reputations result in favorable constituent behaviors for an organization. Some might argue that awareness is just informing people. However, public relations actions selectively expose people to certain information. In turn, that awareness can influence behavior. You learn that wearing a seatbelt can improve your odds of surviving a car crash. Ideally, that information leads you to wear a seatbelt. Information is used strategically in public relations to lead constituents to specific conclusions and ultimate behaviors. If public relations is about influence, it is also about behavior change – how constituents relate to an organization and to one another.

The previous discussion of objectives related to the objective of the public relations department. However, effective public relations departments serve the larger organization as well. Public relations serves the organization by helping it to achieve the organization's strategic plan. This means that public relations must consider how its efforts contribute to larger organizational goals. Think back to the discussion of publicity that opened this chapter. Media coverage about a new product should help to increase sales of that product and boost investor confidence if the organization has stock. Sales and stock valuation are larger organizational objectives that the public relations action of securing positive publicity can enhance. The point is that public relations objectives should be working in concert with organizational objectives and strategic plans.

The first part of planning is identifying what needs to be done – the tasks. A list of what needs to be accomplished is sometimes called the *process objectives*. It is critical to make an inventory of the tasks that need to be done. Forgetting a task can throw off the schedule. It is good to brainstorm the tasks needed as a team. Several minds are better than one. Once you have identified a list of tasks, you need to determine how long each task will take. Every task on your list should be accompanied by a time frame for how long it will take. Next, identify the person or persons responsible for each task (staffing). Finally, you will want to identify any dependencies between the tasks. Tasks are dependent when one task must be completed before another can begin. For instance, newsletter stories must be written before they are inserted into a template for the newsletter.

The second part of planning is organizing all tasks. The list of tasks, time frames, and dependencies must be placed in a useable format. Two common organizing tools for projects such as public relations actions are the Gantt and PERT Charts. We will briefly explain how each structures the information generated from part one of scheduling.

Gantt Charts are named for their inventor, Henry Gantt. A Gantt Chart is simply a bar chart that permits you to plan and monitor a project. The chart lists each task, its duration, start and finish date, and dependencies. Gantt Charts are visually appealing because they allow you to view the tasks quickly. You can also update the Gantt Chart as the project progresses by indicating which tasks have been completed. The Gantt Chart makes it easy to see which tasks are sequential (have dependencies) and which tasks can be performed simultaneously. Tasks that are not dependent on one another can be completed at the same time. For instance, invitations for a charity event can be printed while catering for the event is being arranged. Experts recommend that you only use a Gannt Chart if a project will take less than 30 days and does not involve a large number of complex tasks.

A PERT Chart (Program Evaluation and Review Technique) can handle more complicated and longer-term projects. A PERT Chart emphasizes a visual display of tasks and dependencies. The biggest difference from a Gantt Chart is that the PERT Chart is done more as a diagram or flow chart. To build a PERT Chart, you need to identify all tasks, connect the tasks in the order they need to be completed, and identify dependencies. Both Gantt and PERT Charts can be constructed using software programs such as Microsoft Project and Smartdraw. These programs make organizing a breeze, if you carefully identify the tasks, time frames and dependencies. You can take the information generated in part one of planning and enter it into the computer program. The computer then draws perfect charts and diagrams for you. You can even use the programs to print large versions of a Gantt Chart. Some managers like to post large Gantt Charts on the office wall and mark the progress as it occurs. In a glance, the wall-mounted Gantt Chart shows progress and work still to be done. Microsoft Projects permits quick updates of charts showing what has been accomplished, what still needs to be accomplished, and estimated time to complete the remaining tasks.

A final aspect of planning is calculating the budget. The tasks help you to project a budget. The total budget is the summed cost of the tasks required for the project. How you get the money for your budget varies from organization to organization, but the need to carefully monitor your spending applies to all organizations. Again, there are various software programs to help you organize your budget. Still, the heart of the budget process is in the minds of the public relations people working on the project. You must identify all of the human resources and hard costs. Human resources are the people working on the project. Practitioners need to determine how much time they will spend on the public relations effort and how much to charge for that time. Hard costs are out-of-pocket expenses for materials and supplies. This could even include the cost of a special software program if one is needed for the project. As with planning, there are various software programs to help you organize your budget. Sample budgeting software include SRC's Advisor Series, Outlook Soft, and Prophix. In addition, a program like Microsoft Project allows you to integrate planning and budgets. But three budget factors remain constant across organizations: knowing what goes into developing one, being accurate in your estimates, and learning to stay on budget. Remember, practitioners need to carefully list all expenses at the beginning and try to stay on budget. This includes monitoring spending throughout the project to know if the public relations action is on budget or not.

Step 4: Message design and execution

In the fourth step, *message design and execution*, public relations practitioners create their messages (message design) and send them (execution). This is the creative aspect of the public relations action. The three previous steps help to shape the messages practitioners develop. The message must fit the objective a practitioner is pursuing and the target audience they want to reach. Is the practitioner looking to inform (knowledge objective) or to persuade (attitude and behavior objectives)? A public relations practitioner will use different strategies and resources depending on whether they desire to inform or to persuade. The content of the message must fit, resonate with, the target audience. With which values do the targets identify? Which values might they reject? What do they want from the situation? Practitioners will want to avoid values they dislike, use values they like, and address their goal for the situation in some way. Public relations practitioners should be strategic in the selection of material they include in their messages.

ConAgra remains active in efforts to end child hunger. They supported a 2002 public relations effort based on the theme of parents choosing between feeding their children and paying the rent. The print advertisement message begins, "I tell my children little white lies. I tell them we're skipping lunch today so we have more time to spend at the park … I don't tell them that because I paid the rent I don't have enough money for food." The message ends with "Rent or Food? 1 in 5 kids face hunger because of decisions like this. To help your community call, 800–FEED-KIDS or visit feedingchildren.org. Hunger. A choice no one should have to make." The message uses the value of compassion by emphasizing how many children go hungry because of limited incomes. People can be compassionate by helping to feed the US children facing hunger. The message reflects the belief that the target audience is compassionate so the message will resonate with them.

As with message development, execution (how you send the message) is dependent on the objective and the target audience. For instance, behavior objectives are best accomplished using an interactive medium like meetings or the Internet, while knowledge objectives are easily pursued in print or through other mass media channels. Moreover, practitioners must select a medium or media that is used by their target audience. There is no point in using the Internet if your target audience rarely uses it. But using radio is great if your target audience listens regularly. There is a logic in the development of messages and media selection; they should be consistent with the information the public relations practitioners have already collected and the plan they have developed. Each step in the public relations process flows from and is shaped by the previous steps.

Seattle Public Utilities used a variety of media to convey their message about natural lawn care. Their spokes "fish" was Bert the Salmon. Bert was created to add humor to the message. The media used included radio promotions, Bert lawn signs, advertising during Seattle Mariners televised games, and the "Habit Change Kit" that included printed how-to information along with the video "Natural Lawn Care." We can focus on two media to show the strategic thinking behind the selections. The campaign targeted male homeowners and the television audience for Mariners baseball games is predominantly male – the target is using this medium. Sometimes it is easier to learn a behavior by watching it than simply reading about it. Since the campaign wanted behavior change, the Habit Change Kits contained a how-to video. The media were selected because they reached the target and/or helped to achieve the objective.

We can only hope to scratch the surface of message design and execution in this chapter. The books and articles written on how to develop messages and to select the appropriate channels would fill a small library. Practitioners must craft messages that will appeal and reach their target audience with the ultimate effect of influencing the target. Important factors to consider are the source, the arguments, and the channels. The source is who is perceived to be delivering the message. The source should appeal to the target audience. Sources are appealing if they are credible, similar, or appealing to the target audience (O'Keefe, 2002). Formative research can help practitioners to identify appealing sources for their targets. The more appealing the message, the more likely the influence effort will succeed.

An influence message is an argument. The message has a claim that the practitioner wants people to accept, such as "give blood" or "our company is socially responsible." People need reasons to accept claims, what we call evidence. Statistics, examples, and testimonials are viable forms of evidence to support claims. But claims can be presented in different ways. Make sure your strongest claims appear at the start or the end of the message. People tend to forget the information presented in the middle of messages. The practitioner needs to decide if the conclusions (desired action) should be implicit (implied) or explicit (stated directly) and whether to use a one-side message, a two-side message, or include a refutation of opposing claims in the message.

Finally, the channel selection is critical to having the target audience encounter the message. Channels include newspapers, magazines, brochures, fact sheets, websites, blogs, television, radio, and YouTube, to name but a few. Again, formative research helps practitioners to understand what channels a target audience prefers to read, to listen, and to watch. Research will even indicate preferences within a channel. For example, research can identify what websites the target audience is likely to visit or what cable channels and specific shows they are likely to watch. The practitioners must develop a list of possible channels, then see which channel or channels fit with their budget. Practitioners must maximize the potential of a channel to reach the target audience with the cost of the channel. There is no point using a channel that has limited utility for the target audience or to select a channel you cannot afford.

Step 5: Evaluation

If we are being strategic as public relations practitioners, *evaluation*, the final step, tells us whether or not our strategy succeeded and provides important feedback. Effective evaluation is possible only if there is a measurable objective. The objective is the marker of success or failure. Evaluative research determines whether or not the marker of success was achieved. The measurements used for evaluation depend on the objective. What is the best way to determine the amount of the desired outcome? Awareness and attitudes can be assessed with surveys. Some behaviors can be recorded, such as attendees or amount of blood donated, while others are best determined through surveys. A practitioner might even use archival records such as sales or the amount of plastic bottles recycled. Just remember, if the objective is not measurable, there can be no evaluation. That is another value of a proper objective.

Evaluation has serious ramifications for practitioners on both the personal and professional levels. On a personal level, evaluation helps practitioners refine and improve their writing and planning skills. Practitioners should treat each evaluation as a learning experience and collect feedback about what worked and what failed. Practitioners remember what worked for future reference and try to improve it. Practitioners must also remember what failed so they do not repeat the same mistake. Instead of dwelling on miscues, practitioners should think about alternatives and how they might work more successfully for them in the future. The evaluation dovetails back to research; it provides information about a public relations situation.

Let's say you wanted to generate 10 print media stories on the national level and 20 on the regional level for the opening of your company's new production facility. You exceeded your regional goal with 24 news stories generated from 40 news releases. You would want to see which news outlets used the story so you would be sure to target them with similar news releases in the future. You failed on the national level, with only 3 news stories from 30 news releases. Go back to try to determine why you failed. Could it be the news outlets you targeted rarely cover stories about new facilities or products? Was your news release copy too regional and lacked national newsworthiness? Answering these questions provides formative information for future efforts and will improve your media placement efforts.

Evaluation is not just for practitioners, as it tells their client or their organization if public relations actions were a success or failure, and has professional implications. Successes build a justification for increasing budgets and establishing the importance of a department. Failures pave the way for reduced budgets and elimination of personnel during downsizing. Success can generate more clients while failure can lead to the loss of existing ones. But do not think that not knowing is better than knowing a public relations action failed. Practitioners cannot improve if they are not aware of their errors. A practitioner may just keep repeating the same mistakes. Moreover, a practitioner's organization and clients want information when they make decisions about public relations actions and budgets. Practitioners will have a very hard time arguing for the importance of a public relations department or their utility to clients if they have no evaluation data. A simple word of advice: public relations practitioners should be confident in their abilities and evaluate.

As noted earlier, Silver Anvil Award entries must include evaluation. Here are examples of evaluations conducted by two past winners. ConAgra evaluated the Feeding Children Better effort by recording the amount of food donated to the program. Over 200 tons were collected during the public relations effort; it was a success. Pacific Bell used surveys to evaluate the Giant Pacific Bell Park Pitch effort. Fleishman-Hillard Research and SBC Corporate Market Research were used to survey the target audience. The target's positive perceptions of Pacific Bell increased 18 percent and the jump was attributed to the Giant Pacific Bell Park Pitch.

The Pacific Bell example brings up an important point when the objective is to create change. Pacific Bell wanted a 10 percent increase in positive fan perception. To assess the objective properly, Pacific Bell needed to know what fan perceptions of the company were before and after the public relations action. Any change, be it an increase or decrease, demands that the practitioner know the amount of the desired change before and after the public relations efforts. The "after" is compared to the "before" to determine if the desired level of change was achieved.

Practitioners in the corporate setting must be concerned about return on investment (ROI). ROI is how much an organization gets in return for a capital investment (Hardt, 2005). Public relations is one type of capital investment. Some corporations want a public relations department to document its ROI. Executives want to know exactly what they are getting for the public relations budget. In these circumstances, part of evaluation is providing concrete financial evidence of how public relations is contributing to organizational objectives.

The bigger picture

An individual public relations action does not occur in isolation. Each individual public relations action is connected to relationships and larger organizational

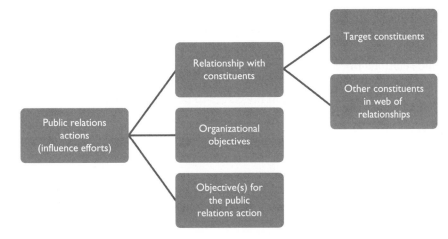

Figure 4.3 Effects from public relations actions/influence efforts

objectives. Failure to appreciate the bigger picture can be harmful to an organization. The harm is that an organization appears to be inconsistent when various units work at cross-purposes.

Our definition of public relations recognizes that mutual influence occurs within a web of relationships. How will the individual public relations actions affect the relationship with the constituencies connected to that action? An action designed to build support among certain constituents of an organization, such as throwing imitation blood on people wearing animal furs, may serve to offend other constituents and damage relationships. How does the individual action help to achieve larger organizational objectives? For instance, what larger organizational objectives is ConAgra achieving through the Feeding Children Better program? You can probably name more than one if you think about it carefully.

Too often, books treat public relations efforts in isolation, just as they treat constituencies, as if each existed in isolation from one another. Each and every public relations effort is part of a larger process. That larger process includes the web of relationships with constituents and organizational objectives. Figure 4.3 illustrates the interconnectedness of public relations actions and the bigger picture. The point is to remember and to appreciate the bigger picture when creating a public relations action.

Summary

The five steps in the public relations process illustrate the strategic aspect of public relations. When public relations practitioners create a brochure, design a website, or create a news release it is not some isolated task but part of a larger process designed to achieve some departmental and organizational objectives. As always, we use the term *organization* to refer to any collective effort, including activists, NGOs, non-profits, and corporations. Regardless of who is doing the public relations, there is still a need to utilize the five-step public relations process. All organizations need to locate problems/opportunities through scanning, understand the situation by conducting research, create plans to guide their actions, craft messages to fit the situation and the plan, and evaluate their efforts to determine the success or failure and to learn for future efforts.

Case Study: The Carl T. Hayden Veterans Affairs Medical Center

The Carl T. Hayden Veterans Affairs Medical Center (VAMC) discovered it had a reputational problem with many key constituencies, including employees, patients, volunteers, and the community. Their environmental scanning was identifying negative perceptions and comments from the key constituents. A negative reputation is a problem that requires attention. A series of survey instruments were developed as the foundation for the formative research to better understand the situation. Surveys data were collected from employees, patients, volunteers, the community, and Veterans Services Officers. The results revealed that the attitudes of employees posed the most serious reputation problem. Only one third of employees said they were proud to work at the center and nearly half reported morale problems.

The formative research resulted in a planning effort that targeted the employees and other key constituencies for a reputation-building effort. Here is a sample of the objectives from the public relations effort:

- To build the VAMC's positive image (reputation) in the community, improving it by at least 20 percent throughout the year.
- To increase the percentage of employees who are very proud and somewhat proud to work at the VAMC by shifting opinions to the positive by 5 percent throughout the coming year.
- To increase employee morale in the "good" to "excellent" category by shifting opinions to the positive by 5 percent throughout the coming year.

Note that the objectives had a specific target and quantity of change, were measurable, and provided a time frame.

The message design and execution used a variety of tactics and communication channels. The community was reached through a cable access TV show about health issues with a focus on veterans called *To Your Health*. There were six episodes of the television show. VAMC also renewed its support for the Veteran's Day Parade and used the event as a media relations trigger. For employees, the "Pride Campaign" was developed that allowed employees to be recognized on-the-spot for efforts in promoting the VAMC. To address morale, outstanding employees were highlighted in the newsletter through the "Role Model Campaign" and "Leaving a Legacy" campaign. A telephone survey found that both the cable access show and parade sponsorship increased favorable views of the VAMC among the community by an average of 21 percent. Employee pride increased 34 percent and morale improved 33.9 percent. All three of the selected objectives were achieved, resulting in the campaign being judged overall as a success.

The effect of the public relations efforts on the bigger picture was not evaluated. Logic would suggest the effort helped to improve rather than damage the web of relationships. Happy constituents will communicate that positive view to others in the web. Improving a reputation and improving morale help to support a variety of larger organizational objectives.

Case questions

1   Explain the rationale for the public relations action at the Carl T. Hayden Veterans Affairs Medical Center.

2   The case study indicated that surveys were used to collect data in the formative research stage. How might focus groups and in-depth interviews also be used to collect information about employees' attitudes?

3   This chapter discussed knowledge, attitude, and behavior outcome objectives. Which were the focus of the public relations at Carl T. Hayden Veterans Affairs Medical Center?

4   Explain how the tactics and communication channels were a good fit for this situation.

Discussion Questions

1   What do we mean when we say public relations is "strategic"?

2   Distinguish between strategy, tactics, goals, and objectives. Develop an example that illustrates them.

3   Describe the five steps in a public relations action. Explain why each is important to the overall public relations action.

4   Distinguish between informal/qualitative research and formal/quantitative research. What are the advantages and disadvantages of each type of research? Develop an example to illustrate how you could use both types of research in formative research.

5   Explain how knowledge, attitude, and behavior objectives are interdependent.

6   Develop a hypothetical public relations action. Explain what you would need to accomplish within each of the five steps of a public relations action.

7   Identify a recent public relations action in your community or school. Try to identify how the action reflected the five steps of a public relations action. How successful do you think this action was? If you were in charge of the action, what methods could you use to evaluate its success? How would you determine its effectiveness?

Agreement between Immokalee workers and McDonald's.

5

Public Relations as Activism

In drama, the terms *protagonist* and *antagonist* are used to describe key characters. The protagonist is the leading or main character in the drama and can be a hero or a villain. The antagonist stands in opposition to the protagonist and is an obstacle to be overcome. As we and others have documented elsewhere, the corporate-centric history of public relations casts corporations in the role of the protagonists and activists in the role of antagonists in the marketplace of ideas. The development of public relations is defined as corporations utilizing public relations to overcome or cope with activists. Consider how the developmental histories of public relations typically note how the muckrakers of the Progressive Era and activists in the 1960s were a catalyst for the growth of public relations. Corporations turned to public relations as a way to win support for themselves and to counter the attraction of activist groups created through their own public relations efforts (Coombs & Holladay, 2007b; McKie & Munshi, 2007).

Even today, many in public relations view the Internet as a threat because it can empower and embolden activists. Many high profile writers in public relations still have a knee-jerk reaction to online activism as a foe that must be vanquished. Consider the terms "rogue sites" or "attack sites" used generically to describe any website that is critical of an organization, or the fear of blogs spreading criticisms of organizations (e.g., Holtz, 1999; Middleberg, 2001). The Internet provides a mechanism for activists to engage in a variety of public relations activities at lower costs and with the potential to reach a larger audience (Coombs, 1998, 2002; Jaques, 2006; Taylor, Kent, & White, 2001; Thomas, 2003). A smaller segment of writers have begun to acknowledge and to study activists practicing public relations. Karlberg (1996) was on the leading edge of interest in activism public relations. Dozier and Lauzen (2000) later reinforced the need to study activist public relations, calling the corporate-centric focus "intellectual myopia" (p. 7). McKie and Munshi (2007) note that the same concerns remain seven years later. Still, the sense of activists as antagonists remains a strong theme in public relations writings (e.g., Werder, 2006).

We place this chapter on activist public relations early on in this book to reinforce the contributions that activists have made and continue to make to public relations. We begin the discussion of activists by defining who they are, including the basic goals activists pursue. We then compare and contrast the public relations activities of corporations and activists.

Who Are Activists and What Do They Want?

As our examples will illustrate, activists are not one group pursuing one ideology. Activists are a diverse group of characters interested in a variety of issues, frequently clashing with one another over how to address the issues. In this section we present a definition of activists as the core of our discussion, followed by a review of how activism is treated in the public relations literature with an emphasis on activists as antagonists and obstacles to organizations.

Defining activists

Activists are a rather unique constituency group. Activists are drawn from other constituencies such as community members, customers/potential customers, investors/potential investors, and even employees/potential employees. So what are activists? A variety of terms are used to refer to *activist groups*, including *pressure groups*, *grassroots organizations*, *social movements*, and *special interest groups*. Larissa Grunig (1992) noted that regardless of the title, these groups all sought "to exert pressure on an organization on behalf of a cause" (p. 504). She provided an early, influential definition: an "activist group is a group of two or more individuals who organize in order to influence another public or publics through action" (p. 504). Activists seek to influence "public policy, organizational action, or social norms and values" (Smith & Ferguson, 2001, p. 292) and employ communication strategically to reach those goals. In short, activists are organized and focused on influence.

It is important to broaden our definitional discussion beyond public relations to writings by activists. A broader view will give us a more accurate conceptualization of activism. Raymond (2003) views activism as a human duty. Activists are those who stand up for a cause. They arise when concerns are not heard. Raymond (2003) sees activism as a sign of a healthy democracy and that activists "provide insight into future values and hopes of society" (p. 209). The essence of activism is "an expression of genuine public interest in participation and shaping society" (Raymond, 2003, p. 211). Thomas (2003) defines activism as "an attempt to change the behavior of another party through the application of concerted power" (p. 129). It would seem that the public relations and activist definitions of "activists" are similar. Activists do engage in strategic influence if they are trying to shape society or change behaviors.

The main difference is that activists view their efforts as a noble cause rather than as an obstacle, as often they are viewed in much of the public relations literature. Activists view activism as a responsibility that serves to better society and even corporations. Raymond (2003) notes, "Activism is a positive influence on corporate policies and practices. It is a 'moral barometer' providing insight into the public's concerns" (p. 221). Raymond's words are echoed in many of the progressive writings about corporate social responsibility and even public relations. Activists can be bellwethers of societal change. Organizations can be at the vanguard of these societal value shifts if they listen to and work with activists.

Communication and public relations would be critical to both organizing and influencing public policy, organizational policies, or social norms and values. Clearly, one avenue pursued by activists is to increase the number of people aware and in support of their concerns. More people equates to more power. Additional power means an increased likelihood of successful influence. Of course, the potential to reach large numbers of sympathetic listeners may be enough leverage to create a change as well. The fear of large numbers of people being drawn to a situation can be powerful. The fear is derived from the threat of reputational damage if constituents learn negative information about an organization.

Activists in public relations research: Antagonists and obstacles

Historically, activist goals have often been in conflict with corporate goals. The muckrakers of the early 1900s wanted public policy and organizational changes that would cost corporations more money and place them under the closer scrutiny of the government. As weak as the Pure Food and Drug Act of 1906 (Wiley Act) was, it did create regulation and compliance with regulations costs corporations money. The Wiley Act set the foundation for meat inspection, prohibited the adulteration of food, and ended the practice of selling spoiled animal and vegetable products (Young, 1981).

In 1992, Larissa Grunig wrote in her chapter entitled "Activism: How it limits the effectiveness of organizations and how excellent public relations departments respond": "This chapter represents an attempt to help public relations practitioners deal in a more than an ad hoc way with the opposition their organizations often face from activist groups" (p. 503). As McKie and Munshi (2007) noted, the chapter's title reinforces the "obstacle" view of activists by referring to activists as limiting organizational effectiveness. Later in the chapter, Grunig writes, "Activist pressure is an extensive problem for organizations" (Grunig, 1992, p. 513).

Grunig's chapter is not entirely negative towards activists. She notes that activists seek to improve an organization from the outside – they can have respectable intentions. However, the way the chapter is written reflects the view of activists as antagonists. Activists are largely outside of the purview of public relations. Public relations practitioners in or working for corporations must deal with activists. Activists themselves are not examined as public relations practitioners. In 1989, James Grunig wrote: "When members of active publics join activist groups, they contribute to the constraints on organizational autonomy that create a public relations problem and bring about the need for a public relations program" (1989c, p. 3). His words echo the corporate-centric history of public relations. Once more, public relations is stimulated by the need to respond to activists. Activists again were not studied as public relations practitioners. Activists are seen as the antagonists to the corporate protagonists. This is a shortsighted view that more recent writings have tried to correct.

Smith and Ferguson (2001) note that James Grunig and Larissa Grunig did not examine public relations by activists because the researchers assumed activists enacted public relations the same as corporate practitioners. It was an unintended oversight rather than a purposeful exclusion. In fact, Larissa Grunig's (1992) analyses of the tactics used by activists is an implicit recognition of activists as practicing public relations. The problem is there is a general lack of recognition and study of activists as practicing public relations. Activists and their potential contributions to public relations become marginalized and largely overlooked. McKie and Munshi (2007) argue that Excellence Theory, the dominant public relations paradigm, is corporate-centric and reinforces the marginalization of activists in public relations. Refer to Box 5.1 for a summary of Excellence Theory.

Smith and Ferguson (2001) posit that to assume activists and corporations practice public relations similarly could be flawed and warrants further study. It is logical that the two groups will differ to some degree, due in part to the resources and constraints they face when engaged in public relations. We have seen a small body of research develop around the public relations practices of activists following the calls of Karlberg (1996) and Dozier and Lauzen (2000). Taylor, Kent, and White (2001) and Reber and Kim (2006) have examined how activists use the Internet in their public relations efforts. Taylor, Kent, and White (2001) note that activists have "unique communication and relationship-building needs" (p. 264) that could shape their public relations practices. Reber and Kim (2006) focus on how activists use online press rooms and provide recommendations for improving their use. Kovacs (2001) studied the public relations activities of activist groups in Britain. Simmons (2003) offers practical advice on how activists can effectively use staged events to attract media coverage. Researchers have slowly begun to embrace activists as public relations practitioners. Still, the notion of activists as antagonists for public relations practitioners remains a strong current in thinking and writings about public relations.

Box 5.1   Excellence Theory

James Grunig headed a research project funded by the International Association of Business Communicators (IABC) called the Excellence study. The idea was to identify how public relations could contribute to the overall effectiveness of an organization (Grunig, 2001). The Excellence study was conducted over a decade and involved both quantitative and qualitative data collection. The end result was a number of books, articles, book chapters, and a normative theory of public relations, Excellence Theory. A normative theory is prescriptive. Excellence Theory prescribes how public relations should be practiced and how public relations departments should be structured (Bowen, 2005b). Excellence Theory is a grand theory because it tries to explain the totality of public relations rather than a specific area of public relations.

Excellence Theory is predicated on ten principles of Excellence that have been reduced to eight variables:

1 Top management must understand the value of public relations.
2 Public relations contributes to strategic planning/strategic organizational functions.
3 Public relations should enact the managerial role by engaging in research and planning.
4 Public relations should use the two-way symmetrical model of public relations. This model emphasizes a dialogue between organizations and constituents.
5 People in the public relations department must have the skills and knowledge to enact the managerial role and engage in two-way symmetrical public relations.
6 Activist pressure can result in organizations communicating with constituents. Activist pressure is one indicator of an organization's effect on its environment.
7 Organizations need a participative rather than an authoritarian culture and structure for Excellent public relations to flourish.
8 Public relations benefits from diversity in terms of race and gender. (Bowen, 2005b)

Obviously, this is only a cursory explanation of Excellence Theory. For more information, refer to J. Grunig (1992) or the Excellence Theory entry in the *Encyclopedia of Public Relations* (Heath, 2005).

It is instructive to explore the theme of activists and antagonists in more detail to further debunk the connection. In biochemistry, an antagonist acts against and reduces the reaction of a chemical substance in the body. Insulin is an example of an antagonist because it serves to reduce the glucose level in a person's blood. Instead of a protagonist, biochemistry has an agonist. An agonist seeks to stimulate a physiological reaction – create an action. Protagonists are the central character in a story around whom events unfold. Interestingly, in drama, a protagonist can be either a hero or a villain. An antagonist can play a useful role when opposing a villain. An agonist can create positive or negative change in a body. Hence, an antagonist can be a positive force. The antagonist may prevent a villain from harming others or an agonist from damaging a body. We would argue that activists as antagonists have themselves brought about some important social changes. Among those favorable changes are ending slavery, winning important rights for women such as voting, helping to end apartheid in South Africa, improving workplace safety, and creating a safer food supply. Being an antagonist does not have to be negative. Still, casting activists as antagonists seems to place them in a lesser role when activists are discussed in public relations. It reinforces a corporate-centric view that limits what we consider to be public relations and how we understand its practice.

Another use of the term protagonist is in designating the primary advocate of a movement or cause. Clearly, activists have long been protagonists in the sense that they have been a driving force in social movements that were effective in large measure because of public relations actions. Oddly, corporations become cast as antagonists when activist groups utilize public relations to seek social change. Corporations use public relations to defend and support the status quo. The growth of public relations in the Progressive Era and in the 1960s was a defensive response. Pragmatically, the activists were the protagonists because they advocated for change. The corporations were the antagonists as they resisted the change. The point here is that the labels of antagonist and protagonist are relative. Who is a protagonist or an antagonist depends upon the situation and who is viewing it. We should avoid thinking of activists as antagonists and reinforcing the corporate-centric view of public relations. Activists are important users of public relations, have helped to pioneer the field's development, and are important constituents or stakeholders in the web of relationships.

James Grunig and Larissa Grunig do recognize that activists can shape how corporations engage in public relations. Activist pressure can help organizations to practice two-way symmetrical public relations. By exercising their power, activists force management in organizations to address their concerns and begin a dialogue with the activists. This is an argument found in the activist literature as well (Raymond, 2003). A variation of a Hegelian dialectic is occurring. Hegel and his dialectical approach were initially presented in chapter 3. To review, a Hegelian dialectic is a system of inquiry that can be used to explain historical developments. The central notion is that progress is a function of conflict. The Hegelian dialectic begins with an idea or thesis. A conflicting idea or antithesis is presented as a counter to the thesis. Synthesis is used to reconcile the common truth in the two ideas and to create progress. Of course, in Hegel's work, each new synthesis becomes a thesis and the process chains out. For our purposes we are taking just the basic process. Figure 5.1 is a visual representation of the Hegelian dialectic.

From the Excellence Theory perspective, activists can serve as the antithesis to the corporation. The synthesis is the realization that an organization needs to

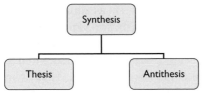

Figure 5.1   Simplified Hegelian dialectic

consider the needs of its diverse stakeholders and practice a more inclusive version of public relations (e.g., the two-way symmetrical model). The public relations practice of the organization evolves. Still, this variation of the Hegelian dialectic, the Excellence dialectic if you will, privileges the corporation. It is how the corporation practices public relations that matters, not the activists, and determines whether or not there will be a dialogue. While recent writings are softening on the view, Excellence retains a sense of being a corporate-centric perspective.

Counter-pressures to collaboration

Not everyone believes activists and corporations should work together. Skeptics on both sides question if such collaboration is a good thing. Nick Nichols (2003) is vociferous from the corporate side of anti-collaboration. Nichols views working with and adopting "demands" from activist groups as appeasement and corporate cowardice. He argues that appeasement does not work and activists have been permitted to dominate society through "pressure, intimidation and even terror" (p. 137). Corporations must fight back against activists by adopting many of the non-traditional public relations tactics of the activists. These views are shared by Ross Irvine, a Canadian public relations practitioner and proprietor of www.epublicrelations.ca.

Nichols (2003) uses the example of how an activist protest rally was disrupted by a corporation funding a mime and a fake car crash. The mime tried to prevent positive media coverage of the event by jumping in front of news cameras when the activists would speak. Two cars faked a crash just as the main activist speaker was to begin, triggering a loud series of car horns.

Nichols patterns his ten power plays on the work of Saul Alinsky. Power plays are "powerful weapons that companies, industry groups, and determined citizens are using to beat the activists and survive in the twenty-first century" (Nichols, 2003, p. 140). Some of his ten power plays include "Flash your brass knuckles: Threaten to use your power" and "Make them sweat your threats." From this perspective, collaboration is viewed as a sign of weakness that will breed more activist demands.

A number of activist writers also question the wisdom of collaborating with corporations. The theme in these writings is a fear of co-optation and distraction. Co-optation occurs when activists are brought into the decision making process as a means of quieting their voices. By working with corporations, activists lose their edge and ability to be critical of the corporations. Activists begin to censor themselves once they are linked to a corporation. Rowell (2002) argues that dialogues with corporations are a way to co-opt critics and are motivated by a desire to pre-empt conflict and negative publicity. This sounds reminiscent of the Excellence dialectic. "The move toward openness and dialogue is not a business strategy, but a public relations strategy – the new phase of sophisticated greenwashing" (Rowell, 2002, p. 33).

A primary concern is that corporations control the dialogues and dictate the terms of dialogues. Corporations decide what will be discussed (what is open to negotiation) and who can be involved (Monbiot, 2002; Rowell, 2002). Activists critical of dialogue believe it is "the most important co-optation tactics that companies are now using to overcome opposition to their operations" (Rowell, 2002, p. 33). The issue is power. Corporations have the power to control if there is a dialogue and potentially the rules governing the dialogue process. In addition, activist identity can be lost through collaborations with corporations. The cause which defines the activists' identities can be lost when the activists' interests are seen to merge with those of the corporations. Consider how negatively members of the Sierra Club reacted when their organization began working with Clorox on its line of green cleaning products. The anger was in part driven by a sense of a loss of identity. The Sierra Club was no longer what some members thought it was and was no longer consistent with their own identities.

The other concern is distraction. Let us return to that phrase *greenwashing*. As mentioned in chapter 2, greenwashing is when an organization pretends to be environmentally friendly. Some surface changes are made to distract people from how the organization still harms the environment. When former activists work with corporations, these former activists give the corporation green credentials even if there is no real commitment to change (Monbiot, 2002). Similarly, corporations can sponsor activists (fund programs) and benefit from the association with the activists – the connection "greens" the corporation's reputation. Wilson (2002) claims that "sponsorship is merely a convenient public relations tool, enabling corporations to manufacture a green veneer while continuing business as usual" (p. 44). Again, the sponsorship does not mean the organization has changed its behaviors but it is viewed as green anyway. Moreover, the sponsors then shape what and how the research is conducted (Wilson, 2002). Clearly, the activists have a strong dislike for public relations, even though public relations is at the core of what they themselves do. Some activists equate public relations with a facade, a false image.

Interestingly, the critics seem to evoke co-optation. Nichols (2003) feels that collaboration should result in an end of criticism – he expects co-optation as an outcome. In contrast, activists fear that co-optation will occur. Can you blame activists for worrying about co-optation when some in corporate public relations (we use the term grudgingly to describe what Nichols and those of his ilk do) see that as the desired outcome? What is striking about these counter-forces to collaboration is distrust. Corporations do not trust the activists to appreciate the changes and activists do not trust that corporations really will make changes. As Moloney (2005) notes, public relations and trust do not always go together. For effective collaboration to occur, corporations and activists need to agree on/negotiate the rules of engagement. The rules must cover how the collaboration will work, who will be involved, and the criteria for reaching a successful outcome. Each side needs to trust the system for collaboration. That is why all parties must work to create an acceptable set of rules for collaborative efforts. Some examples of activist-corporate partnerships include McDonald's and the Environmental Defense Fund (EDF), Rainforest Alliance with Chiquita and Kraft, and the World Wildlife Fund (WWF) with HSBC, Unilever, Lafarge, and Canon.

The collaboration should be viewed as a long-term project. That means activists can still raise concerns and seek additional change. If activists are to be a resource for positive organizational change as Raymond (2003) and others suggest, they have to be allowed to continue to voice their concerns. Activists must remain free to be skeptics and question the status quo. It is the critical voice of the skeptic that can prove valuable to an organization by identifying problems that the organization needs to address. The goal of the collaboration should not be co-optation. The goal should be a continuing engagement with activists where they are free to air their concerns.

We run the risk of sounding too idealistic here. We do not deny there are risks to this public relations version of constructive engagement. There have been and will continue to be abuses of dialogue and collaboration to greenwash and to co-opt. But there also are legitimate efforts by activists and corporations to improve society. The question is how do we facilitate more of the latter and prevent more of the former. Just because we do not have a definitive answer now does not mean we should abandon the question.

Activist Public Relations

To discuss activist public relations, it is instructive to review some of the key resources for activists engaging in public relations, the primary uses of activist public relations, and the public relations tactics often used by activists. Each of these three points helps to illuminate how activists approach and utilize public relations.

Activist public relations resources

Printed public relations advice for activists can be found in Saul Alinsky's (1972) *Rules for Radicals* and Charlotte Ryan's (1991) *Primetime Activism*. Alinsky concentrates on high-profile staged events to bring attention to an organization, its issues, and its demands. It is a highly confrontational approach because Alinsky knew from experience how easy it is for those with power to ignore those without. Ryan (1991) details the value of media coverage and how activists can generate effective media coverage. She provides a carefully thought out and sophisticated approach to media relations. Ryan helped to create the Boston College Movement/Media Research and Action Project (MRAP). MRAP helps groups attempting to create social change to maximize their utilization of the news media.

The Internet has expanded the amount and ease of access to public relations resources available for activists. Two excellent online sites offer public relations advice to activists: the SPIN Project developed by the Independent Media Institute (www.spinproject.org/index.php) and the Green Media Toolshed (www. greenmediatoolshed.org). The SPIN Project offers a wide range of advice for activist public relations, including media relations, online communication, identifying your target audience, and strategic communications planning. The target audience discussion explains the need to segment and avoid using the notion of a general public. Activists learn how to segment and to research a target audience. The discussion of strategic communication planning walks activists through the planning and communication aspects of a public relations action. The SPIN Project clearly articulates a vision of public relations as strategic. As the project website states, "The creation and adoption of a strategic communications plan represents a significant step for any organization."

The Green Media Toolshed is dedicated to media relations, often called media activism. Whatever the name, the focus remains placing one's message in the news media in a positive manner. Topics include how to create releases, how to pitch the media, and media trends. Once more, the emphasis is on strategy. Activists learn how to research a target audience, develop plans, develop messages, send messages, and evaluate results. While each website emphasizes media relations tactics, both the SPIN Project and the Green Media Toolshed present public relations from a rich strategic focus, not just a simple "how to" list of tactics.

We have not provided a comprehensive review of all the resources relevant to activist public relations. What this sample shows is the sophisticated approach activists bring to the utilization of public relations tactics. The public relations resources reviewed here provide instruction on public relations that is comparable to what students would learn in public relations writing and campaign courses. The activist approach to public relations is as complex and strategic as that found in corporate public relations.

Activists as issues managers

As noted earlier, activists organize in order to influence organizational actions, public policy, or social norms and values – they seek to exercise influence. The three targets of influence are related. Activists can talk directly with an organization to influence its actions. If direct contact fails, activists can attempt to force or to pressure the organization into compliance. Public policy can be used to force organizations into change. New regulations or legislation can force an organization to change its behavior. Social norms, as reflected in constituency expectations, can be used to pressure organizations into change. Constituency expectations reflect social norms. Activists can shape social norms so that constituencies expect an organization to behave the way the activists want it to behave. Such pressure is evident in reformation of sweatshop and child labor in the modern apparel industry. Constituents reflected the social norms that child labor is exploitative and workers should be treated as humans. Concern over sweatshop abuses resulted in organizations making voluntary changes and government regulation of the apparel industry in the US and other countries. If constituency expectations change but organizational behavior does not, the organization risks violating constituency expectations and triggering constituency churn. Constituency churn can include boycotts, negative media coverage, and protests.

Given the focus on change, activist public relations is in large part issues management, "the identification or creation of issues and the application of systematic procedures designed to influence the issue's resolution in a manner favorable to the issues manager" (Coombs & Holladay, 2007b, p. 82). The change efforts of activists are a form of issues management. The need for change is the issue and various skills and resources are brought to bear in order to influence the issue. Issues management is the focus of chapter 10, but the basics are introduced here to help explain activist public relations.

Activists can pursue their objectives through a combination of negotiation and pressure. Pressure and activism are closely linked, as pressure about a cause has been a critical element in definitions of activists. The pressure aspect of activism reflects the *catalytic model of issues management*. The catalytic model is premised on systematically expanding the number of people aware and in support of an issue. The catalytic model hinges on legitimacy, awareness, and influence. An issue must be viewed as legitimate (accepted as a public concern) from the start or other people will ignore it. The activist group must also establish its legitimacy to represent the issue – establish its connection to the issue. Activists must answer the question, "What right do you have to speak for this issue?" (Coombs, 1992).

Through the news media, the Internet (websites, email, discussion boards, blogs, etc.), public presentations, and interpersonal communication, the activists spread awareness of the issue to increasingly larger numbers of people. Once others are aware, the focus shifts to influence, as activists try to win support for their preferred resolution of the issue. There is then a transition from awareness to support. Activist groups, like any membership organization, must work to keep their supporters. Part of the communication effort is designed to keep members interested and happy. Moreover, people need to be willing to actively support the issue and not just be aware of it or signal tacit support. This pressure can result in policy changes that force an organization to change (Coombs, 1992; Crable & Vibbert, 1985).

While built for public policy, the catalytic model can also be used to pressure organizations into voluntary change. When managers realize there is public pressure building for change, management may "voluntarily" change rather than wait for regulation to force them into changing. The pressure forces management into a negotiation or a partnership with the activist groups. The Immokalee case study at the end of this chapter illustrates how organizations can be pressured into negotiations and partnerships. If an activist group has established its power, that power can result in negotiations and partnerships without pressure tactics that are visible to constituents.

Raymond (2003) uses the term *copycat action* to describe how activists can win concessions by simply threatening to use a previously successful tactic. The corporation agrees much more quickly to work with the activists and change because management wants to avoid the negative publicity a successful activist effort can create. For instance, Wendy's moved much quicker to work with People for the Ethical Treatment of Animals (PETA) than did Burger King to reform guidelines for meat and egg producers. Wendy's management had seen the power of the Murder King campaign and knew the Wicked Wendy's campaign would result in similar negative publicity. As a result, Wendy's management agreed to the more humane guidelines for meat and egg supplies rather quickly. Early corporate-activist partnerships can also be a result of management trying to get ahead of an issue (Coombs & Holladay, 2006). Effective issues management seeks to anticipate and address issues as early as possible. Grunig and Repper (1992) have argued for early intervention to prevent visible conflict with constituents. Management takes actions because they anticipate the issue could create constituency churn in the future.

The catalytic model, which is detailed in chapter 10, is an exercise in power. Marginalized activists use the catalytic model to secure power as part of an effort to increase their salience to an organization. Mitchell, Agle, and Wood (1997) have identified three dimensions for evaluating the salience of "stakeholders":

1 *Power:* the ability to get an actor to do something she or he would not do otherwise.
2 *Legitimacy:* the actions are perceived as appropriate, desirable, or proper within the context of some belief system.
3 *Urgency:* the extent to which time frame is important; the call for immediate action due to the importance of the claim or the relationships to stakeholders.

Stakeholders exist within a web of relations, so they compete for attention against other stakeholder groups that can hold contradictory or mutually exclusive demands. Thus, stakeholders must work to increase their salience and the likelihood an organization will recognize and negotiate with them. Stakeholder salience is a function of the ability to demonstrate these three attributes. The more attributes the stakeholders are perceived to possess, the greater their salience to management. The stakeholders and the issues they advocate can be prioritized according to their threat level as determined by their ability to damage the organization and their probability of developing momentum. The same process can be used if we term the groups "constituents" rather than "stakeholders." Activists will be perceived to have greater salience when the attributes of power, legitimacy, and urgency are strong (Coombs, 2002).

Through the catalytic model, activists increase their number of supporters by making people aware of an issue and winning support for their side of the issue (power). The catalytic model is rooted in legitimacy, the perception that something is appropriate. For issues management, legitimacy involves having people perceive both the issue and the issue manager as appropriate (Coombs, 1992, 2002). Finally, the catalytic model seeks to build urgency by creating pressure to take action. The catalytic model talks about a felt need for action (Crable & Vibbert, 1985). People are mobilized to demonstrate the need to take action on the issue now.

Summary

Issues management is a broad, strategic subdiscipline of public relations. Issues management is broad because it draws upon a variety of public relations tactics. Issues management is strategic because it requires a carefully planned approach. Chapter 10 provides more details on issues management. We touched on the subject in this chapter to give you a feel for how activists are using public relations. Issues management provides one framework for guiding and analyzing the public relations activities of activist groups. The emphasis on *change* is common to activists and issues management, making the two a natural fit for one another. Clearly, activists are practicing public relations and often in a very complex manner.

Corporate and Activist Public Relations Use: Comparison

The question has been raised about the differences and similarities in how activists and corporations use public relations. The belief is that unique features of activism should result in some difference between the two. A limited amount of research addresses this question directly. However, we can also offer some general comparisons between activist and corporate public relations practices to help answer the question.

Specific research on activist public relations

Reber and Kim (2006) examined how activists used online newsrooms. Journalists are increasingly turning to websites to collect information, making online media relations an important concern. Online newsrooms are one way to evaluate online media relations. Only 32.4 percent of the activist websites examined had online newsrooms while 33.8 percent supplied news releases. The most common media relations material found on websites were the organizational history (70.3 percent) and the organizational mission (54.1 percent). Reber and Kim concluded that activist websites could devote more attention to journalists and media relations so as to build relationships with them. Basically, activist websites need to post more information of interest to the news media, such as news releases. Their findings are not that different from the information generated by an investigation of corporate online newsrooms.

Corporate sites were a little better at providing information the media might want in the proper pre-packaged formats (Perry & Bodkin, 2002). It should be noted that many corporate online newsrooms are designed and often maintained by consultants rather than in-house. One popular online newsroom provider is TEK Group International (www.tekgroup.com/), whose clients include Accenture, Audi, Best Buy, the Public Relations Society of America, Staples, and Walgreens. Few activist groups have the financial resources to outsource their online newsrooms.

Taylor, Kent, and White (2001) have conducted one of the few studies of activist public relations that allows a comparison to similar corporate practices. They examined activist websites for the five dialogic principles: ease of interface (easy to navigate), usefulness of information, conservation of visitors (keep visitors at the site), generation of return visits, and dialogic loop (incorporates interactivity). Their study found that activist sites do cover the first three well, but fared poorly on the last two. These results are similar to those found by Esrock and Leichty's (1999) study of Fortune 500 websites. Their examination of corporate websites found a limited use of interactivity and would fair poorly when judged against the five dialogic principles. However, many of the examples in this chapter have identified activist websites that are very interactive. Taylor, Kent, and White (2001) note their findings are limited by the activist groups they sampled.

Some differences did emerge as well. Corporate websites focus on the media, consumers, and investors, while activists focus on members of the activist organization and could do more to address media. Activists and corporations differ in the conservation of visitors, as reflected in how they connect to similar groups. Activists build credibility through links to other groups and do not try to prevent visitors from leaving their sites as sales-based corporate sites do. Taylor, Kent, and White (2001) found a "high level of interconnectedness between activist organizations" (p. 280). They also noted that activists are good at informing but weak on mobilizing.

Contingency Theory in public relations is a useful perspective when comparing activist and corporate public relations. Contingency Theory centers on managing the conflict between organizations and other constituencies. Conflict is viewed as a positive, motivating force in the relationships. The strategies used in resolving the conflict range from accommodative (each group considers the other's interests) to advocacy (a group argues for its own self-interest). A total of

Box 5.2   Contingency Theory

Glen Cameron and his colleagues have developed Contingency Theory as another grand theory of public relations in an attempt to explain how public relations is practiced. Contingency Theory is based in the conflict between organizations and constituents. How do public relations practitioners respond to this conflict? Contingency Theory places possible public relations responses – what are termed stances – on a continuum from pure advocacy to pure accommodation. Pure advocacy is when the practitioners fight for the self-interests of their organization. Pure accommodation involves surrendering to the interests of the constituents. Public relations practitioners can use a stance from anywhere along that continuum.

The choice of the stance is contingent upon a number of internal and external variables. Contingency Theory is complex, with 86 variables placed into 11 categories on two dimensions of internal and external. The external variables include threats, industry environment, political/social/cultural environment, external publics, and the issue under consideration. The internal variables include organizational characteristics, public relations department characteristics, management characteristics, internal threats, individual characteristics, and relationship characteristics. The researchers continue to refine Contingency Theory and seek to simplify its complex structure (Shin, Cameron, & Cropp, 2006). Contingency Theory recognizes that a public relations response is shaped by many factors and that there are times to accommodate and times to advocate. So when asked what is the best response for a public relations practitioner, the answer is "it depends."

For additional insight, refer to the Contingency Theory entry in Heath (2005) or the Contingency Theory chapter in Hansen-Horn and Neff (2008).

86 different factors are believed to influence the choice of strategies (Cameron, Cropp, & Reber, 2001; Shin, Cameron, & Cropp, 2006). We do not mean to unpack all the intricacies of Contingency Theory here (for additional information about the theory, see box 5.2). Instead, we propose that the use of advocacy, especially aggressive strategies, might separate activist and corporate public relations.

Given the desire for change, it is possible that activists will favor advocacy in their public messages. Activists may spend considerable time trying to pressure corporations into action. The need to create pressure should be reflected in the activist messages, such as those placed on a website, and the use of more aggressive strategies. It is reasonable that activist websites have a much higher percentage of advocacy messages than corporate websites. We would also expect to see a shift to accommodation strategies once a corporation agrees to collaborate with the activists. These are intuitively appealing conclusions but require testing to determine if they are accurate. It should be noted that Contingency Theory and Excellence Theory do not necessarily agree with one another and can provide different views on public relations. Box 5.3 overviews the tension between these two grand theories of public relations.

Box 5.3   Excellence-Contingency Theory Tension

Reading the boxes on Excellence Theory and Contingency Theory should suggest the tension that exists between these two theories. Excellence is highly prescriptive and argues there is one, best way to practice public relations. The best way is to engage in two-way symmetrical public relations. Contingency posits that the best way to practice public relations depends upon the situation. There are times when one-way forms of public relations might be needed or times when two parties will not even engage one another. The answer to how should public relations be practiced is "it depends." The singular and multiple views of public relations effectiveness is a point of contention for these two grand theories of public relations. It is helpful to realize that the theoretical debate exists, as it shapes some of the research in public relations.

There needs to be more research into activist public relations. It would be useful to conduct additional comparative research with corporate public relations. As the name implies, comparative research contrasts public relations efforts in two or more countries. Comparative research would give us a better idea of the similarities and differences in how corporations and activists approach public relations. It would be helpful to know if there are differences in the tactics and appeals the two sides use. Existing evidence suggests there may be more similarities than differences. Understanding what those differences are and why they exist would further our understanding of activist public relations. For instance, are activist messages more likely to reflect the advocacy aspect of Contingency Theory than corporate websites? Public relations has the potential to help marginalized voices be heard. But without a fuller understanding of the factors that shape activist public relations, we cannot maximize this amplification potential.

General Comparison of Activist and Corporate Public Relations

We can draw comparisons between activists and corporate public relations by reviewing how each uses basic elements of public relations. For our comparison, we choose media relations, online activities, direct action, advocacy advertising, and recruitment and mobilization.

Media relations

Activists, like corporations, seek news media coverage through (1) routine publicity and (2) staged events. *Routine publicity* is the practice of outside sources placing information in the news media (Baskin & Aronoff, 1992). The term *routine* is used because the publicity practices are used on a regular basis and are viewed as acceptable by the media. Routine publicity would include news releases, editorials, online newsrooms, and public statements (e.g., press conferences and interviews) (Howard & Mathews, 1985).

Staged events are activities created just for the media and often are called *pseudo-events* (Boorstin, 1978; Graber, 1980). Rallies, demonstrations, protests, and parades are all examples of staged events. Staged events can be disruptive, such as efforts to slow traffic with farm machinery or throwing blood on people wearing furs. Such disruption runs the risk of offending the targets (including the media) of the issue manager (Cobb, Ross, & Ross, 1976; Paletz & Boiney, 1988; Sigal, 1973). Staged events are not routine because they are not publicity tools commonly used by public relations practitioners. *Association* refers to connections between an issue and something already considered newsworthy. Personalities, symbols, and other issues already in the news can be used to help create newsworthiness for an issue (Paletz & Entman, 1981).

Like its corporate kin, activist public relations has a desire to attract media attention. The news media can be used to create awareness and build legitimacy (public acceptance of an issue), and provide a limited opportunity to win support. The news stories can make people aware of an issue. Most people learn about events that do not directly affect them through the news media. As of 2008, most people in the US were still receiving their news from television and print. The Pew Research Center for People & the Press found that 57 percent of Americans receive their news from the television, while 24 percent receive their news from newspapers. It is still a minority of Americans who depend upon Internet sources for their news (Audience, 2008). Few people in the US had heard of Alar before the National Resource Defense Council (NRDC) promoted the issue. Within a month, millions of US consumers were aware of Alar, how it was used on apples, and the reported links to cancer.

When the media report on an issue, they provide a frame for the issue and the related proposals. The topic of framing also is examined in chapter 6 on media relations. A frame is an explanation of how the issue relates to actors, motives, and other issues (Graber, 1982; Hallahan, 1999; Ryan, 1991). Frames organize information and tell people how to interpret an issue. They help publics to evaluate issues and the proposals offered for resolving them (Ansolabehere, Behr, & Iyengar, 1993; Kosicki, 1993). Therefore, it is important for issue managers to attempt to influence media portrayals/frames. Framing is not to be dismissed as inconsequential. Linsky (1986, p. 94) notes: "The way the press frames the issue is as important as whether or not it is covered at all."

The importance of media frames can be traced to people's inability to create their own frames. Few people are able to develop the frames necessary to organize and to analyze political information such as policy issues. Therefore, publics must rely upon other sources to provide frames. In most cases the source of the frames is the media (Bennett, 1975; Paletz & Boiney, 1988; Tuchman, 1981). A small but increasing number of people now turn to Internet sources for their news. By 2005, 23 percent of all Americans were receiving their news from the Internet and the number jumps to 43 percent for broadband users. The vast majority of the Internet news seekers are utilizing the online version of traditional media, with only 9 percent from blogs and 5 percent from listservs (Farrelly, 2006). Framing remains an issue with Internet news sources.

A positive frame can advance an activist's cause while a negative frame can undermine it. Reber and Berger (2005) examined how the Sierra Club used frames. They defined media frames as "structures through which individuals organize and make sense of an ambiguous stream of events and issues in the world" (p. 186). The study examined the frames used in Sierra Club newsletters and compared them to the frames used in regional and national newspapers about the same environmental issues. Framing is important because it helps to build legitimacy for activist groups and shape the public discussion of an issue. In the news stories, environmentalists were the primary sources and the Sierra Club frames appeared more than competing frames. The research suggests that being an important media source provides an opportunity to frame news stories. Reber and Berger found that the Sierra Club is fairly effective at creating the desired frame in news stories because they are a regular source for such stories. However, not many activist groups have the stature to be important sources for the news media.

An issue manager's legitimacy can affect a public's willingness to listen. Media representatives are more likely to listen to and to report from legitimate issue managers, while discounting or ignoring illegitimate ones. A legitimate issue manager has a greater chance to facilitate a positive media frame by explaining how the issue and ways to resolve it should be interpreted. The lack of a legitimate spokesperson can lead to misinterpretations of the issue and the proposal. Constituencies (including the media) will be left to make their own interpretations that may be incorrect. The use of a disruptive media attention tactic increases the likelihood of an incorrect interpretation. Publics may focus on the negative tactics and not on the issue and its related proposal (Goldenberg, 1975; Paletz & Boiney, 1988; Paletz & Entman, 1981). The news reports are a chance to persuade people as well. The activists may have an opportunity to present their persuasive appeals in a news story through quotations or paraphrasing. However, due to the short nature of news stories, the channel offers limited utility for persuasion.

Online activities

Activist are becoming increasingly aware of the power of the Internet in assisting their causes. While traditionally we may visualize activists engaging in public protests, we must also recognize the power of virtual activism to influence others and corporations. Several web-based avenues exist for resistors: web pages, blogs, email lists, discussion groups, etc. If we look beyond online newsrooms we can see the Internet has emerged as an important tool for constituents who want to demand attention for their claims and influence corporate operations (e.g., van de Donk et al., 2004).

Virtual activists can engage in e-activism by using the Internet in numerous ways to affect sentiments, disseminate information, connect like-minded people, and mobilize actions. The Internet-based activities of activists can even become a news source for the traditional media and thereby garner increased attention and credibility. When websites are cited in news reports by mainstream media organizations, the sites and the causes gain legitimacy and extend awareness of the issues. For example, in the US, the Flaming Ford website gained attention when CNN, National Public Radio (NPR), and major news networks cited the website in their news reports. The website was started by a couple living near Atlanta, Georgia. They were angry that Ford would not recall vehicles that were prone to catching fire when they were not running. In spite of federal investigations, Ford had resisted the recall for several years. The problem was in the starter. The couple posted pictures of their burnt car and asked others to post their pictures and stories, too. The website is credited for sparking attention and forcing Ford to recall the defective cars and trucks (Coombs, 1998). In this way the Internet can work in conjunction with traditional media to challenge the activities of corporations (Bennett, 2004).

In some respects activists have been ahead of corporations in using the new media/online media. True to public relations' history of reacting to activists, the early writers about the new media emphasized the need to address activists' online activities, such as rogue websites (e.g., Middleberg, 2001). The corporate foray into blogs followed concern over how activists were spreading messages online. Think about it. Who was blogging first, activists or CEOs? *Buzz marketing* (word-of-mouth campaigns that influence consumers to spread a company's message) was an effort to mimic non-corporate efforts to spread positive messages about the organization online. Consumer anger over a very minor Pentium chip flaw in 1994 exploded on the Internet in under a week and crossed over to the news media in less than two weeks (Hearit, 1999). Serious works on using the Internet for buzz marketing appeared much later.

Organizations continue to be held accountable as activists reveal their errors and lies online. Online activism is an important element in creating organizational transparency. Corporate public relations is learning more from activist online public relations than vice versa. The main lesson activists have learned from corporate online public relations is the creation of online newsrooms (Reber & Kim, 2006).

E-activism works in conjunction with rather than replacing traditional activism. The Internet helps to reduce the costs, time, and effort needed to create an activist action (Raymond, 2003). Thomas (2003) states: "Activists have a demonstrable advantage – in terms of skill and experience – in the effective use of online media as a tool for protest and dissent" (p. 115). The point is that activists are ahead of their corporate counterparts when it comes to communicating online in some ways. A good example of the effectiveness of e-activism is Oxfam's attempt to stop Nestlé from claiming $6 million from the Ethiopian government. Nestlé based the compensation claim on the Ethiopian government's nationalization of a business

27 years earlier. News headlines in December 2002 asked if Nestlé knew it was Christmas. How could a major corporation demand so much money from an impoverished country at Christmas? Oxfam used the Internet to coordinate a response. Within three days, 15,000 negative emails had been sent to Nestlé. The number grew to over 40,000 in a few weeks. After 35 days, Nestlé agreed to give the money to Ethiopian famine relief (Raymond, 2003). Would the money have gone to corporate coffers rather than relief if Oxfam had not generated opposition online?

Direct action

The writings in the public relations and activist literatures suggest a pattern in the relationships between activists and corporations. The initial step is for activists to request a corporation to make changes, an action known as *petition* (Bowers, Ochs, & Jensen, 1993). If the petition is rejected or ignored, the activists escalate their actions to apply pressure to the corporation (Raymond, 2003).

Direct action seeks immediate resolution to the issue and has a long connection to activists. Indirect actions, on the other hand, try to work within the existing system to solve the problem. Traditional and non-traditional public relations tactics are primarily indirect actions. Direct actions are intended to force the decision makers to act immediately. Examples of direct action tactics include strikes, the occupation of space, non-violent resistance/civil disobedience, hackivism (online direct action such as denial-of-service attacks), destruction of property, graffiti, and vandalism. Granted, direct action can also garner media coverage, thus we label the actions *radical* public relations tactics. However, direct action runs the risk of negative news media portrayals and backlash from potential supporters. If the news media report on logging equipment being vandalized but not why it was done, the activists are framed negatively. As Raymond (2003, p. 216) cautions, "Direct action is a tactic of last resort."

Direct action is also more likely to be used by radical activist organizations. Radical activist groups seek fundamental changes to social, economic, or political systems that would radically alter people's lives (Derville, 2005). Consider the violent actions of the Earth Liberation Front (ELF), which include arson and spray painting expensive gas-guzzling vehicles. Or how members of Stop Huntingdon Animal Cruelty (SHAC) used direct action and what are termed secondary and tertiary tactics in efforts to close Huntingdon Life Sciences, Europe's largest contract animal testing laboratory. SHAC has protested at the homes of management and called customers and suppliers to question them about Huntingdon Life Sciences' practices. The protests against suppliers, insurers, and office cleaners are secondary and tertiary strategies because they do not target the organization but those affiliated with it in some way. Radical activist groups are self-directed, their members participate because the issue is part of their identities. The direct actions are used to build group identity and create a sense of personal fulfillment. Derville (2005) notes how disruptive image events – very emotional protests that include a powerful visual component – are more common in radical activist groups.

Radical activist groups will not engage in compromise. SHAC wants an end to Huntingdon Life Sciences and will settle for nothing less. Nor is the Earth Liberation Front (ELF) likely to partner with Monsanto on a project. Extreme measures are being used to end what these groups feel are intolerable situations. However, such radical activists help to open doors for moderate activists. The demands of the moderate activists appear more reasonable in comparison and corporations are more likely to engage the moderate activists in some form of discussion or dialogue (Derville, 2005). Hence, radical activists can be part of the Excellence dialectic.

Radical activists intensify the pressure on corporations to engage with activists, just not with the radical activists themselves. The radicals make corporations and other constituents more likely to view the moderate activists more favorably. Constituents might provide monetary and opinion support for the moderates, thereby increasing their power base. Corporations are more likely to view the moderate activist groups as potential partners for dialogue or at least more willing to listen to their concerns.

Radicals also help to move "the middle." "The middle" means the middle ground or what most people in society would find acceptable or deem legitimate. Crudely, we can think of a continuum of corporate behavior ranging from financial (corporate) to social (activist) concerns. Radical activists help to move the center more toward social concerns. We see this happening with the growth of corporate social responsibility (see chapter 13).

Advocacy advertising

Activist groups with more funding can buy advocacy advertisements. Advocacy advertisements are placed in newspapers and magazines. The advertisements might raise awareness of an issue, seek to persuade people to support an issue, or urge people to contact their political representatives. Often, advocacy advertisements will address pending legislation. The advertisements seek to make people aware of the vote, hope to persuade people to support the activists' position on the vote, and ask people to tell their representatives how they should vote on the issue. The We Can Solve the Climate Crisis activist group uses television and print advertisements to attract constituents to their website and ultimately to their cause. At the website, people learn more about the activist groups and are encouraged to join the fight to solve the climate crisis. Corporate public relations is more likely to utilize advocacy advertisements than do activists, but that gap is narrowing.

Recruitment and mobilization

Like any voluntary or membership organization, activists need to recruit members and donations. There has been some work on how public relations can help in recruiting members and fundraising. The Internet facilitates recruitment just as it can build awareness. Potential members can be reached through special-interest websites, discussion boards, and blogs. People who visit such sites are already interested in a particular issue. Activists are attractive to people when the activist group supports their issue. Activists can use their own websites to raise money by providing links to make donations. The Campaign to Stop Killer Coke (www.killercoke.org), a group that raises questions about Coca-Cola's involvement with the brutal repression of union efforts in Columbia, provides a connection for donations that includes the ability to use PayPal.

Activist groups can build communication networks online. Activists can connect with their membership and with like-minded groups. Direct links are easy and inexpensive to create on the Internet (Coombs, 1998). Activists now have a variety of options for staying connected and activating potential supporters. Activists can use the Internet to create much more expansive social networks than would be possible without the Internet. Kearns (n.d.) argues that the Internet allows for network-centric advocacy. Activists can act quickly with a network-centric approach. People can be activated quickly with mobilization messages. People come together when needed, using their social networks. However, communication skill is needed to keep people connected and to activate them when needed. People must be persuaded to act in support of an issue.

One way that people support an issue is through *grassroots lobbying*. Grassroots lobbying is when citizens/voters demonstrate support for an issue through attending rallies, signing petitions, or contacting political representatives via email, phone, letter, or fax. Activist groups and corporations have both stimulated and directed grassroots efforts. Activists stimulate the grassroots by making people aware of an issue and the need to take action. They direct grassroots by providing a mechanism for taking action. For instance, activist groups can have links on their websites that allow people to email their political representatives, recommend scripts for such messages, or provide downloadable petitions.

The Parents Television Council (www.parents.org), a conservative activist group, has an "action center" on its website. This action center provides guidance on writing letters to public officials and provides contact information. All you have to do is type in your zip code and you are supplied with the names and links that can connect you to your senators, US representative, governor, state senator, and state representative. Grassroots lobbying is a powerful force even though all players know when the grassroots are being stimulated, sometimes called *astroturfing*. The idea is that people are not taking action on their own, they are being prodded into action – hence, the grassroots effort is not genuine. A full discussion of astroturfing is provided in chapter 10. Still, when voters contact a member of Congress, for example, they are taken seriously.

Conclusion: Final Comparison

This chapter has defined activists and considered how they are practitioners of public relations. A key concern has been a comparison of corporate and activist public relations practices. Funding serves to constrain some of the public relations activities used by activists. Due to limited resources, activists will rely more heavily on inexpensive tactics such as publicity, Internet connections, and Internet contagions (word-of-mouth via the Internet). However, activists do take a strategic approach to public relations. Activists utilize complex public relations actions to build support for an issue and to pressure organizations into change or negotiations. There is a sophistication to how activists utilize communication to build power, legitimacy, and urgency, thereby raising their salience to organizational managers.

Activists are more likely to use extreme forms of public relations tactics, including confrontation and outrageous messages, to attract attention as well as direct action. PETA's Murder King campaign is an excellent example. Central to the Murder King campaign was a website devoted to explaining how Burger King needed to use suppliers who treated animals humanely. The first screen was a logo that looked like Burger King's but said "Murder King." Soon after the logo appeared, blood began to run across the computer screen and cover the logo. PETA also held protests at Burger King restaurants. One protest included the actor James Cromwell getting arrested inside a Burger King to maximize media coverage. Corporate public relations is unlikely to stage protests, purposefully get people arrested, or use such extreme language.

There are corporations that utilize more extreme tactics. Nichols (2003) is an exception in his aggressive strategies and tactics for the corporations he represents, embodied in his 10 Power Plays. Another example is how Burger King tried to subvert the efforts of the Immokalee workers. The Coalition of Immokalee Workers (CIW) makes extensive use of the Internet to spread the word about their cause, a point developed further in the case study at the end of this chapter. A key reason for the use of the Internet is the low cost of reaching people. The CIW Internet efforts include posting messages to discussion boards and videos to YouTube. At one stage, two people attacked the Internet postings by the CIW. Their screen names were activist2008 and surfxaholic36. The two would claim the CIW was exploiting the workers and just in it for the money they could get. Here is a sample post: "The CIW is an attack organization lining the leaders' pockets.... They make up issues and collect money from dupes that believe their story. To [sic] bad the people protesting don't have a clue regarding the facts. A bunch of fools!" It turned out the two posters were Burger King employees, including soon-to-be ex-vice president Stephen Grover (Williams, 2008).

Jaques (2006) argues that corporate and activist public relations are becoming more similar. He believes one reason for the growing similarity is the ability of the Internet to level the public relations playing field. Another trend is the professionalization and growing financial resources of activist groups. Large, established activist groups have structures much like corporations. Well-established and funded activist groups such as the Sierra Club practice public relations in a nearly identical fashion to corporations and non-profits. While their financial resources are not similar, the larger activist groups do have the monies to "buy" corporate-style public relations such as advocacy advertising and hiring consultants. It would be worth tracking the convergence of corporate and activist public relations to see how close they are becoming. We believe that if we dig beneath the tactics, the strategies should still differ. The activist devotion to change should be reflected in the style and content of their messages. Activist public relations should be more aggressive in its pursuit of advocacy than its corporate counterparts. If activist public relations loses that aggressive edge, it could be a dangerous sign of widespread co-optation of activist movements.

Case Study: Coalition of Immokalee Workers and American Fast Food

The Coalition of Immokalee Workers (CIW) represents fruit and vegetable pickers in the US state of Florida. Historically, these pickers have lived and worked in what are disgraceful conditions. A 2003 report by the *Miami Herald* was titled "Fields of Despair." The lives of the workers were likened to indentured servants and sweatshop workers. In 2000 the CIW took their case to Yum! Brand, the parent company of Taco Bell. They wanted improved working and living conditions. Yum! Brand's management took no action on the demands. The CIW turned to public relations to advocate change and to leverage their position into change.

The CIW's attack on Yum! Brand centered on a boycott of Taco Bell. Boycotts are effective because they create negative publicity for an organization, rarely because of their economic impact. Hence, the Taco Bell boycott was in reality a public relations effort by the CIW. In 2002 the CIW organized the first Taco Bell Truth Tour. A caravan of workers traveled across the US making stops to raise awareness of the plight of the workers and how corporations make huge profits from the poverty of their workers. The CIW would hold informational rallies and talk to local media on the stops. The Truth Tour ended with a massive march and rally outside Taco Bell's headquarters in Irving, California. The tour and march were repeated in 2003 and 2004.

In 2003 there was even a ten day hunger strike by 75 CIW workers. A number of college students joined the hunger strike to show their support.

In addition to taking their message directly to the people and the news media, the CIW utilized a website to organize its efforts, spread information, and agitate for change. The website facilitated communication between people and groups interested in supporting the CIW, including student and religious groups. The website was also an information portal and an advocacy platform. It kept people informed and connected through the CIW Listserve(sp) and Action Alerts. People could take action by signing a petition, sending an automated fax to the CEO of Taco Bell, or giving a donation to the CIW effort. There were sample public relations materials others could use to further the CIW cause, including sample press releases and flyers.

Student groups formed on numerous college campuses, including Notre Dame, the University of Florida, and UCLA. These student groups brought attention to the CIW cause and pressured their campus to cut ties with Taco Bell. The sample public relations materials at the CIW website were designed to help these kindred groups send out their message. The CIW produced a DVD it sent free to students. The DVD was to be shown to student groups in order to increase awareness and support for the CIW and its battle with Taco Bell. The website also allowed these various student groups to communicate with one another and with the CIW. In a high-profile college victory, Notre Dame cancelled a $50,000 contract with Taco Bell over concerns for worker rights.

The CIW archived some of the publicity generated by CIW efforts and those of student groups around the country. The public relations was working. The news media were covering the CIW's issue and framing it from their perspective – the exploitation of workers for profit. The public relations effort did have the desired effect to pressure Taco Bell management into addressing CIW concerns. On March 8, 2005, Taco Bell agreed to collaborate with the CIW on addressing the issues of working conditions and wages in the Florida tomato industry. Taco Bell agreed to pay an additional penny per pound of tomatoes. That penny would be a "pass through," meaning it would go directly to the workers, not the suppliers. The money would help to improve the wages of the workers in the field. Taco Bell also agreed to work with the CIW to improve the working conditions in the Florida tomato fields. The CIW agreed to end its boycott/publicity effort against Taco Bell.

A relatively small activist group had used public relations to increase its power and to force a major corporation into concessions – concessions the organization was unwilling to even entertain three years before the public relations effort. In 2007 the CIW obtained similar concessions from McDonald's and then turned its attention to Burger King in the summer of 2007. By May 2008 Burger King had joined in an agreement with the Immokalee workers as McDonald's and Taco Bell had. Public relations proved to be an important and powerful tool for these activists.

Case questions

1 Visit the online headquarters of the website for the Coalition of Immokalee Workers at www.ciw-online.org/. What kinds of materials are available? How would these materials enable those sympathetic to their cause to contribute to the activists' efforts?
2 What techniques have they used to bring attention to their cause? How have they used online resources as well as traditional methods to influence corporations and public support?
3 Why was it a good idea for the Coalition of Immokalee Workers to attract student involvement in their cause?

Discussion Questions

1 What are activists? Identify activist groups with which you are familiar. Visit their websites to learn more information about the issues they support.
2 Visit the websites for organizations designed to aid activist groups: the Movement/Media Research and Action Project (www.mrap.info); the SPIN Project (www.spinproject.org/index.php); and the Green Media Toolshed (www.greenmediatoolshed.org). What resources are available on these sites? How do their recommendations for action resemble what you know about the practice of public relations from a corporate perspective?
3 Visit the website for the Ruckus Society, an organization that provides training for activist groups (www.ruckus.org). What evidence do you see of training in public relations?
4 Why are activist groups wary of co-optation? Do you think this is a legitimate concern?
5 Distinguish between routine publicity and staged events. What purposes are served by each?
6 Explain why activist groups usually begin by petitioning corporations and then move to direct action. Provide examples of each.
7 How has the Internet benefited activist groups?
8 Do you agree with the idea that activist groups have more public relations tactics available to them than corporations do? Why do corporations refrain from using some tactics that may be used by activist groups?

Gerry Bell (R) of the National Oceanic & Atmospheric Administration (NOAA) Climate Prediction Center speaking about the 2006 Atlantic hurricane season, Washington, August 8, 2006.

PHOTO MARK WILSON/GETTY IMAGES

6

Media Relations
Shaping the News

As noted in chapter 1, historically, US public relations has been seen as having strong ties to journalism. As the twentieth century began, the mass media became an increasingly important force in shaping public opinion. At that time, newspapers were the dominant mass media. Newspapers could shape public opinion, perhaps even pushing the US to enter the Spanish-American War. Conventional public relations history claims that ex-journalists used their understanding of the media to help corporations turn hostile news media into docile or favorable news media. Ivy Lee, one of the central figures in American public relations, illustrates the career move from journalist to public relations practitioner. After graduating college, Lee worked as a newspaper reporter in New York covering mostly business. In 1903 he left journalism for public relations, or publicity as it was often called. He formed the Parker and Lee public relations firm in 1906. Also in 1906 Lee issued what was believed to be the first news release, a document intended to influence media coverage, on behalf of the Pennsylvania Railroad.

The aura of public relations as publicity, simple efforts to stimulate favorable coverage by the news media, remains today. The *Princeton Review* describes public relations as follows: "A public relations specialist is an image shaper. Their job is to generate positive publicity for their client and enhance their reputation" (Career, n.d.). Public relations may also be called "spin." Spin seeks to only show the positive side of an organization or individual. Spin is a derogatory term, as many view it as deception, with public relations practitioners seeking to hide the negatives while promoting the positives. (For a more detailed discussion of public relations as spin, see Ewen, 2000.)

There are times public relations needs to have information disseminated by the news media. Conversely, there are times when the news media need public relations people to create content for publication or broadcast. This chapter examines media relations, its role within public relations, and various effects of media relations on society.

Public Relations is Not Just Media Relations

We have consistently argued that public relations is more than media relations, a more precise term than publicity or spin. However, the news media remain an important constituency for public relations. *Media relations* involves how representatives of an organization work with representatives of the news media. Media relations is the relationship between the organization and members of the media. The goal of media relations is to garner positive media coverage for an organization. Media relations has a narrower focus than public relations. Media relations is concerned primarily with just one public: the news media. Public relations, in contrast, deals with a wide array of publics, including the news media, government agencies, investors, consumers, community groups, employees, and activists, to name just a few of the key publics. It is fair to say that not all public relations is media relations but that all media relations is a form of public relations. Some organizations take a narrow view of public relations as just media relations. However, that view is not shared by the professional community of public relations, which prefers the broader view of public relations.

Media relations is an essential public relations skill and one of the critical job skills for an entry-level public relations job. What constitutes those skills will be discussed shortly. Media relations helps organizations to achieve a variety of other objectives. For instance, you read an online news story about a new sandwich at McDonald's. By reading the story you are aware of the new product and might be interested in buying it. McDonald's is using media relations to enhance sales. Media relations can support a wide array of organizational objectives. In other words, media relations is a means to an end. The media stories should help achieve other objectives, a point we shall return to in the next section. Modern public relations traces its roots to publicity and, hence, media relations. Publicity bureaus emerged in the late 1800s and grew in stature in the early 1900s. As the name implies, the publicity bureaus worked with newspapers, the emerging news media of the day. However, public relations was practiced much earlier in the 1800s in the reform movements of abolitionists and temperance. These early activists employed a number of strategic communication actions designed to manage their relationships with different publics. Media relations played a very small role in this First Reform Era in the US. Public speeches, sermons, and brochures were the preferred communication tactics (Coombs & Holladay, 2007b). We would argue that public relations pre-dates media relations. However, the term public relations was not officially used until after media relations had been in operation. The overlapping histories of media relations and public relations adds to people equating the two.

Public relations and journalists: uneasy alliance

Public relations practitioners and journalists have a symbiotic relationship. When two organisms live in close association for a long period of time, they are said to have a symbiotic ("living together") relationship. In the symbiotic relationship, at least one member of the pair benefits from the relationship. If the other organism is unharmed, the relationship is commensalism, meaning "at the same table." If the other organism is harmed, the relationship is parasitism (parasites). If both organisms benefit, the relationship is mutualism.

Have you enjoyed or heard of truffles? Truffles are a fungus that have a mutualism symbiotic relationship with plants. Truffles grow on roots and help their hosts to absorb nitrogen and phosphoros from the soil. Barnacles living on whales are an example of a commensalism symbiotic relationship. The barnacles eat the unused food from the whales. Tapeworms living in a human are an example of a parasitism symbiotic relationship. The tapeworm does harm to the human by stealing nutrients.

So what do public relations people and journalists have to do with a discussion of symbiotic relationships? Public relations practitioners and journalists live in close association with one another for their entire careers. There are times when public relations practitioners need to place information in the news media and there are times when journalists must have information from practitioners to complete a story. Hence, the two organisms seem to have a mutualism symbiotic relationship, as both benefit. An example will help to clarify what each derives from the relationship. A television station in a small market wants to cover a national story about a product recall. However, it does not have the financial resources to send a reporter to the company's headquarters. The company distributes a video news release (VNR) that includes exterior shots of their facility and footage of the production process. The company also provides time for satellite interviews with the CEO. The local news station uses the VNR footage and their satellite interview time to create a national story for a very low cost. The news station gets its national story and the company reaches more constituents with information about the recall. Both benefit from the process.

However, some critics argue that the relationship has become parasitism, with public relations being the parasite to the news media's host. We will return to this point later in the chapter.

News media-public relations relationship

To understand media relations it is important to examine the evolving relationship between the news media and public relations. The early process of journalism involved reporters physically visiting a source to develop a story. Of course, telephones could be used, but television frequently demands visuals from the actual location of an event. A story was developed by reporters actively searching for and finding the relevant information and sources. This is a time and cost-intensive way to create news. Budget cuts have resulted in news outlets exploring more cost-effective ways to gather news. Public relations practitioners offer one means of reducing news gathering costs.

There is a symbiotic relationship in media relations. Public relations people want coverage and reporters are looking for low-cost stories. The term *information subsidy* is used to characterize the publicity aspect of media relations. The public relations practitioners are information subsidies because they provide news material at a reduced cost to the reporter. As news outlets continue to reduce costs, they become even more dependent on their information subsidies. However, reporters have the final say in what materials are used and how a story will look. Reporters can edit or use publicity materials to create an unfavorable story about an organization. There is no guarantee that publicity materials will be used exactly as intended by the public relations practitioner.

Media Relations: The Dynamics

The common view of media relations is that the public relations professional wants media coverage for an organization or person. Messages are designed and sent to the news media representative (reporter) in hopes they will appear in a news story. For instance, suppose McDonald's plans to launch a new sandwich and uses media relations to support the marketing and advertising for the new product. The idea is that various news sources will run stories about the new sandwich. The act of public relations people seeking media coverage is known as publicity. The organization is hoping that the media coverage is favorable to the organization and that this positive publicity will help to achieve some larger organizational objective. In the McDonald's example, the larger organizational objective is to increase sales.

At other times, reporters ask public relations people for information, including interview access to organizational management. Reporters usually seek information when they sense a problem (an investigative report) or there is a public crisis. In these situations the goal of media relations is to minimize the damage to the organization. One way to minimize the damage is to present the organization's side of the story through the media. This might involve correcting misperceptions caused by a rumor, or insuring accurate information is disseminated about the cause of an accident that injured employees or damaged property in the community.

The "right" frame should help with the "ends" of good publicity. It helps to achieve some larger organizational objective. In 2004, Majestic Brands launched a new vodka drink targeted at younger women called Cocktails by Jenn, or CBJ. CBJ positioned itself as a fashion accessory. The single-serve drinks were packaged in purse-like totes with trendy designs. The flavors included Cosmopolitan, Lemon Drop, Appletini, and Tropical Blue Lagoon. The new product received extensive media coverage with the primary frame being CBJ as a fashion accessory

(Chang, 2007; Cocktails, n.d.; Set 'em up, 2006). As with McDonald's, CBJ's publicity is designed to create awareness and ultimately sales along with crafting the desired reputation for the brand. Publicity facilitates the achievement of a number of other organizational objectives, including cultivating a favorable reputation, generating investment, and minimizing damage from a crisis.

Media relations seems very simple – place information in the media and respond to the queries. Responding is fairly simple; placing information in the media is not. Media relations involves *uncontrolled media*. Uncontrolled means the public relations person has no control over whether or not the information is used and, if it is used, how the information will be presented. Media placement/ publicity is a two-step process. First, the public relations materials must catch the attention of those in the media. If no one notices the materials, there is no chance that the information will be used. Second, the reporters must present the material the way the organization intended (shape how the information is used). This process of framing is very important to effective media relations. A *frame* is the information selected for the story and *framing* refers to the process of developing frames. Organizations want the information they provide to be presented in a certain way. In other words, they seek to influence the journalist's framing process because the way a story is presented will influence the audience's interpretations of events. Cocktails by Jenn provides an example of shaping interpretations through framing. The publicity efforts for CBJ emphasized that the drink was a fashion accessory (the frame). The news media did run stories about CBJ that noted it was a fashion accessory – the desired frame was used in the news story.

Effective media relations occurs when the news media report the desired information about an organization or person. Organizations rarely subscribe to the belief that "any publicity is good publicity." Stories about corruption, harmful products, or environmental abuses are not good publicity. The question becomes, "What is good publicity?" Good publicity is when a story is created and reflects the desired interpretation or frame of the information. A frame helps people to interpret information by calling attention to specific aspects of an event or story. Frames also can define problems and suggest solutions to those problems (Zoch & Molleda, 2006).

Next, we explore in more detail the two key elements to placing a story: (1) creation of the story and (2) the frame of the story.

Creating a news story

Public relations practitioners are in fierce competition for space in the media. There are only so many pages in publications and so much time in broadcasts for stories. While publicity efforts account for around 40 percent of all news stories in the US and the UK, the vast majority of publicity efforts fail. After being submitted to news outlets, most publicity materials are discarded rather than converted into news stories. The effectiveness of publicity materials is increased by understanding the factors that shape their use, including newsworthiness, tactical skill, and media preferences.

Newsworthiness is the *news value* a publicity piece holds. Publicity material is newsworthy when it reflects the values that appeal to the media personnel and to their target audiences. There are six common news values:

1   Timeliness
2   Impact
3   Audience interest
4   Conflict/oddity
5   Drama
6   Human interest

Timeliness means the information is happening now. News is like food – it spoils if you wait too long to use it. Impact refers to the information having the potential to affect or involve a large number of people. Bird flu, for instance, has a high impact potential because it could affect millions of people around the world. The greater the impact, the larger the audience drawn to the story. Audience interest is specific to the media outlet. It represents the preferences of that media outlet's audience. What kinds of stories will appeal to this audience? Understanding interest is a function of doing the proper research into the media outlets. Conflict or oddity is the most commonly mentioned news value. People are drawn to deviation from the normal – oddities. Conflict is a deviation from the normal that people find entertaining. Court cases have the conflict that the news media and their audiences crave. Conflict is part of the drama news value as well. A good news story is a good story; it has the narrative form of conflict, problem, and denouement. Even when a news story lacks drama, journalists try to infuse it with drama. Reports regularly add dramatic form to increase the appeal of a story. Finally, human interest refers to the allure of ordinary people in unusual situations or with unusual experiences (Bennett, 1988; Gans, 1979; Paletz & Entman, 1981). A cat rescuing a woman from a fire represents human interest. Most of the popular videos on YouTube would fall under the human interest banner.

In addition to news values, there are two other factors that can increase newsworthiness: news pegs and celebrities. A news peg is an event or issue that is already being covered by the media. Publicity material has greater newsworthiness when it can be connected to a news peg. For instance, when the news media are covering global warming, stories about how a company is reducing carbon emissions have a news peg. Celebrities are well-known people and their attachment to publicity materials increases its news value. Audiences seem obsessed with celebrities, as stories of their exploits frequently dominate the news media, whether it be Paris Hilton, Hugh Grant, Prince William, David Beckham, or Michael Jackson. Celebrities can be used as spokespersons or have some other association with a publicity event (Gans, 1979). Actress Meryl

Streep once helped to increase the newsworthiness of an activist group by being the spokesperson at its news conference.

Newsworthiness does not magically appear in publicity materials. Public relations people must skillfully weave news values into their publicity materials. Media relations remains centered around the news release, the core publicity material tactic. A news release is a tactic that is typically one printed page designed to interest a media representative in a story. Even today, public relations practitioners are expected to know the format for a news release and other publicity tactics such as pitch letters and media alerts (Treadwell & Treadwell, 2005). The appendix contains examples of news releases, media alerts, and the format recommended by the FDA for a pitch letter.

Modern public relations practitioners need to know how to adapt these basic media relations tactics to the Internet. Journalists increasingly use the Internet to collect information for stories. Media relations now involves online newsrooms. An organization creates an online newsroom and keeps it stocked with current information that reporters can access at their discretion. Writing for the online environment requires an understanding of the interactive and linked nature of the Internet. These two features should be captured in online media relations materials (Kelleher, 2006). Some organizations create their own VNRs, but most hire firms to produce them. VNRs require an understanding of how to write for television and how to select appropriate visuals for television. The primary knowledge, skills, and abilities of media relations are to understand and to be able to use the various tactics for reaching the news media. Part of content knowledge is knowing the news values and how to incorporate them into publicity materials.

Effective media relations is more than writing. Media relations people must understand which media they need to target and the best ways to reach those media outlets. The media outlets need to reach the target publics of the larger organizational objective. The Cocktails by Jenn example illustrates the need to target specific media. Younger women of drinking age are the target consumers for CBJ. As a result, the media relations effort targeted media outlets that represented this demographic, such as *Cosmopolitan* magazine. Moreover, media outlets vary in how they prefer to receive publicity materials. Many now accept materials sent via email. However, the outlets vary in whether they prefer the publicity materials as an attachment or in the text of the email. Media relations people also must know the deadlines for when materials must reach the media outlets and the types of stories a media outlet uses. Sending personnel profiles to a media outlet that does not use personnel stories is a waste of time and will irritate journalists. On a very basic level, the media relations person has to have a current list of journalists so that they address the publicity materials to the right person. Overall, media relations people must have a thorough knowledge of the media outlets they target (Treadwell & Treadwell, 2005).

In short, a media relations professional must be able to write and to distribute effective publicity materials. This demands that the professional understand the format of various publicity materials, how to feature news values in the content of these messages, and how and when to send which publicity materials to which media outlets.

Why public relations uses publicity

At this point it is relevant to consider why public relations practitioners want media coverage. There is a belief that a news story about an organization is more credible than an advertisement about an organization. The news story is a form of third-party endorsement. We know a company runs an advertisement to aid their own self-interests. However, the news outlet does not have a vested interest in the company. So positive comments in a news story are likely to be more credible than an advertisement. However, research is mixed on whether or not a news story is more credible and persuasive than an advertisement. So we cannot be sure securing a news story will sell product or attract business more effectively than an advertisement. A more sophisticated theory of media relations is needed to appreciate its true value.

Media relations and theory are not commonly used together. Research on media relations has concentrated on what works to get publicity materials into the news media. This research yielded the news values that guide media relations content to this day. Zoch and Molleda (2006) are among the few to unpack the theory that can be used to understand media relations. They argue that framing and agenda building are essential theories for media relations.

Framing was discussed earlier. Frames influence how a situation, event, person, or organization is interpreted. Interpretations are based on the information people receive and frames seek to control the information people receive. If all we hear about a company is how it helps the environment, we will think of that organization as being green. Publicity tactics are framing efforts. The media relations personnel frame their information to highlight the desired aspect of the organization. As noted earlier, good publicity is a news story that reflects the frame presented in the publicity materials. Framing is the theoretical equivalent of spin. However, the news media commonly use the term spin to indicate when someone is only giving their positive view of a situation. Framing is more complex than just telling people the good news. Framing involves selecting the information that an organization hopes its publics will use when interpreting a situation. Zoch and Molleda (2006) offer an excellent discussion of framing theory and media relations.

So why do media frames matter so much in a news story? Most people experience and develop impressions about organizations and events from the news media (Carroll, 2004; Carroll and McCombs, 2003; Meijer, 2004). So what the media covers and how the media talks about it does matter. We use the term *media agenda* to refer to the stories covered by the media. Agenda setting theory posits what the media talk about influences what publics feel is important – the media tell people what to think about (Zoch & Molleda, 2006). Media relations tries to influence this agenda building when they attempt to place items on the media agenda. Thus, agenda building is the second theory Zoch and Molleda (2006) tie to media relations.

Framing and agenda building theories are linked to one another. Media relations people do not simply want to get an item in the news. They want that news story to reflect their preferred frame. Agendas tell people what is important and also how it should be interpreted. Media frames have been proven to shape how people perceive events, individuals, and organizations. That is why media relations is an important aspect of reputation management. News stories help to shape how publics perceive an organization. Shaping news coverage, then, helps to shape an organization's reputation (Carroll, 2004; Carroll and McCombs, 2003; Meijer, 2004). The importance of reputation management will be explored further in chapter 9. The theoretical aspect of media relations is important because it serves to highlight the strategic value of media relations.

Reflections

There is clearly competition among various entities for media coverage. The publicity competition is driven by the connections between media coverage and public opinions. Public relations is the primary mechanism for the publicity competition. One defense of public relations is that everyone, even the most vile corporations and governments, should be allowed to be represented in the publicity competition. However, critics of media relations argue that people and groups do not compete on a level playing field. Those with more money and power naturally have easier access to the news media for placement and framing of stories. While everyone can practice media relations as part of their public relations, not everyone has an equal chance of being successful at media relations. As a result, only certain, privileged voices are heard or seen while marginalized voices remain muted in the distance. Earlier discussions in chapter 5 touched on this point, but now let us push the concern further by examining the propaganda model of media.

Twenty years ago, Herman and Chomsky (1988) articulated the propaganda model of media in their book *Manufacturing Consent*. The propaganda model of the media posits that through a series of filters, the news media will reflect the concerns of the status quo and largely ignore dissenting views. In the model, the status quo is composed of the government and corporations. In terms of media relations, corporations and the government have much easier access to and placement in the news media than marginalized groups such as activists. Although the propaganda model of the media is based on the US media, it can be seen in any country where the economic structure of its news media allows the filters to appear.

Herman and Chomsky (1987) identify five filters:

1   Large corporations owning and operating the media for profit.
2   Dependency on advertisers for revenue.
3   Dependence on government and corporate sources.
4   Negative responses to media content.
5   Enemies/anti-communism.

A full discussion of the propaganda model of the media is beyond the scope of a book on public relations. What we will do is tie elements of the model to public relations and its use of media relations. We will focus on filters 1, 3, and 4 because they are most strongly connected to media relations and public relations.

The news media in the US are a business. Businesses try to reduce costs and increase revenues (filter 1). As noted earlier, the news media need to hold down the costs of collecting and creating the news and increase revenues by expanding their audience. Revenue is derived from advertising and advertising is a function of the number of people who use that news outlet. US news outlets continually seek ways to reduce costs, such as reducing the workforce, and increasing their audience.

Public relations provides a mechanism for reducing the cost of gathering and creating the news. Public relations practitioners create and send a variety of materials to journalists in the hopes that the material is used in a news story. News releases (print and email) and VNRs are the two most common forms of publicity materials/tactics public relations practitioners send to reporters. Most publicity materials are never used. However, research consistently notes that around 40 percent of all news stories are a result of publicity materials. Why do most publicity materials fail yet account for a high percentage of the news? Because the news media receive far more publicity materials than they could ever use, rejection rates are high along with the percent of news that was developed through media relations. Most of the early research on media relations involved how to make publicity materials more attractive to reporters. Out of that research came news values, the elements of a story that are appealing to reporters.

VNRs are an excellent example of how publicity materials feed into the economic needs of the news media. VNRs are professionally created and ready to be aired on television. A typical VNR contains interviews with key personnel in an organization and stock (B-Roll) footage of products, the production process, or exteriors of a facility. A reporter can take the VNR and with a little editing have a finished story that is quickly produced at a low cost. Time and money are saved because the reporter and camera crew do not have to travel to develop the story themselves. So is public relations taking advantage of a weakened news media system? The short answer is "yes." As the news media increasingly need a media subsidy, public relations benefits and may have a greater ability to shape news content. The effect of public relations shaping the news will be debated in this and many other chapters because media relations is a means to many other public relations objectives. The relationship is still a mutualism symbiotic relationship, as both benefit.

The profit orientation filter of the media feeds directly into the source filter. The news media need a reliable and steady source of information for stories. The government and corporations are in the best position to supply this information through their advanced public relations departments. As Herman and Chomsky (1987) noted, "Government and corporate sources also have the great merit of being recognized and credible by their status and prestige" (p. 19). Although many corporate managers complain that activists have easier access to the news media due to the liberal bias of the news media, journalism and public relations research consistently find that government officials and corporations are the dominant news sources. Established activist groups are making some inroads as established sources but have yet to reach the level of access afforded government officials and corporations.

Public relations plays a part in the negative response filter. Negative response includes lawsuits filed against the news media and letters of complaint written to media regulators. For example, Food Lion, a US grocery store chain, sued and won a lawsuit with ABC over an investigative report on its show *Primetime Live* that accused the chain of selling past due meat. Public relations and media relations are involved when the negative response includes front groups. As we discussed in chapters 2 and 4, front groups are designed to look just like grassroots activist groups – citizens banding together to speak out on a public issue. However, front groups are actually funded and staffed by corporations or industry associations. The connection is concealed from others so that the front groups appear to be the people talking, not an industry or specific organization. (For an additional discussion of front groups, see chapter 10.) The Public Relations Society of America decries front groups as unethical, but the US Supreme Court has ruled their use to be legal.

Front groups are common in the battle over environmental issues. In her book *Global Spin*, Sharon Beder (2002) identified how front groups were used to counteract pro-environmentalist news stories. One example is the Foundation for Clean Air Progress, ostensibly a group of citizens dedicated to concerns over air quality. The Foundation for Clean Air Progress is really composed of a number of industry groups, including the American Petroleum Institute and the American Trucking Association. Front groups do exist and are used to disguise the role of corporations or industry in public debates.

So how does a front group fit with media relations? Front groups present their own publicity materials designed to influence news stories. The idea is that front groups can produce stories that counter those currently in the news media when those stories conflict with the interests of the corporation or industry. When unfavorable stories appear about a critical issue, opposing stories are run with the front group as the source. The idea is that the public may be more persuaded by the information coming from front groups. The key is that the front group is the information source. Persuasion research would suggest that information from people like ourselves would be more persuasive than messages from a corporation or an industry. First, the homophily research finds that we are more persuaded by people like ourselves than people who are different from us. Most people have more in common with a citizen who is an activist than with a corporate spokesperson. Second, if a message comes from a corporation or industry, we can identify its self-interest in the topic and factor that into our evaluations of the message. When the message is from a citizen activist in a front group, we are blind to the self-interest and cannot take it into account when evaluating a message. We will elaborate on the potential problems with front groups in the global warming case study at the end of this chapter.

The advertising filter argues that advertisers can use their payments to the media to influence content. A US study found that 90 percent of the newspapers surveyed had been pressured by advertisers to change the content of stories (Propaganda model, n.d.). In 2005, for example, General Motors pulled its advertising from the *Los Angeles Times* over the content of a story. In 1999 British Telecom threatened to remove its advertising from the *Daily Telegraph* after a series of critical articles. There are times when advertisers do try to influence media content.

Lastly, the enemies filter posits that news coverage of foreign events reflects who the government believes are the country's friends or enemies. Neither of these two filters have much to do with public relations, but we wanted to complete the short explanation of the propaganda model of the media.

As we reflect on the concerns about media relations, it is fitting to return to the discussion of symbiotic relationships. Ideally, public relations and journalism live in a mutualism symbiotic relationship. Public relations benefits from positive media coverage while journalists benefit from the low cost and useful "news." The relationship becomes parasitic when public relations disregards the sanctity of public communication and the integrity of communication channels by manipulating news content to its own ends without considering the ramifications for the marketplace of ideas or when transparency is ignored or subverted. The case study at the end of this chapter illustrates the problems of a parasitic relationship.

Should there be greater transparency about the sources of news stories? Yes, but that issue involves far more than public relations. Are the news media becoming too dependent on public relations for the news? Perhaps, but there is no definitive answer to this last question. We can argue that power in the public relations-journalism relationship often tilts in favor of public relations these days. The real concern is how the power is used and that leads us to a consideration of ethics. As described in chapter 2, public communicators and public relations personnel must consider the effects of their actions on society. If public relations exploits the news media in order to silence some voices in a public debate, that is problematic. Effective media relations can be and are conducted in an ethical fashion. There may be greater opportunity for abuse, but that does not absolve practitioners from ethical violations of the public trust committed through media relations.

It is easy to think of media relations as simply distributing publicity materials. But there is a lot of skill, knowledge, and ability that goes into effective media relations. Getting the news media to run a story as framed by an organization takes research about the news media and careful construction of the message to convey the frame in a way that entices the news media to use that frame. If the news story reflects the desired frame, an organization is more likely to achieve the objectives the media relations effort was designed to facilitate, such as reputation management or consumer awareness and purchasing behavior. Of course, organizations can choose to mindlessly produce publicity materials and fail to appreciate its strategic value. That is easier to do but far less rewarding for the organization. While media relations is an essential aspect of public relations it is only a part of it. While closely linked to media relations, a true public relations program involves communication with a much broader range of publics and using additional communication channels beyond the news media. Still, effective media relations can contribute significantly to an organization.

Case Study: Seeding the News Media

Imagine that an organization creates a loyal following of analysts who regularly appear and give their opinions to media outlets. These opinions often are the centerpieces of news stories and serve to frame the reporting. These analysts are considered experts, based on their experience, and generally are trusted by the news media and their audiences. There is no mention that these analysts have a close relationship with the organization. In fact, the organization sends the analysts "talking points" prescribing what to say to the news media on certain topics. The organization even holds briefings for the analysts through their public relations division. The end result is a highly effective publicity effort that creates stories favorable to the organization's view of the world. Such a situation would reinforce the fears of critics that organizations can use public relations to manipulate the news media and deceive other constituencies.

Unfortunately, this is not a hypothetical example. From 2002 until April 25, 2008, the US Pentagon was running just such a covert publicity program. The program is known as the Pentagon military analyst program. A cadre of 75 retired military personnel were recruited for this program and worked as military analysts for a variety of news outlets, including NBC, CNN, and Fox. The analysts not only appeared on television and radio, but wrote op-ed pieces in newspapers that supported the Pentagon's position on key issues such as the Iraq War. The analysts appeared as "independent experts" who just happened to unflinchingly support the Pentagon's position on the Iraq War and other topics.

The program was created by Secretary of Defense for Public Affairs Victoria Clarke, a former Hill & Knowlton executive. The original purpose was to support the Bush Administration's case for war. The analysts were regularly briefed by the Pentagon, given talking points, and even taken on trips to Iraq and Guantanamo Bay so they would have first-hand experience with the topics. The analysts were called "message force multipliers." Their words and views were heard by millions and potentially swayed many listeners and readers. The program was so successful that it was expanded beyond the Iraq War (Barstow, 2008).

To add to the intrigue, a number of the analysts disagreed with the Pentagon but did not dare speak out. Many of them were lobbyists for defense contractors. For instance, Fox analyst Timur J. Eads works with military contractor Blackbird Technology. The list at the end of this case study provides a partial inventory of the analysts and if they represented a military contractor. The Pentagon let it be known the analysts would lose access to the Pentagon if they publicly disagreed with the Bush Administration. William V. Cowan was fired from the program when he disagreed with the Pentagon on Fox News. Lobbyists have much less value when they cannot access the people their clients want to reach. Because others feared retaliation by the Administration, they simply repeated the Pentagon talking points (Barstow, 2008).

The first public whiff of the Pentagon military analysts program was an April 2006 story in the *New York Times* by reporters Mark Mazetti and Jim Rutenberg. The topic received little attention because the focus was on Secretary of Defense Rumsfeld and his imminent resignation. David Barstow of the *New York Times* broke a full exposé on April 20, 2008. On April 25, 2008 the Pentagon announced the program was being suspended pending an internal review. However, the Pentagon claimed no laws were violated, but did not address the concerns of ethical violations and the appearance of impropriety. The Department of Defense has since made all documentation used in the *New York Times* story publicly available on the Internet. In an Orwellian twist, one of the most egregious subversions of the news through public relations was perpetrated by the US government. It should be noted that the program could be reinstated at a future date.

Partial list of Pentagon military analyst program participants

Kenneth Allard	NBC, lobbyist for Potomac Strategies International
Jed Babbin	Fox News and MSNBC, co-founder of the military firm WVC3 Group
William V. Cowan	Fox News, chief executive of the WVC3 Group
Timur J. Eads	Fox analyst, vice president of government relations for Blackbird Technologies, and lobbyist for Science Application International Corporation and EMC Corporation
Rick Francona	NBC, MSNBC, and CNBC
John C. Garrett	Fox News TV and radio, Patton Boggs lobbyist
David L. Grange	CNN
Barry R. McCaffrey	NBC analyst, advisory board member for the Committee for the Liberation of Iraq
Jeffrey D. McCausland	CBS military analyst and lobbyist with Buchanan Ingersoll & Rooney
Thomas G. McInerney	Fox News analyst and board member of Nortel Government Solutions
Robert L. Maginnis	Fox analyst, works in the Pentagon for military contractor BCP International
James Marks	CNN, senior executive with McNeil Technologies
Montgomery Meigs	NBC analyst
Charles T. Nash	Fox News analyst
William L. Nash	ABC analyst
Joseph W. Ralston	CBS analyst, Cohen Group lobbyist
Robert H. Scales Jr.	Fox News and National Public Radio; Colgen, his company, advises military contractors
Donald W. Shepperd	CNN, president of the Shepperd Group, a defense consulting firm
Wayne Simmons	Fox analyst
Martin Strong	Fox analyst

Case questions

1 Describe why the Pentagon's military analyst program was successful in (1) getting into the media and (2) framing the information. For example, consider how news values, news pegs, framing, and agenda building were used strategically by the program.

2 Do the actions associated with the Pentagon's military analyst program meet the criteria of transparency described in chapter 3? Explain.

3 How could the ethical perspectives described in chapter 2 be applied to your analysis of this case? Which ethical perspectives could be used to defend the use of the Pentagon's military analyst program? Which ethical perspectives could be used to condemn the program?

4 What factors might lead journalists to rely on these analysts as information subsidies?

5 How does the use of expert analysts differ from the use of front groups?

6 The case describes how the US government has made available on the Internet all the documentation that was used in the *New York Times* story that exposed the Pentagon's military analyst program. How effective might this information posting be in satisfying critics who claim the program relied on Herman and Chomsky's (1987) propaganda model of media?

Discussion Questions

1 Historically, why is public relations closely linked to journalism?

2 What is media relations? What are the goals of media relations? Why is a news story about an organization often viewed as more credible than an advertisement?

3 Distinguish between controlled and uncontrolled media. Describe the advantages and disadvantages of each.

4 Describe the six common news values (timeliness, impact, audience interest, conflict/oddity, drama, and human interest) and news pegs and celebrities. Why are these important to public relations practitioners? Identify examples of these in traditional print media news stories and Internet stories.

5 Locate several news stories in major newspapers that may have resulted from media relations efforts. What cues lead you to believe media relations affected the stories?

6 What is framing? Why is it important to public relations professionals? Locate a media story and identify the frame(s) used in the reporting. What alternative frames could have been used to shift interpretations of the content of the story?

7 Why is the use of VNRs tempting to journalists and advantageous for public relations practitioners? Under what circumstances might VNRs work against media relations efforts?

Killer Coke campaign online flyer – an example of online public relations.

7

Technological Development and Online Public Relations

Technological advances provide new ways for people to send and receive messages. We have seen the evolution from spoken word to print to radio to television to online communication. Each new communication technology has the potential to contribute to the repertoire of a public relations practitioner by providing yet another online communication vehicle. As you read this book, it is likely some "new" technology is being employed online as a communication tool. Therefore, we do not pretend to have the most up-to-date inventory of the latest communication technology in public relations. Instead, this chapter discusses some of the more recent developments in communication technology found online and their implications for public relations and its effect on society. The next section concentrates on defining some key terms and examining their application to public relations.

Terms and Application to Public Relations

The online communication environment and public relations are a natural fit. Public relations requires two-way communication and online communication vehicles provide ways to talk and listen to constituents. This section begins by identifying and defining some of the major online communication channels. The definitions are followed by a discussion of how such online communication channels can be applied to public relations.

Key terms

Few people reading this book will not have gone online and utilized several of the key online communication vehicles we are about to discuss. Our core list of terms includes the Internet, the World Wide Web, website, email, instant messaging, blogs, wikis, really simple syndication (RSS), listservs, Flickr, and Twitter.

The Internet is the broadest term in our online lexicon. The Internet is the collection of computers connected through fiber optic cables, phone lines, and satellite links. The Internet is the infrastructure that allows the other online communication vehicles to operate and to be available to the millions of people who log on each day.

The World Wide Web, or Web, is the publicly available part of the Internet. Through links, search engines, and browsers, people navigate through the various content other people make available on the Web. This content includes text, graphics, video, and games. A common component of the Web is an organization's or an individual's website. A website is a collection of linked content. The "owner" of the website acts as a manager by deciding what content will appear and how people can navigate through the material. Some websites are locations for building and verifying social networks. The most popular social networking sites are Facebook, My Space, and Friendster.

A wiki is a variation of a website. There is no one "owner" creating content for a wiki. Instead, people collaborate to create the wiki's content. The more technical term is a content management system (Kelleher, 2006). The most famous wiki is Wikipedia, the online encyclopedia. People often do not realize that Wikipedia is open to editing and assume it is an online variation of a published encyclopedia such as *Britannica*. In reality, a wiki entry is only as good and as accurate as the person or persons compiling it. People have been known to exploit Wikipedia for their own ends, a point we will return to when discussing public relations applications.

The most common communication channel on the Internet is email. Email is short for electronic mail and is popular among all age groups that use the Internet (Pew, 2004). Text, pictures, video, and sound can be sent from one computer to another computer via email. An email is typically asynchronous, as people read and respond to messages at different times rather than being online simultaneously. Instant messaging, on the other hand, is done in real time with the participants being online at the same time. For both email and instant messages, people can communicate one-to-one or one-to-many. Listservs are used for one-to-many communication. A listserv is formed when people join a list. By sending an email to one address, the message is disseminated to all the people who subscribe to that listserv.

People congregate online in chat rooms and discussion groups. A chat room allows people to talk to one another in real time. A chat room is a location online, with an address that allows people to discuss shared interests such as a sports team, hobby, or vacation destinations. Discussion groups are where people with similar interests share information as well. However, discussion groups are generally asynchronous. People post messages at discussion groups and others can comment on those messages. Related responses to a message are called a thread. Both discussion groups and chat rooms allow many-to-many communication. These congregations are tempting for public relations because people are coalescing around common interests, values, and ideas. Public relations practitioners also segment people based on interests, values, and ideas. Online, people voluntarily segment themselves and signal their interest in a particular topic, value, or idea, thus making their ideas available for practitioners.

The term blog is short for web log and is a variation of a diary. Most blogs are messages a person posts about a topic. Blogs frequently have a specific focus, such as public relations, or can be whatever an individual wants to talk about that day. The entries are dated, often have archives, and usually have links to other web content. Most blogs allow people to post comments about the blog's messages and for others to connect to other web locations to the blog. Trackback technology is a common method used for letting bloggers know that someone has linked to their blogs. A Pingback is another method for notifying bloggers of links.

Twitter is a slimmed down and portable version of a blog. Twitter allows people to post messages up to 140 characters long. They can even post messages using text messaging from a cell phone. Other people can follow your messages by subscribing to your "feed." Twitter provides yet another avenue for reaching constituents.

Flickr is a website for posting photographs and more. It is the self-organizing aspect of Flickr that is relevant to public relations. People can tag their photographs. A tag is a label that allows other people to find your photographs through searches. Self-forming groups have emerged through Flickr tags. People find others with similar interests, through tags, and form communities by regularly communicating with one another. Public relations professionals may be interested in communities that are relevant to their concerns.

The last of the online communication tools we will discuss is RSS, really simple syndication. RSS is similar to a news feed for a news media outlet. A news feed sends stories to the news media outlet. Individuals can subscribe to a variety of online content including news stories, blogs, and podcasts. Individuals are sent updated information when the content of their subscription changes. The update can be a summary or the complete text of the new information. RSS allows people to be updated when information/content changes.

Basic applications for public relations

The above list of online communication vehicles is not exhaustive. The point is to identify a variety of the online communication vehicles and establish their connection to public relations. Public relations should be two-way communication involving sending and "listening" for information. When combined in this way, public relations permits interaction between constituents. All of the online communication vehicles discussed in this section can be used to deliver information and to "listen" to what others are saying. Websites, wikis, and RSS would be the most sender-oriented vehicles because they focus on creating information for others to browse. The online environment has an enormous potential to allow constituents to listen to one another. Blogs, listservs, chat rooms, and discussion groups are particularly useful in gaining insights into what other constituents are thinking or feeling. These channels are designed to be sites where people can be heard.

Traditional public relations is filled with various means to deliver messages and listen to constituencies. Online communication is unique because of its interactive and linked potential. Both asynchronous and real-time interactions are made easier through the Internet. Email, blogs, listservs, chat rooms, and discussion groups all have the potential to facilitate interaction. For instance, it is cheaper and easier to interact with constituents on a listserv or a blog than to hold face-to-face meetings. Participation in a blog is not limited to geographic location or the time of the meeting, just access to the Internet.

We need to remember that the Internet is an active environment. People search the Internet for information, so they are active in the process. Their searches are facilitated by links between related web content. An example would be a blog that mentions a newspaper article about something an organization did, such as sponsoring an event, launching a new product, or countering arguments presented by an activist group protesting the expansion of their facility. The blog could provide a link to the news story, to the organization, and to other blogs about the action. Moreover, the organization's website would provide additional links to documents that would offer further information about the action. As discussed shortly, the ability to link is one of the defining characteristics of the social media news release when compared to the traditional news release.

The Continuing Evolution of Online Public Relations

To appreciate the impact of the online world on public relations we need to move beyond the simple mechanics of the online communication channels and examine their applications to public relations in more depth. This section focuses on four applications of online public relations that leverage the uniqueness of the online world: (1) online media relations; (2) buzz marketing; (3) potential for dialogic communication; and (4) potential for power acquisition. The first two points are extensions of existing public relations practices into the online environment. The last two offer a more theoretical examination of how the interactive potential of the online environment can alter the practice of public relations and relationships between constituencies.

Traditional media relations goes online

An obvious move for public relations has been to develop online media relations that mirrors traditional media relations. Recall, we discussed media relations in chapter 6. We see evidence of online media relations in social media news releases, online news rooms, and guidelines for pitching bloggers. The social media news release is designed to replace the old, traditional news release. Social media news releases take advantage of the linked nature of the Internet. Shift Communication and Edelman were among the first to promote the use of the social media news release. A social media news release seeks to maximize search engine hits (including blog search engines such as Technorati), provide easy links to multimedia and background information, facilitate people adding your releases through RSS, and include links to add the news release to social bookmarking sites such as Del.iciou.us. The social media news release reflects online communication because it is a portal to additional information, designed to be found by search engines, and facilitates RSS.

Organizations should have online newsrooms to feed hungry journalists. Each year, more journalists turn to online sources when developing stories (Reber & Berger, 2005). Both researchers and consultants are keenly interested in the features of online newsrooms. However, research from both camps indicates organizations are not very effective at providing useful online newsrooms. Frequently the online newsrooms lack relevant content or are difficult to navigate (Bulldog Reporter/TEKgroup International, 2007; Kent & Taylor, 2003; Reber & Kim, 2006). The beauty of an online newsroom is that journalists have access at any time and can look for the information they want instead of waiting for someone to send them information they may or may not want. Effective online newsrooms have both current and archived news releases, contact information for an actual public relations person that can be used any time of the day or night, easy to find additional materials such as biographies, corporate information, and facts sheets, and a functional search mechanism, and are easy to navigate (Bransford, n.d.). Vocus is one of the major providers of online newsrooms. Vocus is a public relations firm that will help an organization build an online newsroom that is consistent with that organization's website. In other words, it does not look like someone else created the online newsroom. If journalists and other constituents are using online information, effective online newsrooms are a valuable commodity to corporations, activists (Reber & Kim, 2006), and any other constituency engaged in public relations.

Finally, if you search online you can find countless lists of advice on how best to pitch bloggers and how to avoid the wrath of bloggers. Box 7.1 reveals the dangers of mis-pitching bloggers. Bloggers can use their space to "out" bad public relations practices and to complain about public relations people spamming them with unwanted news releases and story pitches. Advice for pitching bloggers includes using the right name, understanding what the blogger blogs about, leading with a link, and not sending attachments. The last two are related to the online environment. Capitalize on the linked nature of the Internet and offer links to information rather than sending long attachments that most bloggers do not wish to open (Odden, 2007).

Box 7.1   Bad Blog Pitch

Below are some examples of bad pitches made to bloggers. The errors should be obvious.

- A woman who writes a blog about living with type 1 diabetes has received two very bad pitches. The first involved a pitch for a drug designed to treat type 2 diabetes. The second pitch asked her to imagine what life was like if she had diabetes.
- US NetcomCorporation sent a pitch to a blogger after the Virginia Tech shooting that included the following lines: "For $1 per student per year, services such as AllCall Notification could have provided VT with a method of crisis control capable of reaching every student far faster than email. It should have been in place as part of the school's emergency preparedness plan. There is a tragic lesson for every educator of every school-age student" (Cooke et al., 2007).

The bad pitch of a news release undermines a public relations professional's credibility with his or her targets, be they bloggers or traditional media representatives. But bad blog pitches can take on a life of their own. One blogger was so irate he posted the email addresses of public relations people who sent him bad blogs as a warning to other bloggers. There was also an opportunity to retaliate by emailing the public relations people worthless messages. Retaliation from bloggers is very real. Bloggers post public messages and have no qualms about posting messages about bad blog pitches and outing the offenders. Just visit the website Bad Pitch Blog (www.badpitch.blogspot.com/) to see archived examples of public relations mistakes. Whether the sin be pitching the wrong story or spelling errors, you can find them discussed publicly in this unofficial hall of shame. The Bad Pitch Blog is popular and includes Facebook links as well as references in the mainstream media such as *Businessweek*. The price for bad blog pitches can be retaliation along with public ridicule.

Ideas for new media relations parallel those of media relations. Essentially, you must know who you are sending the news release to, if they are interested in the type of information you are sending, and how they prefer to receive information. In terms of strategy, it truly is the re-creation of traditional media relations online. The main difference is that bloggers typically do not have the same need to depend on public relations for low-cost stories. The Internet is vast and has plenty of no-cost and low-cost information available. The question becomes whether or not it is a good idea to re-create traditional media relations online. We shall return to this question shortly.

Buzz marketing: new life for word-of-mouth

Public relations and marketing professionals have long known the power of word-of-mouth. *Negative word-of-mouth* is the "interpersonal communication among consumers concerning a marketing organization or product which denigrates the object of the communication" (Richins, 1984, p. 697). People can be heavily influenced by comments and information they receive from family and friends (Brown & Reingen, 1987; Herr, Kardes, & Kim, 1991). Furthermore, negative word-of-mouth demonstrates a stronger effect on customer evaluations than positive word-of-mouth (Laczniak, DeCarlo, & Ramaswami, 2001; Mizerski, 1982).

The Internet makes it easier to spread both positive and negative word-of-mouth (Schlosser, 2005). The Internet was the catalyst for the creation of the Word-of-Mouth Marketing Association (WOMMA). With the Internet came the rise of agencies attempting to exploit its word-of-mouth potential under the heading of buzz or viral marketing. WOMMA seeks to set some best practices standards and ethical guidance to protect clients and consumers from those just looking to make some quick cash (WOMMA, n.d.). (For some examples of word-of-mouth efforts online, see box 7.2.) A blog or posting to a discussion group has the

---

Box 7.2   Buzz/Viral Marketing

Lee Dungarees

Lee Dungarees were known as a stodgy brand sold at Sears and J. C. Penney. In 2001 Lee created buzz through an innovative viral marketing effort. A consulting firm identified 200,000 influential online young men aged 17 to 22. These influentials had a high online profile based on email use and other web-based activities. Each influential was emailed one of three grainy, low-quality video clips about a cartoon character. A link was provided for a web that provided additional information. The three clips were different characters in a video game. People could access the game free of charge at the website address. However, to unlock higher levels people had to get codes by buying Lee products. The first day of the campaign saw over 100,000 hits to the website. Lee saw an increase in sales of 20 percent among young men following the campaign. Keep in mind Lee was still using traditional advertising as well. Still, the viral marketing effort seemed to be the contributor to the increase in sales to men aged 17 to 22 (Khermouch & Green, 2001).

KLM Royal Dutch Airlines

In November and December 2006 a video game trailer appeared in social sites in 58 different countries in one of ten languages. The social sites included blogs, forums, YouTube, and Facebook. The flying game featured airplanes and used Pixar-style animation. If people followed the link, they could play a game where they personalized a plane to create their own character, who could then could fly into various adventures. Playing the game introduced players to the sponsor, KLM Royal Dutch Airlines.

The campaign, created by SocialMedia8, provided significant results for KLM. In the first 90 days, over 8 million people viewed the trailer while over 1 million people actually played the video game. KLM experienced an 11 percent increase in awareness, 11 percent increase in likeability, and a 9 percent increase in purchase intention. A little over 878,000 people visited www.klm.com/fortune. There were 160 blog posts and 120 video portal posts about the game. In the end, KLM estimated a 1,200 percent return on investment (ROI) (KLM, n.d.).

potential to reach hundreds or thousands of people. Even emails have been known to reach far beyond their initial senders as people forward them to others.

However, word-of-mouth is a double-edged sword that hurts as quickly as it can help. Fear over the negative comments people might be posting online fueled the desire to track online communication about an organization and still fuels the growing industry built around online messages. Early online "public relations" practitioners claimed to be able to stop negative online comments. In reality they simply tried to intimidate people who created websites that were critical of corporations, what are termed "rogue websites" by some online experts (Holtz, 1999). Alternative names for these critical websites include complaint sites and gripe sites. Unfortunately, other entrepreneurs have followed suit by offering services designed to prevent people from sharing negative information about an organization online. For a brief period of time one expert tried to make a living by offering to alter Wikipedia content an organization did not like (see box 7.3).

Box 7.3   Censoring for Money

Whether we like it or not, Wikipedia is a major information source for Internet users. The danger to Wikipedia is also its strength: user developed content. People log on and create the content millions of other people then read. It is up to users to detect and correct inaccuracies, whether purposeful or accidental. The use of references, footnotes, and linked references give an appearance of thorough research but are no substitute for the critical evaluation of information. A good critical thinker will always consult multiple sources.

The fact that anyone can edit Wikipedia admittedly opens the door for potential abuse. What if corporations edited their own entries to eliminate negative information and positively spun the entry to their advantage? This is a real concern. In 2006, Gregory Kohs started MyWikiBiz.com. His service was writing and editing Wikipedia entries for corporations and non-profits. Kohs' focus was on creating entries for organizations that lacked entries. However, rewriting entries was also a possibility. Wikipedia founder Jimmy Wales eventually blocked Kohs from editing on Wikipedia. Wales felt the paid editing was a problem because it was based on self-interest and lacked authenticity (Bergstein, 2007).

In 2007, news reports revealed that Microsoft had been paying experts to edit Microsoft-related Wikipedia entries to correct errors. Wales condemned the actions, stating that paid entries constituted a conflict of interest. Wales has asked that public relations agencies not edit entries for any of their clients (Quainton, 2007).

How do we know who edits an entry? Enter Virgil Griffith and his Wikipedia Scanner. By visiting the Wikipedia Scanner website, anyone can see who edits an entry. The system traces IP addresses, those identifiers of our email addresses. The IP address can identify when someone from an organization, including corporations and public relations agencies, has accessed and edited an entry. The FBI,

---

Box 7.3   (cont'd)

ExxonMobile, and the Church of Scientology have all edited criticisms from their entries. Search any major public relations firm and a number of edits will appear. You can even search an organization's name to find out what their representatives have been editing. Wikipedia Scanner adds transparency to the Wikipedia editing. Of course, those intent on hiding their identities will find ways to use IP addresses that cannot be linked to their organizations. This is yet another reason to be a critical consumer of information you find on Wikipedia.

Efforts to stifle the free flow of ideas are antithetical to public relations and create suspicion about online public relations. We will explore the issue of censoring as part of the discussion of the Internet as a site of resistance.

The concern over negative online content has even spread to video as organizations worry about what might appear on YouTube or other sites where people can post videos. KFC had a firestorm of negative publicity when videos showing rats in a New York restaurant appeared on YouTube. In reality, most online content is seen by very few people. The skill is in determining what to respond to and what to leave alone, as well as how to constructively address the negative material, a theme that will reappear in the remainder of this chapter. A point we would like to make here is that suppressing the negative comments is not the best practice.

Interactive potential of the Internet:
dialogic communication

From the first writings on public relations and the Internet, people have touted the potential of the Internet to facilitate interaction between organizations and constituents. Social networking sites, listservs, email, instant messaging, chat rooms, discussion groups, and blogs (with response features) all permit interaction, whether it be asynchronous or in real time. Public relations was urged to make organizational websites interactive for constituencies by including email links, listservs, chat rooms, employee blogs, or even discussion groups. In reality, few organizations reach a high level of interactivity. Few websites go beyond providing content for constituents and providing a mechanism for feedback through email or blogs. We see relatively little effort to engage in discussion over time online (Kent & Taylor, 1998).

Kent and Taylor (1998, 2002) explored the use of *dialogue* as one of the principles informing online public relations. In dialogue, people interact with an eye toward reaching a mutually satisfying resolution. Kent and Taylor (1998) posit that web-based public relations should (1) utilize dialogic principles, (2) provide useful information to visitors, (3) encourage return visits, (4) provide an intuitive interface, and (5) keep visitors on the site by not providing links to other websites.

Kent and Taylor (2002) elaborated on the dialogic principles by identifying five tenets of dialogism. Those five tenets are:

1   *Mutuality:* collaboration between the parties involved.
2   *Propinquity or engagement:* an immediacy and willingness to communicate.
3   *Empathy:* supportiveness and recognition of the other.
4   *Risk:* vulnerability created by shared information.
5   *Commitment:* willing to keep engaged in the process.

The dialogic approach seeks to develop relationships. The interactive nature of the Internet makes it a potentially effective tool for relationship building through dialogic communication. However, Kent and Taylor's (1998) research found websites were frequently lacking interactivity and the dialogic principles.

The power acquisition potential of the Internet: Internet contagions

The potential for creating power is another framework that has been used to examine online public relations. The basic argument is that the Internet provides a mechanism where even powerless constituencies have the *potential* to build their power. By building power, other constituencies, including corporations, begin to listen to these once-marginalized and powerless constituencies (Coombs, 1998; Coombs & Holladay, 2007a; Heath, 1998). Again, the word *potential* is important. Just because constituents use the Internet does not mean they will gain power. The Internet is littered with constituencies failing to gain power.

Internet Contagion Theory (Coombs, 2002; Coombs & Holladay, 2007a) is one framework for understanding how the Internet can be a source of power. The theory holds that constituents can use the spread of information on the Internet to build power in their relationship with organizations. A basic premise is that organizational management only has the time and resources to handle the most salient constituents. Following the work of Mitchell, Agle, and Wood (1997), salience is a function of *power* (the ability to get an entity to do something it otherwise would not), *legitimacy* (the concern is acceptable to others), and *urgency* (pressure to take action). Power is the central and most scarce of the three resources.

Through leveraging the Internet, constituents can take actions designed to increase their power by maximizing their centrality in the web of relationships. The Internet provides a low cost and easily accessible means for forging a variety of communicative links with other constituents. Power is built as a constituent creates multiple communication points (e.g., websites, listservs, and blogs) to an increasing number of other constituents. The constituent will be able to more readily disseminate information and to mobilize other constituents to take action (urgency). Of course, the cause must be perceived to have legitimacy or others are unlikely to follow. Internet Contagion Theory proposes that constituents build power by constructing active and expanding webs of relationships predicated on the use of Internet-based communication channels.

The Internet as site of resistance

The Internet has been likened to a lawless frontier. There are few rules and people can build new lives and even new identities. But like most frontiers, with settlement comes domestication and rules. The Internet has slowly shifted from an exploratory network for sharing information to a tool of commerce. Internet sources are gaining in terms of respectability for political and other news. The Internet is becoming yet another social institution (Wood & Smith, 2001).

Still, the Internet holds a potential for marginalized groups that is missing in most other social institutions. Consider how journalists have long consternated over "citizen journalists," average people who post news stories. Established journalists fear this unfettered access to information because it is the job of the journalist to interpret and frame information for the masses. There is a not-so-subtle elitism to journalists' concerns about citizen journalists. More importantly, citizen journalists show how even an individual can still carve out a niche for communicating with others in this increasingly domesticated Internet. The Internet frontier still has opportunities and a wild side.

One view of the revolution online is the development of a parallel or alternative structure to the traditional news media. People can post information online about news events, companies, products, or services. These messages can appear on blogs, websites, discussion boards, or any other mechanism for placing ideas online. People are no longer limited by the filters or the space/time limitations of the news media. There are alternative sources of information. Public relations has gravitated toward the online environment because of these alternative sources of information. Practitioners realize these alternative sources can be powerful factors when people make decisions about how they will interact with an organization. In addition to messages from the organization and the news media, people have an expanded network of "interpersonal communication" to shape interactions with an organization. We will return to concern over this expanded interpersonal communication network in the next section.

Marginalized groups frequently lack the numbers and financial resources to speak their minds in a way that allows others to hear them. These groups often just speak to themselves. The Internet is a mechanism where marginalized groups have the potential to move from intra-group to inter-group communication. Their words can spread beyond their own members. The words *potential* and *can* are important qualifiers. The challenge of any communicator is to create a message that can spread and to access the most effective distribution points. Potentially hundreds, thousands, millions, or no people can encounter an Internet message. The challenge is to convert that potential into reality, a point we will address later in this chapter.

Wood & Smith (2001) wrote about *discursive resistance* on the Internet. Marginalized groups go unheard because of the very loud voices of the status quo that dominate traditional communication channels such as the news media. Discourse is "communication that shapes or influences human relations" (Wood & Smith, 2001, p. 169). Public relations, as we define it, qualifies as discourse. Discursive resistance "is a process through which text, oral, non-verbal communication, and other forms of meaning-making are employed to imagine alternatives to dominant power structures" (Wood & Smith, 2001, p. 169). Think of discursive resistance as the marginalized group's critique of dominant groups. The Internet provides a forum for communicative resistance. Marginalized groups can present their positions, concerns, and critiques where others can experience them.

Marginalized groups have other communicative avenues for resistance, including advertisements, flyers, books, and meetings. However, the cost-to-reach ratio is not very attractive. Traditional communication tactics have limited reach and can be costly for marginalized groups. The Internet has a relatively low cost given the amount of information that can be stored and the various forms of media that can be used (print, video, and audio). Moreover, there is the potential to reach all those people who log on and navigate the Internet.

It is important that we respect the notion of discursive resistance as we move public relations online. Marginalized groups can create a discursive space online that they are denied or cannot find in the real world (Mitra, 2004). The Internet provides an opportunity for voice – people can take a position and speak on an issue. People seek a space where their voice can be concretized (Watts, 2001). Voice in the real world is too often dependent on possessing the traditional trappings of power such as status and money. Access to voice is itself a form of exercising power. The Internet provides a location where traditional power holds less sway and the normally powerless can create discursive space where their voices can be heard.

Critiques of organizations are a type of resistance created by offering alternative views of how organizations should behave or fit with society. Consider the Parents' Television Council's (PTC) efforts "to promote and restore responsibility and decency to the entertainment industry in answer to America's demand for positive, family-oriented television programming" (Frequently, 2005). The PTC campaigns target the issues of broadcast decency, cable choice, advertiser accountability, and video game violence. The PTC argues for an alternative where television and video game content is less violent, less sexual, and more strongly promotional of traditional family values. Clearly, the PTC hopes to change a number of organizations, including producers of television shows and video games, distributors of television programs, the Federal Communication Commission (FCC), and television advertisers. Not everyone will agree with the PTC's agenda, but we all must respect their right to voice their concerns and articulate their view of reality.

Discursive resistance raises the issue of *constituency churn*. Constituency churn is when members of a constituency actively oppose an organization and seek to attract others to support their cause. Researchers in reputation and stakeholder management recognize constituency churn as a cost for organizations and seek ways to buffer an organization from "churn." We see this view reflected in chapter 5's discussion of activists as obstacles. Churn occurs when there is a gap in what constituencies expect from an organization and how an organization behaves. Sethi (1979) was among the first to note the role of expectation violations creating problems in the organization-constituency relationship. Heath (1994, 1997) has discussed violations of expectations in issues management, while Hearit (1995a, 1995b) has applied the idea to crisis management. Activists frequently seek change when expectations are violated; as the name implies, this constituency favors action. Hence, activists are a likely source of constituency churn, but customers, employees, the media, and investors can all produce churn as well. Once more, we need to alter our frame of reference and embrace rather than try to quell constituency churn.

Reflections on Public Relations Migrating Online

Discussion about online public relations will reflect the four extended applications of public relations discussed in this chapter: traditional media relations online, word-of-mouth, dialogic communication, and power acquisition.

The most interesting aspect of bloggers as citizen journalists is their lack of accountability. Bloggers generally are not trained in media ethics, nor are they bound by ethical codes that (usually) prevent abuses in traditional media. A serious concern is bloggers who are paid with cash or goods to write positive comments about a product, person, or organization. Companies such as Marqui and USWeb freely admit to paying bloggers, but recommend (but do not require) bloggers to disclose their self-interests. Edelman, considered a leader in online public relations, gave bloggers expensive new Acer laptop computers so that the bloggers could review Microsoft's Vista. Such gifts raise two concerns. First, the new high end laptops ensured the smooth operation of Vista by avoiding the problem of downloading Vista to an old system. Second, receiving a laptop that costs over $1,000 can lead to questions about objectivity. The blogosphere was a-buzz over how the Edelman-Acer-Vista effort was ethically challenged.

Some bloggers have articulated codes of ethics to guide other bloggers. Box 7.4 contains two samples. As always, codes are nice but do they mean anything? There are literally millions of bloggers. How many have read any blogger ethical codes? How many would feel the need to be bound by such codes? Public relations has two professional codes for practitioners that are binding to less than half of all practitioners in the US. How are people to know when a voice they hear/read is authentic or paid for by a corporation? We once more open public relations to the charge of corrupting a channel of communication. Even if most

Box 7.4   Blogger Codes of Ethics

There is no formal organization that can shape blogger ethics because anyone with Internet access can blog. However, a number of bloggers have posted their blogger codes of ethics. Two such codes are presented in this box.

CyberJournalist.net created a model blogger code of ethics based on the Society of Professional Journalists Code of Ethics:

Be honest and fair
Bloggers should be honest and fair in gathering, reporting, and interpreting information. Bloggers should:

- Never plagiarize.
- Identify and link to sources whenever feasible. The public is entitled to as much information as possible on sources' reliability.
- Make certain that weblog entries, quotations, headlines, photos and all other content do not misrepresent. They should not oversimplify or highlight incidents out of context.
- Never distort the content of photos without disclosing what has been changed. Image enhancement is only acceptable for technical clarity. Label montages and photo illustrations.
- Never publish information they know is inaccurate – and if publishing questionable information, make it clear it's in doubt.
- Distinguish between advocacy, commentary, and factual information. Even advocacy writing and commentary should not misrepresent fact or context.
- Distinguish factual information and commentary from advertising and shun hybrids that blur the lines between the two.

Minimize harm
Ethical bloggers treat sources and subjects as human beings deserving of respect. Bloggers should:

- Show compassion for those who may be affected adversely by weblog content. Use special sensitivity when dealing with children and inexperienced sources or subjects.
- Be sensitive when seeking or using interviews or photographs of those affected by tragedy or grief.
- Recognize that gathering and reporting information may cause harm or discomfort. Pursuit of information is not a license for arrogance.
- Recognize that private people have a greater right to control information about themselves than do public officials and others who seek power, influence or attention. Only an overriding public need can justify intrusion into anyone's privacy.
- Show good taste. Avoid pandering to lurid curiosity.
- Be cautious about identifying juvenile suspects, victims of sex crimes, and criminal suspects before the formal filing of charges.

Box 7.4   *(cont'd)*

Be accountable
Bloggers should:

- Admit mistakes and correct them promptly.
- Explain each weblog's mission and invite dialogue with the public over its content and the bloggers' conduct.
- Disclose conflicts of interest, affiliations, activities, and personal agendas.
- Deny favored treatment to advertisers and special interests and resist their pressure to influence content. When exceptions are made, disclose them fully to readers.
- Be wary of sources offering information for favors. When accepting such information, disclose the favors.
- Expose unethical practices of other bloggers.
- Abide by the same high standards to which they hold others. (Bloggers' code of ethics, 2003)

Rebecca Blood, author of *The Weblog Handbook: Practical Advice on Creating and Maintaining Your Blog* (2002), has written about ethics. Her ideas on ethics are frequently referenced and linked to by other bloggers. She presents six principles for blogger ethics:

1   Publish something as a fact only if you believe it is true, not speculation.
2   Link to materials online that you reference in your writing. The links allow readers to better evaluate your interpretation of the material.
3   Publicly correct any misinformation. Correct your mistakes and note if you have linked your writings to incorrect information.
4   Each posting should remain intact. Do not rewrite or delete an entry. Instead, add to the original entry to maintain the integrity of the message.
5   Be sure to disclose any conflict of interest. Make it clear if you have a personal stake in the issue under discussion.
6   Indicate when you use or link to a questionable or biased source.

---

public relations professionals bring their ethics online, those without ethics will be there inflicting more damage on the industry's reputation.

Another point that parallels traditional media relations is the ability for those with more power and money to limit the voice of the marginalized. Commercial messages now dominate the Internet – and we are not just referring to the advertisements that appear magically on our screens or the marketing software that tracks our online movements. The contents of web pages are mostly commercial and the search engines we rely upon are profit-making centers. How wealthy are the people at Yahoo and Google? Money can allow organizations to manipulate search results. A website can move up in a search by being mentioned on blogs.

If bloggers are paid to mention a website, that web mention will improve its search ranking. Organizations have already begun to effectively buy higher search rankings (Search, 2006). Known as search engine reputation management (SERM), companies such as Converseon can keep critics and competitors from appearing on the first page of a search for a corporation's name or prominent product. Why does this matter? When was the last time you visited a link on the second page of your search results? If you have, you are among the small minority of people who do. The first page or top ten listings seem to be the limit for most people.

Suppose you are a group critical of bottled water. Due to the content of your site, it appears in the top three when searching "bottled water." A major bottled water company creates ten websites and heavily promotes them online, including buying bloggers. Your web page suddenly is bounced to the second page and oblivion. This can and has happened to activist groups. Their voice is less likely to be heard if those with power and money can manipulate search engine results. As a public relations practitioner, you need to decide where you stand on these online tactics and what will guide your practice of online media relations.

The concerns with word-of-mouth online are derived from paying bloggers. *Floggers* is the term created for those who create fake blogs. Fake blogs are created by people who readers think are speaking their own mind but are really working for someone else. There is a slight difference from just paying bloggers. Floggers try to create the illusion of impartiality through the omission of affiliations and work for an organization rather than just taking a fee. Once more, the channel of communication is corrupted, as readers have difficulty identifying authentic voices from corporate shills. Floggers re-create the problem of front groups online. Front groups (see chapter 10 on issues management) claim to represent average citizens when in reality they are funded and directed by corporations or associations (Fitzpatrick & Palenchar, 2006). Floggers pretend to be independent when they really work for an organization.

Edelman created a firestorm in the blogosphere that helped to create the terms flog and flogger with their fake blogs for Wal-Mart. The case study at the end of this chapter details the Edelman-Wal-Mart flog case. The key concern was that Edelman employees were blogging for Wal-Mart but not divulging they worked for Edelman or Wal-Mart. People visiting the website were led to believe the bloggers were writing simply because they liked Wal-Mart – they were believed to be independent supporters (PR, 2006). The failure of transparency led to charges of unethical behavior. The flogs were a clear violation of the fledgling word-of-mouth code of conduct from the Word of Mouth Marketing Association. The second point in the code is "Honesty of Relationship," which includes having word-of-mouth advocates disclose their relationships to marketers in their communications (WOMMA, n.d.). Edelman could not plead ignorance of the code. Sadly, Edelman personnel had violated the very word-of-mouth code of conduct they helped to create and to promote. How likely are violations from the myriad of practitioners that do not know of the code nor have any attachment to it?

Once more, missteps by practitioners create the impression that public relations views the online environment as a site of exploitation rather than a site for public discussion of ideas.

Consider the ammunition critics of online public relations have gained from the examples reviewed thus far. Edelman, Microsoft, and Wal-Mart are giants in their fields and recognized around the world. These corporate behemoths are imprinting the online environment with very negative messages about online public relations. Edelman is especially problematic. If purported leaders of understanding and leveraging online public relations behave in this way, how will those with lesser knowledge and scruples behave? It seems critics have a reason to fear that public relations could corrupt the authenticity of online messages, thereby eroding the trust people place in such messages. The up-side is that people should bring a skepticism to online messages and seek to verify online information. Everyone must be a careful and critical consumer of online information by seeking to vet sources and verify information before assimilating that information into their lives. We address this point in more detail in chapter 15.

As with traditional media relations, the discussion is dominated by corporate use of online public relations. However, all constituents, especially activists, are communicating online as well. They can also use traditional media relations and word-of-mouth. Activists may at times be in a better position than corporations to leverage these two online applications of public relations. The greater credibility enjoyed by activists as opposed to corporations makes them more attractive sources to many bloggers and a more authentic voice for starting word-of-mouth efforts. But transparency and disclosure remain ethical concerns. The Internet provides for a mix of corporate and constituent voices not found in traditional media. However, issues of power and access still remain.

Dialogic communication remains more of a potential than a reality. Studies of corporate websites, environmental activist websites, and non-profit websites find very little dialogic communication (e.g., Kent & Taylor, 2003; Taylor, Kent, & White, 2001). The potential increased interaction among constituents has yet to be reached. However, examples of dialogic communication online can be found, such as opportunities to vote on issues found at the Cooperative Bank in the UK (www.co-operativebank.co.uk/servlet/Satellite?cid=1170748476664&pagename=CB/Page/tplStandard&c=Page). The challenge is discovering a way to allow dialogic communication online to flourish. Part of that challenge is the issue of power. By allowing all constituencies a voice, organizations are forced to share some power, because there is power in being able to influence the topic of discussion. Dialogic communication requires a movement away from the controlled messages organizations typically develop. Constituencies raise questions and topics an organization may want to avoid but cannot when everyone else can "see" the question and whether or not there is a response. It is much easier and comforting for an organization to simply control the content of the website and respond privately to emails. Organizations must embrace the risk of public discussion of ideas and the loss of power associated with the commitment to dialogic communication.

The Internet remains a potential source of power for the powerless (Coombs, 1998; Coombs & Holladay, 2007a; Mitra, 2004). While many once-marginalized voices have harnessed the Internet to build power and be heard, there are scores that go unnoticed in the expanses of cyberspace. Building power through the Internet is not a given, it remains a challenging task. Knowing the ways the Internet can increase power is a necessary but not a sufficient condition for being heard. Contagion Theory helps groups *understand* ways they can utilize the Internet to generate power, but effective *execution* is still required. There are helpful online sources such as the Green Mediashed to help the marginalized understand their routes to power and skills needed to navigate those routes. The status quo is threatened by efforts to build power and reacts in ways designed to suppress online voice. While difficult in the wide-open online environment, suppression of dissent is still a very real possibility through lawsuits and the manipulation of search engines. The potential for power acquisition remains, but is not a given.

Dialogic communication and power acquisition online are both tempered by the digital divide. The digital divide refers to the separation between those with access to communication technologies (computers and the Internet) and the resources and skills necessary to utilize them and those without. The digital dividing lines include socioeconomic status (rich vs poor), race (white vs minorities), and geographic location (urban vs rural). The digital divide is a concept that has global implications (Baran, 2008). Every country must wrestle with this issue. Some experts conceptualize the digital divide in terms of information inequity. For our purposes, it is the power, or lack thereof, associated with access and Internet usage.

Dialogic communication and power acquisition on the Internet become bounded by the digital divide. Even if organizations increasingly develop dialogic-oriented websites, many constituencies will not have the opportunity to participate in the discussion. Groups cannot build power on the Internet if they cannot access the Internet or lack the skills to utilize its power potential. So long as groups are excluded from access and/or lack the skills to employ Internet resources, elements of society will not enjoy the benefits of dialogic communication online or power acquisition. Public relations cannot be expected to completely solve the global problem of the digital divide. However, we should be cognizant of it and seek to reach those on the far side of the divide when developing Internet dialogic programs. Moreover, those activists with access should continue their efforts to extend the reach of the Internet and to provide skills training for those crossing the digital divide.

Conclusion

It is not surprising that public relations has tried to re-create media relations online. The short-term view of public relations is to harness any communication channel for disseminating a message. So why not pitch bloggers, place media relations materials online where journalists are searching, and try to generate buzz with clever websites or videos? After all, here are pre-segmented publics that are fairly simple to reach. But public relations practitioners do so at their own risk if they fail to appreciate their new environment. On the most basic level, public relations must bring its real-world media relations principles and ethics to the online world. If you are to pitch bloggers, understand what information they want and how they want to receive it. Utilize the linked nature of online messages, do not simply repeat traditional strategies online. Finally, respect the online audience through transparency and authenticity. Clearly state affiliations when posting messages and disclose any connections to an organization, product, or service you might be discussing.

The long-term view of public relations seeks to understand how communication channels can help to build relationships and co-create meaning. Public relations must become better at utilizing the potential of the Internet to provide dialogic communication. However, the idea of surrendering power to constituencies is easier said than done. Public relations practitioners should honor the discursive space of online resisters. Use online monitoring as a way to listen to various constituents. Do not employ tactics designed to silence a voice simply because you do not like what it is saying. Identify those constituents you need to engage more directly to address their concerns, if you can. Chapter 5's focus on activism and chapter 13's discussion of corporate responsibility elaborate on the need to engage contrary voices. The Internet is becoming increasingly commercialized and tame. However, there is still room in the online universe for people to voice their concerns. As a communication discipline, public relations should seek to protect the right for all to speak on the Internet. Online public relations should be the domain for any and all constituents to present their voices.

Case Study: Edelman, Wal-Mart, and Fake Blogs

It began as a small website where a couple posted blogs about their journey across the US in a recreational vehicle (RV). Jim and Laura, the couple blogging, were stopping at Walmarts on their trip because Wal-Mart is RV-friendly, often letting people park overnight in their lots. The blogs told of the happy workers and shoppers they met. Jim even posted pictures on their "Walmarting Across America" blog. At a time when Wal-Mart was under fire from critics in the news media and online, the blog was a welcome breeze of support from the average person. That

was until a *Business Week* magazine reporter exposed that Jim and Laura were hired by Edelman to promote Wal-Mart. The firestorm of criticism, most directed at Edelman, began.

The fake blog or *flog* was a symbol of the ultimate blog corruption. The bloggers were not authentic and not transparent. Bloggers should be transparent and state their potential conflict of interests and if they are working for someone. It is only then that readers can determine if comments are authentic or manufactured. But the story gets worse. Another media report revealed that another pro-Wal-Mart blog site, "Working Families for Walmart," had Edelman employees blogging when the site describes itself as giving voice to the millions of Americans who know Wal-Mart makes a difference in their lives. Now, the vast majority of the posts were authentic, but the revelations of Edelman employees writing for the site cast a pall over the entire online blogging effort to show public support for Wal-Mart.

The tragic nature of this online fiasco is three-fold. First, Edelman prides itself on being a leader and expert in the area of online communication. CEO Richard Edelman has an active blog and Edelman hired self-promoted blog expert Steve Rubel to head their leading-edge online public relations. Richard Edelman helped to draft the code of ethics for the Word of Mouth Marketing Association. This code was violated by the flogs because they failed to disclose a relationship between the bloggers and a marketer. Public relations bloggers generally condemned Edelman for such a lapse in judgment. The great experts had bungled a major online effort worse than anyone could have imagined.

Second, the response from Edelman took a few days, which is a very long time in the online environment. Edelman eventually blogged an apology: "I want to acknowledge our error in failing to be transparent about the identity of the two bloggers from the outset. This is 100 percent our responsibility and our error; not the client's" (Gunter, 2006). An apology is good, but in addition to being too slow it missed some of the key points as to why bloggers were upset. Also, Rubel's comments showed a disturbing lack of knowledge about the project. Edelman failed to appreciate the seriousness of its transgression. Transparency and authenticity should be an important concern for bloggers. This was more than an error, it was a serious violation of online protocol and reinforced stereotypes of public relations people as emphasizing exploitation over conversation. Rubel was a supposed "big name" blogger Edelman brought in to help with online public relations. He chimed in even later in the event, basically saying he was not

involved with the project. Granted, Rubel cannot be on every account, but he could have done better. There was nothing about why it was wrong or how he might help to fix it. Wouldn't you expect a founding blogger to have some ideas about proper blogging?

Third, there was no need for flogs. Millions of Americans do shop and love Wal-Mart. That is not an exaggeration – look at the sales numbers and growth. If you provide a forum for Wal-Mart fans to speak, they will send messages. You have to believe that if you build it they will blog and blog in support of Wal-Mart. Authentic voices exist and could have been used. Instead, Edelman violated the ethics policies its CEO helped to write and wasted their online effort to show support for Wal-Mart. Wal-Mart management may have the strongest reason to be angry about the flogs. Wal-Mart lost an opportunity to turn their shopping supporters into a force for positive commentary online. Instead, that resource was squandered and Wal-Mart became the subject of additional negative comments in the traditional and online media.

Case questions

1 Why were the Wal-Mart flogs criticized by the public? Do you think they were justified in their concerns about them?
2 Do you think Edelman's responses were sufficient in this situation? What could – or should – Edelman have said in order to satisfy those who viewed the flogs as abusing the online environment?
3 To what extent would you hold Wal-Mart accountable for the flogs? How should Wal-Mart be involved in discussions of the flogs?
4 Are there any circumstances where bloggers would not have to reveal their connections to organizations or their products and services?

Discussion Questions

1 Compare the social media news release to the traditional news release. What are the advantages and disadvantages of each?

2 Describe how public relations practitioners can use online media relations, buzz marketing, the potential for dialogic communication, and the potential for power acquisition in their public relations actions.

3 Visit an organization's online newsroom. Evaluate the usefulness of the information provided. Would journalists and other interested parties find the information helpful? What additional information would you like to be made available at the site?

4 Suppose your organization learns a video featuring one of its products has been posted on YouTube. The video humorously shows someone being injured by misusing the product. The video is moderately popular, as demonstrated by numerous hits. Although no one has contacted the organization about product-related injuries, you fear this may happen, especially because the video may spawn copy-cat incidents. What should you do?

5 What does Internet Contagion Theory seek to explain? How can activists use ideas associated with the theory to enhance their power?

6 What is discursive resistance? Why should public relations professionals be concerned with online discursive resistance?

Newspaper ad from the campaign to prevent online sexual exploitation.

8

Social Marketing

Do you know who Smokey the Bear is? Have you ever heard or seen a message telling you not to drink and drive, to donate blood, or to wear your seatbelt? If the answer is "yes," you have experienced social marketing. This chapter is unique in that it covers an area of public relations whose utilization is not explicitly corporate-centric.

The roots of social marketing are traced to G. D. Wiebe (1952) who posited the idea of selling brotherhood like soap (Andreasen, 2003; Salmon, 1989). Generally, *social marketing* involves the application of marketing principles to sell ideas, attitudes, and behaviors. More specifically, social marketing takes a *health* and *safety* focus that seeks to change behaviors that will help individuals and society. Social marketing is "the application of commercial marketing technologies to the analysis, planning, execution, and evaluation of programs designed to influence the voluntary behavior of target audiences in order to improve their personal welfare and that of the society of which they are a part" (Andreasen, 2003, p. 296).

This chapter explores the area of social marketing and its connection to public relations. The first section defines a set of related terms and discusses the public relations aspect of social marketing. The second section examines the development of social marketing, followed by a reflection on its use in society.

Social Marketing and Public Relations

Wearing seatbelts, adopting children, and protecting kids from online predators have all been the focus of social marketing campaigns. In each case, the public relations effort seeks to help people and to benefit society. The objective is *behavior change* among a target audience. The change could include accepting a behavior, rejecting a behavior, modifying a behavior, maintaining a behavior, or ending a behavior.

The focus on behavior change is considered a significant step in the development of social marketing. Originally, Kotler (Kotler & Roberto, 1989; Kotler & Zaltman, 1971) included the acceptance of social ideas as part of social marketing. Andreasen (2003) argues that including social ideas places social marketing with health education and communication efforts and allows it to be confused with social advertising and public relations. We need to explore this point to clarify what social marketing is and its relationship to public relations.

Andreasen (2003) draws a distinction between *education campaigns* that use information to change attitudes, *social marketing* efforts that create behavior change, and *legislative behavior* that is mandated. Obviously, legislative behavior change is very different. Laws or regulations force people to change their behaviors. In the US, for example, it is illegal to drive a car without a seatbelt due to state laws. Public relations is used to inform people of the required change and the penalties for failure to comply. For instance, people in the US still receive messages to wear their seatbelts, but they are reminded it is the law and they can be ticketed if they do not wear one.

The distinction between education campaigns and social marketing may not be as clear as Andreasen (2003) would like us to believe. It may be a matter of degree at best rather than a stark contrast. Andreasen places public education with public relations. Information is sent to people to change their attitudes and even behaviors. Andreasen therefore establishes a distinction between public information campaigns and social marketing. Salmon (1989) articulates the counter-argument that the two concepts are similar because they both represent attempts at planned change. Public relations has a long association with public information campaigns (Botan, 1997; Rakow, 1989; Salmon, 1989).

Public information is a misnomer. These campaigns sought behavior change not just to create awareness or to inform. The information is strategically used to influence behaviors. For example, a message shows a bloody scene of an automobile accident and information on how a seatbelt saves lives. What conclusion would you draw from this message? Information frames reality and the choices people make. For instance, defining the problem dictates the entire process because it shapes possible solutions (Salmon, 1989). As Rakow (1989) notes, information is used to control how people think and act. Information can shape how people see a situation or if they know about a situation at all. For instance, people cannot take action on a social problem if they do not know one exists.

Early public information campaigns were crude, relying heavily on *public service announcements* (PSAs). A PSA is a non-commercial message designed to benefit society by promoting a desirable behavior or a specific public interest. The form of PSAs frequently mirror those of advertisements. Examples would be efforts to increase seatbelt usage and to encourage people to seek screenings for colon cancer. Box 8.1 gives an extended example of colon cancer screening. The PSAs highlight the belief that a simple message in the mass media will create

Box 8.1   Colon Cancer Detection Campaign

Physicians chase down a character in a red suit in what seems like a parody of the television show *Cops*. The scene concludes with the physicians catching Polyp Man. The short television spot ends with the tagline, "Get the test, get the polyp, get the cure." The message is a PSA for colon cancer screening. Such humorous messages try to persuade men and women over 50 years old to get screening tests for colon cancer. Such tests are at times uncomfortable, so why get them? The survival rate for colon cancer is 90 percent when it is detected early. The American Cancer Society estimates that only 44 percent of the people who should get the screening actually do. If everyone did get screening, the number of deaths from colon cancer would be cut in half (Cohen & Falco, 2002).

Polyp Man began his run in 2002. He made personal appearances and variations of the messages were developed from African-American and Hispanic/Latino-American targets. In one ad for African-Americans, Polyp Man interrupts a picnic and is then chased and caught by doctors. But humor for colon cancer? Earlier, more serious messages about colon cancer had failed. One featured tombstones as a scare tactic. The idea was that humor might be a better way to get people to talk about and to take action on screenings (Cohen & Falco, 2002). The Ad Council's testing showed Polyp Man was successful at increasing screening (Polyp 2003).

social change. There is evidence that mass mediated messages such as PSAs can be successful in some situations. However, we also know that mass mediated messages are often not enough. Interpersonal and more direct communication often are required (e.g., Maccoby & Solomon, 1981). The complexity of the social change effort and channels utilized sheds additional light on Andreasen's (2003) distinction between education and social marketing.

Andreasen (2003) uses the example of sudden infant death syndrome (SIDS) prevention as an example of education that tells people to place babies on their backs. The campaign simply conveys basic information via mediated messages to offer simple solutions to a problem. However, social marketing is anchored in behavior change. McGuire's (1981) model for persuasion can help to clarify the relationship between education and social marketing. McGuire's model is summarized in box 8.2. Social marketing often begins as exposure to information but always ends in behavior change. If a target does not know there is a problem there can be no change. Hence, the first step is awareness. *Awareness* begins with exposing people to a message, attempting to get people to attend to the message and ultimately comprehend the message. Next, the emphasis shifts to *attitude change* and *remembering the message*. Finally, the target *engages in the desired behavior*. Where the target audience currently resides in McGuire's model dictates what actions are necessary to move them to behavior change. Again, there are shades of differences between education and social marketing.

Box 8.2   McGuire's Information Processing Steps for Attitude and Behavior Change

McGuire (1981) has articulated 12 steps to behavior change that include both informational and attitudinal changes. The 12 steps are a sequence that can be followed to change behaviors. Not all change efforts will follow all 12 steps in the exact order prescribed by McGuire. However, McGuire's steps offer useful guidelines for social marketing because the endpoint is behavior change. The 12 steps are listed and defined below along with a running example:

1   *Exposure to the message:* the target audience has an opportunity to encounter the message in some fashion. The message appears in a medium they watch or read or appears at a website they utilize.
2   *Attending to the message:* the target actually experiences the message in some fashion. Messages routinely compete for people's attention in their daily lives. The target attends to the message when they see or hear it.
3   *Liking the message:* the target is interested in the message once they attend to it. People like/are attracted to messages that are consistent with their attitudes or values (selective attention) and messages that meet their needs.
4   *Comprehending the message:* the target understands the message once they attend to it. It must be in a language the target can understand and structure so that it is easy to comprehend. Understanding a language includes how the readability level fits the target and the actual language used by the target.
5   *Skill acquisition:* the target learns how to do something. Many behavior changes require people to master a new skill such as evaluating the fat content from food labels or learning how to quit smoking.
6   *Yielding to the message:* the target has a favorable attitude toward the object of the message. This is attitude change or creation of a new attitude. People accept that a low fat diet is good for their health.
7   *Memory storage:* the target remembers the desired information in the message. Efforts are made to make the message more memorable so that people can recall and use the information at a later date. People remember how to find fat content information on product labels.
8   *Information search and retrieval:* the target can recall the information when it is relevant. People remember that low fat is better for their health and look for the fat content label on the food they buy.
9   *Deciding on the bases of retrieval:* the target applies the recalled information when making decisions. This allows the recalled information to influence decision making. People consider fat content when choosing products.
10   *Behaving in accord with the decision:* the target makes choices based in the recalled information. People choose between two products by selecting the one with the lower fat content.
11   *Reinforcement of the desired act:* the target finds their needs are satisfied by the new behavior. People must find the low fat diet meets their needs.
12   *Post-behavior consolidation:* the target collects information that reinforces their decisions and actions. There is a need to provide additional reasons for the behavior change. People see additional information about the benefits they can derive from a low fat diet.

Education is limited just to the delivery of a simple message designed to address attitudes and easy-to-execute behavior changes. More elaborate messages and behaviors that are challenging to alter are the province of social marketing. The more elaborate messages and actions require greater sophistication that can be supplied by marketing. We would argue that to be effective, even simple education efforts require careful planning based on principles used in public relations and marketing. The same holds true for social marketing. Public relations theories and principles can inform social marketing due to its overlap with marketing. This will be discussed later in this chapter.

There is a *pro-social bias* in social marketing public relations. Social marketing is designed to produce social consequences that make society a better place and the target audience better off than before the communicative effort. In fact, social marketing can be used to correct social problems created by corporate public relations and marketing. For instance, Edward Bernays joined anti-smoking efforts in his later years in part to combat the smoking-related problems he helped to facilitate by promoting smoking among women in the 1920s and 1930s. We should note it is unfair to blame Bernays for the spread of smoking among women. Though he liked to take credit for popularizing smoking among women through his "green campaign," Bernays merely helped to amplify the already-increasing demand among women for cigarettes. Refer to box 8.3 for more information on Bernays, women, and smoking.

Box 8.3   Edward Bernays Promotes Smoking Among Women

It was less than 100 years ago that a woman was arrested in New York for smoking a cigarette in public. At the turn of the twentieth century, cigarettes were a gendered product. Men were the purveyors of this dirty and nasty habit (Amos & Haglund, 2000). Unfortunately for the health of women, cigarettes would not last as a gendered product. By 1916, cigarette consumption by women was on the rise (Brandt, 1996; Tate, 1999). Cigarettes made smoking cleaner, easier, and more appealing to women. Cigarette smoking was also emerging as a weapon against traditional sex roles for women (Amos & Haglund, 2000). In 1916 the *Atlantic Monthly* ran an article equating cigarettes and emancipation for women (Brandt 1996). By the 1920s, cigarette smoking had already reached the middle class (Ewen, 2000; Tate, 1999). Enter Edward Bernays and George Hill to leverage this shift in sex roles to further gender-neutralize cigarettes.

Edward Bernays' career and legacy in public relations was haunted by his association with George Hill and the American Tobacco Company. Bernays, the father of public relations, used promotional tactics to help win acceptance of women smoking in public. Even books written in the 1990s painted Bernays as tainted by luring women to the deadly cigarette. They were highly critical of how he had used public relations to harm society (Ewen, 1996; Stauber & Rampton, 1995). His obituary in

Box 8.3   (*cont'd*)

the *New York Times* noted he was "instrumental" in garnering public acceptance of women smoking (Edward, 1995).

Hill saw women as a gold mine. They represented a large, relatively untapped market for his company and dominant brand Lucky Strike. In 1928 Bernays was hired to help Hill mine this vein of gold. Lucky Strikes had already increased in popularity with women using the message "Reach for a Lucky instead of a sweet." The message appealed to the developing trend of women being weight conscious. The success is indicated in the subsequent 200 percent market share increase (Amos & Haglund, 2000).

According to the lore, Bernays needed to find a way to increase the acceptance of women smoking in public, especially among society's elite. Bernays was the nephew of Sigmund Freud and a strong believer in psychoanalysis. After consulting with the psychoanalyst A. A. Brill, Bernays hit upon the theme of cigarettes as freedom, "torches of freedom." In 1929 Bernays hired a number of young women (debutantes) to smoke their "freedom torches" while walking in the New York City Easter parade. The publicity event drew a great amount of media interest. In turn, the pseudo-event is used as evidence that Bernays made smoking in public acceptable for women (Amos & Haglund, 2000; Brandt, 1996; Ewen, 2000).

While he was a player in the progression of women smoking, too much credit is often given to Bernays. The evidence suggests that women smoking cigarettes and the link to freedom existed before Bernays' involvement in the campaign. Cigarette smoking was becoming popular among women well before Bernays and Hill entered the equation in 1928 (Brandt, 1996; Ewen, 2000). Bernays did not create the trend, he merely added to the speed and breadth by which it spread across the United States. Bernays took an existing shift in the sex roles and amplified it in an effort to gender-neutralize cigarettes, step one of gender neutralization.

The real genius of Bernays is found in step two: appeals to the opposite sex. During the 1920s and 1930s, Lucky Strike was wedded to the color green for its product. Hill had spent millions of dollars marketing the green Lucky Strike packaging and deemed the color green as an integral part of the Lucky Strike brand. Green posed a barrier for gender neutralization. Green was not a part of women's fashion during this time. Hence, the Lucky Strike packaging clashed with women's clothing. If cigarettes are to be accessories, the packaging needs to fit with fashions. Lucky Strikes were clashing with women's fashion and causing women to select other brands to match their clothes. Marketing research discovered that many women did not buy Lucky Strikes because the package clashed with their clothing (Tye, 1998). Hill was adamant about his commitment to green; thus he tasked Bernays with making green a popular color in women's fashion. If women wore green, Lucky Strike would work as an accessory.

Edward Bernays crafted a very advanced, six-month promotional campaign designed to make green the "in" color of women's fashion. The campaign was based on careful formative research. Bernays knew the problem was that women were not wearing the color green. Hence, the goal was to have women wear green. But Bernays thought beyond fashion to ensconce women in green. Green would

Box 8.3   (cont'd)

surround women through fashion and home design. The next step was defining the target audience for the promotion. Bernays enlisted the assistance of fashion opinion leaders, fashion and accessory makers, department stores, interior designers, and home furnishing buyers.

For fashion advice, women of this time turned to New York City debutantes and fashion magazines. Women would be encouraged to wear green if the debutantes were seen in green and fashion editors were praising green. Women cannot wear green if there are no dresses and accessories (scarves, gloves, shoes, etc.) in green, so manufacturers needed to be on board. Department stores were necessary to deliver the green goods to women. The interior designers and home furnishings buyers rounded out the target by weaving green into the fabric of woman's lives (Ewen, 1996; Tye, 1998).

The execution of the green campaign was a complex logistical challenge. Bernays began by recruiting the Onondaga Silk Company. Bernays convinced Onondaga President Philip Vogelman that green would become the "in" color. If Onondaga was at the front of the green wave, the company would have a sales advantage. Bernays used Onondaga to reach fashion editors, department stores, and interior designers. Vogelman was instrumental in arranging for fashion editors to attend the Green Fashions Fall Luncheon at the Waldorf-Astoria. Green dominated the menu with green beans, asparagus-tip salad, and olivette potatoes. A psychologist spoke about the wonderful qualities of green and an art professor from Hunter College lectured about the use of green by great artists. Following the luncheon, newspaper stories began to appear that touted green as a color to look for in this year's fashions.

The Color Fashion Bureau was established by Onondaga and Bernays. The Color Fashion Bureau's purpose was to address green and home décor. The belief was that women would not want clothing that clashed with home furnishings. The Color Fashion Bureau sent over 6,500 pro-green letters, on green paper, to home furnishing buyers, department stores, and interior designers. Oddly, the Color Fashion Bureau became a source for fashion information. In the few months after its creation, the bureau received information requests from 77 newspapers, 95 magazines, 83 furniture and home decoration manufacturers, 301 department stores, 175 radio stations, and 64 interior designers. The requests were evidence that the green message was gaining traction. Other evidence included major department stores utilizing green clothing in window displays and a major art gallery holding an exhibition of green paints (Ewen, 1996; Tye, 1998).

The most visible element of the green campaign was the Green Ball. Through the Green Ball, debutantes would be shown wearing green and fashion magazines would support the pro-green message. Bernays knew a successful ball would be a function of the hostess. Bernays selected Mrs. Frank A. Vanderlip, the wife of the former National City Bank chairman. She was well connected in New York City social circles. Bernays appealed to her sense of charity to win her support for the Green Ball. Mrs. Vanderlip was the chairwoman of the Women's Infirmary of New York. Bernays promised the proceeds from the ball would go to the Infirmary, along with a $25,000 pledge from an anonymous donor. The one constraint was that the

---

Box 8.3   *(cont'd)*

event had to feature green and all attendees must wear green gowns. Thus the Green Ball was born.

The Waldorf-Astoria served as the site for the Green Ball. Mrs. Vanderlip recruited the elite of New York society to the cause, including Mrs. James Roosevelt, Mrs. Walter Chrysler, and Mrs. Irving Berlin. *Harper's Bazaar* and *Vogue* featured the Green Ball on their covers. Other prominent newspapers and fashion outlets covered the Green Ball as well. Green was establishing itself as an important color in fashion. Of course, Bernays proclaimed the green campaign a success (Ewen, 1996). Moreover, independent historians generally agree that green did become the "in" fashion color in 1934 (Tye, 1998). We do not know if green becoming a fashion color increased the sale of Lucky Strike. However, the major barrier to women not buying Lucky Strikes was removed. Appeals to the opposite sex role, promoting a color, were used to reinforce cigarettes as a product women could use. The appeal was not overly gendered, so there was little risk of a backlash from male smokers.

With some basic definitions in place and relationships established between social marketing and related areas, it is time to examine the development of this pro-social public relations application.

The Development of Social Marketing

In the 1970s, Kotler and Zaltman posited that the principles of marketing products to consumers could be used to effectively market social concerns. Thus the field of social marketing was born and continues growing to this day. The core of social marketing is the application of a program-planning process and concepts from marketing to social concerns. In this section we review some of those concepts and develop the link between public relations and social marketing.

At the center of social marketing is the target audience, the people the communicative effort is trying to reach. Marketing uses various methods to divide people into segments or subgroups. Common segmentation factors include lifestyles, values, and behaviors. Dividing a target audience into segments increases the effectiveness of a social marketing effort. By grouping similar people into a segment, social marketers are better able to develop a message that resonates with that segment. A variety of messages can be created for a campaign, with each designed to speak to the values and/or behaviors of a specific target audience segment (Grunig, 1989a).

The campaign to prevent cyberbullying illustrates targeting multiple targets. The campaign targets children and parents with different messages. Children can be the victims or witnesses of cyberbullying, while parents may lack awareness of the problem. Social marketers, like public relations practitioners, must have a detailed understanding of a target audience if they hope to succeed. It is by understanding the needs and desires of the target audience that successful social marketing and public relations messages are created. Marketing and public relations share this target audience focus.

Following consumer marketing, social marketing has four P's, also known as the *marketing mix*: product, price, place, and promotion. *Product* would be the benefits associated with the desired behavior. Each social marketing effort involves the target audience assessing benefits and costs. What benefits do they derive from the behavior change and what are the associated costs? The behavior change can be as simple as wearing a seatbelt or as complex as modifying a diet to consume less fat. *Price* is the cost of the behavior for the target. The price can be the effort or the financial costs associated with the behavior, such as buying condoms. But even effort has costs, as new behaviors can take time, reduce pleasure, or even create embarrassment (Grier & Bryant, 2005). Target audiences implicitly use exchange theory to compare product and price. If the price (cost of the behavior) exceeds the product (benefits of the behavior), the target audience is unlikely to adopt the desired behavior. For example, people may ask themselves, "Is getting an inoculation worth possibly preventing the disease?"

Place is the action outlet. An action outlet is the location that the target audience will enact the behavior, collect necessary items, and receive training, if necessary (Grier & Bryant, 2005). Action outlets include how and where targets can physically access a behavior such as an immunization shot and where they can be trained so that they can successfully execute more complex behaviors. The County of Sacramento has an action outlet in its Provider Car Seat Safety Training. This is a three-hour session where people learn how to properly install car seats for children. Adults are given detailed instruction on proper installation and given "hands on exercises in vehicles and with car seats" (Car, n.d.). Training is critical because the National Highway Traffic Safety Administration (NHTSA) estimates that as many as 4 out of 5 child car seats are installed improperly, making them a safety hazard rather than a safety aid (Car, n.d.).

Finally, *promotion* refers to the various channels used to deliver the social marketing messages, including advertisements, PSAs, print materials, websites, special events, and interpersonal communication. Promotion is the most visible part of social marketing, leading many people to think that social marketing is just promotion. The social marketing campaign to protect children from online predators employs various Internet sites, newspaper advertisements, radio PSAs, and television PSAs (Weinreich, n.d.).

Public relations is consistent with the marketing mix. Marketing emphasizes consumers while public relations considers consumers one of many constituents. Hence, public relations has long been adapting the marketing mix to other constituents, such as those in need of pro-social messages. Early public relations research frequently examined public information campaigns that would now be called social marketing (Salmon, 1989). Public relations practitioners must understand what motivates a target audience, including how the target is likely to evaluate the costs and benefits associated with a message. Public relations is more than promotion; it shares a mindset and methodologies with marketing, and by extension, social marketing.

Social marketing moves beyond the simplistic thinking of only using a PSA, often untested, to a mix of principles and theories for creating messages and methods of delivering those messages. Have you ever heard of the PSA "This is your brain. This is a drug. This is your brain on drugs. Any questions?" This PSA was launched by the Partnership for a Drug-Free America. The message saturated US television starting in 1987 with a person frying eggs. For a brief time, the message became a cultural icon, with t-shirts sporting the message. Then came the parodies of the message in print, television, and music recordings. The message lives on in the Museum of Television Broadcasting and the Smithsonian, as well as various sites on the Internet.

The question is whether or not the "This is your brain on drugs" message was effective. There is disagreement on the assessment. There is evidence to support awareness and comprehension, but little to support behavior change. In fact, many in the target audience found the message amusing rather than persuasive (Alexander, 2000). One problem was the campaign lacked a theoretical focus. Instead, the emphasis was a catchy phrase and visuals. We can agree that there was success on some level, as the message spread like a virus through the popular culture. But as the message spread, it became less effective as a warning or behavioral deterrent and more effective as entertainment. Later, anti-drug campaigns shifted focus to coping strategies such as how a child could say no to drugs. According to the Government Accountability Office, US government-sponsored anti-drug campaigns as a whole have done little more than raise awareness (GAO, 2006). Public relations can do so much more than create awareness when designed and executed properly.

Social marketing, as with marketing and public relations, follows a multi-step process. We can use a five-step process from these allied fields as a base for social marketing: scanning, formative research, program development, implementation, and evaluation. *Scanning* includes efforts to search the environment for information. The search is designed to find information that suggests possible problems or opportunities that should be addressed. Social marketers are looking for negative consequences that are in need of remediation. *Formative research* is a thorough analysis of the potential problem or opportunity. Formative research provides the evidence needed to develop the remainder of the social marketing effort. Data collected in formative research include specifying the target audience, understanding the segments, and developing specific objectives.

The data generated in formative research is used in *program development*. Planning documents are created to guide the project and to develop the messages for the social marketing effort. Public relations people gravitate toward the creative aspect of program development. However, creating effective messages is a complex process. Effective practitioners do not just come together and start generating ideas. Creativity must be guided by research and planning if it is to be useful. Program development can include pre-testing a message to ascertain how the target segments might react to it. The last element of program development is distributing the messages.

Once the target segments have been exposed to the message and the campaign is completed, evaluative research can begin. *Evaluative research* answers the question "Did it work?" For social marketing, the ultimate concern is did the desired behavior change occur. Monitoring is another element of evaluative research. Monitoring is research conducted during the campaign to determine if the desired effects are being achieved. If there are problems, the social marketing effort can be modified and, hopefully, its effectiveness improved. Evaluation demands a measurable objective. We cannot judge success if we do not have a standard for success or failure. Specific, measurable objectives are the standards used to assess success or failure. (For more information on objectives, see chapter 4.)

Theoretical Guidance for Social Marketing

Though connected to public relations, social marketing is an important topic in health communication. Both fields share a desire to better understand how to precipitate positive social change. A number of theoretical frameworks for structuring social marketing efforts are discussed in the health communication literature. This chapter will discuss three of those theories to illustrate the strategic nature of social marketing: (1) the theory of planned behavior, (2) the extended parallel process model, and (3) the trans-theoretical model of behavior change. These three theories provide a mechanism for organizing and guiding social marketing efforts.

Theory of planned behavior

The theory of planned behavior (TPB) is an extension of the theory of reasoned action (TRA). TRA argues that behavior intention is a function of one's own attitude and one's subjective norm. A subjective norm is composed of how those important to you view the behavior. Common sources of subjective norms are peers and family. Research can identify both attitudes and subjective norms, making behavioral prediction more accurate. The relative importance of attitude and subjective norm to a behavior can vary. Moreover, social marketers must consider the need to address subjective norms as well as attitudes in their campaign efforts. In TRA, behavior change can be a function of attitude change, normative change (subjective norm), or a shift in the relative weight of attitude or subjective norm (O'Keefe, 2002).

TPB adds perceived behavioral control (PBC) to the behavior prediction and change equation. Essentially, PBC is the degree of difficulty or ease of performing a behavior. PBC is strongly associated with *self-efficacy*, a person's belief that she or he can perform a behavior. The greater the sense of PBC, the more likely a person is to engage in a behavior. Perceptions of resources and obstacles shape a person's PBC. Resources are factors that facilitate the desired behavior (O'Keefe, 2002). Examples of resources include knowledge and training. Obstacles are factors that block a desired behavior. Examples of obstacles include money and lack of knowledge or skills. It stands to reason people are less likely to attempt a behavior if they think that behavior is difficult and that they are likely to fail when attempting to enact the behavior. Social marketers must assess PBC and factor it into their campaign design efforts.

Extended parallel process model

The extended parallel process model (EPPM) provides guidance for designing effective health messages, including those used in social marketing. EPPM uses the notion of fear appeals. A *fear appeal* warns people that bad things will happen if they do not engage in the desired behavior. A fear appeal needs a threat – something bad will happen – and a recommended response that will help to avoid the threat. An example would be people dying because they do not monitor their blood pressure (threat), so monitor your blood pressure (recommended response).

A fear appeal triggers a cognitive appraisal (Leventhal, 1970). People think about the fear and decide to use either a fear control or danger control process. A *fear control* process involves people trying to control the fear by such measures as avoiding it. A *danger control* process involves people seeking to alleviate the danger. People engage in behaviors designed to reduce the threat. Social marketing messages should promote danger control (Witte, Meyer, & Martell, 2001).

EPPM explains how people evaluate threats and how those evaluations shape behaviors. Social marketing messages trigger two evaluations: threat and efficacy. The appraisal of these two factors will shape if the person responds with the fear process or control process. People appraise a threat for perceived susceptibility and perceived severity. *Perceived susceptibility* determines if the threat can affect them. *Perceived severity* is the amount of danger the threat possesses. People will not react to a social marketing message if the threat is not serious and/or they feel the threat will not affect them. People are motivated to act when the threat can affect them and/or is serious. Motivation is a function of the perceived threat (Witte, Meyer, & Martell, 2001).

If people are motivated, they then assess the efficacy of the recommended response. People evaluate both the efficacy of the recommended response (response efficacy) and their self-efficacy relative to that response. *Response efficacy* determines whether or not people believe the recommended response will actually avoid the threat. If the people do not believe a recommended response will work, they will not follow the advice. *Self-efficacy* is whether or not people believe they can enact the recommended response. When response efficacy and self-efficacy are high, people try to enact the recommended response (danger control). If either or both are low, people will try to control the risk through denial or avoidance (fear control) (Witte, Meyer, & Martell, 2001). EPPM explicates how fear can be used successfully in a social marketing effort.

Trans-theoretical model of behavior change

The trans-theoretical model of behavior change (TTM) is unique because it views behavior change as occurring over time. The temporal aspect of TTM results in five stages:

1 *Precontemplation stage:* the person has no intention of changing behaviors in the near future (typically in the next six months).
2 *Contemplation:* the person thinks about making a change in the next six months.
3 *Preparation:* a person is planning a behavior change in the next six months but may not know how to create the desired change successfully.
4 *Action:* a person takes action designed to make changes.
5 *Maintenance:* a person works to prevent a relapse and keep the gains she or he has made (Prochaska & Velicer, 1997).

The second aspect of TTM is process of change. Researchers have concentrated their study on ten processes:

1 *Consciousness raising:* people need to understand the negative consequences of a behavior and the benefits of a change.
2 *Dramatic relief:* people must experience the emotions and feelings associated with the problem behavior.
3 *Self-reevaluation:* people assess their self-image with and without the problem behavior.
4 *Environmental reevaluation:* people assess how the presence or absence of the problem behavior affects their social environment.
5 *Self-liberation:* people decide they can change and commit to the change.
6 *Social liberation:* people must increase the opportunity for non-problem behaviors.
7 *Counter-conditioning:* people must learn to substitute a healthy behavior for the problem behavior.
8 *Stimulus control:* people attempt to remove stimuli connected to the problem behavior and replace them with cues for the healthy behavior.
9 *Provides consequences* for engaging in or avoiding the problem behavior.
10 *Helping relationships:* others support people's attempts to change (Patten, Vollman, & Thurston, 2000).

Social marketers must appreciate how the ten processes fit with the five stages when designing their efforts.

This section was designed to give you a quick taste of the theories utilized in social marketing. The idea was to illustrate three commonly used frameworks for developing social marketing efforts. Social marketing should be a strategic effort guided by theory, not just some public service announcements blasted at people. The sophistication of the social marketing theories is further evidence of evolution from the often simplistic public information campaigns of the 1950s and 1960s.

Sponsors of Social Marketing

It would be remiss to discuss social marketing without considering where the money comes from to create the messages. In most cases social marketing messages are carried in the media free of charge. But it costs money to create professional messages. Most often, the government and private voluntary organizations (PVOs) are the sponsors of social marketing efforts. Government money drives many governmental and PVO-created social marketing efforts. The Ad Council, a PVO, provides talent to many national campaigns in the US. The Ad Council uses volunteers from the communication industries to create messages for select campaigns. They are selected because of limited time and resources – the Ad Council cannot cover all social issues in the US.

Some PVOs use their own funds. Environmental Defense, for instance, uses PSAs on radio, television, magazines, newspapers, billboards, and the Internet to lead people to their website for fighting global warming. The American Institute of Certified Public Accountants uses the same media mix to teach people financial literacy, including the value of saving money. At times, social marketing can blur into advocacy by an activist group. Consider the above example of global warming. Some people would see this as advocacy because they do not believe the problem is real, while others see it as addressing an important societal concern.

Corporations become involved through funding, but can also take more direct roles in social marketing campaigns by running their own campaigns and by supporting marketing efforts on related causes. Since it is solely related to social marketing, we present a discussion of cause marketing in box 8. 4. Tobacco (e.g., Philip Morris USA) and alcohol (e.g., Anheuser-Busch) companies run their social marketing efforts related to underage smoking and drinking, drunk driving, and responsible consumption of alcohol. Below, we examine the motivations behind these efforts.

Reflections

Saying that social marketing is pro-social can result in people not reflecting and examining the practice in greater detail. It is "doing good" for society, so everything must be okay. We suspend critical judgment because the outcomes benefit society. While social marketing does seek to help society, there are two

Box 8.4   Cause Marketing

Have you ever bought a product and a percent of what you paid was given to charity? If so, you have participated in cause marketing. In cause marketing a corporation works with a charity by linking donations to purchases (Dean, 2003/2004). A corporation donates a specific amount of money or products to a charitable cause each time a customer makes a purchase. An example is the Red Campaign. By buying products or services, consumers help to provide AIDS drugs to African AIDS patients. Corporations including the Gap, Motorola, Emporio Armani, Hallmark, Converse, Apple, and American Express have agreed to donate a percent of the income generated by certain products or services to the Global Fund. The people at the Global Fund buy the AIDS drugs and distribute them to African patients in need. The idea is that consumers use their purchases to make the world a better place.

Cause marketing is designed to help all of the three key actors: customers, charities, and corporations. Customers receive their desired product or service and know their purchases helped others. Purchases serve a social benefit as well as an instrumental benefit to consumers. It is a way to feel good about your purchase: you get the I-Pod and patients in need get medicine. The charities benefit because they receive donations. The donations are typically monetary, but could be goods as well. The corporation benefits from sales and reputation. The corporations will make some money from the sale of the cause marketing products or services, but less than they normally would. Constituents should think more positively about the corporation (a more favorable reputation) because the corporation is helping society through a charity (Dean, 2003/2004). If constituents like a particular charity, they might extend that liking to the corporations that support that charity. For cause marketing, guilt by association is a positive.

related issues for reflection: (1) Who benefits from social marketing? and (2) Who creates the social marketing efforts?

Who benefits from social marketing?

The simple answer to this question is society. But society is a vague concept. In reality, specific elements of society, the target audience, benefit from social marketing. As Salmon (1989) recognizes, social change is value laden. Not all problems in a society receive attention. So there is an issue of who receives attention and who is ignored or marginalized. As the research in health campaigns reveals, those of low socioeconomic status are at the greatest risk of health problems, but campaigns benefit the healthy rich, reflecting the gap between rich and poor (Dutta-Bergman, 2005). Marginalized groups find their powerlessness extends even to social marketing efforts. Societal improvements rarely include helping those who may need help the most.

Charles Salmon (1989), an expert on campaigns, noted "social marketing efforts necessarily comprise certain values and interests, often individual freedoms, in order to promote values and interests deemed more socially, economically, or morally compelling by the organization sponsoring the change" (p. 20). Salmon is concerned that freedom can be lost when we seek pro-social changes. Seatbelt laws are a perfect example. Some people see seatbelt laws as an infringement on their freedom. They are no longer free to drive without a seatbelt. The point is we must be sure to balance the benefits and costs of social corrections and not accept changes blindly.

Social marketing is a frame for explaining social issues. By promoting a solution, social marketing messages are defining the problem. Perhaps there is an agenda behind the social marketing effort. McLaren (2000) notes how major environmental problems were reduced to simple littering in the 1970s. Was properly disposing of trash really going to solve the major environmental concerns of the day? McLaren is very critical of social marketing: according to her, it is "concerned more with public relations than the purported cause" (para. 6). Let us say that public relations is used improperly as substance over style. Her point is that social marketing can be a symbolic action designed to create quiescence. People take some small action and believe they have helped to solve a much larger problem when in fact they have not.

Imagine you are watching television. A message appears talking about a vaccine that can "protect against 4 types of human papillomavirus (HPV): 2 types that cause 70 percent of cervical cancer cases, and 2 more types that cause 90 percent of genital warts cases" (Important, n.d.). The message goes on to urge young women to get the vaccine to protect themselves. You might assume you have seen a PSA that was part of a social marketing effort to reduce cervical cancer. In reality you were exposed to part of a marketing campaign by Merck, the manufacturer of Gardasil, the vaccine shown to reduce the risk of cervical cancer. There is some debate over the side effects from Gardasil and concern about longer-term effects from the vaccine, but there is support for the vaccination from the Centers for Disease Control (CDC) in the US and the National Cancer Institute. Given that Merck is promoting a public health concern, should this be considered a social marketing campaign even though there is a strong link to selling a product? There are times when the line between product marketing and social marketing becomes very blurry. Such blurring is problematic when people pursue a behavior thinking it is in their interest when corporate interests really are the big driver. We are not saying that is the case with Gardasil. Instead, we use the case to remind people to be critical consumers of social marketing messages. Corporations may not always have your interests as the highest priority.

Who creates the social marketing efforts?

Rarely are target audiences involved in the creation of social marketing efforts. Social marketing suffers from the same sender-orientation that plagues other public relations endeavors. Some group or organization decides what social concern to address and how to address it. The more powerful organizations control the social marketing efforts, resulting in voicelessness for the powerless. In turn, the "real" problems are often overlooked or the solution is simply cosmetic, helping only a limited range of high-profile victims. Underlying problems and those in deep trouble remain out of sight and out of mind. We are not saying social marketing does no good. The concern is whether or not it does enough good and *whose* good. We believe social marketing can do more and for more people.

Dutta-Bergman (2005) strongly advocates doing more for more. He argues that social marketing does not address changing structures that would promote greater social change. Structures refer to the capabilities to provide basic resources such as food, shelter, and clothing. Public relations can be used to mobilize a community so that they can work together to resolve structural problems and improve the community as a whole, not just select parts of the community. Rakow (1989) makes a similar point. Public relations facilitates collective action by providing a conduit by which people can discuss issues and participate in decision making. We should consider how public relations can be used to develop such empowering collaborations designed to remove structural barriers. We believe a close examination of existing activist efforts to address such concerns may yield insights and potential models for future actions.

Social marketing must also return to its roots of audience focus by taking a cultural-centered approach, especially when global action is required. International efforts should not reflect Western values but be embedded in the values of the culture being served. The marginalized must be given a voice in the definition of the problem and development of the solution (Dutta-Bergman, 2005). This point is the intersection of who benefits and who creates social marketing. First, we need to expand the target audience to include the marginalized who are in need but frequently ignored in social marketing. This would involve considering a wider scope of social problems. Second, those in the target audiences should be part of the process. As with risk communication (see chapter 11), those impacted by the public relations efforts should be involved in the process. Their insights should improve the effectiveness of the social marketing efforts.

A final point to consider in this reflection is the idea of competition in marketing. Products and services have competition, others jockeying for attention and use. Frequently, competition is overlooked in social marketing. Because an effort is pro-social, we think that no one argues against it. However, factors do conspire to prevent social change, otherwise it would be easy to accomplish. Hence, there is competition. Forces in people's lives work against social marketing efforts, including the opinions and actions of significant people in our lives. For instance, the theory of reasoned action argues that subjective norms influence how people will behave. Subjective norms include what people close to the person think about the desired behavior (Albarracin et al., 2001). For example, a person is unlikely to stop smoking if friends and family members view smoking positively and are unsupportive of efforts to stop.

However, we can look to the roots of social marketing for competition as well. Marketing can create undesirable consequences (Hastings & Saren, 2003). Let us return to cigarettes and alcohol as an example. Both products are legal for adults but can produce serious health consequences. That is why governments, including the US and the UK, carefully monitor and restrict the marketing of cigarettes and loosely monitor alcohol marketing efforts. However, US tobacco companies make extensive social marketing efforts against teen smoking and alcohol companies engage in similar efforts against underage drinking. Why? The answer is that their advertising and marketing campaigns are seen as targeting this "illegal" constituency. By spending significant amounts of money on high-profile anti-youth consumption efforts, the companies can argue they are trying to solve the problem, not creating it.

Such social marketing efforts are part issues management and part reputation management. If the tobacco and alcohol companies are addressing the problems on their own, there is no need for additional government intervention. The social marketing is part of an effort to self-regulate, thereby precluding additional regulation of the industries. (Preventing regulation is pursued further in the discussion of issues management in chapter 10.) Moreover, tobacco and alcohol companies can use the social marketing to bolster their reputations. This is no small task given they are known as sin industries and hazard industries. Still, they are legal industries that attempt to construct favorable reputations in part by addressing social problems they have helped to create. But if you are managing a reputation, that last part is not a featured element of your messages. When a corporation is involved in a social concern, look closely to determine if the interest is self-preservation or societal beneficence.

Conclusion

If we call something social marketing it has to be good. Right? The answer is yes and no. Because social marketing is pro-social it should be doing some good for someone in society. The question is how much good, for whom, and which good. Social marketing messages should lead us to think about the social problem. People must consider if the real problem is being addressed, if more could and should be done, and who benefits from the program and who does not. Social marketing may do good, but it may include some harm if we assume a complex problem is solved by a simple solution. Granted, some problems are simple to solve: wear your seatbelt and learn how to install a child's car seat properly. But other social problems are complex. Social marketing messages should sometimes act to stimulate further discussion of a social problem and not end it. Critically examine the social messages you encounter to determine if the solution is really effective or simply a distraction from the real problems.

Case Study: Deleting Online Sexual Predators

Today, children and parents generally accept the Internet as a part of life. Young people heavily use the Internet for social networking and parents hope the children will also use the Internet as a research tool for schoolwork. In the US. an amazing 61 percent of 13–17 year olds have a personal profile on a social networking site. About half the users post pictures of themselves on these sites. Unfortunately, there is more involved here than innocent fun and sharing information with friends. Social networking sites have also become the location of choice for child predators. Teen girls face the greatest risk. The odds are 1 in 7 that a youth will receive a sexual solicitation or be approached via the Internet. Of those solicitations, 70 percent target girls (Online, n.d.).

Starting in 2004, the US Department of Justice and the National Center for Missing & Exploited Children partnered to address the plague of online sexual exploitation. The first round of messages targeted parents. The message objective was to make parents aware of the dangers their children faced online. One message contained the story of 12-year-old Janine Marks who went to meet a "boy" she met in a chat room at the mall. It was an adult predator, not a boy. Janine was not harmed, but the story reinforced the tagline, "Every day, children are sexually solicited online." Other messages included a sheet of abbreviations to help parents understand the messages their children were sending and the chilling reminder that the Internet can allow predators into our homes. The first set of messages encouraged parents to monitor more carefully and to get involved in their children's online activities. Ad Council research found that parents were significantly more likely to talk to their children about online chatting if they had seen the PSA (Results, n.d.).

The second round of messages targeted teens to warn them of the dangers of forming relationships online with people they really do not know. The focus was on the dangers of posting personal information and photographs. As one line states, "Think before you post" while the tag line says, "Don't believe the type." Young girls are reminded that most of what they post can be seen by predators. The emphasis has been on young girls since they are the primary victims of online predators. The website linked to the campaign provides advice on ways to avoid dangers online and advice on how to detect when a predator is pretending to be a youth. There is even an interactive game called "ID the Creep" that reinforces the warning and skills the social marketing effort is trying to convey to youths (Online, n.d.). Online sexual predators are a problem and efforts such as these are designed to improve society by making the online experience less dangerous for children.

Case questions

1 Visit the NetSmartz website sponsored by the National Center for Missing & Exploited Children at www.netsmartz. org/. Compare the messages directed toward parents and guardians, educators, law enforcement, teens, and kids. What resources at the site seem consistent with ideas discussed in this chapter?

2 Discuss how the five steps (scanning, formative research, program development, implementation, and evaluation) were used – or could be used – in the deleting online sexual predators case.

3 Consider how the three theoretical frameworks for structuring social marketing efforts could be applied to this case:

theory of planned behavior, extended parallel process model, and trans-theoretical model of behavior change. Is one a better fit with the goals of the program than the others? Why?

4 Explain how outcome objectives could be used in this case.

5 Go online to view examples of current PSAs related to online exploitation (enter search terms like "online sexual predator").

The Ad Council, the National Center for Missing & Exploited Children, and the US Department of Justice often partner to produce these PSAs. Compare these to PSAs sponsored by Facebook or Myspace. Why might these two social networking sites partner with organizations like the National Center for Missing & Exploited Children to create PSAs related to online predators?

Discussion Questions

1 What is social marketing? How does it differ from traditional marketing?

2 Develop an example to illustrate how the four P's (product, price, place, and promotion) from the traditional "marketing mix" can be applied to social marketing efforts.

3 Describe how the five steps (scanning, formative research, program development, implementation, and evaluation) could be applied to a hypothetical social marketing campaign.

4 Distinguish between the three theoretical frameworks for structuring social marketing efforts: theory of planned behavior, extended parallel process model, and trans-theoretical model of behavior change. Identify examples to illustrate how they could be used to guide the development of social marketing efforts.

5 Identify examples of contemporary social marketing campaigns. How have the campaigns used traditional media and online media? How effective do you perceive these to be? Have you ever been influenced by social marketing?

6 Examine current social marketing efforts. How easy is it to identify the sources of the messages? Critically evaluate the message sources and message contents to assess if they seem to be promoting a health concern or selling a product.

7 Suppose you wanted to develop a social marketing campaign at your school. What issues might social marketing efforts address? What behaviors would you like to change? Select one specific idea and discuss how would you implement this social marketing effort.

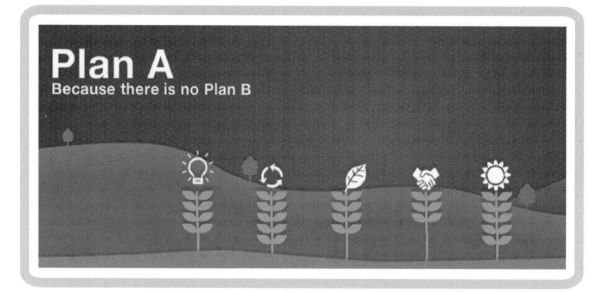

"Plan A because there is no Plan B" – Marks & Spencer publicity.
REPRODUCED BY KIND PERMISSION OF MARKS AND SPENCER PLC

9

Reputation Management

Each March people eagerly look to see who made the cover of *Fortune* magazine when the "America's Most Admired Companies" issue is released. It is a point of honor to be ranked number 1 and be featured on the cover. Inside the magazine are the full rankings, complete with who is moving up and who is dropping down the list. The issue now includes the 50 "Most Admired Global Companies" as well. The "Most Admired Companies" is one of the first and most recognized indicators of corporate reputation and relies heavily on financial performance factors. The concept of reputation and the need for reputation management seems to increase in stature each year.

Unlike social marketing, reputation management is dominated by a corporate-centric perspective. The bias toward using financial factors to assess reputations supports this corporate-centric evaluation of reputations. It is interesting how reputation, roughly defined as how constituents perceive an organization, has quickly moved from the periphery to the center of business and public relations thinking. This dramatic shift is a direct result of researchers documenting the many benefits that accrue from a positive "corporate reputation." Moreover, the conceptualization of reputation began with a financial focus and has slowly progressed to include a strong social component as well.

Of course, the principles of reputation management can be modified and applied to any type of organization, but the vast bulk of the research centers on corporate reputation. Public relations is pivotal in efforts intended to influence how constituents perceive an organization – in determining its reputation. This chapter documents the development and evolution of reputation management by examining the transition from image to reputation, illustrating the reputation management process, and considering how reputations are measured.

From Image to Reputation: The Quest for Respectability

In 2001, Hutton, Goodman, Alexander, and Genest proclaimed that reputation could be the new face of public relations. Given the current acceptance of reputation as a core element of management, this does not seem startling. However, if we were to go back to the 1980s and early 1990s, the statement would have been very controversial. By reviewing the history of reputation in public relations we gain a greater appreciation for how reputation management is practiced today.

The earliest discussions of reputations emerged in the 1950s and 1960s with the works of Kenneth Boulding and Martineau (1958). Back then, the term *image* was in vogue rather than reputation. These earlier works noted that different stakeholder groups would view organizations differently, that an image (reputation) has dimensions, and that an image (reputation) is a result of information stakeholders receive about an organization. Interestingly, many public relations researchers in the 1980s seemed to think they had "discovered" the idea that reputations were multi-dimensional and varied by stakeholders. In reality, public relations was reinventing a wheel created nearly two decades earlier. The important point to remember is that these early observations about image remain salient in today's reputation management discussions.

So why did public relations have so little interest in the development of images, and later, reputations? It seems odd indeed that public relations was not more central to the development of reputation management given the focus on stakeholder perceptions. The term *image* itself was frequently viewed as problematic in public relations. Important figures in both public relations practice and research expressed distaste for the term. Edward Bernays (practitioner) and James Grunig (researcher) felt image was too shallow and should be avoided. Their views reflect what Botan (1993) refers to as the instrumental view of image. The instrumental view of image treats image as "a manipulative representation often lacking substance or accuracy" (p. 72). The instrumental image is a false front projected by management and designed to manipulate how people perceive and react to the organization. An image is a triumph of style over substance. An organization "is" whatever it claims to be, free of the tethers of reality. As the field of public relations was struggling for legitimacy, many experts felt it was best to steer clear of image and the baggage associated with the term.

The problem with avoiding image is that it also had a more relevant conceptualization for public relations: that images are subjective knowledge about an entity (Botan, 1993). This view of image is what eventually became known as reputation. Loosely, a *reputation* is how constituents perceive an organization. In more technical terms, a reputation is the *aggregate evaluation constituents make about how well an organization is meeting constituent expectations based on its past behaviors* (Rindova & Fombrun, 1999; Wartick, 1992). The key factor is that a reputation is an *evaluation* constituents make about an organization's performance. Constituencies vary in what standards they use for making evaluations of reputation, a point we will return to when we discuss measurement issues. The focus on constituency perceptions places constituencies in a position of power – their perceptions decide the reputation. Hence, a substantive view of reputation requires corporations to treat constituencies in a way deemed appropriate by the constituencies. This point will echo throughout this chapter.

Marketing researchers were much quicker to see the potential in this more substantive view of image. Their research moved the field toward a richer understanding of image that evolved into reputation management. Several pieces of evidence support the dominance of marketing in the development of reputation management. A review of the primary public relations journals finds scant research on image or crisis prior to 2000. What research there is does little to advance our thinking of reputation much beyond what was known in the 1990s. If we examine the marketing literature we can see a very different picture. Researchers there are trying to operationalize reputation and both understand and document its effects on organizations. An excellent example is Fombrun's work to create the reputation quotient, the founding of the Reputation Institute in 1997, and the inauguration of the journal *Corporate Reputation Review* in 1997 as an outlet for research about reputations. Consequently, if you search the influential books published about reputation in the late 1990s and early 2000s, the titles are dominated by marketing researchers and include books such as *Fame and Fortune* (Fombrun & van Reil, 2004), *Corporate Reputation and Competitiveness* (Davies et al., 2003), and *Creating Corporate Reputations* (Dowling, 2002).

Public relations research and practice are still trying to catch up and establish their relevance to discussions of reputation. Oddly, practice seems to be leading research. Major public relations consulting firms embraced reputation and began conducting their own research before academic researchers. This could be because the practitioners saw the economic value of understanding reputations and offering that service to their clients. Again, it seems strange that public relations has been so far removed from reputation management. Public relations seems well positioned to address concerns of constituency perceptions of the organization. Given the nature of the field, public relations should be able to shed light on what those perceptions are, how they were formed, and what can be done in efforts to change those perceptions. Instead, public relations is subjected to public comments such as reputation being "too important" to leave to public relations. Given public relations' late appreciation for reputation management, that might be an apt comment. Still, public relations does have knowledge and skills that can aid reputation management. It needs to work harder to refine and present those ideas to a broader audience.

Reputation management: the value

As alluded to above, corporations have shown a growing interest in reputation because of the many benefits it can yield. A reputation is an intangible asset, meaning no one can touch it but it still has value. There is no single, accepted way to calculate the value of a reputation. However, research has connected to a number of valued outcomes for organizations (Alsop, 2004; Carmeli, 2004; Davies et al., 2003; Dowling, 2002; Fombrun & van Riel, 2004). Among the benefits a positive reputation can bring to an organization are:

- Attracting customers
- Motivating employees
- Generating investment interest
- Increasing job satisfaction
- Garnering positive comments from financial analysts
- Generating positive news media coverage
- Attracting top employee talent
- Improving financial performance

By anyone's standards reputation represents an impressive collection of corporate benefits. Reputation is an asset that stretches across a variety of constituents, including employees, investors, customers, and the media. It would seem that constituents are drawn to a positive reputation and more likely to enter into mutually influential relationships. A favorable reputation makes a corporate public relations person's job much easier.

However, a positive reputation is a double-edged sword. Yes, it provides advantages to a corporation, but it serves as a weakness, too. Management invests a great deal in a positive reputation, so they want to protect this investment or asset. Constituents who can threaten the reputation asset are seen as a threat. Moreover, constituencies are also the final arbiters of reputation – they decide if a reputation is positive or not. Constituents can derive power from the ability to damage a corporation's reputation and to render an unfavorable evaluation.

Reflect back on chapter 5 and the way activists used public relations, such as promoting boycotts, to pressure corporations into change. In general, public relations efforts such as boycotts cause change because they threaten a reputation, not because people stop buying a product or using a service. The boycott is a publicity point used to make other constituents aware of inappropriate or unacceptable behavior by a corporation. As other constituencies learn about the corporation's unsavory behavior, their evaluations of the corporation's reputation declines. Corporations that trade on their reputations frequently must negotiate with constituents as a means of protecting their reputation assets. For example, Yum! Brands and McDonald's now pay a penny more a pound (behavior change) to the Immokalee workers who pick their tomatoes because of concerns over their reputation, not because of any financial threats the workers posed. It is rare that an asset can be so beneficial yet be such a source of vulnerability for a corporation. The fact that reputations are composed of constituency evaluations is what makes reputation assets so volatile.

Reputation seems to relate well to social capital. Recall, social capital is a function of social networks and the benefits derived from those relations. A positive reputation attracts constituents and makes it easier to form relationships with them. For instance, potential supporters are more likely to affiliate themselves with an entity they view positively than one they dislike or know little about. Moreover, positive relationships are a sign of healthy relationships in the web of relationships. A favorable relationship would indicate current constituents are predisposed to helping an organization by providing resources. You are much more likely to help a neighbor you know and like than one you hardly know or one you dislike.

Reputation management: the process

Reputations are built on the information constituents receive about an organization, hence they are built through the constituent-corporation relationship (Fombrun & van Riel, 2004). While the focus is on corporations, the process holds for how people form reputations about any type of organization, including activist organizations. Reputations are formed through the various ways constituents experience a corporation. We can divide the information received (i.e., the ways corporations are experienced) into four categories: (1) interactions with the organization, (2) controlled messages from an organization, (3) uncontrolled media reports about an organization, and (4) second-hand information from other people (Balmer & Soenen, 1995; Meijer, 2004; Money & Hillenbrand, 2006).

Interactions with the organization would include buying a product or using a service. The individual has a first-hand experience with the organization. Controlled messages are those sent by an organization and include advertising, websites, brochures, newsletters, and packaging. Constituents realize controlled messages will serve the self-interests of the organization.

Most of the information constituencies receive about organizations is derived through the news media. As discussed in chapter 6 on media relations, a great deal of news media reports are stimulated and shaped by public relations efforts. Still, the news media messages often appear to have less of a self-interest motivation than the controlled messages. After all, the news media selected the content, or so it might seem. Because so much information is delivered via the news media it is an important component of reputation management (Carroll, 2004; Carroll & McCombs, 2003; Meijer, 2004). The risk of negative publicity damaging a reputation is also great, once more providing power for constituencies. Carroll's (2004) research found that the news media influence reputations through agenda setting. News media coverage influences which organizations people think about (the first-level agenda setting effect) and what attributes they use to evaluate an organization's reputation (the second-level agenda setting effect). This is consistent with the ideas about framing discussed in chapter 6. The news coverage shapes people's interpretations and subsequent evaluations of organizations.

Meijer (2004) uses priming and issue-ownership theory to expand on the value of news reports to reputation formation. *Priming* in reputation management involves the news media telling people what points are important for forming an organization's reputation. People prefer short cuts, or heuristics, when making evaluations rather than trying to sift through all the information they know about an organization. Meijer's data revealed that the more the news media reported on an issue, the more people used that issue when making evaluations about an organization's reputation. News media coverage primes people to utilize certain issues when evaluating an organization. This parallels Carroll's research on the second-level agenda setting effect.

Issue-ownership theory is premised on using issues that favor an organization. If an organization rates favorably on an issue, it owns that issue. An organization's reputation will be more positive if the news media cover issues an organization owns. Meijer (2004) found that news stories about organizations frequently mention issues. Suppose an organization is known for sustainability efforts. When news stories mention sustainability and the organization, the organization's reputation should be enhanced. Issue-ownership theory involves two parts. First, the news story makes an issue salient. Second, the salient issue shapes evaluations of the organization/its reputation.

Second-hand information centers on word-of-mouth. Constituencies have a variety of ways to tell others how they feel about an organization. As discussed in chapter 7, online social media such as blogs and social networking sites are increasingly being used to shape reputations. Remember how an entire industry has developed to help organizations track and monitor what constituencies are saying about them online. As with news media, agenda setting, priming, and issue-ownership theory can help to explain how second-hand messages influence reputation. Add to that the fact that word-of-mouth messages, especially from trusted sources, have proven to be powerful persuaders (Brown & Reingen, 1987; Schlosser, 2005).

Following the dynamic outlined above, a *favorable reputation* occurs when constituents receive largely positive information and have positive experiences with an organization. Constituents take the information they collect and compare it to some standard for organizational performance. Skilled reputation managers have tried to influence not only the information the constituents receive but also their standards for evaluation. The comparison allows constituents to determine whether or not an organization is meeting its expectations (standards). Essentially, constituents are trying to determine if an organization exhibits the values that are important to them. Meeting expectations should translate into positive reputations. When expectations are not met, expectation gaps occur and result in negative reputations. Expectation gaps and negative reputations are problematic for organizations (Reinchart, 2003). Not only do "negative" organizations miss out on the benefits of a reputation, but they also are more susceptible to additional reputation damage (Coombs & Holladay, 2004).

Constituencies may be indifferent, however. They may choose to ignore the expectation gaps and continue their relationship with an organization. They also may privately express their concerns to the organization in hopes of creating change. However, two unpleasant reactions can occur. First, constituents may choose to end their relationship with the organization. Thus the organization loses some resources and support. Second, constituents may become outraged and publicly oppose the organization. The opposition is designed to punish the organization and try to force it to change its ways. As described in chapter 6 on media relations, conflict is a news value and journalists may report on conflicts between organizations and constituencies.

Another way researchers and practitioners discuss expectation gaps is through the concept of alignment. *Alignment* occurs when the expectations of the constituencies and the behaviors of the organization are in sync. For instance, many of the customers at the Body Shop appreciate the organization's commitment to sustainability. Customer expectations align with the organization's behavior. Misalignment can occur in different ways and is illustrated in figure 9.1. *Fundamental misalignment* is when the organization's actions do not reflect the expectations of the constituency – the organization is not living the desired values. The organization must change to meet expectations and/or work to alter constituency expectations. *Perceptual misalignment* is when the constituents do not realize that the organization is living the desired values. In this situation the organization's behaviors actually match constituent values and expectations, only the constituents are not aware of this. The organization must try to locate the barriers preventing their desired messages reaching constituencies and improve on how it communicates its behaviors to constituencies. Reputation managers must vigilantly monitor the reputation for any expectation gaps, work to identify emerging gaps, and seek to facilitate alignment.

However, we must resist thinking there is one, monolithic reputation for an organization. Because different constituencies can employ different criteria for evaluating an organization, this can produce a diversity of reputations. Moreover, even those in the same constituency group can receive differing information, have different experiences, or perceive similar information or experiences differently. Yes, the term *different* was overused in the last sentence, but the repetition was necessary to make the point. That is why a reputation is an aggregate of constituent perceptions. An *aggregate* means that a number of evaluations are combined and averaged. With any aggregate data there are variations among the individual respondents but the average is used to inform decision making.

Effective reputation management

With the evolution from image to reputation there has been a shift in what constitutes effective reputation management. In general there has been a shift from

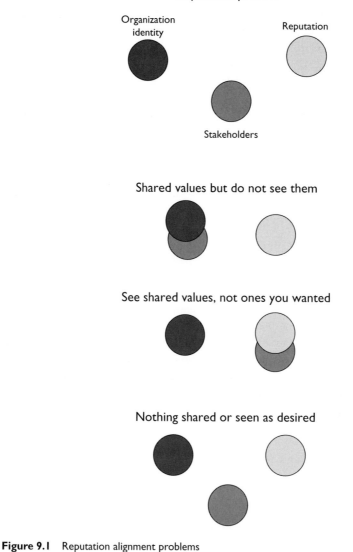

Figure 9.1 Reputation alignment problems

image making to reputation management. Image involved organizations crafting the desired image they wanted. Again, the image could be divorced from reality and the behaviors of an organization. Reputation places greater emphasis on the constituents. Constituents define the reputation. Granted, organizations can influence the constituent perceptions that are reputations. Still, organizations must be cognizant of how they are being viewed and the actions upon which those perceptions are predicated.

Effective reputation management is a matter of identity-reputation alignment. The reputation fits with the desired organizational identity. *Organizational identity* is conceptualized as how people in an organization define that organization – who the organization thinks it is. Management should select an identity that will (1) be beneficial to the organization and (2) reflect the organization's behaviors and values (Dowling, 2002). When constituents "see" the organization the way the organization "sees" itself, there is *identity-reputation alignment.*

Organizations should benefit from this alignment. If constituents perceive the organization as desired, the reputation should be positive and constituents will react to the organization favorably. We use the phrase *should be* for a reason. Constituencies must feel that the reputation is desirable. That is to say, constituents must respond favorably to the identity chosen by the organization and communicated to the constituencies. Identity and reputation can align, but if constituencies dislike the identity, the reputation does not benefit the organization. Ideally, the constituencies see a desirable part of themselves in the reputation and identity. There is an element of co-creation of meaning happening here. Organizations must select and communicate identities that will resonate with constituencies if they hope to reap the full benefits from a reputation. Organizations work with constituencies to discover the elements that should be in their identities. Then, communication with constituencies helps shape how that identity becomes translated into a reputation.

Another way to consider the situation is through the use of *values*: which behaviors and ends are important to people. Recall, we also discussed values in chapter 2 on the origins of ethics. Identities and reputations are reflections of values. An organizational identity should embody values that are consistent with constituents. Through communication, constituents learn the organization's values and form reputations for the organization. If the organization's values align with the constituent's values, a relationship is more likely to develop and to be maintained. The reputation is co-created with constituencies. The core values of the reputation are drawn from both the organization and the constituencies. Moreover, communication allows the organizations and constituents to form the organization's current reputation.

An extended example should help to clarify the co-creation aspect of reputation. The Cooperative Bank in the UK is known as an ethical bank. Its ethical policy states: "This is the Ethical Policy of the Cooperative Bank and smile.co.uk. It is based on extensive consultation with our customers and reflects their ethical concerns about how their money should and should not be invested. It also informs our choice of partners and suppliers." Ethical behavior is the core value and the constituents help to define what is ethical behavior. Table 9.1 lists some of the values embodied by the Cooperative Bank. The list of values includes human rights, the arms trade, corporate responsibility, genetic modification, social enterprise, ecological impact, and animal welfare.

The Cooperative Bank realizes that values change over time and seeks to stay abreast of what constituents value. It regularly seeks customer consultation and uses the information to revise the Ethical Policy. There is a link on the website for customer consultation as well as the Ethical Policy Questionnaire to solicit specific feedback about individual policies. Clearly, the Cooperative Bank is

Table 9.1　Sample values from the Cooperative Bank

Human rights
Through our investments, we seek to support the principles of the Universal Declaration of Human Rights. In line with this, we will not invest in:
- any government or business which fails to uphold basic human rights within its sphere of influence;
- any business whose links to an oppressive regime are a continuing cause for concern.

Arms trade
We will not invest in any business involved in:
- the manufacture or transfer of armaments to oppressive regimes;
- the manufacture of torture equipment or other equipment that is used in the violation of human rights.

Corporate responsibility
We advocate support for the Fundamental International Labor Organization Conventions. In line with these, we will seek to support businesses which take a responsible position with regard to:
- fair trade labor rights in their own operations and through their supply chains in developing countries. We will not support:
- irresponsible marketing practices in developing countries;
- tobacco product manufacture;
- currency speculation.

Genetic modification
We will not invest in businesses involved in the development of genetically modified organisms (GMOs), where, in particular, the following issues are evident:
- uncontrolled release of GMOs into the environment;
- any negative impacts on developing countries; in particular, the imposition of "Terminator" technologies;
- patenting; in particular, of indigenous knowledge;
- cloning; in particular, of animals for non-medical purposes.

co-creating the meaning of ethics (core values) with its customers. Since these ethics are the basis of its identity and reputation, the Cooperative Bank is co-creating its reputation with customers as well.

Obviously, the Cooperative Bank appeals to a certain type of customer, one that holds the ethical values that guide the bank. People simply wanting a strong return on their investment will not be as strongly attracted to the Cooperative Bank as those concerned about social issues. If the Cooperative Bank decided to focus on profit at the expense of ethics by ignoring human rights and other ethical policies, its core supporters would leave the bank. Profit at the expense of ethics is counter to the values of a large segment of its current customer base. A shift away from those values would alienate core customers. In turn, the ethical customers would seek out a bank more consistent with their values, a bank whose reputation embodied their view of ethics.

Reputation: measurement

There is no one, perfect measure of reputation. However, Berens and van Riel (2004) reviewed the various measures and found trust to be a core element. *Trust* involves constituents believing that the organization takes their interests into account when taking action and making decisions. We will review a few major reputation measurement systems to illustrate the dimensionality of reputations and why various constituents will perceive reputations differently. We will discuss the Reputation Quotient, *Fortune* magazine's "Most Admired" and "Best Places to Work," and the *Corporate Responsibility Officer*'s "Best Corporate Citizens." Table 9.2 lists the evaluative dimensions for each of these reputation measures.

Charles Fombrun and Harris Interactive created what was originally called the Reputation Quotient (RQ). The RQ evaluated 20 attributes grouped into six dimensions: emotional appeal, products and services, financial performance, visions and leadership, workplace environment, and social responsibility. Table 9.3 provides details for each dimension. The RQ was revised and became the RepTrak Pulse with 23 "performance indicators" clustered into seven core

Table 9.2   Evaluative dimensions for popular reputation measures

Most Admired Companies
- Innovation
- Financial soundness
- Employee talent
- Use of corporate assets
- Long-term investment potential
- Social responsibility
- Quality of management
- Quality of products/services

Best Places to Work
- Trust, includes credibility and respect
- Fairness, includes justice and equity
- Pride
- Comaraderie

100 Best Corporate Citizens
- Climate change
- Governance
- Employee relations
- Environment
- Finance
- Human rights
- Lobbying
- Philanthropy

Table 9.3   Dimensions for the Reputation Quotient (RQ)

1   Emotional appeal
- Good feeling about the company
- Admire and respect the company
- Trust the company

2   Products and services
- Stands behind products/services
- Offers high-quality products/services
- Develops innovative products/services
- Offers products/services that are good value

3   Vision and leadership
- Excellent leadership
- Clear vision for the future
- Finds and takes advantage of market opportunities

4   Social responsibility
- Supports good causes
- Environmentally friendly
- Treats people well

5   Financial performance
- Shows profitability
- Low risk investment
- Strong prospects for future growth
- Outperforms competitors

6   Workplace environment
- Well managed
- Seems like a good company to work for
- Seems like it has good employees

dimensions: products and services, innovation, workplace, governance, leadership, citizenship, and performance. The Global RepTrak is an international version of the assessment that can be adapted to the culture where a reputation is being evaluated (Company methodology, 2007). Note how financial concerns dominate both the RQ and the RepTrak. Three of the six RQ dimensions and four of the seven RepTrak dimensions are financially based. Social concerns appear in social responsibility (later, citizenship) and the workplace. The focus on financial dimensions is a common theme in the measures of reputation and reflects the corporate-centric focus of this discipline.

In the US the best-known reputation measure is *Fortune*'s annual "Most Admired Companies" list. *Fortune* also publishes a "World's Most Admired" list (formerly "Global Most Admired"). The "Most Admired" list is based on eight key attributes: innovation, financial soundness, employee talent, use of corporate assets, long-term investment value, social responsibility, quality of management, and quality of products/services. Executives, directors, and security analysts are surveyed to create the "Most Admired" list. The "Most

Admired" list has been used extensively in US-based research examining the effects of reputation on economic outcomes for organizations (e.g., Berens & van Reil, 2004; Fombrun & Shanley, 1990). Again, the dimensions are predominantly financial. Of the eight, only social responsibility does not have a strong financial bent to it. The financial focus is reflected in the survey respondents. Security analysts and directors would have the knowledge and skill necessary to evaluate the seven financially focused dimensions for the "Most Admired" survey. The evaluative dimensions and respondents are clearly corporate for the "Most Admired." This corporate-centric bias is not a criticism. Rather, it is useful to examine the assumptions of these reputation measures when we evaluate their utility and their results.

Fortune's "Best Companies to Work For" is another US-based measurement with a focus on employees. The Great Place To Work Institute compiles the "Best Companies to Work For" list by reviewing entries and surveying employees. Organizations must self-nominate and agree to participate in research in order to be considered for the list. Five dimensions are used to create the list: (1) credibility: management listens to employees and provides regular information about the organization's direction and plans; (2) respect: the employees receive the training and equipment necessary to do their jobs; (3) fairness, equitability in compensation, benefits, and promotions; (4) pride in the organization; and (5) camaraderie between employees. Credibility, respect, and fairness are all considered elements of trust (Trust, 2009).

In the UK, the "Sunday Times Best Companies to Work For" is a reputation measure with an employee orientation. Best Companies Limited administers the survey to organizations that apply. Again, there is a self-nomination process. Employees evaluate their organizations in five areas: (1) leadership: how employees feel about top management; (2) well-being, level of stress and work-life balance; (3) belonging: feelings about the organization they work for, not the people they work with; (4) giving back: how much the organization and employees give back to the community and society in general; and (5) personal growth: employees feel challenged and stretched on their jobs (Sunday Times, 2007). The two workplace-based reputation measures shift from financial to worker interests, which can result in a much different ranking of organizations when their reputation scores are compared to one another.

Finally, there is *Corporate Responsibility Officer*'s "100 Best Corporate Citizens." According to *PRWeek*, it is the third most important corporate ranking to CEOs behind the two *Fortune* magazine lists. KLD compiles the "100 Best Corporate Citizens" list based on an evaluation of company materials, media coverage, government and non-governmental organization (NGO) information, public documents, and ten global social responsibility research databases. The ratings cover the three dimensions of environment, social, and governance. The environment dimension is composed of climate change, products and services (effects on environment such as ozone depletion), and operations and management (pollution prevention, recycling, hazardous waste, regulatory problems, and emissions).

The social dimension is composed of community (charitable giving, volunteer programs, and negative economic impact), diversity (in management, promotions, work-life balance, gay and lesbian policies, and women and minority contracting), employee relations (health and safety, retirement benefits, unions, and employee involvement), human rights (labor rights and relations with indigenous people), and products (benefits to economically disadvantaged, safety, and anti-trust issues). The governance dimension includes reporting (transparency and political accountability) and structure (compensation of management and ownership) (Socrates, 2007).

The "100 Best Corporate Citizens" relies almost exclusively on social concerns with little reliance on financial. Social issues are broadly defined to include the environment, treatment of the community, and treatment of workers. The dimensions are much more constituent oriented than corporate-centric. It could be possible that the top companies on the "Most Admired" and RepTrak lists could be very different than those on the "100 Best Corporate Citizens" list. Different evaluative dimensions can result in different rankings. Still, great companies could score highly on both assessments.

Organizational reputations are perceptual evaluations. Any evaluation requires some expectations against which an organization is judged. The various dimensions assessed in the reputation measures we have reviewed here are expectations. Reputations can be based on multiple expectations/dimensions. Multiple dimensions are used to develop a richer understanding of the reputations. Organizations can vary in how people perceive the various expectations/dimensions. For instance, an organization might be viewed favorably on social concerns but unfavorably on the environment, or rated positively on financial performance but negatively on social responsibility. Having multiple expectations/dimensions allows managers to determine where their reputation is weak and needs work and where it is strong and should be maintained. Also, it should be noted that the dimensions assessed by the reputation measures may not be the ones all constituencies would value. Along the same lines, constituencies may place different weight on different dimensions rather than considering all the measurement dimensions to be equal.

The list of dimensions in table 9.3 illustrates how reputations are measured using multiple dimensions/expectations. Clearly, different constituencies can perceive the dimensions differently. Moreover, the dimensions are not relevant to all constituencies. Investors would find the RQ and "Most Admired" dimensions as salient for their evaluations. Employees, unions, communities, and some activists would see greater utility in the "Best Companies to Work for" lists, while activists, communities, and some employees would find the "100 Best Corporate Citizens" salient dimensions for making evaluations.

Another point that emerges from review of reputation measures and discussion of reputation management is how heavily corporate-oriented it is. First, all of the measures reviewed here emphasize financial rather than social concerns. Second, the research has tied reputations to corporate benefits. This is not to say the ideas cannot be adapted and applied to non-profits, charities, and NGOs. Charities and NGOs are rated by some groups. For instance, Charity Watch rates charities based on the percent of spending on charitable programs and how much money is spent to raise $100 (Criteria, n.d.). Some experts note that donations and volunteers should be drawn to non-profits with more favorable reputations. However, there is scant research in non-corporate applications of reputation management. We really do need to expand our knowledge of reputation management in the non-corporate realm.

Edelman publishes an annual Trust Barometer that assesses the level of trust people around the world place in various institutions. We include the Trust Barometer in the discussion of reputation because trust is a core element in many reputation measures (Beren & van Reil, 2004) and the research includes corporations and NGOs. The Trust Barometer covers 17 developed and developing countries. When asked, "How much do you trust each institution to do what is right?" a total of ten countries ranked NGOs the highest, while seven ranked business in general the highest. As part of their research, Edelman asked people if they heard information about a company from a list of sources, how credible would each source be. For the CEO of a company, 41 percent in developing countries and 26 percent in developed countries rated the source as credible. The credibility was higher for NGOs, as 49 percent of respondents in developing countries and 47 percent of respondents in developed countries rated the source as credible. Public relations executives scored low as a credible source of information about a company, with 27 percent in developing countries and 14 percent in developed countries rating them as credible (Edelman Trust Barometer, 2007). Globally, NGOs seemed to enjoy a fairly positive reputation. However, the Edelman Trust Barometer is very general and does not examine the reputations of specific NGOs. Still, it is one of the few sources of data about non-corporate reputations.

Reflection

As noted earlier, reputation management has a strong corporate-centric focus. Most research and application of reputation management is for corporate consumption. There is limited activity related to the reputations of activists and non-profits. It is not that reputation does not have an effect on activists and non-profits. Rather, it is assumed that corporations have more problems with reputations than activists or non-profits. The available data would seem to corroborate that conclusion.

The historical development of reputation management reflects the shifting view that corporations must attend to needs beyond just financial concerns. Corporations have a variety of constituents and must address these varied needs. Simply put, the growing interest in corporate social responsibility (see chapter 13) indicates that corporations must address social needs. What is critical in reputation management is the realization of the need to move beyond the financial markers of reputation and to integrate more social markers into the evaluation of reputation. Clearly, early reputation measures privileged financial concerns over all else. More recently, reputation experts have begun to extol the virtues of social concerns as key elements of a reputation and recognized how social concerns can be used to form beneficial corporate identities and reputations.

Public relations should seize upon the social aspect of corporate identities and reputation. Practitioner insights into constituents' social concerns can be incorporated into identity and reputation efforts. Furthermore, public relations can be used as part of communication efforts to make constituents aware of what a corporation is doing to fulfill or to exceed its social requirements. To be a more proactive force, reputation management must embrace the co-creation of meaning by working with constituents to understand and develop viable reputations. Chapter 13 will elaborate on how the co-creation perspective can be used in reputation management as part of its application to corporate social responsibility. Reputation management has the potential to benefit both the corporation and society when it shifts from a financial-only to a social-inclusion focus.

Case Study: Marks & Spencer

Marks & Spencer is a large retail company based in the United Kingdom. It has over 600 stores in the UK and over 200 stores spread across 34 other countries. You can buy clothes, houseware, and groceries at a Marks & Spencer. Retail is highly competitive, so it is important to create a distinct identity that will appeal to customers and become manifest in a positive reputation. Marks & Spencer has developed its "Look Behind the Label" campaign and "Plan A" commitments to craft, identify, and stimulate a reputation based on caring for its customers and the planet.

Plan A is the overarching guide to Marks & Spencer's social responsibility. Plan A has five pillars:

1   *Climate change:* try to become carbon neutral by 2012.
2   *Waste:* have no packaging or clothing in landfills by 2012.
3   *Sustainable raw materials:* get key resources from the most sustainable sources available.

4   *Fair partner:* improve the lives of people in the supply chain.
5   *Health:* give customers healthier choices in food. (Plan A, 2007)

Plan A incorporates a number of different issues and dimensions constituents might use to evaluate Marks & Spencer's reputation. Plan A provides a broad view of corporate social responsibility rather than focusing on one or two points. The five pillars will appeal to the values and identities of a variety of constituents, thereby leading them to identify with Marks & Spencer and to judge its reputation favorably.

Marks & Spencer backs its identity with the required actions. In 2007 it reduced CO_2 emissions from its stores and offices by 55,000 tons. Marks & Spencer are actively engaging customers in reducing the use of plastic bags and recycling clothing (Plan A, 2008). In 2008 Marks & Spencer formed a partnership with the charity Oxfam to further the goal of clothes recycling. Marks & Spencer has begun using recycled wood in many of its products and has been recognized by the Marine Conservation Society for its work in sustainable fishing. Marks & Spencer works with the World Wildlife Fund (WWF) to better understand and develop sustainable sources for many key ingredients. Marks & Spencer only serves fair trade teas and coffees in its cafés, is a heavy user of fair trade sugar, and provides the greatest retail support for fair trade cotton products by purchasing one third of the world's fair trade garments. By spring of 2008, 100 percent of the food produced by Marks & Spencer was free of artificial colors and its labels already use the Food Standards Agency's traffic light system that is easier for customers to understand than other food labeling systems.

Look Behind the Label is a promotional aspect for many of the Plan A activities. Through signs in the stores and information on its website, Look Behind the Label informs customers of the positive changes Marks & Spencer is making to help customers and the planet. Customers benefit from less salt, no artificial colors, no genetically modified organisms, elimination of hydrogenated fats, and clothes that are easier to wash and wear for a longer period of time (What we're doing, n.d.). The planet benefits from reduced energy consumption, support for people in the supply chain, and the preservation of resources. Look Behind the Label is the communicative link between Marks & Spencer's actions and its constituents. Constituents must be aware of the actions being taken if they are to believe an organization's identity is true and accept it as the organization's reputation. Public relations is part of the communication mix that allows constituents to "see" what the organization is doing, thereby helping to shape its reputation. Marks & Spencer wants its constituents to know what it is doing to become a retail leader in a variety of social responsibility-related initiatives.

Case questions

1   What are your reactions to Marks & Spencer's efforts as described in the case study?

2   Visit the Marks & Spencer website to read more about Plan A and Look Behind the Label (www.marksandspencer.com/gp/node/n/42966030/275–6449955–4366703). Look for recent updates to the initiatives described in the case study. How does Marks & Spencer try to inform constituents of its efforts?

3   The case describes how Marks & Spencer is working with Oxfam, a UK NGO. What are some reputational advantages associated with working with Oxfam? How would Oxfam benefit from this collaboration?

4   Visit Oxfam's home page (www.oxfam.org.uk/) and enter "Marks & Spencer" as a search term to see recent reports of their collaboration. In addition to those efforts described in the case study, how have Marks & Spencer and Oxfam collaborated?

5   The case study describes how Marks & Spencer supports fair trade by carrying Fairtrade certified products and serving Fairtrade products in its cafés. What reputational benefits does Marks & Spencer derive from being associated with fair trade? Visit the website for the Fairtrade Labeling Organization (FLO) International (www.fairtrade.net/) to learn more about fair trade products and how products become eligible for the Fairtrade designation. The FLO is the international certifying body, while TransFair USA is the US arm of FLO. Its website is at www.transfairusa.org/.

Discussion Questions

1   What is a corporate reputation? Describe the benefits of a positive reputation. Why are these important to organizations?

2   What roles do constituency perceptions play in reputation? How can public relations be involved in reputation assessment and reputation management?

3   Describe the four categories of how corporations are experienced (interactions with the organization, controlled messages from an organization, uncontrolled media reports about an organization, and second-hand information from other people). Give examples to illustrate the categories.

4   Think about organizations you perceive to have highly favorable and highly unfavorable reputations. What factors have contributed to your evaluations? How do these factors compare to ideas discussed in this chapter? How do your personal evaluative dimensions compare to those used in formal assessments of reputation?

5   Visit *Fortune* magazine's website (money.cnn.com/magazines/fortune) and click on "rankings" to examine the most recent rankings in the US of "Most Admired Companies" and "Best Companies to Work For." The site also links to the "World's Most Admired Companies." Also visit the *Sunday Times* to see the "Best Companies to Work For" (www.timesonline.co.uk/tol/life_and_style/career and_jobs/best_100_companies/). What are your reactions to these rankings? Examine the factors that comprise the basis for the rankings.

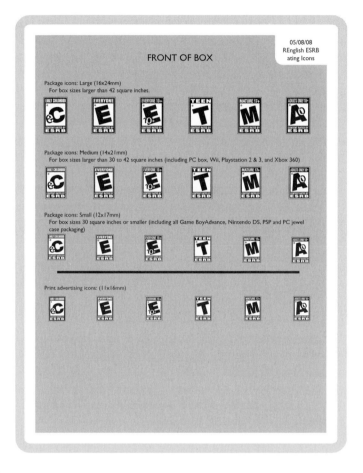

ESRB rating symbols.

10

Issues Management

Similar to reputation management, issues management was developed in the corporate sector. In the 1970s, corporate executives were bewildered by a series of public policy losses to activist groups. How were these activists able to stimulate regulatory changes that constrained corporate behavior? Why was the old lobbying emphasis ineffective for corporations? The concern over public policy losses resulted in the creation of issues management, a systematic and often more proactive approach to addressing public policy concerns.

While issues management has been applied outside of the public policy realm, that remains its dominant arena of application. As evidenced by the discussion of activist public relations in chapter 5 and Internet contagions in chapter 7, issues management is no longer the sole province of corporations. This chapter examines the development of issues management along with the various perspectives for how to approach it. Given the serious consequences policy decisions can have on society, it is incumbent that we consider the abuses of issues management as well.

Historical Overview

Environmental groups began to acquire resources and power in the late 1960s. As their popularity and numbers increased, they leveraged their newly found clout into new environmental regulations. Environmental awareness was emerging in the US, the UK, and other nations. Globally, a number of clean air and clean water regulations were created. Generally, people believe helping the environment is a positive step, especially in light of today's concern over global warming, a topic we return to in chapter 11. But corporations were paying a price for environmental regulation. They were required to spend money to reduce the pollution they spewed into the air and belched into the water (Beder, 2002). Vogel (1989) described the situation facing corporations as follows: "From 1969 to 1972, virtually the entire American business community experienced a series of political setbacks without parallel in the postwar period. In the space of only four years, Congress enacted a significant tax-reform bill, four major environmental laws, an occupational safety and health act, and a series of additional consumer-protection statutes" (p. 59). Public policies were reflecting activist views of reality, not corporate views.

Corporations had long enjoyed powerful political influence, particularly in the US. Now that political power was being challenged, public distrust rapidly increased as well. The confluence of these two factors troubled corporate America. The old practice of simply paying a lobbyist to fix a political problem was becoming increasingly less effective. Corporations needed a new model for dealing with public policy issues. Grefe and Linsky (1995) observed that corporations adopted strategies from activists as they began to use coalitions, grassroots organizing, and publicity to influence policy decisions.

Beder (2002) refers to the shift in corporate public policy practices as the "first wave of corporate activism" (p. 16). The name reflects the co-optation of public-interest activist tactics. Corporate activism was well funded and operated through newly developed public affairs departments. In public relations we refer to this new practice as *issues management*. Howard Chase, an insurance executive, coined the phrase and developed the first model for corporate use. Chase saw the need to find a better way to engage in public policy decisions because he too viewed the old ways of simply paying lobbyists as ineffective. Chase envisioned issues management as a means of providing organizations with a louder and more effective voice in the public policy matters that touched their industries (Jones & Chase, 1979).

Issues management and public policy

Issues are basically problems ready for some resolution (Jones & Chase, 1979). These problems initially were those located in the public policy arena. Hence, issues management began as a process by which an organization can act upon public policy issues that might impinge upon its ability to operate (Heath, 1990; Nelson & Heath, 1986). Issues managers were charged with locating potentially important public issues, then taking actions designed to have the issues resolved in a way favorable to their organization (Jones & Chase, 1979).

The example of plastic bags can be used to illustrate this point. People are concerned about the environmental threat posed by plastic bags. The concern has been translated into initiatives to ban the use of plastic bags by retailers in many cities such as Seattle, WA and Malibu, CA. Instead, people would be given paper bags or use their own cloth bags. The American Chemistry Council (ACC), a trade association for chemical companies including those involved in plastic, has opposed bans on plastics bags. It argues that more recycling is needed. The ACC claims that plastic bags take less energy to recycle than paper bags and that ultimately plastic bags are the more environmentally friendly choice if they are recycled (Proposed, 2007). The ACC is pushing policy options that choose recycling over bans or the rejection of bans. If communities choose recycling over bans or simply reject bans, it would be a more favorable resolution to the plastic bag issue for the ACC and its members.

It is instructive at this point to briefly discuss public policy making, since it is a focal point for the origins of issues management. *Public policy making* involves how legislative and regulatory decisions are made. The classic model of public policy making has four steps: (1) agenda setting; (2) policy formation; (3) implementation; and (4) policy evaluation. At any given time, there are more issues than there is space and time for politicians to discuss and act upon them. The end result is that policies compete for the attention of policy makers. An issue is said to be on the policy agenda when policy makers begin to officially discuss the issue. *Agenda setting* can include the process of having an issue rise to the level of consideration by politicians. The *policy agenda* represents the list of issues that political actors are considering.

How this policy agenda is created is the subject of much debate. A full discussion of the debate on how to conceptualize the influence on the public policy making process is beyond the scope of this chapter, but must be addressed at least in a cursory manner. A simplistic view of agenda setting begins with the *media agenda*, the stories being covered by the news media. The media agenda influences the public agenda or the issues people consider important (Iyenger & Kinder, 1981). The policy agenda is influenced by the *public agenda* (Cobb & Elder, 1972; Manheim, 1987). However, the relationships between the media, public, and policy agendas are not always linear. The three agendas all interact with one another and are influenced by external factors. Figure 10.1 provides depictions of both the simple linear and more complex relationships between the various agendas involved in policy making. Suffice it to say, policy making involves different groups jockeying to place their issues on the agenda.

Once an issue is on the policy agenda, the discussion can shift to the policy options for addressing the issue: *policy formation*. Policy is formulated as the policy options are considered and one is chosen, if the politicians decide to take action. Policy makers can decide to do nothing about the issue. In some cases, inaction is a preferred option for issues managers. The plastic bag example illustrates this idea. If local communities decide not to pursue bans on plastic bags, the ACC wins because that is its preferred option. Again, various actors, including issues managers, try to influence policy formation. When a decision is made, some administrative unit *implements* the policy (policy implementation stage). This is when the policy is executed and translated into operations. At this stage, the policy becomes real and affects people's lives (Barrett, 2004). Then, at some future point, an *evaluation* of the success or failure of the policy is made (policy evaluation stage).

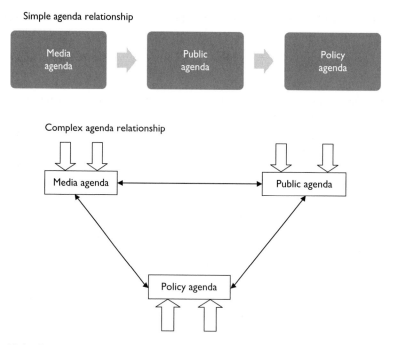

Figure 10.1   Representations of agenda relationships

The early focus on public policy can create the impression that issues management was all about the self-interest of corporations. After all, issues management was developed to protect corporate interests. However, Chase (1982) himself saw issues management as a two-way phenomenon. Issues management requires collecting information about concerns to understand why corporate behavior and societal expectations are misaligned. Corporations might realize they need to change their policies to better represent public expectations rather than manage the issue. The issue can provide insights to managers on how the organization needs to adapt to changing public sentiments. Issues management is not just about adapting the environment through public policy; it also includes adapting the organization to a changing society. Still, initial discussions of issues management focused more on adapting the environment to meet organizational needs. This included efforts to prevent public policy changes designed to better align corporate and societal interests.

Issues management beyond public policy

As time passed, issues management began to extend beyond the policy arena. Grunig and Repper (1992) argued that public policy oriented issues management is too short sighted. Their argument was premised on the difference between a problem and an issue. Issues were problems, points of contention, that were being aired in public view. Issues managers should not wait until a problem becomes an issue before they take action. Earlier involvement in the problem could prevent public debates over issues and allow for problem resolutions that are less acrimonious and more palatable to both organizations and their publics (Grunig & Repper, 1992). The management literature on strategic issues management supports this claim by emphasizing the existence of non-public policy applications of issue management (Dutton & Ottensmeyer, 1987).

Robert Heath is the most prolific and influential issues management scholar. His writings reflect the spread of issues management beyond the public policy arena. Heath's seminal book, co-authored with Richard Nelson, *Issues Management* (1986), emphasized public policy. Heath (1997) noted issues management's focus is on public policy issues – issues that have the potential to become regulation or legislation. As he observed, issues management is about "strategic and ethical public policy formation" (p. 44). However, Heath began to conceptualize issues management in terms of Sethi's (1979) notion of the *legitimacy gap*. Issues arose when there was a gap between how organizations behaved and how constituencies expected them to behave. These gaps could be addressed through public policy or through corporations voluntarily making changes after engaging with constituencies who desire a change.

Heath (2005) more recently defined issues management as "a strategic set of functions used to reduce friction and increase harmony between organizations and their publics in the public policy arena" (p. 460). Heath argues that issues management cannot be pursued at the risk of alienating the organization's public. Issues management is not the unbridled pursuit of self-interest. In addition, other authors have begun to apply the process of issues management beyond the public policy arena to other aspects of public relations (e.g., Botan & Taylor, 2004). The shift is noticeable as writings on issues management increasingly focus on shared interests (e.g., Jaques, 2006). Moreover, there is a greater awareness of issues outside of the public policy realm.

Throughout the issues management literature scholars have recognized the importance of values as well as issues of policy (Heath, 1997). Two groups can disagree because their values lead them to different evaluations of an issue. Managing values-based issues is often a matter of adjusting organizational policies voluntarily rather than through public policy. Corporate social responsibility (CSR), the subject of chapter 13, provides an excellent illustration of issues management centered on values. Through CSR, corporations are adapting to societal values as Chase suggested. Of course, when value issues go unheeded, the next step is often the conversion of the value issues to public policy issues. After all, can we legitimately say all policy issues are not rooted in values?

We can return to the notion of the legitimacy gap to complete the discussion of issues management extending beyond public policy. An issue can form when constituencies and organizations diverge in terms of expectations and behaviors. The issue may be managed in a "private" policy when the management and constituents reach an agreeable solution. The issue may escalate into a public discussion or remain more discreet. If a resolution is reached without government involvement, the issue management effort resulted in private policy. The efforts by the Immokalee workers that changed how corporations pay for tomatoes (discussed in chapter 5) illustrates private policy resolutions. If government gets involved and creates public policy designed to alter behavior, there is an involuntary public policy resolution. Ultimately, issues management transpires in a mix of public policy and private policies.

Perspectives on Issues Management

While a macro view of issues management's history provides an informative foundation, our understanding will be enhanced by a closer examination of the concept that informs its application to public relations. In 2003, Taylor, Vasquez, and Doorley categorized issues management research into four schools of thought: (1) systems, (2) strategic, (3) rhetorical, and (4) engagement. We will apply these four categories to our analysis of the issues management body of knowledge.

Systems approach

The systems approach reflects the need for organizations to minimize surprises and to employ a systematic response to public affairs. Systems theory recognizes the interdependence of an organization and its environment. There is a sensitivity to the external sociopolitical environment's impact on organizational operations and success. Chase's initial work in articulating issues management embodies the systems approach (Chase, 1982; Heath & Nelson, 1986). The systems approach is the foundation for issues management and is premised on a number of models that enumerate the steps in the issues management process. *Process* is the key word here because the systems approach centers on delineating the issues management process. Ewing's (1980) definition of issues management illustrates the systems approach: "the identification of emerging issues, prioritization, policy development, operation implementation, communication to the appropriate stakeholder, and evaluation of the results" (p. 14). In a systems approach, communication is simply a tactic to be employed by issues managers/public relations practitioners (Taylor, Vasquez, & Doorley, 2003).

While many models emerged from the systems approach, the Jones and Chase model (technically the Chase/Jones Process Model) was the first and most influential (Chase, 1980; Jones & Chase, 1979). Essentially, all later models were derivations of the Jones and Chase model. Their model is actually a systematic perspective for addressing issues, thus it transcends being "just a model." Jones and Chase (1979) conceived of issues management as a proactive venture whereby public relations could influence the formation of public policy. Issues were "unsettled matters which are ready for decision" that influenced the organization's operating environment (Jones & Chase, 1979, p. 11). Management's ability to "manage" issues in large part helps to shape the organization's operating environment and its ability to survive and/or thrive. The connection to the environment is a clear signal that the Jones and Chase model was grounded in systems theory.

The Jones and Chase model of issues management includes five steps: (1) issue identification, (2) issue analysis, (3) issue change strategy options, (4) issue action program, and (5) evaluation of results. Scanning is the focal point of issue identification. Managers use various methods to search the environment for emerging issues, what are termed trends, and actual issues. Ideally, scanning should locate an issue before it fully emerges. The earlier issue managers engage an issue, the increased likelihood of their success in influencing its resolution (Coombs, 1992). Once issues managers identify potential issues, an initial prioritization is performed by predicting the potential impact of each issue on the organization (Jones & Chase, 1979).

Research dominates the issue analysis step. The issues managers thoroughly research an issue by examining its origin and evolution. The research provides the information necessary to refine the predictions for how the issue could affect the organization. Issues can be threats and/or opportunities because the impact could be positive, negative, or a mix of both. A final prioritization of the issues is based upon the research. Prioritization is necessary because organizations only have the resources and time to address a limited number of issues. The final prioritization indicates what issues should provide the greatest return on an issues management investment.

Once a set of issues has been identified, issues managers use the issue change strategy option step to select the most feasible and practical plan for responding to each individual issue. Three issue change strategy options are identified: (1) reactive, (2) adaptive, and (3) dynamic. The reactive change strategy option involves simply preparing for the effects of the issue. The issue manager does not try to influence the development of the issue but readies for the changes the issue will bring. Perhaps an issue was identified too late and the opposition is too powerful. Whatever the reason, the reactive strategy recognizes there are times when issues cannot be managed, but that organizations can benefit from being prepared for the effects of the issue.

The adaptive strategy change option is accommodative and has issues managers offering alternative courses of action. The issues manager tries to influence the resolution of the issue by providing options to existing policy proposals. Policy proposals are the different ways an issue can be resolved. For instance, many industries favor self-regulation rather than governmental-based regulation. The movie ratings system in the US is an example of self-regulation. The dynamic change strategy option is the most proactive, as the issues manager anticipates the issue and is the first to make a policy proposal. Ideally, that policy proposal will result in the most desirable issue resolution for the organization. In fact, Jones and Chase (1979) believed the dynamic change strategy option was their only truly proactive change strategy option.

The change strategy options can be illustrated by returning to the plastic bag issue. If the plastic industry chose to adapt to bans on plastic bags by creating reusable plastic shopping bags, that would be reactive. Companies would adjust to the ban by shifting to products that would be viable under the ban. The industry response of offering recycling as an alternative to bans is an example of an adaptive strategy. The plastic industry creates an alternative to the existing proposal to ban plastic bags. Had the plastic industry discussed recycling requirements before there were public discussions of a ban, the dynamic strategy would have been in play. An issue manager has to be the first to publicly present a policy option to be dynamic.

Communication appears primarily at the issue action program step. This is when issues managers begin to communicate the organization's position on the issue to the relevant constituencies. A policy option is selected that is consistent with the change strategy option. The policy option becomes the keystone of the issue action program because it provides the boundaries for executing the program. With a policy option in place, issues managers set the goals and objectives for the issue action program and assemble the means and resources necessary to pursue the objective. Communication is one of the resources. Issues managers must decide what to communicate, when to communicate, and when not to communicate. A communication program is created based upon the target constituents and the tactics selected for reaching them (Jones & Chase, 1979).

Taylor, Vasquez, & Doorley (2003) observe that Jones and Chase (1979) focused on the tactical aspect of communication. A wide range of communication tactics can be employed in issues management and the Internet has increased those tactical options. The most common communication tactics in issues management include grassroots lobbying, direct lobbying, advocacy/issue advertisements, publicity (traditional and online), websites, listservs, email alerts, and coalition building. The first three warrant further attention because of their uniqueness to issues management. *Direct lobbying* is personally meeting with government decision makers or a member of the decision maker's staff. You present your case directly to the decision making group. *Grassroots lobbying* is when citizens/voters send their opinions to decision makers. Today, most grassroots lobbying is enacted through email and telephone contact, but some people still write postal letters. *Advocacy/issue advertisements* are paid messages that deliver a group's position on an issue (Heath & Nelson, 1986). Advocacy/issue advertisements typically appear in elite publications read by business and governmental leaders, such as the *New York Times* and the *Washington Post*. However, some will appear in mass audience publications, such as *USA Today*, when the objective is to generate widespread grassroots support.

The evaluation of results is based on comparing the desired outcome of the issues management effort to the actual outcome. Was the issue resolved the way the organization desired? The actual results are the policy decisions – the selection of a policy option. Bear in mind that "no action" is a viable policy option. Efforts to develop self-regulation are dependent on governments deciding not to regulate an industry themselves. Success is measured in terms of how closely the actual results match the intended results (Jones & Chase, 1979).

The Jones and Chase model was the first articulation of a distinct framework for managing issues. While not perfect, the model helped to establish issues management as a distinct area within public relations and influenced the development of later models (Coombs, 1990).

Strategic approach

The strategic approach is based primarily on research from management under the heading of strategic issues management (Ansoff, 1980; Dutton & Ashford, 1993; Dutton & Ottensmeyer, 1987). Strategic issues management seeks a way to improve an organization's ability to survive by becoming more adaptable (Ansoff, 1980; Taylor, Vasquez, & Doorley, 2003). It was also an effort to connect issues management with business strategy development (Jaques, 2007). An issue is "a forthcoming development, either inside or outside the organization, which is likely to have an important impact on the ability of the enterprise to meet its objectives (Ansoff, 1980, p. 133). The strategic issues management model is similar to the Jones and Chase model: (1) issues are detected, (2) issues are prioritized, (3) strategies are created and implemented, and (4) feedback from the strategies is collected (Dutton & Jackson, 1987).

As Taylor, Vasquez, & Doorley (2003) note, the strategic approach is a complement to the systems approach. The key difference is the focus on decision making. Strategic issues management is concerned with how managers interpret issues (strategic issue diagnosis) and the effects those interpretations have on decision making. Moreover, strategic issues management was not bounded by public policy, as issues managers could address a wide array of issues that arose externally and internally.

Rhetorical approach

The rhetorical approach conceives of issues and communication rather differently than the systems or strategic approaches. Issues are "created" whenever people attach significance to a situation or a problem. This is in contrast with conceiving of an issue as something you simply "find" (Crable & Vibbert, 1985; Taylor, Vasquez, & Doorley, 2003). Granted, the rhetorical approach still includes scanning and finding issues, but it allows the opportunity for people to create new issues. Issues are created when people craft clusters of arguments that support a preferred resolution to questions or concerns that involve demands for scarce resources (Crable & Vibbert, 1985). An issue becomes more than a problem; it becomes a *set of arguments to resolve demands for scarce resources*.

An example will help to clarify the difference between an issue as a problem and an issue as a set of argument clusters. Let us consider the situation of improper disposal of medical waste. As a problem the issue could be defined as

"Dangerous situations exist when medical waste is disposed of improperly." The focus of the issue is on the dangers presented by the situation. From a rhetorical perspective, the issue could be defined as "Medical facilities should be responsible for the safe disposal of their waste." The rhetorical issue definition reflects an issue being a distinct type of argument created through communication. The issue's definition should include the preferred resolution of the demands for scarce resources. In this case, the issue's resolution is placing the burden for resources on the medical facilities.

Communication becomes the focal point of issues management because communication is the mechanism by which an issue is managed. Communication is used to move an issue through its life cycle. The rhetorical perspective holds that issues move through a life cycle characterized by five levels of status, reflecting the importance an issue holds for people: (1) potential, (2) imminent, (3) current, (4) critical, and (5) dormant (Crable & Vibbert, 1985). Figure 10.2 is a visual representation of an issues life cycle as presented in Crable and Vibbert's (1985) catalytic model of issues management. Communication is used to move an issue from one status level to another. It should be noted that an issue can stall at any status level and slowly fade away. Reviewing the five status levels will illustrate the role of communication issues management.

The potential status level occurs when a person or persons deem a situation as significant. The communicative strategy at the potential status is definition. Issues managers must define their issues. Definitions provide boundaries for the future discussion of the issue (Crable & Vibbert, 1985). The boundaries dictate what constitutes a justified argument for the issue. A return to the medical waste issue will clarify the boundary notion of an issue's definition. We originally defined the medical waste issue as "Medical facilities should be responsible for the safe disposal of their waste." What if we had defined the issue as "States should be responsible for overseeing the proper disposal of medical waste by trash haulers." The shift in definitions alters how the issue is argued. The original definition limits the debate to points that address the medical facilities' role in the situation. The "state" definition shifts the arguments to the government's responsibilities and the role of trash haulers.

The definition of the issue controls the issue's focus and boundaries. An issue has potential status when someone or some group has articulated a set of arguments about how to resolve a concern. Jaques (2004) echoes the value of an issue's definition when he observes, "a well-chosen definition establishes a firm foundation for effective issues management" (p. 199). Definitions help to control the terms of the issue's discussion and it is a distinct advantage when the definition favors your option for resolving the issue.

The issue moves to the imminent status level when other people begin to accept that the issue is justified – worthy of their time and attention. Legitimacy is the key communicative strategy for the imminent status and helps to establish the issue as a public concern. An issue has legitimacy when people accept that it is worthy of their attention and appreciate the connection between themselves

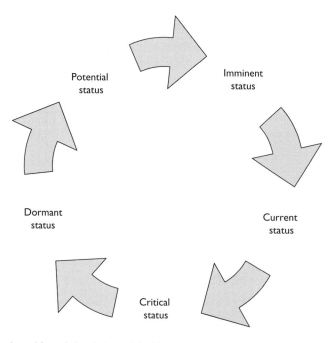

Figure 10.2   Issue life cycle/catalytic model of issues management

and the issue. In essence, legitimacy involves people accepting the issue as a public concern. Issues managers promote legitimacy as a means of reaching the imminent status level. They must convince others that their issue matters and should be a public concern. In the catalytic model, the goal is to keep increasing the number of people aware of and concerned about the issue. The movement from potential to imminent status level requires an expansion of the issue beyond the creators of the issue.

Coalition formation is a common means of taking an issue to the imminent status level. Coalitions form when groups with similar interests decide to work together on an issue. Groups can pool resources, including people and money, to increase their power and potential for success. Chapters 5 and 14 both include sections that address the development and utility of coalitions by activist groups and NGOs.

The issue moves to the current status when a wide number of people are aware of and concerned about the issue. Knowledge and understanding of an issue are spread to more and more remote constituents as the issue information is disseminated through channels with expansive communication linkages. Common channels for reaching the current status include mass media coverage and online discussions. *Polarization* is the key communicative strategy for the current status. Polarization involves representations of the heroes and villains – who is good and who is bad. The issues managers must convince the broader audience that they are the heroes. The idea is to force people to take sides. Issues and

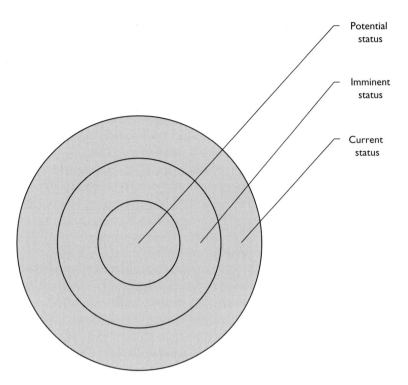

Potential
status

Imminent
status

Current
status

Figure 10.3   Progressive expansion of public interest

policy options are presented as dichotomization. In other words, there are sides
and people must choose a side. Obviously, the issues managers try to portray
their side as the heroes and the opposition as the villains to attract supporters.
The progression from potential to current is a steady expansion of the number of
people interested in the issue. Figure 10.3 illustrates this progressive growth of
interest in an issue.

An issue reaches the critical status level when there is pressure for a decision.
People feel a need for the issue to be resolved in some way. *Identification* is the
key communicative strategy for the critical status. Rhetorician Kenneth Burke
explains identification thus: "insofar as their interests are joined, A is identified
with B. Or he [she] may identify himself [herself] with B even when their interests
are not joined, as he [she] assumes they are, or is persuaded to believe so" (Burke,
1969, p. 21). When people realize they have common interests or simply perceive
they have common interests, identification can occur. Through identification,
people are persuaded to support a particular side of the issue. Issues managers
use communication to convince constituents that their side of the issue best captures the constituents' values and concerns. Once a decision is made, an issue is
considered resolved and moves to the dormant status. However, issues can be
revived at any time; that is why they are resolved rather than solved.

Collectively, these five status levels are often referred to as the *catalytic model* of issues management. The catalytic model derives its name from Crable and Vibbert's catalytic change strategy option. They felt even Jones and Chase's (1979) dynamic strategy was somewhat reactive because an issue is not addressed until it develops. The catalytic issue change strategy option allows an issues manager to create the issue, not simply wait for it to appear. An issues manager creates an issue by recognizing its importance and crafting a definition of it. The catalytic change strategy option is the most proactive because the issues manager creates the issue and begins its discussion. Others must then react to the issue crafted by the issues manager (Crable & Vibbert, 1985). The change strategy options presuppose issues managers find existing issues rather than creating issues. The term catalytic was then applied to the model of the five status levels, resulting in the final catalytic model of issues management portrayed in figure 10.2.

The four communicative strategies are the core of the rhetorical approach and explain how an issue is managed. Issues managers use the four communicative strategies to "move" an issue through the status levels. In turn, public policy is influenced if the issues manager successfully affects how the issue is resolved. Keep in mind an issue management effort could end at any status level due to (1) resolution or (2) lack of interest. An issue can be resolved at any status level if the parties involved agree on a resolution. For instance, an issue at the imminent status might catch the attention of management in an organization. The management meets with constituents pushing the issue and resolves the issue through engagement. The same process can occur at the current level as well. For example, when Burger King changed requirements for vendor contracts following PETA's "Murder King" campaign, that was private policy making. This returns us to the idea that issues can be resolved through private policy making. Simply stated, a policy decision is not the only way to resolve an issue.

Moreover, an issue can go dormant at any time from any status level if the issues manager fails to move the issue to the next status level. Interest in the issue simply fades and eventually disappears from public view as it returns to the dormant status (Crable & Vibbert, 1985). If an issue stagnates at a status level, interest will begin to wane. The issue attention cycle research documents that over time the news media and public lose interest in issues and they fade from public view and consciousness (Downs, 1972; McComas & Shanahan, 1999; Peters & Hogwood, 1985).

The issue attention cycle has five stages: (1) pre-problem, (2) alarmed discovery and euphoric enthusiasm, (3) realizing the cost of significant progress, (4) gradual decline of public interest, and (5) post-problem stage. The process begins when there is an undesirable social condition that goes unnoticed (pre-problem). Through some event or reason, the social condition is recognized and the media are keen to cover an issue (alarmed discovery and euphoric enthusiasm). Then people realize the cost of solving the problem is high (realizing cost of significant progress). The realization of costs leads to loss of interest (gradual decline of public interest) and eventually social concern is replaced by another concern

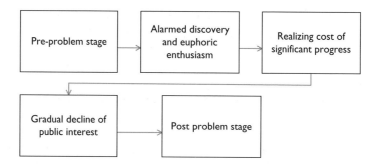

Figure 10.4   Issue attention cycle

and the news media move on to other stories (post-problem). The progression of the issue attention cycle is shown in figure 10.4. An issues manager must keep generating interest in an issue and broaden the audience for it, otherwise the issue is destined for dormancy.

Engagement approach

Taylor, Vasquez, & Doorley (2003) argued that there should be a fourth school of thought in issues management that they term the engagement approach. Engagement seeks to use a dialogue between an organization and its publics to manage an issue. Engagement is premised on three principles. First, organizations attempt to maximize their outcomes. Second, publics are a resource vital to the success of an organization. Third, a favorable relationship between an organization and its publics is highly valued. Through dialogue, organizations and publics resolve issues by seeking a convergence between their interests. An issue can create competition and conflict that could adversely affect the organization-public relationships. Therefore, effective issue management always considers the implications of the issue's resolution on those relationships. Engagement tries to move beyond the conflict and competitive elements of early issues management writings and to embrace the more recent cooperative view of issues management. Issues management should not be seen as a competition between organizations and publics, but rather as an opportunity to resolve an issue together in a cooperative fashion.

Summary

Issues management is not one thing, it is a complex amalgamate of concepts from public relations, mass communication, and management. At its core, issues management seeks to influence how issues (problems) are resolved. The rationale for issues management is that an issue resolution can seriously affect an organization for better or worse. Issues managers utilize communication to minimize the worse and maximize the better. However, issues management must be tempered and not be an unabashed pursuit of self-interests. Overly aggressive issues management can alienate constituents and create long-term harm for an organization (Heath, 2005).

Obvious Abuses of Issues Management

The discussion of issues management should highlight that this is a public relations function played for high stakes. Hence, it is important to consider the downside of issues management when it is abused. Issues management, as with public relations as a whole, is premised on the open exchange of ideas. Policy making should be born through the open discussion of multiple viewpoints. It should function within the marketplace of ideas. Issues management is a mechanism for participating in the public discussion. Unfortunately, two very obvious abuses have occurred in issues management, designed to subvert open discussion: (1) front groups and (2) strategic lawsuits against public participation (SLAPP).

Front groups and astroturf

In late 2007 an advertisement appeared in Kansas newspapers condemning the governor's failure to support the construction of new coal-power generating facilities. The advertisement claimed the governor had made Hugo Chavez, Mahmoud Ahmadinejad, and Vladamir Putin very happy. The sponsor of the message was named Kansans for Affordable Energy. Sounds like a reasonable group – just average people wanting energy they can afford. But if you dig deeper the real sponsors were Peabody Energy (a coal company) and Sunflower Electric Power Corporation (a group that wants to build the new coal-powered facilities). So why were these corporate names omitted as sponsors when they paid for the message? The answer is self-interest.

Self-interest means that a person or group has something to win or lose in a given situation. A corporation has a self-interest in selling its products or services, for instance. Self-interest is an obvious source of bias. Constituents should be more alert to the intentions of a message when the source of the message is pursuing its own self-interests. People reading the message would see it as self-interest if Peabody Energy or Sunflower Electric Power Corporation were the sponsors. Self-interested messages are less persuasive to people, especially policy makers (Fitzpatrick & Palenchar, 2006). Hence, front groups are used to mask self-interest.

Front groups "are created to pursue public policy objectives for organizations that disguise their connection (e.g., financial support) with the effort while attempting to appear independent" (Fitzpatrick & Palenchar, 2006, p. 203). As discussed in chapters 2 and 3, front groups raise questions about ethics and transparency. The policy focus is what leads us to include front groups in this issues management chapter.

Unfortunately, public relations has a long association with front groups. In fact, a Supreme Court case recognizing the legality – but not the ethicality – of front groups was a result of public relations efforts. The case involved the use of front groups by Carl Byoir, an important figure in the history of corporate public relations, to support efforts for the railroad to pass legislation that would have given them a competitive advantage over the trucking industry. Byoir created a number of front groups to create the illusion of grassroots support for the railroads. These groups included Garden Clubs against Big Trucks, Save Our Highways Club, and Taxpayers Opposed to Pavement Destruction. These groups wrote letters to legislators and editorials, and even took out advertisements in support of the railroads. The names imply concerned citizens, not the railroads themselves. No one would guess from their names that these groups actually represented the self-interests of the railroads. A front group was exposed by a disgruntled railroad employee who leaked the information (Wilner, 2008). The Supreme Court decision stated: "We can certainly agree with the courts below that this technique, though in widespread use among practitioners of the art of public relations, is one which falls short of the ethical standards generally approved in this country" (*Eastern Railroad Presidents Conference et al., v. Noerr Motor Freight, Inc., et al., 1961*, p. 141).

This association with public relations remains today, as recent exposés on front groups link their creation to public relations agencies (Apollonio & Bero, 2007; Mayer, 2007). Apollonio and Bero (2007) used R. J. Reynolds' own documents to prove it used the public relations firm of Mongoven, Biscoe, & Duchin to create the front group Get Government Off Our Backs (GGOOB). GGOOB appeared to be comprised of ordinary citizens upset about government regulation. GGOOB, funded and directed by R. J. Reynolds, used publicity, rallies, and grassroots pressure to help prevent perceived anti-tobacco regulation by both the Food and Drug Administration (FDA) and the Occupational Heath and Safety Administration (OHSA). Mayer (2007) characterized front groups as "designed by public relations firms to look like spontaneous outpourings of grassroots public sentiment" (p. 96).

Front groups are deployed because corporations and industries often lack the credibility of the public interest activist groups that may oppose them on an issue. A front group creates a false impression of impartiality from concerned people. That is more persuasive than a statement from a corporation or industry with a vested interest in the issue. Such obvious self-interest can lead political policy makers to discount a message (Apollonio & Bero, 2007). But the deception of front groups harms both society and public relations as a profession. The quality of policy making is eroded because an issue does not have a fair hearing in the marketplace of ideas. If interests are hidden, people cannot properly evaluate the information presented to them – the marketplace of ideas is corrupted. Public relations suffers because the image of the deceptive practitioner is reinforced when a front group is exposed. Public relations needs to take a stand against utilizing front groups in issues management or any other public relations endeavors.

Front groups are often part of astroturfing, a concept first introduced in chapter 5. Astroturfing is when a group artificially generates grassroots support for an issue. With astroturfing, people are hired to generate citizen support for an issue. People are contacted, typically by phone or email, and asked to support the issue. The reason this is "fake" is that the people would not have contacted the government if they had not been prompted by the astroturfers. Moreover, the astroturfers make it as easy as possible for people to send a message to the government by automatically connecting them on the phone or by supplying email links and templates for messages. The argument in favor of astroturfing is that the concern over the issue did exist, the astroturfers were just facilitating its expression. All grassroots efforts try to encourage other people to join their causes. But with astroturfing the entire process is artificial. There is no core of citizens who began the movement. Instead, the core of the movement is people paid to create grassroots pressure. The true originators of the messages are hidden from view. There is a lack of transparency and authenticity, and the presence of hidden motives with astroturfing. It is not always easy for government officials to separate astroturf messages from grassroots messages. In addition, astroturfing makes concern for the issue appear stronger than it really is.

Strategic lawsuit against public participation

A strategic lawsuit against public participation (SLAPP) is a term referring to any effort designed to prevent an individual or organization from expressing opinions to the government on public issues. Clearly, issues management involving policy issues hinges on people expressing their concerns and opinions to the government, a right protected by the First Amendment in the US. Still, a large number of individuals and groups have been sued for various expressions such as writing letters to the editor, testifying at a public hearing, reporting a legal or regulatory violation, demonstrating about a policy, or lobbying a member of Congress. Any of the aforementioned actions are tactics that could be used in issues management (What is a SLAPP? n.d.).

A SLAPP is typically based on common torts (grounds for civil cases based on injury, damage, or some other wrongful act) such as defamation (includes libel and slander), business torts (including interference with contract, business, and economic expectancy), judicial torts (includes abuse of process and malicious prosecution), conspiracy (joining with others to commit a tort), nuisance, and constitutional or civil rights violations (includes due process, equal protection, and discrimination) (Canan & Pring, 1988). Outrageous conduct is also used as grounds for a SLAPP. Most SLAPPs are dismissed. However, even the threat of a SLAPP can serve to silence people for a time or chill discussion because others fear lawsuits if they speak out. SLAPPs are meant to be lost by the organization filing them because their true purpose is to quell discussion.

SLAPPs seek to punish people for engaging in issues management through the public discussion of policy – punishing people for exercising a legal right! SLAPPs and other efforts to prevent public discussion are anathema to public relations and a pox on the profession. Public relations, including issues management, should seek to maintain the right and opportunity for everyone to be heard, even if you do not like what some people have to say. Access to the marketplace of ideas should be open and attempts to deny access should not be made under the guise of "public relations."

Reflections

The outcome of issues management is to affect behaviors by changing policies. The idea is that policies constrain and shape the behaviors of organizations. Thus, altering policies will change behaviors. The policies can be a result of external or internal change. Government policies represent external change that "force" organizations into changing behaviors, while internal change is a result of organizational leaders making "voluntary" changes. The Corporate Average Fuel Economy (CAFÉ) standards for the automobile industry are external, while the movie rating code is internal. The government tells automobile manufacturers what the average fuel economy must be for their collection of vehicles, while the movie industry polices its own ratings. While issues management emphasizes the need for engagement and harmony, policy decisions have an oppositional theme that lurks just below the surface. It is incumbent on issues managers to be aware of the possible abuses and ethical concerns that this oppositional theme can invite.

Issues by definition are points of contention and involve different sides. While sides can often work together, there are still differences that could prevent successful engagement and result in some constituents losing in an issues management effort. The oppositional theme demands that we address the role and implications of power in issues management. The discussion of power in issues management centers on the power differences among the constituents involved. Since its early days, critics have argued that corporations have an unfair power advantage in issues management. That power advantage is based on corporations having greater resources (status and financial resources) and skills than the constituents that might oppose them in an issue management contest. One example is the claim that "deep pockets" (strong financial resources) allowed corporations to dominate public discussions of an issue by buying advertising space and generating extensive publicity. As discussed in chapter 7 on technology, the Internet has helped to level the playing field to some degree, but typically corporations still are the most powerful actor in the issues management contest.

However, as noted earlier, unbridled use of their power in issues management works against corporations. An abuse of power could result in restrictions on corporate issues management and/or damage important relationships with constituents. Therefore, it is not in a corporation's best interests to recklessly pursue its own self-interests. In a way, self-interests should help to keep corporate power in check. While it might be the case that corporations will not abuse their power and have a stake in engagement, that does not ensure a fair and impartial field for issue management contests. Power can be wielded with a velvet glove. Constituents may even seem to win an issue but be a victim of symbolic actions – actions that do not really change any behaviors. Issues are political in nature and politicians often use symbolic acts to create quiescence. Some issue resolutions are symbolic gestures meant to reassure publics and to create quiescence. One example from the US is the Pure Food Act that was passed in light of Upton Sinclair's exposé of the meat packing industry in the popular book *The Jungle*. As noted in chapter 5 on activism, the Pure Food Act was intended to reassure an angry populace, not to be functional policy that really improved the safety of meat.

Symbolic issue resolutions can reflect the engagement approach. The organization maximizes outcomes while maintaining a positive relationship with its constituencies. It will appear that the interests of the organization and the constituents have converged. When the big pharmaceutical companies created a voluntary code of conduct for direct to consumer (DTC) advertising, it was a win-win situation. The DTC issue was a concern that direct advertising to consumers was "selling sickness." People would seek medication they did not need or be treated for illnesses that did not really exist (Moynihan & Cassels, 2005). DTC became "regulated" without the need for government intervention. Consumers would now be protected from the abuses of DTC. Right? Well, not exactly. The practice of DTC remained with slight modifications. The only substantive change was a delay between when a DTC advertisement was submitted to the Food and Drug Administration (FDA) and when it would be sent to consumers. This delay would give the FDA a chance to demand changes if the advertisement was deemed inappropriate in some way. Prior to the voluntary code, DTC advertisements were sent to consumers simultaneously with the submission to the FDA. Since the FDA could take up to six months to review the advertisements, the "inappropriate" versions could circulate publicly for six months or more before being corrected.

So where is the problem? At the time of the voluntary DTC code there was intense pressure on Congress to take action on the industry's abuses. Using the catalytic model as an analytic tool, the issue was at the critical status level with pressure for a decision. The amorphous American public supported some reform. The voluntary code reassured Congress and the public that DTC was now okay and quiescence ensued. The interests of the pharmaceutical industry seemed to converge with its constituents. In reality, the convergence was between the pharmaceutical industry and some of its constituencies. Activist groups' concern with the existence of DTC advertising and the selling of sickness in the US was not part of this convergence. But without the larger American populace clamoring for change, interest in DTC advertising reform evaporated from public view.

Again, we need to consider the oppositional theme and power in issues management. Different constituents might oppose an organization on an issue. Organizational management will prioritize these constituents and when convergence is deemed appropriate, seek convergence with the highest priority constituents. As discussed in chapter 5, constituent priority is predominantly a function of power. Hence, even when an engagement perspective is used, less powerful constituents can remain on the margins. We cannot please all of the constituents all of the time. As a result, we still must be cognizant of power differences in issues management.

A final concern in issues management is the use of emotions to override logic and the rush to action. In rare cases, an issue emerges very rapidly, often precipitating a crisis in its wake (Heath, 1994). A hallmark of these firestorm issues is that emotion drives the action. The Alar case provides an excellent example. In the late 1980s a series of studies began to link Alar to cancer. Alar was the trade name for daminozide, a chemical that helps fruit stay on the plant or tree longer so that it looks better for market. Uniroyal produced Alar and the primary crop for application was apples. By 1989 there was evidence that Alar could be a carcinogen when heated. So, if Alar was still on apples when they were converted into apple juice and apple sauce, there was a risk of cancer. The precise degree of that risk is debated to this day, a point that is revisited in chapter 11. Search Alar online to learn more about the debate.

In 1989 the National Resource Defense Council (NRDC), an environmental activist group, created an issue out of Alar that focused on banning Alar. Alar was defined as a cancer risk to children that should be banned. Working with the public interest public relations agency Fenton Communications, the NRDC launched its issues management effort in February 1989 on the popular news show *60 Minutes*. The following day the NRDC held a number of press conferences about the dangers of Alar featuring celebrities such as Meryl Streep to attract additional attention. Basic media relations was used to expose millions of people to the Alar issue. The Alar issue moved very rapidly from potential to critical status as opinion polls and letters to the FDA showed people wanted the product banned. Further evidence was the sharp decline in the sales of apples and apple-related products due to the fear of Alar and cancer.

In June 1989 Uniroyal agreed to stop making Alar. In November the Environmental Protection Agency (EPA) decided to ban Alar. This followed a tentative EPA statement to ban Alar after a May 1989 study linked Alar to tumors. As noted by an earlier March 1989 EPA statement (see Box 10.1), the EPA was not convinced by the science of the cancer risk at that time. In fact, many in the food industry believed the risk was not strong enough to warrant a ban and blame. Many writers in support of the chemical industry talk about the "Alar scare," "Alar myth," or "Alar hoax" (How chemical industry, 1998). Most people's views of Alar are actually ideologically based, including whose data one finds convincing. The point of the Alar case is the role of emotion. Emotion to ban Alar moved ahead of the science. The March 1989 news release offers further evidence that public pressure for a ban existed before the EPA had the science to impose a ban.

Box 10.1   Alar Use on Apples

P89–12
FOR IMMEDIATE RELEASE

Food and Drug Administration
Chris Lecos – (202) 245–1144

The following statement is being issued jointly by Frank E. Young, M.D., Ph.D., Commissioner of the Food and Drug Administration, Dr. John Moore, Acting Deputy Administrator, Environmental Protection Agency, and John Bode, Assistant Secretary for Food and Consumer Services, US Department of Agriculture:

In the last few weeks there has been a growing public controversy over the potential harmful effects of a chemical called Alar, which is used by apple growers to retain the crispness of their fruit as it goes to market. It is used primarily in the growing of Delicious, Staymen, and McIntosh apples.

The federal government believes that it is safe for Americans to eat apples, and the responsible federal agencies are working together to reassure the public of this fact.

Recently, the Natural Resources Defense Council has claimed that children face a massive public health problem from pesticide residues in food. Data used by NRDC, which claims cancer risks from Alar are 100 times higher than the Environmental Protection Agency estimates, were rejected in 1985 by an independent scientific advisory board created by Congress. Alar has been used for decades in apple growing, and it has been the subject of many studies on possible harmful side effects.

A recent progress report on preliminary results from an ongoing study shows that a breakdown product of Alar caused certain kinds of tumors in mice. Based on this report, EPA has begun the process to phase out Alar in apple growing if the final data, which will be independently reviewed, demonstrate a need for cancellation. Cancellation could then occur by July 1990.

EPA believes the potential risk from Alar is not of sufficient certainty and magnitude to require immediate suspension of the use of this chemical. EPA and others have pointed to lack of scientific validity in the suggestion by the NRDC that the risk is much greater than has been stated by EPA.

The Food and Drug Administration of the Department of Health and Human Services, the agency responsible for monitoring pesticide residues in food, has found either no residues or residues that are far below EPA's tolerance. Both FDA and EPA believe that Alar use over this interim period is safe and does not pose a health risk to the American public. Available data show overwhelmingly that apples carry very small amounts of Alar. In addition its use has decreased dramatically over the past several years; estimates are that 95 percent of the apple crop was not treated in 1988.

It should also be noted that risk estimates for Alar and other pesticides based on animal testing are rough and are not precise predictions of human disease. Because of conservative assumptions used by EPA, actual risks may be lower or even zero.

The FDA, EPA, and the US Department of Agriculture believe there is not an imminent hazard posed to children in the consumption of apples at this time, despite claims to the contrary.

Therefore, the federal government encourages school systems and others responsible for the diets of children to continue to serve apples and other nutritious fruit to American children.

Box 10.1   *(cont'd)*

This is an issue that will continue to be monitored closely by the responsible federal agencies that have acted in the past to cancel pesticide uses which pose a cancer risk.

Daminozide (Alar) pesticide canceled for food uses
[EPA press release – November 7, 1989]

The US Environmental Protection Agency today announced that it intends to approve the request of Uniroyal Chemical Co. Inc. of Bethany, Connecticut, to voluntarily cancel all food-use registrations of the pesticide daminozide (trade name Alar). EPA will order a prohibition on all sales, distribution, and use of daminozide products labeled for use on food crops, including existing stock, effective three days after publication in the *Federal Register*, which is expected on November 15.

The cancelation order will require Uniroyal to complete and submit final reports of three cancer studies involving a breakdown product of daminozide, unsymmetrical dimethylhydrazine (UDMH). The only study that is still ongoing is scheduled to be reported to the Agency by January. EPA also announced today that it will terminate the special review of daminozide for food uses. However, the special review of daminozide for use on ornamental plants, the remaining registration, will continue. After receipt and review of the remaining UDMH studies, EPA will complete a final assessment of dietary risk attributable to any residues remaining from past use, as well as a non-dietary risk assessment for exposure resulting from use on ornamentals.

Uniroyal voluntarily halted the sales and distribution of daminozide food-use products in June and agreed to buy back all existing stocks, including those held by users. In today's action, Uniroyal offered to extend the recall and reimbursement program for existing stocks of daminozide products until November 30 for growers and December 31 for retailers. Uniroyal will notify all distributors, grower organizations, and trade associations about the extended recall and reimbursement period. EPA plans to monitor the progress of the removal of daminozide from the marketplace.

EPA proposed to cancel all food uses of daminozide in May based on evidence that UDMH causes tumors in laboratory animals and that lifetime dietary exposure to this product may result in an unacceptable risk to public health. The Agency's proposed cancelation action on daminozide was based in part on a 12-month interim report of a two-year feeding study on mice using UDMH which showed that this chemical causes tumors.

In September, EPA proposed to lower the allowable residue level of daminozide in apples from the current 20 parts per million (ppm) to 5 ppm on November 30, 1989. On November 30, 1990, the tolerance would be lowered to 1 ppm and after May 31, 1991, any detectable levels would be illegal. Similar actions were proposed for the remaining food uses of daminozide. EPA proposed the tolerance-reduction action in part to insure that imported foods comply with the same residue requirements as domestic foods while daminozide is removed from the marketplace.

The cancelation order will place certain conditions on exportation of existing stocks of daminozide. Existing stocks of daminozide currently labeled for food uses may be

Box 10.1   *(cont'd)*

exported under the following provisions: the stocks will be repackaged into products for non-food uses before being sold; the stocks will be shipped on pallets that are either shrink-wrapped or containerized in such a way as to maintain their integrity; and, the pallets will be clearly marked "Not registered for use in the United States of America." Section 17 of the Federal Insecticide, Fungicide and Rodenticide Act, which contains the provisions for exporting canceled pesticides, will be applicable.

Uniroyal will also be required to notify EPA at least 20 days before shipment of existing stocks and provide the name(s) of the importing country (including the specific destination within the importing country) and port of entry, the countries of final destination (if different from importing country), specific amounts of shipment, product name(s), unit size(s), date of shipment, and expected date of arrival. EPA will contact the importing countries to determine whether the shipments are acceptable.

Uniroyal will also be required to follow the notification/acknowledgment provisions of section 17 before exporting any new stocks of daminozide labeled for food use, including the information that daminozide is not registered for food uses in the United States.

Daminozide is a plant-growth regulator and has been registered since 1963. In addition to apples (on which it was primarily used) and ornamentals, it was also registered for use on cherries, nectarines, peaches, pears, Concord grapes, tomato transplants, and peanut vines. On fruit trees, daminozide affected flower-bud initiation, fruit-set maturity, fruit firmness and coloring, preharvest drop, and market quality of fruit at harvest and during storage.

Source: www.epa.gov/history/topics/food/02.htm

One criticism of activist groups in issues management is they can amplify or distort the fear in order to generate emotions and support for their side of an issue. (See chapter 11 on risk communication for more on this topic.) As with criticisms of corporate abuse of power in issues management, there are times when the criticism of activist fear-mongering is accurate. Issues managers must be cognizant of the ethical use of fear when building support for their side of the issue. Issues management can become a forum where different views are aired for public consumption. However, issues managers must be mindful of the potential subtle abuses of power and fear that can serve to distort the discussion and unfairly influence the outcome of an issues management effort. These concerns are in addition to the obvious need to prohibit the use of front groups and SLAPPs to gain a communicative advantage.

Conclusion

Issues management was the brainchild of corporate interests that targeted public policy decisions. Interest in issues management was shaped by and a reaction to successful efforts by activists that we could legitimately call issues management. As issues management matures, it is spreading beyond public policy and corporate interests. Activists are utilizing the same issues management models and tactics as corporations. Concepts applied to understanding policy decisions are used to track and to manage social issues and corporate social responsibility efforts. In fact, Botan and Taylor (2004) suggest that issues management should be used as a model for the practice of public relations itself. Public relations is experiencing a renewed interest in issues management and that interest is justified.

Issues management brings with it issues of power that should not be ignored. Influencing policy decisions or corporate policies is a significant effect of public relations. Power used improperly can corrupt decision making. Issues managers should follow rules for transparency to avoid the appearance of hidden interests and ultimately the corruption of the process. Issues management should be scrutinized carefully to determine whether or not the participants are "playing fair" and multiple voices reaching all constituents. When decisions matter, the process of decision making should be examined carefully to prevent abuse.

Case Study: Entertainment Software Ratings Board

If you play or purchase video games, have you ever noticed the ratings on a game's packaging? The rating system, in which participation is voluntary, is implemented by the Entertainment Software Rating Board (ESRB), which is the non-profit, self-regulatory body established in 1994 by the Entertainment Software Association (ESA). The ESRB assigns computer and video game content ratings, enforces industry-adopted advertising and marketing guidelines, and helps ensure responsible online privacy practices for the interactive entertainment software industry. The ESRB ratings are designed to provide consumers, especially parents, with concise, impartial guidance about the age-appropriateness and content of computer and video games so that they can make informed purchase decisions about the games they deem suitable for their children and families (About, n.d.).

There are six possible age ratings for a video game:

- "Early Childhood" means a game is appropriate for those three and older. The game should contain no content a parent would find offensive.
- "Everyone" means a game is suitable for those six and older. These games may contain minimal cartoon, fantasy or mild violence, and/or infrequent use of mild language.
- "Everyone 10+" has content appropriate for those ten and older. These games may contain more cartoon, fantasy or mild violence, mild language, and/or minimal suggestive themes.
- "Teen" games have content suitable for those 13 and older. Titles in this category may contain violence, suggestive themes, crude humor, minimal blood, simulated gambling, and/or infrequent use of strong language.
- "Mature" means a game is appropriate for those 17 and older. Titles in this category

may contain intense violence, blood and gore, sexual content, and/or strong language.

- "Adults Only" games have content that should only be played by persons 18 years and older. Titles in this category may include prolonged scenes of intense violence and/or graphic sexual content and nudity.

Games that are designated "Rating Pending" have been submitted to the ESRB and are awaiting final rating. (This symbol appears only in advertising prior to a game's release.)

The ESRB's age rating symbols, which provide guidance about age appropriateness and are found on the front of virtually every game sold at retail in the US and Canada, are one part of the ESRB's two-part rating system. The second part, content descriptors, are found on the back of a game's package and indicate elements in a game that may have triggered a particular rating and/or may be of interest or concern. Box 10.2 provides a list of ESRB content descriptors along with their definitions.

So who are the ratings mainly for, parents or gamers? Of course, the answer is parents. The rating system was designed to help parents make choices about games and to find games appropriate for their children. Parents can review the age rating symbol and content descriptors

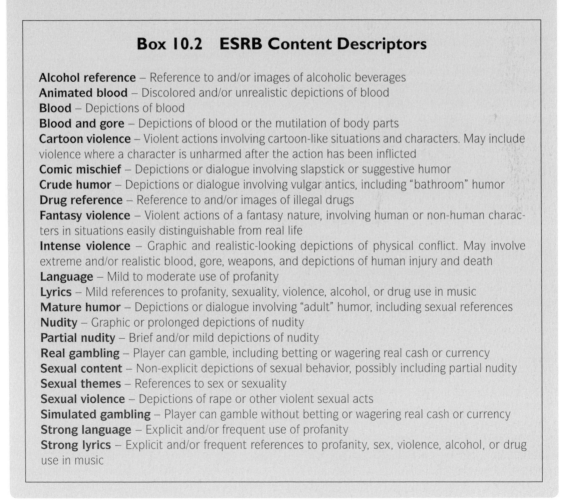

Box 10.2   ESRB Content Descriptors

Alcohol reference – Reference to and/or images of alcoholic beverages
Animated blood – Discolored and/or unrealistic depictions of blood
Blood – Depictions of blood
Blood and gore – Depictions of blood or the mutilation of body parts
Cartoon violence – Violent actions involving cartoon-like situations and characters. May include violence where a character is unharmed after the action has been inflicted
Comic mischief – Depictions or dialogue involving slapstick or suggestive humor
Crude humor – Depictions or dialogue involving vulgar antics, including "bathroom" humor
Drug reference – Reference to and/or images of illegal drugs
Fantasy violence – Violent actions of a fantasy nature, involving human or non-human characters in situations easily distinguishable from real life
Intense violence – Graphic and realistic-looking depictions of physical conflict. May involve extreme and/or realistic blood, gore, weapons, and depictions of human injury and death
Language – Mild to moderate use of profanity
Lyrics – Mild references to profanity, sexuality, violence, alcohol, or drug use in music
Mature humor – Depictions or dialogue involving "adult" humor, including sexual references
Nudity – Graphic or prolonged depictions of nudity
Partial nudity – Brief and/or mild depictions of nudity
Real gambling – Player can gamble, including betting or wagering real cash or currency
Sexual content – Non-explicit depictions of sexual behavior, possibly including partial nudity
Sexual themes – References to sex or sexuality
Sexual violence – Depictions of rape or other violent sexual acts
Simulated gambling – Player can gamble without betting or wagering real cash or currency
Strong language – Explicit and/or frequent use of profanity
Strong lyrics – Explicit and/or frequent references to profanity, sex, violence, alcohol, or drug use in music

---

Box 10.2 *(cont'd)*

Strong sexual content – Explicit and/or frequent depictions of sexual behavior, possibly including nudity
Suggestive themes – Mild provocative references or materials
Tobacco reference – Reference to and/or images of tobacco products
Use of drugs – The consumption or use of illegal drugs
Use of alcohol – The consumption of alcoholic beverages
Use of tobacco – The consumption of tobacco products
Violence – Scenes involving aggressive conflict. May contain bloodless dismemberment
Violent references – References to violent acts

Source: www.esrb.org/ratings/ratings_guide.jsp#descriptors

---

to determine if they are comfortable with their child(ren) being exposed to a particular type of material. The "Mature" rating leads many parents to question whether or not to buy it for their children under 17. Of course, more "extreme" ratings may have the effect of increasing the interest of those under the age of the rating. Merchants are affected by this rating system as well. Video game retailers, the vast majority of which support the ESRB rating system, display information about the ratings in their computer and video game departments and enforce voluntary store policies not to sell or rent "Mature" titles to those under 17. In fact, according to a study conducted by the US Federal Trade Commission (FTC) in 2008, national retailers are enforcing those store policies 80 percent of the time, far surpassing the rating of restriction for other types of entertainment media such as films, DVDs, and music.

The ESRB actively promotes its rating system and works to help parents and adults to use the system effectively to determine appropriate game buying and playing for children. In 2003 the ESRB began the "OK to Play? Check the Ratings" campaign to further educate consumers, mostly parents, about the rating system. Public service announcements (PSAs) continue to be disseminated through various media outlets

including print, television, radio, and online. The ESRB print PSAs are placed in publications such as *TV Guide*, *Better Homes and Gardens*, *Good Housekeeping*, *Entertainment Weekly*, *Disney Adventures*, *AARP*, *Popular Mechanics*, *Electronic Gaming Monthly*, *Game Informer*, *OXM*, *Xbox Nation*, *Computer Gaming World*, *Game Now*, *PSM*, *Computer Games*, *Game Pro*, *Official PlayStation Magazine*, *GMR*, *Pocket Games*, and *Nintendo Power*. Many radio networks have run the radio PSAs, including Metro Source, American Urban Radio Network, CNN Radio, USA Radio Network, ABC Radio Networks, Westwood One, Univision Radio, Radio Bilingue, Radio Lazer, and the Hispanic News Service. The ESRB has also produced national and statewide TV PSA spots. In 2006 the ESRB partnered with the Parent Teacher Association in the US to distribute over 1.3 million educational brochures in Spanish and English to all PTAs throughout the country. In 2008 the partnership was continued via the distribution booklets to all 26,000 PTAs nationwide, which included information about ESRB ratings, parental controls, and online safety.

As with the movie industry, the video game industry in the US and many other countries has avoided government regulation through effective self-regulation. However, the issue of video game content is an excellent example of how an issue can arise repeatedly. When a game with controversial content appears, like the notorious Grand Theft Auto (GTA) series of games, the issue returns to the forefront, driven in large part by advocacy groups and activists, many of which pressure government for controls over content. GTA is a flashpoint for video game regulatory issues because of its reputation for the extreme use of realistic violence and references to sex.

Grand Theft Auto: San Andreas created additional controversy in 2005 when hackers found code on the game's disc that could be unlocked using an unlicensed third-party modification program, called a "mod." Installing this "mod," dubbed "Hot Coffee," allowed the player's character to engage in virtual sex. Following an investigation by the ESRB, versions of the game that included the locked-out content on the disc had their Mature rating revoked, and were labeled "Adults Only." This action was taken in part because people could easily find the "mod" on the Internet and use it to activate the locked-out sex mini-game. A new version of the game that lacked the locked-out content and retained its original "Mature" rating was soon made available. Immediately following the conclusion of its investigation, the ESRB clarified its disclosure policies to require that any pertinent content that exists on a game's disc, whether or not it is accessible through normal gameplay, must be disclosed during the rating process. The ESRB also eventually increased to up to $1 million the fine it is able to impose against companies for an egregious failure to disclose pertinent content during the rating process.

In general, the video game industry in the US has been successful in defeating each new legislative initiative designed to control video game content, and the ESRB rating system is a major weapon in that ongoing battle. While the rating system has been shown through research to be a useful resource for parents, groups such as Common Sense Media feel video game content has gone too far and that it is too easy for children to find ways to access games intended for older players. The concern of critics like these arises largely from the contentious yet unproven notion that video game violence has a negative effect on children, including claims that violent video games lead to real violence. These groups want restrictions on the violence in video games and laws restricting the sale of certain games. Whether you agree or disagree with video game anti-violence groups, their interests are not served by the ratings system. These groups are not part of the convergence of public interests surrounding video game content.

Video game content is an international concern as countries as diverse as Germany, China, Argentina, New Zealand, Japan, Poland, South Korea, and Australia grapple with the issue. In the United Kingdom, the Entertainment & Leisure Software Publishers Association (ELSPA) handles the content rating system. Starting in 2003, the ELSPA adopted the Pan European Games Information (PEGI) developed by the Interactive Software Federation of Europe (ISFE) that was modeled on ELSPA guidelines. PEGI is voluntary and had been widely adopted in Europe. The PEGI system is a combination of age appropriateness and content descriptions. The age ratings are 3+, 7+, 12+, 16+, and 18+. Games are not to be sold to those under the specified age. There are seven content descriptor categories: bad language, discrimination, drugs, fear, gambling, violence, and sex, nudity, erotica, and pornography.

Case questions

1   Why is voluntary self-regulation, like the application of the ESRB rating system, preferred to forced regulation?
2   How could the educational component, including the partnership with the Parent Teacher Association, be effective in preventing regulation?
3   What might the anti-violence campaign do to become more relevant to the debate?

Discussion Questions

1   What provided the impetus for the development of issues management as a public relations function?

2   Explain how Chase viewed issues management as a two-way phenomenon. How is this perspective consistent with this text's definition of public relations?

3   Discuss how both issues of policy and issues of value are important to issues management. Develop examples of both kinds of issues. How might these be interrelated?

4   Describe the four schools of thought reflected in issues management research: systems, strategic, rhetorical, and engagement. Explain distinguishing characteristics of each and how each contributes to our understanding of issues management.

5   Describe the five steps included in the Jones and Chase model of issues management, an early model grounded in systems theory.

6   Explain how the rhetorical school of thought conceives of issues as being "created" and issues as sets of "argument clusters." Describe the five levels of status associated with Crable and Vibbert's catalytic model of issues management.

7   Explain how the engagement approach to issues management emphasizes cooperative views of the issues management process.

8   Describe front groups and how they may influence the issues management process. Explain why front groups can be seen as unethical. How are front groups associated with astroturfing?

9   Identify contemporary examples of organizations engaging in the issues management process. How do you know they are trying to manage an issue? What tactics and channels are they using to manage the issues?

Biohazard symbol sign in front of rusted drums.

11

Risk Communication

Some hazardous wastes, such as organochlorines, pose a problem for disposal. The mixture of carbon, chlorine, and hydrogen is difficult to break down. The compound accumulates in the fatty tissue of animals such as fish. If ingested, it can build up over time, creating a health risk for people who might consume those fish. While the use of organochlorines is being phased out, a large amount still exists due to previous commercial use, including agricultural production. Governments and corporations need a solution beyond just storing the compound because storage runs the risk of leaks or other types of unintentional releases.

One disposal option is incineration. The organochlorines are eliminated by being burned at a high temperature. Imagine you live in a town where there is a proposal to build a hazardous waste incinerator whose primary purpose is to dispose of organochlorines. Stories and talk around town focus on the creation of new jobs and the value of safely disposing of hazardous wastes that plague society. But then "safety" talk emerges as people begin to wonder about the incinerator. Are the emissions from the incinerator really safe? What are the risks of contamination during transportation or storage? Would employees be safe? A potential clash is developing between the supporters and opponents of the incinerator proposal. Risk communicators will play an important role in resolving the conflict brewing over the hazardous waste incinerator.

Risk communication, a discussion between risk creators and risk bearers, is a valuable tool for addressing concerns people have over the various risks they face, including chemicals, manufacturing processes, or potential disease outbreaks. In this chapter we begin by defining the key terms used in risk communication, move to an examination of its evolution and best practices, and then review the outcomes of risk communication.

Key Terms

Risk communication can be a very technical area where science and various constituencies intersect. It is instructive to begin our discussion by defining how we use some of its key terms, including hazard, risk, and threat. *Hazards* are "events or physical conditions that have the *potential* to cause fatalities, injuries, property damage, infrastructure damage, agricultural loss, damage to the environment, interruption of business, or other types of harm or loss" (Multihazard design, 1997). Because hazards have the potential to inflict harm, they are closely associated with – but not synonymous to – risk. Hazards are sources of risk such as personnel, products, the production process, facilities, social issues, competitors, regulators, and customers (Barton, 2001).

Risk is the potential to do harm or more generally the potential exposure to loss. The "potential" of a risk can be quantified as a threat. The notion of *threat* is inherent in the definition of risk and can be conceptualized as the magnitude of negative consequences from an event and the likelihood of the event happening. Some experts have established the following formula: *Risk = Likelihood × Consequences*. The threat posed by the risk is a function of the likelihood of the event multiplied by the consequences of the risk. Efforts to quantify the risk are known as risk assessment. Risks can be one of three varieties: (1) natural risks such as severe weather, (2) actions of others such as producing hazardous waste, and (3) lifestyle choices such as unsafe sex (Heath & Coombs, 2006).

Risk expert Peter Sandman has a popular way to explain risk: *Risk = Hazard + Outrage*. For Sandman (1998), *hazard* involves the statistics that quantify the risk in terms of likelihood and consequences (what other experts termed risk), while *outrage* comprises all the other elements that constituents link to the risk. Table 11.1 presents a complete list of Sandman's outrage factors. Outrage typically includes a dose of anger as well. Sandman's point is that people depend on assessments of risk that are not completely scientific. Hence, risk is often a matter of the outrage attached to a risk rather than the true threat from that risk. In other words, people often assess risk in a subjective way rather than in a scientifically objective manner. We will return to outrage in the discussion of the objectives of risk communication.

We face many hazards in our daily lives that create risk, such as taking a shower, driving a car, riding the subway or bus, and eating food. Each of these risks can be roughly quantified. Has anyone ever told you that statistically it is safer to fly in an airplane than to ride in a car? If so, you were given an assessment of the risk threat of automobile and airplane travel. According to the National Safety Council, the odds of dying while a passenger in a car are 1 in 19,216 while the odds of dying as a passenger in an airplane are 1 in 432,484. Odds are you do not know nor even think about the various hazards and risks you face every day. What are the odds you will be injured in the shower? The answer is 1 in 1,500. The odds are higher for injuries from your pillow, bed,

Table 11.1   Peter Sandman's main outrage factors

1   *Voluntariness:* people are more accepting of voluntary risks while coerced risk creates outrage.
2   *Control:* people feel less outrage when they have some control over the mitigation and prevention of the risk.
3   *Fairness:* people experience greater outrage when they suffer greater risks but not greater benefits than others.
4   *Process:* people feel great outrage when an organization does not consult them before decisions and appears not to listen to their concerns. Put another way, lack of trust builds outrage.
5   *Morality:* people dislike the idea of acceptable risk and language that frames the risk in terms of cost-risk tradeoffs.
6   *Familiarity:* people experience greater outrage when the risk is new or strange to them and less so with familiar risks.
7   *Memorability:* people can more easily imagine risk and feel outrage when the risk is easy to remember or to visualize.
8   *Dread:* people experience great outrage when the risk produces greater dread. Examples of high dread are illnesses with long latency or risks that are difficult to detect.
9   *Diffusion in time and space:* people are more outraged by risks that can affect clusters of people than risks that affect widely dispersed people.

Source: www.psandman.com/articles/facing.htm

or mattress at 1 in 650 (The odds of dying, 2007). Risk communication enters the equation when people are or should be thinking about the risk threats they face. You are a *risk bearer* when you are exposed to a particular risk. For instance, living near a nuclear power facility makes you a risk bearer for the hazards endemic to that industry.

Risk communication defined

Palanchar (2005) defines *risk communication* as "a community infrastructure, transactional communication process among individuals and organizations regarding the character, cause, degree, significance, uncertainty, control, and overall perception of risk" (p. 752). By unpacking the key elements of the definition, we gain a greater understanding of this relatively new area for public relations. At the core of the definition is the transactional process. Risk communication is a *dialogue* between organizations creating risks and the constituents that must bear the risk. In general, organizations explain what the risk is (e.g., character, causes, and degree) while risk bearers try to voice their concerns and fears about the risk. But the dialogue covers an array of issues such as the uncertainty surrounding the risk and the ability to control the risk. A risk can be difficult to quantify or risk bearers may find there is little they can do to control the risk.

The *community infrastructure approach* seeks to build and maintain the risk discussion. A participatory atmosphere is created whereby risk bearers have a say in decisions and feel they are a viable part of the process. As Rowan (2005) notes, organizations must be willing to share power with risk bearers. But why community? Risk communication in the US was born from the Emergency Planning and Community Right-to-Know Act of 1986, title 3 of the Superfund Amendments and Reauthorization Act of 1986 (SARA) (Palanchar & Heath, 2007). SARA was in part a reaction to the devastating tragedy of Bhopal, India in 1984. The Union Carbide facility in Bhopal released methyl isocyanate (MIC) gas killing over 3,800 people and crippling thousands more. SARA posits that people should know about the chemical risks in their communities. US chemical companies are required to inform community members (people living near a facility) about the types and amounts of chemicals they manufacture, store, transport, or release into the community. Hence, the community became the focal point of risk communication (Palanchar, 2005).

Research by Heath and Palanchar has identified a number of variables that influence how people communicate about risk. We shall review a few of those key variables and their relationships to risk communication. The variables related to risk communication include support, harm and benefits, risk tolerance, uncertainty, trust, control, involvement, and knowledge.

At its heart, risk is about uncertainty. Risk involves the likelihood of an event occurring. That can be difficult to quantify. Government experts, for instance, find it difficult to quantify the risk from terrorist attacks. Greater uncertainty arises when a risk is difficult to quantify. Uncertainty is an important motivator for risk communication. People seek additional information when faced with uncertain situations. Self-interest and altruism also prompt people to become involved in risk communication. If a risk involves them or someone or something they care about (altruism), people are more likely to seek out risk information and become involved in the risk communication process.

One goal of a risk-creating organization is to have constituents support the organization even when a risk exists. Are you familiar with the phrase "sour gas"? If you were in the natural gas industry or lived near a sour gas well you would be. Sour gas is natural gas that contains high amounts of hydrogen sulphide, a toxic, flammable substance that smells like rotten eggs. Small amounts of hydrogen sulphide occur naturally; a common source is flatulence. The danger is that this chemical is toxic to animals and humans even in relatively low concentrations. However, over 30 percent of the natural gas in Western Canada is sour gas (Sour gas, 2008). The challenge for gas companies has been to convince people to allow the companies to place sour gas wells on their property and process the gas near where they live. People in parts of Canada have accepted the risk from gas companies and allowed them to extract and process the potentially dangerous sour gas near where they live, work, and play. It was a long and difficult process that included extensive meetings between the gas industry, government, communities, and other constituents. Eventually, a committee composed of the various constituents developed a plan that was acceptable to all involved. The extraction and processing of sour gas in Western Canada was a triumph of risk communication.

Risk communication is a means of converting risk-based opposition to support for an organization. Harms and benefits play a part in support decisions. Constituents will not support a risk-creating organization if they either see no benefit to the risk or do not feel the benefits outweigh the risks. Of course, people will perceive risk differently because they vary in terms of risk tolerances. People can accept different levels of risk in their lives. People can look at the same risk and come to different conclusions about the likelihood of the risk and the degree of harm. Some people like to parachute out of airplanes while others view it as suicide. Similarly, some constituents can accept the risks from hazardous materials in their community because it provides jobs, while others reject those same risks.

Knowledge is a key element of risk communication. Experts attempt to share knowledge with risk bearers. The problem is that experts and constituents often disagree on what the knowledge means. Again, people will see risks differently and not all will agree with the scientific assessment of the risk. Bisphenol A (BPA) serves as a perfect example of differing perceptions of risk. The primary use of BPA is to create clear, shatter-resistant plastic bottles. These bottles are used in a wide range of products that people eat or drink, including most baby bottles. In 2008 a study reported that BPA was linked to cancer and to alteration of brain functions in animals. Wal-Mart then announced it was phasing out any baby products containing BPA, while the government of Canada announced a 60-day comment period for the potential ban of BPA in baby bottles. The story spread rapidly through the news media and people began talking about not using plastic containers any more, especially for children's products and for drinking water (ACC, 2008; Paul, 2008). People feared the BPA would be absorbed into the food or drink they and their children consumed.

The Environmental Protection Agency (EPA) had not taken action on BPA as of Summer 2009. The reason is that there is extensive research that says BPA is safe to use in food and drink containers. That data says the BPA does not leech into food or drink. The European Food Safety Authority and the Japanese Ministry for Health, Labor and Welfare concurred with the EPA on the safety of BPA at the time this chapter was written (ACC, 2008). Undoubtedly, the risk debate over BPA will continue for years. The debate is fueled by perceptions of risk and data about risks. People differ in how serious they perceive the threat of BPA to be and differ in their interpretation of the findings of the various studies.

Just because people are told the degree of risk involved and ways to abate the risk, this does not mean they will accept the risk and support the risk-creating organization. Trust is a part of that equation. Trust is earned as constituents learn over time that a risk-creating organization is keeping them informed and allowing them to be meaningful participants in the risk communication process. The gas companies in Canada alluded to earlier did not win the community's support for sour gas overnight. The support was a result of a long process of risk communication using a community based process.

Control is one of the most important variables in risk communication and is multifaceted. First, constituents must believe they have some control over the risk communication process. Constituents gain control by having a voice in decisions that help to control the risks and potential negative consequences from the risk. Second, constituents must believe the managers in the risk-creating organization are acting properly to control their operations. Constituents trust that management is taking all the necessary steps to keep them safe.

Risk communication evolution and best practices

William Leiss (1996) reports that risk communication has evolved through three stages. Stage one was a source-oriented or technical information model with an emphasis on quantifying risk estimates. Risk communication was seen as simple; people just needed to understand the risk and they would accept it. The information being communicated in this iteration of risk communication was very technical. Community members were told the quantifiable risk of each chemical at a facility. There was no focus on how risk bearers felt about the risks or if they even understood the risk information. The technical information model was not very effective.

The second stage saw a shift from information to persuasion. Risk communication tried to persuade risk bearers to increase their acceptance of the risk and support for the organization. Risk communicators began to realize the importance of risk-bearer perceptions of risk. Effective persuasion demands an understanding of the audience's view of the situation. Still, little was done to address community concerns about risk, such as the ability to control the risk. Communities were more targets than partners in the risk communication process (Palanchar & Heath, 2006).

The third and current stage of risk communication uses dialogue to increase understanding between organizations and risk bearers. The dialogue allows organizations to gain a greater understanding and appreciation of the perceptions of risk bearers. How do risk bearers "see" the risk? What are the risk bearers' concerns about the risk? Risk bearers are not just part of a dialogue, they become part of the effort to manage the risk. Risk communication still involves information and advocacy. Palanchar and Heath (2006) provided an excellent set of guidelines for responsible advocacy in risk communication. Table 11.2 provides a summary of their ethical use guidelines for risk communication.

Risk communication outcomes

So what are the potential desired outcomes from risk communication? We can identify three basic outcomes: (1) awareness of a risk, (2) protective actions to

Table 11.2   Palanchar and Heath's (2006) ethical guidelines for risk communication

---

1   Develop emergency response measures designed to mitigate severe outcomes from a possible risk event. Create those plans in consultation with the community members.

2   Appreciate and try to understand that people will want to exert control over potentially negative effects.

3   Acknowledge that risk assessments are uncertain. Work with community members to address concerns that are bred by this uncertainty.

4   Community members should be active participants in decision making systems about risk assessment and risk management.

5   Trust with community members is built over time through collaboration and community outreach.

6   Communications should address both the harms and benefits involved. Realize that people will not always perceive the risks and benefits the same as you.

7   Develop an appreciation of how the community values and how they are experiencing the risks. This is accomplished by having the community participate in risk assessment and communication.

8   Try to understand how community members are approaching the decision making process and adjust the risk assessment frame to match their perspective.

---

take if a risk becomes manifest, and (3) correction of perceptions when a risk is overestimated.

Cleary, the intent of SARA was to make communities aware of the risk they face and to help them avoid those risks. Awareness of lifestyle risks is essential to social marketing (see chapter 8), so we will concentrate here on the risks created by organizations. For risks created by organizations, constituents need to be aware of the nature of the risks they face. What are the chemicals? How might the chemicals harm them? People should know what they are likely to encounter in their lives.

Awareness should segue into protective actions. Once people know what could happen, they need to understand what they should do if that risk does occur. For instance, some hazardous chemicals require people to shelter-in-place. People are to stay inside, turn off their air conditioning or heating, close their windows and doors, and try to seal the house from outside air. They should not evacuate nor should they attempt to retrieve their children from school. Being outside is hazardous so constituents must learn the value of staying inside and how to shelter-in-place properly. This is not an easy task since people naturally want to flee and to take their children with them. Protective actions add to a sense of control. Constituents realize there are actions they can take to reduce their threat from the risk. SARA included provisions on risk-creating organizations developing safety plans and sharing them with the community.

Public safety should be a basic concern of any organization. However, the 2005 tragedy at a BP facility in Texas City, Texas showed that management often disregards public safety in pursuit of profit. On March 23, 2005 employees were starting up the isomerization (ISOM) unit after a temporary shutdown. An explosion occurred that killed 15 workers and injured another 170. The investigations quickly pointed to mismanagement at BP as the cause. The US Chemical Safety Board, the group that investigates chemical accidents in the US, found that management had allowed an unsafe culture to develop as rules were ignored and safety processes not followed. Management had encouraged workers to bypass steps in the recommended restarting procedures for the ISOM, including turning off a safety warning device. Moreover, cost cutting efforts by BP had eroded the safety practices and preventative efforts at the Texas City facility (US Chemical, 2005).

Finally, risk communication can be used when constituents overestimate a risk, what Sandman refers to as high outrage and low hazard risks. The outrage generated by the risk far exceeds the proper assessment of the hazard. The goal becomes outrage management. More specifically, the emphasis is on outrage reduction, or what Sandman (2006) calls the "Calm down!" side of risk communication. Risk communication is used to help people to properly evaluate the hazard – the perceptions of the risk move closer to the scientific assessment of the hazard. An important part of outrage management is listening to the concerns of the outraged constituents. Risk-generating organizations need to acknowledge the outrage and to promote the efforts they have taken designed to reduce the source of the outrage. Even misperceptions must be acknowledged (Sandman, 2003).

Sandman's discussion of outrage management echoes the Excellence dialectic discussed in chapter 5. The process begins when some constituents are outraged about the risk-generating organization. This means the risk-generating organization is or has done something that created the outrage. It might be a series of chemical releases from improper handling of equipment or storage of extremely large amounts of a hazardous chemical. The point is the process starts with a legitimate reason for the outrage. The outrage becomes amplified in some way, such as through news media coverage or Internet discussions. Typically, some actor, often an activist group, seeks to promote the outrage as a way to pressure an organization to change its behaviors.

The risk-creating organization then makes substantive changes designed to address the outrage and communicates the changes to the constituents. From our earlier examples of outrage sources, safety training might be improved and enforced or the organization might store less of the hazardous chemical on site. Some real change is made designed to reduce the risk and the outrage it generates. Sandman notes that the risk-generating organization should emphasize how the actions it took reflect the demands made by those amplifying the outrage. Outrage should lessen if the risk-generating organization can demonstrate it has met the demands of its critics (Sandman, 2006). As with the Excellence dialectic, a challenge from the constituents focuses attention on a "problem" that is then redressed by the organization.

Summary

Risk communication provides another example of how public relations uses messages to either create arousal or quiescence. At times people need to know about a risk and take actions related to that risk. This is when people need to be aroused by concern about the threat posed by a risk because they fail to see or evaluate a situation as a risk. At other times people are outraged disproportionately to the risk. People perceive a risk as much greater than it really is. This is when people need risk messages designed to promote quiescence because they are overly concerned about the risk. Both arousal and quiescence in risk communication center on the proper evaluation of risk. This is the tricky part because the scientific data are the most common baseline for the proper evaluation of risk. However, we know that most constituents will not see the risk exclusively through the lens of science, and hence arrive at varying risk assessments. The challenge is to discover what the proper evaluation of the risk is by achieving some consensus on the risk assessment.

Best practices

The best practices recommendations for risk communication reflect the current dialogue stage of risk communication. A variety of risk experts have presented lists of best practices (e.g., Covello, 2003). Our discussion highlights a number of points that appear on several inventories of risk communication best practices:

1 Involve constituents as partners in the risk communication process by granting them power in the decision making process. Try to involve constituents early on and reach out to all those who might be affected by the risk.
2 Listen to the constituents to understand their concerns about the risk. Find out what they know about the risk, how they feel about the risk, and what they want done about the risk. Part of listening involves validating the emotions the risks evoke from constituents. Their emotions are real and should not be dismissed or ignored.
3 Acknowledge when there is uncertainty about the risk. There are times when science cannot provide specific risk assessments. Be honest when the science is unclear or perhaps contradictory. The uncertainty provides an opportunity to engage constituents because uncertainty is a motivator for seeking information and being involved in the risk communication process (Covello, 2003).
4 Be honest and open with information. Do not try to minimize or exaggerate a risk and release all information as soon as possible (Palanchar & Heath, 2007).

5   Avoid technical language. Present the risk information in ways constituents can understand. Graphs and other visuals can help to explain risk information (Covello, 2003).

The best practices demand that constituents be a part of the process if risk communication is to be effective. One-way messages from the risk-generating organization will not work. Gone should be the days when experts tell constituents they have misperceived the risk and win acceptance of the risk by enlightening those trapped in ignorance. Risk communication involves a purposeful exchange between interested constituencies (Lang, Fewtrell, & Bartram, 2001) that empowers the risk bearers. Of course, not all risk communication will involve best practices. The next section considers potential pitfalls in risk communication.

Individual risk

The preceding discussion of risk involves corporate issues, or how corporations and their constituents address risk. We can talk of individual risk as well, although that falls more within the purview of health communication and chapter 8 on social marketing. People make choices about the risks they take in their own lives. Risky behaviors by individuals include smoking, drug use, unsafe sex, and other behaviors that increase the risk of damaging one's own health. People will smoke but be upset by emissions from a nearby factory. The issue is control. People can control if they smoke but not the emissions from the smoke stack. Voluntariness, one of Sandman's outrage factors from table 11.1, is another reason for this seemingly usual risk acceptance.

Still the question remains why individuals engage in these "accepted" risky behaviors. One answer is *sensation seeking*. Marvin Zuckerman (1979) is one of the proponents of the sensation seeking explanation for risky behavior. Some people are driven by the need for novel, varied, complex, and intense experiences. These people are sensation seekers. People with the sensation seeking personality trait are more likely to engage in a range of risky behaviors including smoking, drug use, and indoor tanning (Bagdasarov et al., 2008). (We return to the risk of indoor tanning in the second case study at the end of this chapter.) Sensation seeking can be identified through the use of scales, including Zukerman's Sensation Seeking Scale (Form IV) and evaluation of monoamine oxide in the blood (D'Silva & Palmgreen, 2007).

Problem behavior theory is a larger framework that includes sensation seeking as one of the explanatory factors for risk taking. Problem behavior theory posits that risky behaviors are a function of the interaction between three systems: personality, environment, and behavior. Sensation seeking is a key component of the personality system. The environment system includes peer and parental approval. The behavior system is comprised of specific actions, including problem behaviors and conventional behaviors (Bagdasarov et al., 2008). If you look back to chapter 8 you will see elements of the problem behavior theory in the discussion of the theories that inform social marketing. The discussion of individual risk taking ends here because an extended discussion would require a stronger component of health communication than we intended to include in this book. However, a short discussion of why people engage in risky behaviors makes for a more well-rounded discussion of risk communication.

Reflections

Risk communication was created from a pro-constituency perspective. The idea was to help people by making them better informed about the risks in their lives. The risk information would help people to make choices and potentially to cope more effectively with the risks they must bear. Still, there are concerns about how various groups might abuse risk arousal and quiescence. Those concerns are addressed in this section.

A critical issue in risk communication is the inappropriate hype and inappropriate reassurance over risks. This returns us to the use of risk communication to create arousal and quiescence. Constituents are very likely to act against a risk-generating organization when they are aroused. As a result, risk-generating organizations have a stake in risk quiescence. However, other constituents have stakes in risk arousal. News stories of risk can agitate an audience and concern over a risk can build activist membership rosters and entice financial donations. Concerns are generated by both the overplay and underplay of risk.

Sandman (2006) observes that half-truths are commonly used to create both risk arousal and quiescence. For arousal, risk "promoters" carefully select what information to report and what information to ignore. In essence, omission is used to exaggerate the risk and create greater outrage. As an example, we can return to the Alar issue from chapter 10 on issues management. If you were to go on the Internet today and search "Alar" you would find any number of websites that claim the Alar risk was overstated and there was no scientific reason to ban it. The argument is that the test results were reported selectively and the risk of Alar was embellished by activists and the news media. The basic argument is that the Alar risk was distorted to secure its ban. You can find other websites that claim Alar was a true risk. The point is that defenders of Alar have some evidence that the Alar outrage outweighed the scientific hazard it presented. The same holds true for the more recent debate over BPA discussed earlier in this chapter.

Would activists and the news media present half-truths (selected data) to promote a risk and create outrage? Sandman (2006) clearly states the answer is yes. He refers to groups that promote outrage as the "outrage industry." While anchored by the activists and news media, corporations will join the outrage industry when the outrage can give them an advantage over their competitors. In the mid-1990s the Schering-Plough Corporation supported efforts by the Food and Drug Administration (FDA) to label phenolphthalein as cancer causing (a carcinogen). Phenolphthalein was the primary ingredient in laxatives at the time. Schering-Plough Corporation knew of the early FDA tests linking phenolphthalein to cancer and replaced it in their laxative Correctal. Schering-Plough Corporation used newspaper advertisements to alert consumers to the danger and that their competitors, in particular Ex-Lax, still used the carcinogen in its products (Canedy, 1997). Schering-Plough Corporation was creating outrage as a competitive advantage in the laxative market.

Sandman (2006) argues that corporations use half-truths or selective information to reassure people about risks, too. Information is omitted to create quiescence. Sandman notes many of his corporate clients use the omission of information to calm people while complaining how opponents are using the same tactics to create outrage. The advantage, according to Sandman, lies with those who create outrage. The premise is that people are more accepting of alarming half-truths than reassuring half-truths. One explanation for the difference is that the activists and news media generating outrage have greater credibility than the corporations seeking to reduce the outrage.

Exaggerations can hurt both sides when they are revealed. However, people feel the exaggerations for reassurance are more problematic. There is an underlying altruism in the outrage exaggeration while self-interest underlies the reassurance exaggeration. Still, groups that overstate a risk can harm their credibility to some degree (Sandman, 2006). When groups hide the true nature of a risk from people that is deemed worse than exaggerations designed to reduce a risk. It seems worse to hide a risk that could harm people than to overplay a risk. Any time half-truths and exaggerations occur there are ethical concerns to address. Activists should consider the ethics of overstating a risk just to win the day. Responsible risk communication, as outlined in table 11.2, should apply equally to corporations and activists. It is dishonest to overstate a risk even if the goal of protecting people seems noble. Moreover, Palanchar and Heath (2006) reviewed research that indicates risk bearers often have difficulty finding information or identifying relevant information when faced with a sea of data. Too much information can be as troublesome as too little. Both situations can lead to people being poorly informed about risks that are important to them.

People should be given the full picture of the risk so they can make informed choices. Once more we invoke the marketplace of ideas concept. The marketplace of ideas is diminished and decisions flawed when choice is based on half-truths and exaggerations. We cannot accept "the ends justifying the means" simply because we agree with the ends. All constituents should be bound by the ethical advocacy of risk communication.

Another way to influence risk arousal and quiescence is the definition of the risk. Here language and symbols are used to manipulate people's risk perceptions. If a risk sounds bad, people are likely to perceive it as bad. Hence, attach a negative label for arousal or a positive label for quiescence. Alar and phenolphthalein were labeled carcinogens. Nobody wants to be associated with cancer. The classic critical public relations treatise *Toxic Sludge is Good for You* noted how the industry wanted sludge referred to as a "biosolid" because it had a more positive and acceptable ring (Stauber & Rampton, 1995). Symbols are powerful, too, in shaping perceptions of risk. Alar was linked to children because the main products tied to the Alar risk were heavily child-consumed, such as apple juice and apple sauce. People should look behind the labels and symbols to the "facts." It falls to the consumers of the risk communication to determine if the label fits the risk and how well the symbols embody the risk. That task is easier if the various risk communicators are employing ethical advocacy in risk communication.

It is important to return to the idea of the appropriate or proper risk assessment. Ideally, risk assessment is co-created through a dialogue between the risk-generating organizations and the risk bearers. Such a process demands that constituents share control of the process. However, we must be cognizant of the role of power in the risk communication process. Sharing control and power are not always a comfortable fit for corporations (Rowan, 2005). Typically, the risk-generating organization can dictate the terms of the risk communication process because they have the greater power. Risk bearers receive as much power as the organizations are willing to surrender. That is why it is important for risk bearers to be able to draw from and to utilize their own power to ensure fair treatment in the process. Risk bearers must be able to flex their muscles if the risk-generating organization is not extending to them a true partnership in the risk communication process. It is naive to assume that all risk-generating organizations will automatically share power and control. Risk bearers must be prepared to fight for their place in the risk communication process.

The evidence of power imbalance and risk is found in the area of environmental justice. The idea of creating support by accepting a risk may fall prey to economic pressures. The economically disadvantaged may accept a risk because of the financial gain, not because a risk is truly acceptable to them. The risk is sold as an economic gain. Examples can be found in the news about toxic waste incinerators and hazardous waste storage facilities being sold on economic value over risk. Even worse is when the powerless groups have risk thrust upon them with little knowledge or say in the situation, a key concern in the area of environmental injustice.

Statistics in the US demonstrate that powerless groups (e.g., the poor and minorities) are the ones who commonly live, work, and play in heavily polluted areas (Skelton & Miller, n.d.). This problematic statistic reveals a situation known as *environmental injustice*:

> An environmental injustice exists when members of disadvantaged, ethnic, minority or other groups suffer disproportionately at the local, regional (sub-national), or national levels from environmental risks or hazards, and/or suffer disproportionately from violations of fundamental human rights as a result of environmental factors, and/or denied access to environmental investments, benefits, and/or natural resources, and/or are denied access to information; and/or participation in decision making; and/or access to justice in environment-related matters. (What we have, n.d.)

Multinational corporations have made environmental injustice a global concern.

Environmental justice is the counterweight to environmental injustice. The Environmental Protection Agency (EPA) defines environmental justice as the "fair treatment and meaningful involvement of all people regardless of race, color, national origin, or income with respect to the development, implementation, and enforcement of environmental laws, regulations, and policies" (Basic information, n.d.). Risks are a part of society and cannot be avoided completely. Farmers are at risk from the equipment and chemicals they use. The US government creates environmental hazards, for example, in the Defense Department. The medical community produces large amounts of hazardous waste during the course of treating patients.

The question is whether or not society bears the risks equally or disproportionately. Two ideas form the foundation for environmental justice: fair treatment and meaningful involvement. Fair treatment holds that no group of people should be forced to bear the negative environmental consequences created by corporations or the government. Meaningful involvement returns us to the reason risk communication emerged as a field. Decision makers should seek out the risk bearers, give them a chance to actually participate in the decision making process, and permit the risk bearers' contributions to influence policy decisions (Basic information, n.d.).

The discussion of meaningful involvement raises concerns about power that underscore the need for environmental justice and the role of risk communication in the process. Many of the environmental injustice situations are past sins. Sandman (1998) recommends that risk-generating organizations openly admit past oppression of the powerless as part of a dialogue to address what can be done now. The topics of environmental justice and environmental injustice reveal the negative consequences of improper risk communication and the value of responsible risk communication.

Conclusion

Risk communication is the embodiment of mutual influence within a web of relationships. The field was born from government regulation designed to aid communities. Effective risk communication requires corporations to share power with constituents. Old models of corporations just explaining risks to win support from risk bearers were failures. Risk communication succeeds with constituent cooperation and input. But risk and risk communication are dangerous weapons. Any constituency, not just corporations, can manipulate risk communication to win support for a cause. This might involve under selling or over selling a risk. We all suffer when truth is a victim of unethical risk communication. Risk communication is one aspect of public relations that affects our lives. It is incumbent upon all of us to understand and to be able to discern between ethical and unethical risk communication.

Case Study: Global Warming Risk

Some people accept that the environment is itself a constituent. Although it cannot speak for itself, the environment is affected by the actions of corporations and other constituents. Among the threats to the global environment are global warming and ozone depletion from chlorofluoro-carbons (CFCs). But are these risks real? We have traveled throughout Europe to attend public relations conferences in order to expose ourselves to new ideas and perspectives. Along the way we were frequently asked how our president could deny the existence of global warming. After all, the vast majority of scientists around the world agree that global warming is a problem exacerbated by human activity. Our president was not alone in his denial; he was joined by many influential conservative politicians and corporations.

The tide began to shift in the US in 2007 when the president and many large corporations were suddenly converted as they saw the light of global warming. But how could so many people resist the evidence of global warming for so long? The answer lies in risk communication and shaping perceptions of risk. Conservative groups, funded by large corporations, run what are called "think-tanks." A think-tank employs scientists to research topics of interest to the sponsors. Ideally, a think-tank is independent and allows the results to emerge from the science. In reality, most think-tanks "find" the results that support the beliefs of their sponsors (Beder, 2002). If a large oil company wants a study that reports burning fossil fuels is not a significant contributor to global warming, amazingly enough, that is what its think-tank finds!

Large corporations from around the world have used think-tanks and minority opinion scientists to dispute the global warming problem. Conservative think-tanks such as the Competitive Enterprise Institute (CEI) in the US and the Institute of Economic Affairs (IEA) in the UK have argued against global warming. They rely on the very small group of scientists who do not believe in global warming, such as Ronald Bailey, who authored *Ecoscam: The False Prophets of Ecological Apocalypse*. The idea was to cast doubt on the certainty of global warming. If there was doubt, there was no reason to take steps designed to reduce human actions that contributed to global warming. People need to believe in a risk for there to be arousal (Beder, 2002). Not surprisingly, such actions would be expensive to a number of corporations. The idea was to use risk communication to create quiescence.

McKie and Galloway (2007) likened the global warming debunking to US tobacco company efforts to deny the link between cigarette smoking and cancer. For decades, the tobacco industry funded scientists who denied the link when the vast majority of evidence indicated smoking did lead to cancer in humans. Ethics prohibited definitive cause-effect studies for smoking and cancer. Proving cause and effect would require purposely exposing some people to cigarette smoke (a treatment group) while a similar group was not exposed (control group). If the smokers (treatment group) had higher incidents of diseases than the control group, a cause-effect relationship would be proven. However, the cost would be too high for a such a study because you would be condeming some people to horrible deaths. However, the results from correlational studies were overwhelming. The correlational studies simply showed smoking is linked to, or correlated with, various diseases. Further discussion of the design and statistics can be found in books on research methods. The point is, correlational studies provided the tobacco companies grounds for disputing the link between smoking and various diseases. Eventually, tobacco companies relented and spent billions of dollars to settle lawsuits from the victims of tobacco smoking.

McKie and Galloway (2007) argue that groups who use dissident scientists to dispute global warming are on the same slippery slope. There will be a day of reckoning when the corporations are held accountable for their efforts to delay action on global warming. That day appears to be near at hand. On July 18, 2007, the top 160 companies in the US issued a statement calling for the need to address climate change (Lobe, 2007). Even the US President George W. Bush finally seemed to think global warming might be real.

Books by Beder (2002) and Hager and Burton (1999) detail the efforts to derail interest and action on global warming. Public relations played a significant role, including efforts to reassure people the risk was not great – outrage management. We will never know the evironmental damage these risk communication efforts allowed to transpire because they slowed action on efforts to curb global warming. The EPA states the ozone layer "has been gradually depleted by man-made chemicals like chlorofluorocarbons (CFCs). A depleted ozone shield allows more UV from the sun to reach the ground, leading to more cases of skin cancer, cataracts, and other health problems" (Stratospheric ozone, 2007). Yet many of the same conservative think-tanks are parading minority opinion scientists that claim there is nothing to fear from ozone. Among the voices are Ralf Schauerhammer, author of *The Hole in the Ozone Scare: The Scientific Evidence that the Sky Isn't Falling*. His ideas have been amplified in the US by conservative radio show host Rush Limbaugh, meaning they are reaching and influencing millions of people (Beder, 2002). The anti-ozone scientists note there has been no measurable effect of ozone depletion on US cities. While true, there is strong evidence to show the effects on Australian cities and other cities located where the ozone layer has thinned.

So why try to convince people there is no ozone problem – use risk communication to reassure people? The answer is the cost of replacing CFCs as part of the effort to protect the ozone layer. If the ozone depletion is debatable or untrue, there is no reason to be aroused

or to take action. We should wait for a definitive answer. The problem is a definitive answer does exist. Again, the vast majority of scientific data support ozone depletion and the link to CFCs. Dissident scientists and minority views are used as a counterweight to a mountain of evidence. But if doubt is created, people are more likely to be quiescent and CFCs remain in use. In turn, the ozone layer is further eroded, the environment compromised further, and people are placed at a greater risk from sun exposure.

The point of this case study is to reveal the power and effects of inappropriate risk communication. By using obscure scientists and biased studies to cast doubt on a library full of scientifically vetted evidence is unethical and harmful. Those who warned about global warming were derisively called "climate pornographers" and were accused of just trying to scare people. Delays in taking action on smoking by denying the link to cancer resulted in health damage and deaths that could have been prevented. The same has happened with global warming and is happening with ozone depletion. Risk communication is used as a form of denial to reassure constituents and to prevent actions. In this case, the actions could affect the interests of many corporations, so they are involved in the calming risk communication effort. As McKie and Galloway (2007) note, the efforts to deny global warming do more harm than good. Unfortunately, the public relations industry is drawn into the controversy because public relations is a primary mechanism for the denial messages. Risk communication is a valuable tool for society only when it is used appropriately.

Case questions

1   Describe your reaction to how the risks of global warming have been portrayed in the news media. Apply Sandman's risk equation in your answer (*Risk = Hazard + Outrage*).

2 Why is risk communication, especially dialogue, problematic in the case of global
   warming? Why is it difficult to identify the
   risk bearers of global warming? Why is it
   difficult to identify who or what organizations should be responsible for risk
   communication?
3 Conduct an Internet search on chlorofluoro-
   carbons (CFCs) to read what various organizations are saying about their impact on the

environment. What groups seem to downplay
the risks of CFCs? What groups seek to highlight those risks?
4 If you have seen the 2006 documentary *An
   Inconvenient Truth*, how do you think it may
   have influenced current public opinion on
   global warming? To what extent do you
   believe some of the information in the documentary? Evaluate its effectiveness in terms
   of the risk communication process.

Case Study: Tanning Risk

You have probably seen messages in print, on
television, or on the Internet warning about
excessive sun exposure. Most physicians will
warn patients against excessive sun exposure
because of the risk of skin cancer or melanoma.
Patients with high risk factors for skin cancer are
told to avoid the sun as much as possible. The
advice means people should wear sun screen
and/or protective clothing when in the sun and
limit overall exposure to the sun. People also
should avoid overexposure to artificial sunlight
from tanning beds because the same risk of
skin cancer exists. The American Academy of
Dermatology (www.aad.org) even sponsors a
website as part of its social marketing effort to
warn people of the dangers of indoor tanning.
The campaign is called "Indoor Tanning is Out."
Here is a sample of its message:

Indoor tanning before the age of 35 has been associated with a significant increase in the risk of melanoma.
Yet on an average day, more than one million Americans
use indoor tanning salons. Research shows 70 percent
of indoor tanners are female, primarily 16 to 29 years
old, an age group that's particularly at risk for developing skin cancer. (Indoor tanning is out, 2008)

The campaign includes print and radio messages
that feature the stories of cancer survivors who
had high exposure to indoor tanning.

Sun exposure does allow the skin to produce
vitamin D. So there is one argument for some sun
exposure. In 2008 a number of pro-tanning sites
began to appear on the Internet, including the
sister sites Smart Tan and Tanningtruth. The term
sister is used because the sites were developed
by the same group. These pro-tanning sites extol
the value of vitamin D through tanning and
debunk the hype of skin cancer. Indoor tanning is
recommended at both sites. Smart Tan encourages people to use tanning beds so they can get
the necessary vitamin D. It also provides information about tanning products and the online version of Tanning Trends, the indoor tanning's smart
business source. Would you be surprised to learn
the sites are developed and operated by the tanning industry? Tanning salons are businesses and
collectively qualify as an industry. The Smart Tan
site is designed for those who work in the tanning
industry and provides information about products, training, advertising, and trends. The Smart
Tan site also provides a link to tanningtruth.com
so that business owners can access information
about tanning to share with their clients.
Presumably, this information will help them discuss tanning risks with their clients.
   Here is how Tanningtruth defines itself:

TanningTruth.com is a public information site dedicated to teaching a responsible, balanced and effective message about sun care. Sunlight is free – the sun
has no public relations firm touting its many benefits.

And because $35 billion is made annually by parties who use "sun *scare*" tactics – overstating the risks of sun exposure while ignoring the benefits – it's more important than ever for the public to hear the full story. That's the charge of TanningTruth.com. (About us Tanning Truth, n.d.)

The Tanningtruth site is aggressive. There is no industry talk or information, the focus is on debunking the scares over skin cancer. Here is a sample message: "Scaring people out of the sun is a multibillion-dollar business. Smart Tan coined the term 'sun scare' in 1996 to properly identify those who were distorting the truth about sunshine's complex relationship with human health in order to scare you out of the sun. Some 'sun scare' groups profit by marketing a distorted sun abstinence message" (How commercialism, n.d.). The site tries to convince people that the risk of tanning – natural or artificial – is overstated. In the discussion of their position statement, the site offers the professional indoor tanning salon as a solution in the battle against sunburn and even proposes tanning as a part of your skin care regimen. Even worse, it claims the scare is being used simply to sell you products such as sun screen.

In chapter 8 we discussed social marketing. The American Academy of Dermatology's website is social marketing because it promotes benefits to society. The Tanningtruth site is pseudo-social marketing. It appears to be in the public interest but is designed to advance an industry's interest, seemingly to the detriment of society. The point of this chapter is risk and how risk is perceptual. Clearly, both the American Academy of Dermatology and Tanningtruth are trying to shape perceptions of risk about tanning in general and indoor tanning specifically. How people ultimately evaluate that risk can have significant ramifications on their health. Risk can be contested, even when it involves such a well-documented risk such as the link between tanning and skin cancer.

Case questions

1 Visit the websites of Smart Tan (www. smarttan.com) and Tanningtruth (www. tanningtruth.com). How are risks from indoor tanning explained? Does the tanning industry seem to be acting ethically when it claims that a risky behavior is good for you?
2 Visit the website of the American Academy of Dermatology (www.aad.org). How does this group explain the risks of sun exposure and indoor tanning? Do you believe this group is acting ethically when it offers advice on sun exposure and indoor tanning?
3 What other sources could you consult to assess the health benefits and risks of tanning?

Discussion Questions

1 Why are public relations professionals involved in the risk communication process?
2 Distinguish between the terms *hazard*, *risk*, and *threat*. Describe the three varieties of risk.
3 How does Peter Sandman, an expert in risk communication, explain his risk equation: *Risk = Hazard + Outrage*? Explain the variables in the equation and how they relate to public relations functions. See table 11.1 for an inventory of Sandman's outrage factors.

4 Why is it important for organizations to create a dialogue with community members (risk bearers)? What are the goals of risk communication? What are the three basic outcomes desired from risk communication?
5 Discuss how the ideas associated with the community infrastructure approach are consistent with our definition of public relations as the management of mutually influential relationships within a web of constituency relationships.

6 Consider Palanchar and Heath's (2006) ethical guidelines for risk communication (table 11.2). To what extent are these adequate guidelines for risk communication? Would you add any guidelines? What are the implications of these guidelines for public relations practitioners?

7 Are you aware of any risks you might confront due to where you live? Have you received any risk communication messages? If so, how would you evaluate those messages using the "best practices" described in this chapter?

8 Visit the website of an organization you believe will be engaging in risk communication (e.g., manufacturing facilities, power companies, waste management facilities, etc.). What risk communication is available at the site? How would you evaluate the adequacy of the information? If you lived near the facility, would this information be helpful to you?

A bird's eye view of the wreckage at the BP facility in Texas City, March 24, 2005, after the March 23 explosion.
PHOTO WILLIAM PHILPOTT/AFP/GETTY IMAGES

12

Crisis Communication

Millions of fast food tacos are served without incident each week (if you do not include indigestion and cholesterol). In December 2006, Taco Bell was faced with an outbreak of *E. coli* centered in New York and New Jersey. The Centers for Disease Control (CDC) reported 71 cases, including 53 requiring hospitalization. The onset of the illnesses ranged from November 20 to December 2. Taco Bell closed restaurants linked to the outbreak and carefully examined their locations and foodstuffs for the cause. Initially, green onions (scallions) were thought to be the cause, but the CDC eventually indicated the lettuce was the most likely source of the contamination. The Food and Drug Administration (FDA) worked to track down the supplier and possible source of the contamination (Bridges, 2006). With the incident occurring near New York City, a media frenzy surrounded the outbreak. Taco Bell management had to address the problem quickly.

Greg Creed, President of Taco Bell, was visible and vocal during the crisis. One of his statements read:

> I want to reassure our customers that our food is perfectly safe to eat. Food safety is Taco Bell's number one priority, and we have taken immediate actions to safeguard the public's health from the moment we learned of an *E. coli* outbreak associated with our restaurants. Our team of experts, including Dr. Mike Doyle, a world-renowned food safety expert who is consulting with us, has been working around the clock with the CDC, FDA, and state and local health authorities since the date of the first onset to try to pinpoint the source of this outbreak. We continue to be deeply concerned for those who have become sick. (Taco Bell, 2006)

Taco Bell acted quickly and compassionately to address the situation.

Strangely, that same month witnessed customers at Taco John's restaurants in Minnesota and Iowa contracting *E. coli*. Again, tainted lettuce was suspected.

Taco John's announced a change in suppliers, launched a review of their process from farm to fork, and reassured customers their food was safe in a number of full-page newspaper advertisements. About 77 people were affected by the outbreak. The CEO of Taco John's, Paul Fisherkeller, expressed concern for those affected by the outbreak. He also visited the affected areas and ate at Taco John's to demonstrate his confidence that his company had resolved the problem (Lohn, 2006). No link was ever found between the two taco *E. coli* outbreaks, even though both were tentatively linked to lettuce.

These two cases share a very active and effective crisis management effort. In each case the crisis response was helpful in restoring confidence and addressing the concerns of victims. Improper crisis communication would have intensified the problem. People are very concerned when the food they eat has the potential to make them seriously ill or even kill them. Hence, crisis communication becomes critical. But the need for crisis management extends far beyond restaurants, as any organization that has constituents can suffer a crisis. Organizations must be prepared to manage crises at least as competently as was shown in the examples used to open this chapter. This chapter explores the vital area of crisis management by reviewing key concepts, followed by an explication of why crisis management is a public relations practice.

Background

As with public relations itself and the various subdisciplines covered in this book, there is no one accepted definition of crisis or crisis management. In this section we present the definitions for the key terms that guide this chapter: crisis and crisis management.

Crisis

Coombs (2007b) defines *crisis* as "the perception of an unpredictable event that threatens important expectancies of stakeholders and can seriously impact an organization's performance and generate negative outcomes" (pp. 2–3). The key aspects of the definition are *unpredictable, expectations, serious impact/negative outcomes,* and *perception.*

Managers anticipate crises but they cannot predict a crisis. We might know a crisis is likely to happen but we do not know when, so we must be prepared for one at any time. Crises typically violate how constituents expect an organization to act. Lettuce should not poison consumers, trains should not derail, and chemical companies should not release toxic clouds. Violating expectations creates angry constituents who will alter how they interact with an organization. The term *crisis* should be reserved for serious events or threats. A crisis has the potential to disrupt the entire organization (Coombs, 2007b). Along with serious impact is the potential to cause negative outcomes. Business disruption is a negative outcome, but so too are deaths, injuries, property damage, negative publicity, reputation loss, and environmental damage. Many of these negative outcomes are interrelated. Injuries and property damage, for instance, can generate negative publicity and reputation loss. A crisis is a serious threat that can disrupt organizational operations and/or has the potential to create negative outcomes.

The definition we selected moves away from a crisis as just an objective event and considers the subjective nature of a crisis as well. An industrial accident, an airline crash, and major fire are all objective and easy to spot as crises. But some crises originate in the perceptions of constituents. Constituents are elevated in their importance as their perceptions help to determine whether or not a crisis exists. If constituents believe a crisis exists, they react to the organization as if there is a crisis. Hence, an organization is in a crisis if key constituents perceive a crisis. If key constituents view an organizational practice as inappropriate, there can be a crisis.

Constituents told PepsiCo to redesign the labels for their snack chips to make it easier to see the ingredient olestra in 2006. The situation was considered a crisis because one prominent constituent, the Center for Science in the Public Interest, threatened a lawsuit. The controversy brought negative publicity to PepsiCo, including alerting the public to the potential dangers of an ingredient in their chips. Some people react badly to olestra and experience vomiting and cramps. Even though business operations were not at risk, there was the threat of serious negative outcomes to PepsiCo in the situation, raising it to the level of a crisis. PepsiCo managed the crisis by agreeing to change the label (Frito-Lay target, 2006; Frito-Lay to, 2006).

Crisis management

Crisis management can be defined as "a set of factors designed to combat crises and to lessen the actual damage inflicted" (Coombs, 2007b, p. 5). The general goal of crisis management is to prevent or lessen the negative effects of a crisis. In turn, crisis management serves to protect constituents, organizations, industries, and the environment from harm. Crisis management is not one "thing." Rather, it is a set of factors that form a process. The crisis management process can be divided into three parts: pre-crisis, crisis event, and post-crisis. The three parts are related to one another; they are not stand-alone elements. Pre-crisis work prepares for the crisis event. Post-crisis work reviews the crisis event and suggests ways to improve the pre-crisis preparation. Figure 12.1 shows how the three parts form a process.

The pre-crisis phase is the domain of prevention and preparation. The best way to manage a crisis is to prevent one. Crisis managers work with others to identify potential crisis trigger events and work to prevent these from occurring. For example, an organization replaces a toxic chemical in its production process with a non-toxic substance that achieves the same results. A potential hazardous chemical release or poisoning is averted. In 2007 the Chinese manufacturer of

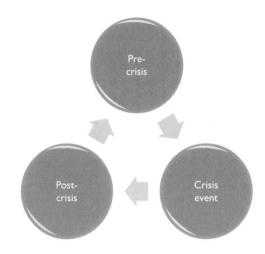

Figure 12.1   Crisis management process

Aqua Dots used a hazardous chemical instead of one of the approved chemicals in the manufacturing process. The end result was very sick children, as the chemical on the toy became the date-rape drug GHB when ingested. There were a number of reports of seizures and even one case of a coma (Spin Master, 2007). Prevention seeks to eliminate trigger events or reduce the likelihood of one occurring.

Because there is no possible way to eliminate all risks, organizations must be prepared for the time when a crisis does unfold. Preparation involves the creation and testing of the crisis management plan (CMP), assignment and training of the crisis management team, and the assignment and training of the crisis spokespersons. A CMP is simply a rough guide that reminds the crisis team what might need to be done during the crisis, specifies certain responsibilities, and pre-collects information that will be useful during a crisis. It is not a "how-to" manual. Each crisis is different and requires the crisis team to adapt to the situation. Exercises are essential to determine if the CMP, crisis team, and spokespersons are prepared for the task. It's better to find and correct a weakness through training in an exercise than in an actual crisis.

The crisis event is when an organization is in a crisis situation. The crisis team is mobilized and the CMP used as a reference tool. The organization must respond to the crisis under the watchful eye of its constituents. A key goal in this phase is recovery from the crisis, both for victims of the crisis and the organization itself. The crisis response includes what the organization says and does after the crisis hits. Crisis communication plays a vital role in containing the damage from a crisis and addressing constituent concerns about the crisis.

The post-crisis phase covers the end of the crisis management effort. A crisis is nearing an end when operations are close to business-as-usual. Two key tasks remain in the post-crisis phase. First, constituents must be updated on the recovery from the crisis. Examples include reporting the results of investigations into the cause of a crisis, settling lawsuits related to the crisis, and announcing when a facility is returning to full operations. Second, the crisis management effort must be evaluated. Management must determine what went well and poorly. The strengths are maintained while the weaknesses are targeted for improvement and become the focal point in future training and exercises (Coombs, 2007b).

Crisis Management as a Public Relations Practice

The purpose of this section is to summarize the lessons provided by the vast research and writings on crisis management. The lessons will be divided into five categories: preparation, communication channels, spokesperson training, initial response, and reputation repair response.

Preparation

Management must be prepared for the time when a crisis eventually hits an organization. No organization is immune from a crisis and no management should delude themselves into believing they are crisis resistant. Preparation allows for a more effective crisis management effort that protects constituents and the organization from undue harm. The four central aspects of preparation are the crisis management plan, the crisis team, exercises, and pre-drafted messages.

The crisis management plan (CMP) is the core of preparation. An organization must have a CMP that is updated at least once a year. A CMP saves time with the pre-assignment of tasks and pre-collection of information. Time is not wasted executing tasks that could have been completed before the crisis occurred. However, an out-of-date CMP with the wrong information wastes time. Personnel and organizations change and a CMP must keep pace.

A crisis management team develops and utilizes the CMP. An organization must have a crisis management team that has been trained for the task. The crisis team is cross-functional, meaning it has people from different function areas within the organization. Different function areas are included because of the knowledge and skills each can bring to the crisis team. Core members of the crisis team include public relations, operations or manufacturing, legal, and security. Other people are added when their skills are needed, such as IT if the crisis involves the computer system (Coombs, 2007b).

A crisis team and CMP are of no value until they are tested through exercises. Exercises can be simple or complex, but all serve to test a part of or the entire crisis management effort of an organization. The organization should conduct exercises once a year to test the CMP and provide valuable practice for the crisis team. Crisis teams are shown to improve their decision making through practice (Coombs, 2006). Exercises can help to find holes in CMPs and any weaknesses in team members before a crisis hits. Again, it is better to find problems when there is nothing on the line than during an actual crisis.

Some messages can be pre-drafted before a crisis hits. Crisis managers can anticipate the basic messages needed in a particular crisis. The crisis team should pre-draft messages when possible, such as templates for news releases, and have a dark website ready with various crisis-relevant content. The legal department should pre-approve the messages. Once more, time is saved as tasks are completed before and not during the crisis. Saving time allows the crisis team to spend more time on the current demands of the crisis (Coombs, 2007b).

Communication channels

The preparation phase mentioned websites. A website is an excellent channel for reaching many constituents and can be updated quickly (Corporate Leadership Council, 2003). Reporters and other web-savvy constituents will look for online crisis information, so do not disappoint them (Taylor & Kent, 2007). The online crisis information can be a special website developed for the crisis or simply a section of the current website devoted to the crisis. Research has shown organizations have lagged in the utilization of websites in crises (Lackluster, 2002; Taylor & Perry, 2005). Today, it is vital for a crisis response to include either a unique website or part of the organization's current website.

Intranet sites are useful during a crisis, too. The organization's Intranet site can be an invaluable resource for keeping employees informed about the crisis. Informed employees, in turn, become communication channels to family and friends. The Intranet can also reach customers and suppliers if they are a part of the organization's extended Intranet. American Airlines effectively used its Intranet site to update employees after 9/11 (Downing, 2003). But not all employees or other constituents in need of immediate information have Internet access.

Mass notification systems are becoming more popular as the technology that drives them improves. An organization should utilize mass notification systems when rapid deployment of messages is required. Mass notification systems send short messages to a pre-selected group of people through multiple and often redundant channels, including telephone and email. For instance, a list of names, contact information, and groupings are placed in the system. Each person could have multiple contact points, including land lines, mobile phones, and email. People are grouped so that messages can be sent to types of constituents such as employees, people living near a facility, or customers. A mass notification even allows for people to send short responses. An excellent use of mass notification is when the area around a facility needs to be evacuated. Residents can be contacted with the notification to evacuate and information about the location of evacuation centers, and can send a reply indicating they have been notified.

Spokesperson training

During a crisis, one or more individuals may speak for the organization to constituents, primarily the news media. The spokesperson is a conduit for conveying crisis-related information from the crisis team to constituents. Proper training is required so that the spokesperson does not make the crisis worse for those involved. There are four critical lessons that emerge from the literature on spokesperson training:

1   The spokesperson should avoid the phrase "no comment" because constituents hear "I'm guilty and hiding something."
2   Avoid jargon and technical language and seek clarity in the message. Confusing messages do not help constituents at risk; people may assume the lack of clarity is intentional. People are not helped if the information intended to promote their safety is presented in a way that they do not understand. This can be as simple as translating crisis messages into various languages or making sure the message is suitable to the readability level of the constituents. The comprehension error is compounded when people feel the obfuscation is intentional. The perception of malice makes the failure to translate much worse.
3   Fully brief all potential spokespersons on the latest information so that they are consistent when questioned.
4   A spokesperson should not display lack of eye contact, nervous gestures, or repeated vocal disfluencies (ums, ers, uhs). These displays are common signs of nervousness, but also may be mistakenly interpreted as signs of deception (Coombs, 2007b). The spokesperson is to be a source of clear information that constituents need. He or she should not create an unflattering portrait of the organization due to incompetence. The media relations knowledge base is a valuable resource to tap for spokesperson training.

Initial crisis response

The initial crisis response is the first set of messages coming from the crisis team/organization. Recommendations encompass both style and content.

Three common pieces of advice are offered for the style of an initial crisis response: be quick, accurate, and consistent. An initial crisis response must happen fast; most experts recommend a response within the first hour. A quick response demonstrates an organization is in control of the situation (Arpan & Roskos-Ewoldsen, 2005; Carney & Jorden, 1993). But what if you do not really have anything to say? Just tell constituents what you know so far and indicate updates will be provided as information becomes available. The Internet has intensified the pressure for a quick response. People now expect information faster, including crisis information.

Accuracy means the crisis team only reports what it has verified. The pressure for speed can breed accuracy errors, so it is important to not let time pressures outweigh verification. Accuracy bleeds into consistency because correcting inaccuracies creates the appearance of inconsistency. Never speculate during a crisis response. If the speculation is wrong, the organization looks inconsistent, incompetent, and perhaps deceptive. Accuracy facilitates consistency. Keeping spokespersons informed also facilitates accuracy and consistency. Spokespersons with the same information will give similar answers when asked the same questions (Coombs, 2007b).

A final style response recommendation is to use all the available channels of communication. This includes sending messages through the news media, websites, Intranets, emails, and mass notification systems. Using multiple channels increases the odds of constituents receiving the crisis information they need.

Content of initial response

The number one priority in a crisis should be constituent safety. Although in some crises constituent safety is not an issue, in most crises it is. Most crises create victims or potential victims, those that are harmed or could be harmed in some way by the crisis. Constituents who can become victims in crises include employees, customers, people living or working near a facility, investors, and suppliers. Constituents could be at risk from dangerous products, harmful food, hazardous chemicals, or fire. The initial message must convey what is termed *instructing information*. Instructing information tells constituents how to protect themselves from the danger posed by the crisis (Sturges, 1994). Telling people what peanut butter was covered in the recall or of the need to shelter-in-place are examples of instructing information. Instructing information must do more than inform, it should move people to action. Constituents are only protected physically if they act upon the instructing information. Therefore, instructing information must be clear and indicate how following the advice will help people protect themselves.

Adjusting information is a secondary priority in an initial crisis response. Adjusting information helps people to cope psychologically with the crisis (Sturges, 1994). Examples of adjusting information include expressions of sympathy/concern for victims, corrective action, and counseling for stress and trauma. Crises produce psychological stress for victims and potential victims. Constituents need to know what happened, what is being done to address the crisis, and what steps are being taken to prevent a repeat of the crisis. What happened and what is being done is a matter of updating constituents as the crisis team collects information about the crisis. The final point is known as *corrective action*. Corrective action is reassuring, as people realize the crisis is less likely to happen again (Sellnow, Ulmer, & Snider, 1998). Corrective action may need to be delayed because it can take days, weeks, or months to discover the exact cause of a crisis (Ray, 1999). No corrective action can be taken until a cause is known. You cannot solve a problem until you know what that problem is.

Counseling for stress and trauma should be provided for victims, their families, and the crisis team. Airlines have a strong program in place for counseling after an airline accident. Counseling is provided to survivors, families of victims, and to the airline personnel working the crisis (Business Roundtable, 2002; Coombs, 2007b). Expressing sympathy or concern seems rather simple, but can be beneficial to victims. Constituents will expect the organization to acknowledge the victims in some fashion. This expectation is primarily an expression of concern for the victims (Patel & Reinsch, 2003). Even though expression of sympathy and concern may seem automatic, not expressing them would be problematic. In other words, not expressing concern and sympathy would harm an organization in crisis. So why would organizations not offer sympathy? The answer is "legal concerns." Some attorneys try to use expressions of concern/sympathy against organizations by arguing it is evidence that an organization has taken responsibility for a crisis. A few states have enacted laws that prevent statements of sympathy/concern from being used as evidence of accepting responsibility in crisis-related lawsuits (Cohen, 2002; Fuchs-Burnett, 2002).

Reputation repair in post-crisis communication

The most heavily researched area of crisis communication is reputation repair. The research tries to determine the most effective way for organizations to protect their reputations following a crisis. As detailed in chapter 9, reputation is a valuable intangible resource that organizations need to protect. The focus of the reputation repair research is how various crisis response strategies can be used to protect or to repair a reputation following a crisis. Four areas of research have emerged that explore reputation protection after a crisis: corporate apologia, image restoration theory, rhetoric of renewal, and situational crisis communication theory.

Corporate apologia was the first approach to reputation protection and crises. Keith Hearit (1994, 1995a, 1995b, 2001, 2006) has written the most extensively on the topic. Social legitimacy – the consistency between organizational values and stakeholder values – is the cornerstone of corporate apologia. A crisis serves to threaten social legitimacy because an organization appears to be incompetent (e.g., a transportation accident) and/or to have violated stakeholder expectations (e.g., unfair labor practices). The social legitimacy violation is a form of character attack. Corporate apologia is intended to protect an organization's character by seeking "to present a compelling, competing account of organizational actions" (Hearit, 2001, p. 502). Social legitimacy is also a type of constituent expectation. Constituents expect organizations to embody "their" values. The corporate apologia research produced one of the first lists of crisis response strategies, the communicative response options available to crisis

Table 12.1   Corporate apologia crisis response strategies

Denial: the organization denies any wrongdoing.
Counterattack: the organization denies wrongdoing and claims the accuser is the one at fault.
Differentiation: the organization attempts to distance itself from guilt for the crisis. There is an admission of responsibility, but factors are identified that limit the organization's responsibility.
Apology: the organization accepts responsibility and promises not to do it again. This is a form of dissociation.
Legal: the organization allows the legal team to handle the crisis and avoids public statements.

managers. Table 12.1 defines the crisis response strategies that have emerged from Hearit's work on corporate apologia.

Image restoration theory (IRT) was developed by William Benoit and fuses corporate apologia with the account-giving literature in interpersonal communication. Once more the crisis response pivots on the organization's account (explanation) of its behavior. IRT holds that communication is goal directed and that one of the goals of communication is to protect one's reputation (Benoit, 1995). IRT was not specifically designed for crisis communication, but has been applied to a wide array of crisis case studies (e.g., Benoit & Czerwinski, 1997; Brinson & Benoit, 1996).

IRT provides a list of five crisis response strategies: denial, evading responsibility, reducing the offensiveness of the crisis, corrective action and/or promise to take action to prevent a repeat of the event, and mortification. Table 12.2 provides complete definitions of the IRT strategies and sub-strategies. IRT researchers create rhetorical case studies by identifying what crisis response strategies were used to manage a crisis. The researcher then draws conclusions about why the crisis management effort was a success or failure. The conclusions are speculative because they are subjective interpretations of the events (Coombs, 2007a). Therefore, we must be skeptical when examining the recommendations emerging from the IRT research. The dominant recommendation that emerges from IRT research is that mortification (publicly accepting responsibility for the crisis) is the preferred response to a crisis (Brinson & Benoit, 1999; Tyler, 1997).

The rhetoric of renewal emphasizes the positive view of the organization's future rather than dwelling on current discussion of responsibility. The emphasis is on helping victims, an accommodation focus. The rhetoric of renewal is about an organization creating a new direction and sense of purpose after emerging from a crisis (Ulmer, Sellnow, & Seeger, 2006). It is an extension of accommodative strategies, adjusting information, and compensation.

There are limits to when the rhetoric of renewal can be used, meaning it is not an option in every crisis. Research suggests four criteria are necessary to permit

Table 12.2   Image restoration theory crisis response strategies

---

Denial
- Simple denial: did not do it.
- Shift the blame: blame someone or something other than the organization.

Evading responsibility
- Provocation: response to someone else's actions.
- Defeasibility: lack of information about or control over the situation.
- Accidental: did not mean for it to happen.
- Good intentions: actor meant well.

Reducing offensiveness
- Bolstering: reminder of the actor's positive qualities.
- Minimize offensiveness of the act: claim little damage from the crisis.
- Differentiation: compare act to similar ones.
- Transcendence: place act in a different context.
- Attack accuser: challenge those who say there is a crisis.
- Compensation: offer money or goods.

Corrective Action: restore situation to pre-act status and/or promise change and prevent a repeat of the act.

Mortification: ask for forgiveness; admit guilt and express regret.

---

the use of renewal: (1) the organization has a strong pre-crisis ethical standard; (2) the constituency-organization pre-crisis relationships are strong and favorable; (3) a focus on life beyond the crisis rather than seeking to escape blame; and (4) a desire to engage in effective crisis communication (Ulmer, Sellnow, & Seeger, 2006). The rhetoric of renewal highlights the value and nature of positive crisis communication and reinforces the value of understanding the crisis situation when selecting a crisis response strategy. Events before and during the crisis determine whether or not a rhetoric of renewal can be used effectively as a crisis response.

Situational crisis communication theory (SCCT) combines elements of the rhetorical approaches to crisis communication with Weiner's (2006) conceptualization of attribution theory (Coombs, 2004a, 2007c). Attribution theory holds that people search for causes when negative and unexpected events occur. For constituents, crises are negative and unexpected events, making them perfect for triggering attributions of cause and responsibility (Coombs, 2004b). While management and even constituents can anticipate a crisis might occur, they cannot predict when one will occur. Hence, we can classify a crisis as unexpected. Typically, people attribute the cause of the negative event to either the person involved in the event or the situation. The attributions of cause and responsibility shape the affect generated by the event and future interactions with the person or organization involved in the event (Coombs & Holladay, 2005, 2007c).

For crisis management, stronger attributions of the organization as the source of the cause lead to greater attributions of crisis responsibility. In turn, stronger crisis responsibility leads to increased anger toward the organization in crisis, reduced

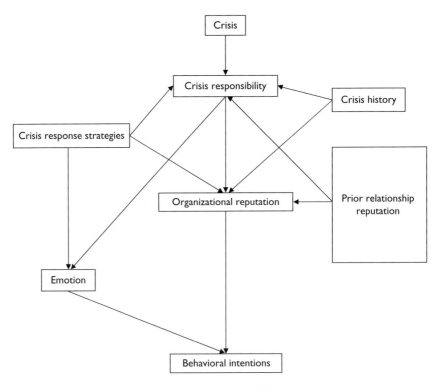

Figure 12.2   Situational crisis communication theory model

purchase intention, increased intentions to engage in negative word-of-mouth, and increased threat to an organization's reputation (Coombs & Holladay, 2007c; Jorgensen, 1996). SCCT seeks to establish the level of threat posed by a crisis and selects crisis response strategies that should provide the maximal reputation defense for that threat level. Crisis responsibility is the primary threat to the organization's reputation. Therefore, SCCT relies heavily on crisis responsibility for the assessment of the reputational threat. Figure 12.2 illustrates the various relationships advanced in SCCT.

Following Sturges' (1994) advice, SCCT recommends a base response of instructing and adjusting information prior to any efforts designed to repair the organization's reputation. SCCT utilizes a two-step process to assess the reputational threat of a crisis. The first step is the initial crisis assessment. The initial crisis assessment is based on how the crisis is being framed. Most crises tend to fall into specific crisis types. Research has shown the common crisis types cluster into three groups: victim crises (very weak crisis responsibility), accidental crises (minimal crisis responsibility), and intentional crises (very strong crisis responsibility) (Coombs & Holladay, 2002). Table 12.3 provides a more detailed list of the common crises found in each of the three crisis groups. If a crisis manager knows the frame/crisis type, they will have a general idea of the amount of

Table 12.3   SCCT crisis types by attribution of crisis responsibility

---

Victim crises: minimal crisis responsibility
- Natural disasters: acts of nature such as tornadoes or earthquakes.
- Rumors: false and damaging information being circulated about your organization.
- Workplace violence: attack by former or current employee on current employees on site.
- Product tampering/malevolence: external agent causes damage to the organization.

Accident crises: low crisis responsibility
- Challenges: stakeholders claim that the organization is operating in an inappropriate manner.
- Technical error accidents: equipment or technology failure that causes an industrial accident.
- Technical error product harm: equipment or technology failure that causes a product to be defective or potentially harmful.

Preventable crises: strong crisis responsibility
- Human-error accidents: industrial accident caused by human error.
- Human-error product harm: product is defective or potentially harmful because of human error.
- Organizational misdeed: management actions that put stakeholders at risk and/or violate the law.

---

crisis responsibility constituents will be attributing to the organization. SCCT takes a receiver/constituent perspective because the emphasis is on how constituents will view the crisis.

The second step is to determine if either of the *two intensifiers* of the reputational threat appear in the situation. The two intensifiers are crisis history and prior reputation. If an organization is known to have had similar crises in the past, the crisis responsibility and reputational threat are intensified. Constituencies may not have long memories, but one feature of crisis media coverage is revealing if the organization has had past crises (Coombs & Holladay, 2004). A prior negative reputation also serves to intensify crisis responsibility and the reputational threat (Coombs, 2006). If either of the intensifiers exists in the crisis, the initial threat assessment is revised upward. In practical terms, a victim crisis should be treated as if it is an accident crisis, while an accident crisis should be treated as if it is a preventable crisis. But what "treatment" is recommended by SCCT?

As noted at the beginning of the discussion, SCCT seeks to match the crisis response strategy to the situation. Roughly, the greater the reputational threat, the more accommodative the crisis response strategy. SCCT arrays crisis response strategy according to the level of accommodation. Accommodation is a function of focus on the victim and the amount of responsibility the crisis response strategy seems to accept for the crisis. Table 12.4 details SCCT's conceptualization of crisis response strategies, while table 12.5 outlines the key matches or recommendations from SCCT. Keep in mind that SCCT is premised on instructing and adjusting information being delivered prior to any attempt to repair the reputation.

Table 12.4   SCCT conceptualization of crisis responses

Deny strategies: seek to eliminate crisis responsibility
- Attack the accuser: confront person or group claiming a crisis exists.
- Denial: claim there is no crisis.
- Scapegoat: blame someone else for the crisis.

Diminish strategies: seek to minimize the crisis responsibility
- Excuse: deny any intent to do harm and/or claim inability to control the event.
- Justification: seek to minimize perceptions of damage from the event.

Rebuild strategies: seek to repair the reputation
- Compensation: offer gifts or money to victims.
- Apology: accept responsibility and ask for forgiveness.

Reinforcing strategies
- Bolstering: remind people of past good works by the organization.
- Ingratiation: praise people who help address the event.

Table 12.5   SCCT crisis response strategy recommendations

1   All victims or potential victims should receive instructing information, including recall information. This is one half of the base response to a crisis.
2   All victims should be provided an expression of sympathy, any information about corrective actions, and trauma counseling when needed. This can be called the "care response." This is the second half of the base response to a crisis.
3   For crises with minimal attributions of crisis responsibility and no intensifying factors, instructing information and care response is sufficient.
4   For crises with minimal attributions of crisis responsibility and an intensifying factor, add excuse and/or justification strategies to the instructing information and care response.
5   For crises with low attributions of crisis responsibility, and no intensifying factors, add excuse and/or justification strategies to the instructing information and care response.
6   For crises with low attributions of crisis responsibility and an intensifying factor, add compensation and/or apology strategies to the instructing information and care response.
7   For crises with strong attributions of crisis responsibility, add compensation and/or apology strategies to the instructing information and care response.
8   The compensation strategy is used anytime victims suffer serious harm.
9   The reminder and ingratiation strategies can be used to supplement any response.
10   Denial and attack the accuser strategies are best used only for rumor and challenge crises.

Unlike IRT, SCCT does not automatically recommend the most accommodative strategies. Most crises with low levels of crisis responsibility do not benefit from the most accommodative crisis response strategies (Coombs & Holladay, 1996). In fact, crisis managers risk a boomerang effect if a crisis response is too accommodative for the crisis. Constituents begin to think the crisis must be worse than they thought if the organization is responding so strongly (Siomkos & Kurzbard, 1994).

Summary

Crisis management should be a fairly comprehensive process. Public relations plays a role throughout this process, including preparation, communication channels, spokesperson training, initial response, and reputation repair response. Public relations generally is part of the crisis management team so it should have a hand in creating the CMP and be involved in exercises and training. The responsibility for training and preparing crisis spokespersons also falls to public relations. The expertise of public relations personnel makes them an excellent resource for information about communication channels, initial responses, and reputation repair responses. However, it falls to the public relations personnel to make sure others in management realize, appreciate, and utilize this crisis expertise. Do not assume that being placed on the crisis management team means you are treated as a member of management. Others on the team may assume you are a technician placed on the team to draft messages rather than to serve as an integral part of the team.

Reflections

It is fair to say that crisis management is very corporate-centric. True, a few case studies have examined non-profits and the principles are meant to apply to any type of organization. Still, the research skews toward corporate targets and corporate outcomes such as purchase intentions. What is more striking about crisis management is the running tension between organizations and constituents. This dialectical tension unfolds in a variety of topics in crisis management, including full versus partial disclosure and defensive versus accommodative crisis response strategies. We shall consider each of these dialectic tensions and how they coalesce around the general organization versus constituent theme.

Crisis experts disagree on the issue of full disclosure versus partial disclosure. Full disclosure argues that crisis managers reveal everything they learn about the crisis to their constituencies. The one limitation is proprietary information. Management should never disclose the information that provides their competitive edge in the marketplace (proprietary information), again a corporate-centric mandate. In cases of full disclosure, information is provided even if it can harm the organization either through loss of reputation and/or financial loss due to lawsuits stemming from the crisis. For instance, the crisis managers learn that part of the cause of the crisis was management negligence. Revealing this information will result in lawsuits that the organization will lose.

The partial disclosure argument is frequently attributed to a legal focus and a need to protect financial assets. Constituents only need to know the information that affects them directly, such as safety or financial loss. Disclose any information that impacts constituents, especially physical safety issues, regardless of the legal consequences. Any other information is discretionary, meaning crisis managers can choose to disclose or not to disclose it. Crisis managers do not disclose the information if it could threaten loss of financial assets due to lawsuits (Fitzpatrick & Rubin, 1995; Kaufmann, Kesner, & Hazen, 1994; Twardy, 1994; Tyler, 1997). Of course, the argument becomes whether or not specific information is important to constituents or poses a financial threat. And what happens when information relates to both? The answer should be to disclose the information, but that is not guaranteed.

Moreover, partial disclosure can create the impression of stonewalling. Stonewalling is when crisis managers purposefully withhold information. In such cases the crisis manager becomes an impediment rather than a conduit in the crisis communication process. Constituents can feel deceived when later reports indicate that crisis managers knew certain information but failed to disclose it to constituencies (Lyon & Cameron, 1999). Today's transparent world makes it difficult to hide undisclosed information, a point first considered in chapter 3. Of course, later disclosures of withheld information will receive much less attention than the crisis. However, it still will undermine the relationships among constituents. Ethical concerns arise as the nature of the crisis-related information takes on shades of gray. Crisis managers must realize there is a serious potential for exploitation when a partial disclosure course is charted.

Defensive crisis response strategies seek to protect an organization and minimize crisis responsibility, while accommodative strategies emphasize helping victims and assuming responsibility. Accommodative strategies are financially more costly for organizations. It costs more to offer compensation or to pay lawsuits after an apology than to deny a crisis or emphasize an organization's lack of control over a crisis. In a way the defensive-accommodative debate is a conflict between financial and social concerns. Accommodative strategies cost money but demonstrate social concern, while defensive strategies are the opposite.

SCCT makes explicit statements about crisis response strategies. Defensive strategies have a place in crisis management, but in very limited situations. What happens when crisis managers place financial interests over social interests and utilize defensive strategies when accommodative are suggested? The result is actually a less effective crisis response that should eventually cost additional financial resources. In addition, one could argue using defensive strategies instead of the recommended accommodative strategies is an ethical breach as well. Crisis managers should pay a price when they underbid with defensive strategies but may feel the short-term financial gain is defensible. Box 12.1 illustrates the dangers of misinterpreting and abusing crisis response strategy research.

Box 12.1   Dangers of Denial

We must be careful when we interpret the results of studies examining denial in a crisis. Denial, claiming no responsibility, has limited utility in crisis communication. However, reading some studies can lead people to believe it plays a much larger role. Some studies will compare denial to other crisis response strategies, such as apology, and draw conclusions that claim denial is a more effective strategy. The problem with these studies is that they do not consider if the organization is responsible for the crisis. If management even suspects it is somewhat responsible, denial should be avoided.

Kim et al. (2004) conducted a series of studies comparing denial and apology. What is noteworthy is the effect of guilt on response selection. When responsibility is ambiguous, denial was better (created more favorable perceptions) than apology for an integrity violation – there had been a violation of accepted rules. Apology was better than denial for a competence violation – failure of skill and execution. However, if someone first used denial and later was found to be responsible, denial made the situation worse. So be wary when a study finds for the superiority of the denial response strategy. Check to see if the study considered the issue of guilt. Using the denial strategy when there is suspicion of guilt is unethical and ultimately detrimental to a crisis manager.

There also exists the danger of misusing the rhetoric of renewal. The rhetoric of renewal is future oriented and avoids discussions of blame or responsibility. Crisis managers could utilize renewal to shift the focus away from responsibility when they know the organization is to blame. The organization then avoids the damage from discussion of blame if it can keep the focus on a positive future. The point is that there is potential for the results of crisis management research to be misused as justifications for less expensive (in the short term) responses. Crisis managers must consider the broader scope of their crisis response strategy selection.

Another concern with crisis management is that it simply seeks to re-establish the status quo. The idea is a quick fix to the problem to restore business-as-usual. Granted, there may be additional safeguards added by an organization following the crisis. At best that is "status quo plus." There is rarely a larger grappling with the industry or societal problems that usher forth the crisis. An exception would be airline accidents. Ray's (1999) examination of airline accidents shows a pattern of correcting large-scale concerns as a result of accidents. One example is precautions against wind sheers after the Delta Flight 191 crash and investigation. However, airline accident crises are more the exception than the rule.

The US Chemical Safety and Hazard Investigation Board is dispatched to the sites of chemical accidents to discover their causes. Its arrival is part of the media coverage about the crisis. It takes weeks or months to find the cause. When the board releases its reports, very little media coverage ensues.

Constituents learn little about the cause of the accident unless they frequent the board website. Often, constituents do not learn the crisis was a result of management misconduct rather than an industrial accident. More importantly, industry recommendations from the board are under-reported in the media. In 2005 an explosion destroyed the entire West Pharmaceutical facility in Kinston, NC. The US Chemical Safety and Hazard Investigation Board found the cause to be rubber dust and eventually issued a white paper about the dangers of organic dust in manufacturing facilities. There was no widespread media coverage and no new regulations.

Once more, we fall victim to the issue attention cycle. When they involve danger, crises are "sexy" and garner media coverage. Reports about causes and policy implications are not sexy and are regularly ignored by the news media. Even when a crisis touches a nerve, such as *E. coli* in shredded lettuce or lead in toys, interest fades as the story moves from effects on victims to how to solve the problem. Addressing problems in the food chain or toy supply chain is complex and involves both industry and society concerns. Interest wanes before anything substantially changes. The lack of attention is often facilitated by effective crisis management. Constituents think "The company took care of the problem, so why should we worry?" The Mattel CEO appeared in a video, apologized, and explained a new inspection policy. The toys will be lead-free now, won't they? Experience says no; toys containing lead continue to make their way to children. The underlying conditions that caused the problem persist, but by "remedying" a few surface symptoms we believe the disease to be cured.

On one level effective crisis management is a symbolic resource used to create quiescence on potential issues. On another level it helps constituents and corrects some flaws. This shows a connection between issues management and crisis management. There are times when crisis management serves as a symbolic action that creates quiescence when the more appropriate reaction should be action through issues management. The challenge is to find ways to move a concern from crisis management to issues management when the situation warrants it.

Underlying the discussion of problems with crisis response strategies is a limited consideration of constituents. Kent (in press) rightly notes that most definitions of crisis favor a corporate perspective. In most definitions a crisis is something that happens to an organization. There is too little consideration for how constituents are affected by crises. We tried to avoid the corporate-centric bias by using a crisis definition that does feature constituents and the negative effects crises can have on them. However, it is easy to read through the crisis communication literature and emerge with a belief that only the organization really matters in a crisis. We must guard against such a corporate-centric view of crisis communication.

Finally, Kersten (2005) observes that crisis management is too dependent on rationality. She reviews literature that emphasizes how irrational, psychotic, and dysfunctional organizations can be. The argument is that if irrationality facilitates the crisis, why should we suddenly expect management to behave rationally?

Kersten's point resonates with anyone who has reviewed the many cases of bad crisis management. Many assume crisis management is fairly easy to enact because it seems logical to intelligent people. However, irrationality goes a long way in explaining why an organization refuses to speak to any constituents or chooses to attack constituents rather than inform them.

We should not be so surprised when even experts mismanage a crisis. In 2007 a public relations firm went over 24 hours before responding to a serious crisis it had created through an overly aggressive marketing campaign. The case involved small electronic signs designed to promote Cartoon Network's show *Aqua Teen Hunger Force*. The signs were magnetically attached to various structures in a number of major cities. In Boston the signs created a bomb scare resulting in traffic closures and the city spending over $500,000 on a response. Turner Broadcasting Company, the parent company of Cartoon Network, apologized and agreed to pay over a million dollars to cover the costs of the response. Interference, Inc., the public relations/marketing company hired by Turner and responsible for the campaign, chose silence. The company even told the two men they hired to hang the signs to say nothing (Lavoie & Lindsay, 2007; McCall, 2007). How could a public relations firm not meet one of the most basic tenets of crisis management – to respond quickly?

We would add that "irrational" responses (or lack of responses) may be coupled with concerns over legality. Managers worry too much about possible legal issues and too little about proper crisis management that in and of itself should help to reduce total legal and financial costs.

It is easy to criticize crisis management as a weapon corporations use to defend themselves from danger. Public relations people spin the crisis narrative by providing select pieces of information to constituents. The emphasis is on protecting organizational assets and making the crisis disappear as quickly as possible. This is how some crisis managers operate. However, effective crisis management should emphasize constituency safety and err on the side of disclosing too much information rather than too little. Crisis managers must recognize the tensions that can push them towards spinning a crisis rather than managing it. We as constituents must demand information and hold organizations accountable for spinning a crisis. Furthermore, we must reflect on a crisis to see if it was an isolated incident or a sign of some larger issue that should be addressed. There are times when a crisis should be the launch pad for issues management. But someone or some group has to use the crisis as an opportunity to showcase the need for larger reforms.

Conclusion

While created by a desire to protect corporations in crisis, there is a pro-social aspect to crisis communication. Effective and ethical crisis communication places constituents at the center of the equation. Constituent safety should be the first priority during a crisis. Efforts to protect the organization are secondary and only considered after constituent safety has been addressed. This chapter has condensed a large body of research into an easy-to-digest format. The idea was to present the critical findings from the crisis communication body of knowledge. The danger with summarizing research is that the results can be misused and even abused. There is a serious concern that crisis managers will only select the results that can be used to defend corporations in crisis and lose sight of the need to address constituent concerns. As consumers of crisis messages we must examine responses to determine if the reply demonstrates the necessary respect for constituents or is simply an effort to protect corporate assets.

Case Study: Thomas & Friends Threaten Children

In June 2007 the RC2 Corporation, in cooperation with the Consumer Product Safety Commission (CPSC), announced a voluntary recall of specific wooden railway vehicles and set components for Learning Curve's Thomas & Friends Wooden Railway products. The recall was extended to five additional railway items in September. The recall was a result of lead paint found on the toys. Eventually, over 1.5 million toys were subject to the recall. The toys were manufactured in Dongguan City, China. The RC2 Corporation discovered the problem during a routine pre-distribution screening process. Lead paint poses a serious hazard for young children. Once the lead paint was discovered, production stopped, and the recall process began (Oneal, 2007).

Recalls in the US are formulaic. Announcements are distributed to the news media and placed on the CPSC website. Posters also are sent to retail outlets that sell the product. The announcements provide instructing information that helps consumers to identify if they have one of the recalled products and what they should do with it. The RC2 Corporation wanted all the products returned so that they could be destroyed. By July 2007, 48 percent of the toys had been returned (Oneal, 2007). The RC2 Corporation recall was aggressive. The company

actively promoted the recall to get the products away from customers by talking with the media. The RC2 website had a special recall section where consumers could obtain additional information and assistance. (It should be noted that most recalls do not go much further than the initial news release to the media.)

Here is a part of the recall crisis response from RC2 Corporation:

The trust you have placed in the Thomas & Friends Wooden Railway brand is very important to us. We want you to know that we fully understand and share your concerns and are dedicated to safeguarding your children and that trust. Since our recall announcement a few weeks ago, we've focused on three primary objectives:

1 Recovering products subject to the recall.
2 Determining what happened.
3 Conducting a thorough review of our processes and procedures to prevent it from happening again.

We are making progress on all three objectives, and we deeply appreciate your patience and loyalty during this time. (Recall of wooden vehicles, 2007)

RC2 was including adjusting information by initiating a discussion of corrective action as it sought to prevent a repeat of the problem.

HIT Entertainment produces Thomas & Friends, so they were drawn into the vortex of the crisis recall. HIT Entertainment stated:

HIT Entertainment is very sorry for the recent recall of a number of items in the Thomas & Friends Wooden Railway range. The RC2 Corp. recall arose because the surface paint on the affected products contained lead in excess of CPSC standards. Lead can be harmful if ingested in large quantities. We fully understand that everyone expects that every single product that bears the Thomas & Friends brand must be safe for children. In this case some of the products manufactured under license by RC2 Corp. have fallen short of that expectation. (RC2, 2007)

HIT Entertainment extended its response into adjusting information by expressing concern and it also pledged corrective action.

The Thomas & Friends crisis response began with instructing and adjusting information. One minor problem was the lack of concern and compassion in the initial recall announcement from RC2. In its defense, most recall announcements contain only adjusting information. However, the company can and should provide additional statements that express concern for the victims, especially when the safety of children was at risk. The recall became an emotional issue in the news media and parents reported how upset their children were to have their toys taken from them. It would have been helpful for RC2 to demonstrate more heart from the very start with statements to the news media and on its website. Considering RC2 talks about "passionate parenting," management should have been more attentive to the emotion dimension of the crisis.

RC2 also used compensation by providing small gifts for customers who returned products, in addition to refunds on the toys. On the downside (and ironically), some of the free gifts had to be recalled themselves. Consumers were directly sent messages notifying them of the recall. RC2 had a list of people to whom it had sent the tainted gifts. It distributed this message from CEO Curt Stoelting and President Pete Henseler: "We are deeply apologetic for and embarrassed by this turn of events, and remain determined to make it up to you and restore your confidence" (Prichard, 2007).

The Thomas & Friends crisis helps to draw attention to the blind spot of product recalls: secondary markets. Recalled items often are sold at garage sales or on eBay. The buyer and seller may be unaware of the recall. Moreover, recalled products have no effective registration system that offers an additional avenue to reach consumers. eBay has been working with the CPSC to warn people about recalls. eBay now has a statement warning sellers to check if a product is under a recall and notes penalties if a seller is caught listing a recalled item. Here is some of the text from the eBay site:

eBay strongly supports the efforts of the US Consumer Products Safety Commission (CPSC) to protect consumers against potentially hazardous goods. eBay does not permit the listing of items that have been identified by the CPSC as hazardous to consumers and therefore subject to a recall. Violations of this policy may result in a range of actions, including:

- Listing cancellation
- Limits on account privileges
- Account suspension
- Forfeit of eBay fees on cancelled listings
- Loss of PowerSeller status

However, eBay acknowledges it is difficult to police every item sold. Thus the focus is on buyers and sellers educating themselves about recall. Toward that end the CPSC has a page on eBay with links to its site, along with links provided at eBay's own recall information page (Konrad, 2007; Recalled items, 2007).

After the Thomas & Friends recall there were larger recalls from Mattel involving lead paint in toys manufactured in China. While Mattel and RC2 both promised greater care in inspections and suppliers, there was no industry-wide effort to fix the problem. China makes over 80 percent of the toys in the US market. Fears of unsafe Chinese-made toys lingered during the 2007 Christmas shopping season. Consumers saw no systematic efforts by the toy industry or the US government to correct the larger issues surrounding toy safety in China. With recalls of toothpaste, medicines, and other products made in China, the concern is spreading over the safety of products from China. However, we cannot say that crisis management efforts have contributed to altering the status quo. The Thomas & Friends case illustrates how crisis management is symptom-specific rather than an effort to eradicate the larger disease a crisis might symbolize. This is no small point. One benchmark for crisis communication success is issues management prevention. In some cases enough may have been done and increased scrutiny and change are unnecessary. Organizations learn from the crisis and make the required corrections. But there are times when larger reform may be warranted. Crisis management is dangerous when it is used for symbolic reassurance at a time when tangible action is required.

Case questions

1 What could RC2 do to prevent a repeat of the toy recall?
2 What communication challenges are faced in recalls in general and in the RC2 case specifically?
3 How would you evaluate the effectiveness of the RC2 crisis responses?
4 In the future, suppose more RC2 toys were found to contain lead paint. How would the crisis communication challenges be different in that situation than in the case described here?
5 What issue(s) might appear as a result of this crisis and the Mattel crisis? (Recall chapter 10 on issues management.) How might the issue(s) affect toy distributors in the US?
6 What did you think of eBay's response? What else could eBay have done in this situation?

Discussion Questions

1 What are the elements in the definition of crisis? Explain how constituent perceptions determine if an organization is experiencing a crisis.
2 What is crisis management? Describe the primary concerns in the three parts of crisis management: pre-crisis, crisis event, and post-crisis.
3 Describe the purpose, contents, and characteristics of a crisis management plan.
4 Explain the importance of the initial crisis response. Why should the response be quick, accurate, and consistent? Why is the "no comment" response a poor choice? Explain the importance of instructing and adjusting information in a crisis response.
5 Reputation repair has been a major focus of crisis communication research. Explain the contributions of four areas of research: corporate

apologia, image restoration theory, renewal, and situational crisis communication theory. How do they help us understand the role of public relations in reputation repair? Describe the utility and limits of these four approaches.
6 Our description of crisis management has been corporate-centric. Can you identify circumstances where crisis management might be important to activist groups?
7 Consider a recent crisis that appeared in the news or consider a crisis that you believe was handled well and one that was handled poorly by the organization. How would you describe the crisis management effort? How would you evaluate the effectiveness of the crisis management effort? How did the crisis seem to affect the organization's reputation?

Picking Fair Trade coffee beans in the Kamuli region of Uganda.

13

Corporate Social Responsibility
A New Driver for Public Relations

Visit your local Starbucks and you will find a variety of information that extends beyond just coffee. There often are announcements about community events. There are brochures detailing Starbucks' social contributions, including information about Fairtrade coffee and their CAFÉ practices (another system for guaranteeing fair prices to coffee growers).

For a time, BP no longer meant British Petroleum but "beyond petroleum." Part of the profit from sales of items ranging from IPods to designer sunglasses is used to help provide vital pharmaceuticals for AIDS patients in Africa through the RED Campaign. Major home improvement retailers, such as Home Depot, sell lumber certified by the Forest Stewardship Council. The certification provides evidence that the lumber was harvested from well-managed sustainable forests. Hewlett Packard has an active program for recycling used computer equipment and plans to develop new products that will create less waste and be easier to recycle. Read any business magazine and count the number of reputation advertisements that promote how "green" (environmentally friendly) a company is.

All these things provide evidence that corporate social responsibility (CSR) is a core concept in society. Constituents expect and companies must deliver on their social obligations to society. The role of a corporation is no longer just to make money for investors. Corporations now must honor their obligations to all constituents, including their effects on society as a whole. We now hear managers talk about the "triple bottom line." The bottom line is triple because it now must account for financial, social, and environmental performance (Elkington, 1994). Managers are cognizant that their constituents demand evidence of how a corporation benefits and harms society. This chapter develops the connections between CSR and public relations. It starts by wrestling with conceptualizations of CSR, then moves to a focus on expectation gaps and CSR. Finally, the sometime-problematic relationship between CSR and public relations is explored directly.

Conceptualizing Corporate Social Responsibility

Social concerns are the domain of CSR. CSR centers on managing the relationship between a business and society. Unfortunately, there is no one, universally accepted definition of CSR. However, there is some agreement surrounding the parameters of CSR. Howard Bowen, considered the "father of corporate social responsibility," recognized that organizations should operate in a manner consistent with the values and objectives of a society. Corporations should think beyond financial and legal responsibilities to ethical and philanthropic responsibilities (Carroll, 1999). Corporations should consider a wide range of stakeholders beyond the privileging of investors. In the broadest sense, CSR is the recognition that organizations have responsibilities beyond shareholders, including social concerns (Husted & Salazar, 2006; McWilliams, Siegel, & Wright, 2006).

CSR can be narrowed further with a focus on how the operations of an organization impact society. These social impacts are broad, including such issues as poverty, environmental damage, sustainability, human rights, treatment of workers, disease control/eradication, and treatment of indigenous peoples. Organizations seek to be a net contributor to society (Werther & Chandler, 2006). CSR becomes operationalized as the actions an organization takes to further the social good (McWilliams, Siegel, & Wright, 2006). A working definition of CSR is *the management of actions designed to affect an organization's impacts on society*. Expectations of the social concerns that constitute corporate social responsibility vary greatly within and between different countries and stakeholders. Because of the wide array of social concerns, CSR actions can take a variety of forms. For example, Chiquita ensures its banana production has a minimal impact on the environment, Unilever provides special small sachets of detergent for low income customers, and Home Depot helps to build local parks.

One additional factor needs to be considered when discussing CSR: the voluntary nature of the actions. Some experts maintain that true CSR involves actions that go beyond those required by law (Doh & Guay, 2006; McWilliams & Siegel, 2001). Simple compliance with legal or regulatory requirements would not be viewed as socially responsible. Others view compliance as a minimal level of CSR because the organization is not being irresponsible (Werther & Chandler, 2006).

Kolb and Pinske (2004) use a modification of Clarkson's (1995) reactive-defensive-accommodative-proactive (RDAP) scale to categorize CSR related to climate change. Their three categories are (1) defensive, (2) opportunistic/hesitant, and (3) offensive. Defensive organizations resist change through political actions (such as lobbying) and non-compliance with requirements. Opportunistic/hesitant organizations accept the changes and prepare to make the changes.

However, these organizations are cautious and do not discuss the issues publicly. Offensive organizations are leaders in the field who are the first to take action on the issues and can even urge governments to implement more stringent standards (Husted & Salazar, 2006; Kolb & Pinske, 2004). Corporations can have their CSR actions rated according to the timing of their involvement in social concerns. Research suggests the most effective CSR programs, from an organizational perspective, are those that could be classified as offensive.

The Value of Social Concerns for Corporations

Researchers rely heavily upon an accounting perspective to justify CSR when attempting to prove its economic value. This perspective holds that CSR is an investment that would pay financial as well as social dividends. Such a view reflects the continuing influence of the shareholder priority in business. It also reflects the reality that organizations that do not make a profit cease to exist. The need to justify CSR through an accounting perspective is alive today (Werther & Chandler, 2006). The results of research testing the effect of CSR on the bottom line have been mixed (Husted & Salazar, 2006). However, if we probe beyond the basic correlations between CSR/social concerns and financial gain, we develop a richer picture of what attention to social concerns can mean for corporate performance.

Financial returns

Husted and Salazar (2006) argue the benefits of CSR are tied to the timing of CSR. Organizations that were forced into compliance, either through regulation or activist pressure, did not see financial rewards from CSR. Organizations that viewed CSR as integrated into their strategy (strategic social investment) did see financial returns. Strategic CSR could improve productivity and profits. One reason social concerns provide economic benefit is that they offer a means of differentiating an organization from its competitors. Organizations often seek ways to separate themselves from their competitors (Dowling, 2002; Hatch & Schultz, 2000; Husted & Salazar, 2006). People are drawn to the organization because of its unique characteristics. CSR can be used to create distinctiveness in an organization's identity and serve as an appeal to stakeholders.

However, we must temper our enthusiasm somewhat when it comes to polling data on social consumers. Regularly, 80 percent or more of consumers in Europe and the US say they want to purchase based on social concerns. The reality is most consumers are driven by price and taste. Witness the continued rise of Wal-Mart. Less than 20 percent of consumers really purchase based on social concerns and about 5 percent do so regularly (Cowe, 2006; Devinney et al., 2006; Doane, 2005). Wal-Mart labels this group the "conscientious objectors" and estimates they are 14 percent of the US market (Leaks, 2007). Still, the percentage is growing and now making social buying an increasingly viable marketing strategy. Just do not think that group is 80 percent or more of your potential consumers.

CSR's social concerns can provide the desired differentiation from competitors through involvement in social issues. Cause marketing, where an organization pairs up with a non-profit to promote a social concern, is a common tactic for connecting with social issues. Typically, a percentage of sales or donations are given to the associated charity (Barone, Miyazaki, & Taylor, 2000; Lichtenstein, Drumwrigh, & Braig, 2004; Menton & Kahn, 2003). Refer to box 8.4 in chapter 8 for additional information on cause marketing.

Reputation returns

The discussion of differentiation raises the link between social concerns and reputation. CSR/social concerns can yield reputational benefits for an organization. Basically, a reputation is an evaluation constituents make about an organization (Davies et al., 2003). That is why we generally talk about favorable and unfavorable reputations. Reputation is the external counterpart of identity. The organizational identity is who or what the organization believes itself to be. Reputation assesses how constituents perceive the identity. Ideally, an organization seeks to align its identity and its reputation; how it views itself is similar to how people perceive it (Dowling, 2002; Hatch & Schultz, 2000). Identity and reputation serve to differentiate an organization from its competitors and to give it a competitive advantage when constituents are drawn to the identity (Barney & Stewart, 2000; Dowling, 2002).

In general, CSR can contribute to a favorable reputation. Brown and Dacin (1997) were the first to link CSR to favorable reputational results. Reputation itself is related to attracting customers, generating investment interest, recruiting top employee talent, motivating workers, increasing job satisfaction, generating more positive media coverage, and garnering positive comments from financial analysts (Alsop, 2004; Davies et al., 2003; Dowling, 2002; Fombrun & van Riel, 2004). Schnietz and Epstein (2005) found that a reputation for CSR can protect against stock decline during a crisis.

CSR benefits the organizational reputation by using social concerns to connect the corporation to important constituent concerns. These shared values of social concern can promote constituent-organization identification. Constituents often use organizations as a key part of their social identities. Identification occurs when constituents feel a sense of oneness with the organization. Shared values are one of the ways of connecting with constituents (Bhattacharya & Sen, 2003). Identification can develop when the values inherent in the organization's reputation are consistent with the values of the constituents (Dutton, Durerich, & Harquail, 1994). CSR embodies values that can serve as a basis for identification. CSR actions convey values to constituents. To the degree that CSR actions reflect the values of the constituents, identification is facilitated (Lichtenstein, Drumwrigh, & Braig, 2004).

Avoiding constituent churn

Ideally, constituents are either favorable or neutral towards a corporation. Either way, the constituents accept the current relationship. Constituent churn occurs when they mobilize against an organization. Marquez & Fombrun (2005) use the term *stakeholder churn*, but we altered the term to fit the focus on constituents. Constituents can force corporations into altering their behaviors (Crossley, 2003; Higgins & Tadajewski, 2002; Tucker & Melewar, 2005). Examples include Shell with the Brent Spar disposal and PepsiCo with human rights. Constituent protests forced Shell to abandon plans to sink its Brent Spar oil buoy in the North Sea. Instead, they disposed of it on land. PepsiCo severed all ties with operations in Burma/Myanmar because of protests by constituents, a case that will be discussed in more detail shortly (Coombs, 1998). As Husted and Salazar (2006) found, forced changes related to social concerns do not benefit a corporation. Constituent churn can represent a cost for a corporation on many levels. One catalyst for constituent churn is a misalignment between corporate and constituent values, what we term expectation gaps.

Expectation Gaps

Constituents hold certain expectations for how corporations should behave. In essence, constituents define what constitutes CSR by indicating which social concerns are appropriate. In turn, corporations must work within those constraints. Corporations can try to negotiate and to shape expectations, but the process is driven by the constituents. Sethi (1979) used the term *legitimacy gaps* when referring to disconnections between constituents and corporations. A legitimacy gap appears when a corporation does not do what constituents expect a corporation to do. Legitimacy carries specific connotations, so we have opted to use the more general term of *expectation gaps*. This section defines expectation gaps, shows the problems they can generate, and reviews ways issues management can be used to anticipate them.

Expectation gaps: what are they?

Problems arise when there are gaps between the social concerns constituents expect a corporation to honor to be socially responsible and what social concerns a corporation actually embraces. There are two types of expectation gaps: perception and reality. *Perception gaps* exist when a corporation has changed policies and practices to meet expectations but those changes have not been communicated to constituents. Constituents keep pressing what the corporation's management views as an old issue. Research in the United Kingdom has found that corporations do a rather poor job of communicating their socially responsible actions to constituents (Dawkins, 2004). Public relations can be used to communicate the changes and bridge the perception gap.

Reality gaps occur when corporate policies do not meet constituent expectations. A reality gap is an actual risk for a corporation that must be managed before it damages the corporation. Allowed to fester, a reality gap will lead constituents to utilize their influence to force change on the organization (constituent churn), possibly through government regulation or legislation. Corporations benefit more from voluntary CSR efforts than from mandated ones. Hence, management should prefer to find and address the gaps without the need for government intervention or other constituent pressures.

Negative consequences of expectation gaps

Constituent churn is a negative consequence of expectation gaps. When constituents mobilize against a corporation, the corporation's operating environment becomes hostile and counterproductive. Boycotts, protests, attack websites, negative word-of-mouth, and the general negative publicity from constituent churn can hinder a corporation's ability to operate effectively.

PepsiCo's eventual exit from Burma/Myanmar illustrates the negative consequences of expectation gaps. In 1993 social activists began protesting PepsiCo's operation of facilities in Burma/Myanmar. The position was that revenues from PepsiCo operations helped to fund the SLORC government and its abusive violation of human rights. Through the use of the Internet and the media, the Free Burma Coalition, the NGO activist organization, raised awareness of PepsiCo and Burma/Myanmar. Soon the investors and some large customers, most notably Harvard University, joined the activists in calls for PepsiCo to leave Burma/Myanmar. Constituents were coalescing in the network to pressure PepsiCo to change. In 1997 PepsiCo severed all ties with operations in Myanmar. Constituent pressure was the primary reason for this business decision. Constituents redefined operating in Burma/Myanmar as socially irresponsible. This redefinition was the reason for Levi-Strauss and Liz Claiborne leaving Burma/Myanmar as well (Coombs, 1998; Cooper, 1997).

Positive potential of expectation gaps

A more positive alternative for constituents and corporations is the anticipation and prevention of expectation gaps. We will use the example of Chiquita to illustrate the prevention of gaps. Chiquita is one of the largest banana growers and sellers in the world. Since 1992, Chiquita has been part of the Rainforest Alliance's Better Banana Project. The Better Banana Project tackles a variety of social and environment issues related to Latin American banana farms, such as the environmental impact of farming practices. By 2000, Chiquita had achieved Rainforest Alliance certification on 100 percent of its Latin American banana farms. As a result of the Better Banana Project, Chiquita also sells Rainforest Alliance certified bananas in nine European countries. In 2003 Cyrus Freiheim, the chairman and chief executive officer of Chiquita, stated: "Adopting the Rainforest

Alliance standard had been one of the smartest decisions Chiquita has ever made. Not only have we helped the environment and our workers – through better training and equipment – but we also learned that profound cultural change is possible" (Corporate conscience award, 2003).

The odds are that many constituents have never heard of the Better Banana Project or thought much about banana farming practices in Latin America. The Rainforest Alliance and other activist groups have been thinking about it for over a decade. As a major banana seller, Chiquita knew this concern could grow and eventually become an expectation gap. Through public relations, Chiquita informed stakeholders globally about its practices. News releases and website postings were utilized by both Chiquita and the Rainforest Alliance to spread the message. Chiquita changed practices and used public relations to communicate its actions and prevented an expectation gap.

Its social concerns leadership can provide a means for Chiquita to differentiate itself from its competitors. Chiquita can craft a CSR-based reputation that will separate it from competitors and will be attractive to certain constituents. Contrast this to being viewed as a corporation that failed to meet its obligations on a social concern. Being a leader on a social concern is much more beneficial than being an object of scorn for failing to be a good steward. PepsiCo, who used a defensive approach to CSR, would happily trade places with Chiquita.

Anticipating expectation gaps through social concerns

One critical difference between PepsiCo and Chiquita is that Chiquita anticipated an expectation gap, the cornerstone of a strategic approach for using social concerns. So how does one anticipate gaps? Issues management (see chapter 10) is a process of proactively identifying and defusing problems before they escalate into public conflict (Heath, 1997; Roper & Toledano, 2005). To be proactive, issues management scans for potential problems. The idea is to identify trends that can evolve into issues (Jones & Chase, 1979). Essentially, scanning is a process of systematically listening to stakeholders. Each trend or potential issue is evaluated to see if it warrants further attention and action. Likelihood and impact are the criteria used to judge trends. *Likelihood* represents the odds that the trend will develop into an issue. *Impact* represents the negative consequences the issue could have on the corporation. Generally, likelihood and impact are rated on a scale of 1 to 10, with "1" being the lowest and "10" being the highest score (Coombs, 2007b).

An expectation gap is a type of issue. Managers are "listening" to constituents for potential gaps. Social concerns are a key source for potential expectation gaps. Societies change their views of what social concerns are important over time. Managers need to anticipate what social concerns are likely to emerge. These potential gaps are then evaluated for likelihood and impact. Those potential gaps that rate the highest become targets for actions – the organization changes actions to prevent an expectation gap. Obviously, projecting social concerns is not a hard science, so there is room for error. Anticipated social concerns may not emerge, while a social concern that was rated low might emerge. Still, careful analysis can increase the likelihood of successfully identifying the "right" social concern. Strategic use of social concerns in CSR programs is one method of preventing expectation gaps. The next section explores the idea of prevention in greater detail.

Strategic Use of Social Concerns: Preventing Expectation Gaps

It is easier to identify a potential expectation gap than it is to prevent one. Prevention requires a greater expenditure of resources than scanning. This section details one process for preventing expectation gaps as a form of social concern-based business strategy.

A matter of values

Social concerns are at heart a matter of values. A social concern indicates what constituents feel is important – what they value. Every society is composed of a cluster of values. There is never just one social concern/value. Over time, the importance of various social concerns/values can ebb and flow. "New" social concerns can emerge as a focal point while "old" ones fade into the background. In recent years ethics has emerged as a key value for corporations in the US, but has already begun to show some signs of fading. Similarly, a corporation is a collection of values. While the organizational identity will privilege one or a few values, many other values are manifest throughout a corporation. The organizational identity simply emphasizes certain values. Expectation gaps are a reflection of societal and corporate values being out of alignment, either perceived or real.

Mechanism for preventing gaps

One way of preventing gaps is to make sure values remain aligned. Drawing from scanning, managers anticipate what values may rise in importance among its key constituents. Managers then use a two-step process to prevent a gap from forming. First, managers engage in values advocacy. Values advocacy involves publicly promoting a value (Bostdorff & Vibbert, 1994). Managers create and send messages that emphasize how important an issue or set of issues is. Each issue will embody one or more values. For instance, United Technologies ran a series of advertisements that promoted dependability and denounced irresponsibility (Bostdorff & Vibbert, 1994). Most reputation-building advertising is simply values advocacy. Values advocacy helps to increase the likelihood that a value will emerge as important. The organization serves to amplify an emerging concern for the "promoted" value.

Second, the organization must take actions that embody that value or values and communicate those actions to stakeholders. Action is the key. Stakeholders look to the words and deeds of an organization to determine if the organization does embody the espoused values (Bostdorff & Vibbert, 1994). Figure 13.1 illustrates

Step 1: Emerging value is identified and selected

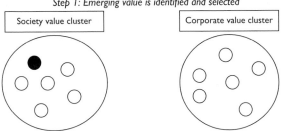

Step 2: Same value is developed in the corporation

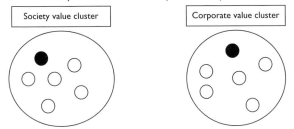

Step 3: Selected value is promoted, including corporation's use of the value

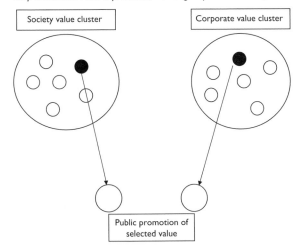

Step 4: Stakeholders perceive their connection to the corporation through overlapping values

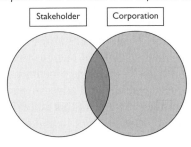

Figure 13.1   Gap prevention/alignment

the gap prevention process. Successful alignment will create a favorable operating environment for the organization and accrue the financial and reputational benefits discussed earlier.

Summary

The idea of a tradeoff between social and financial concerns being reduced to the bottom line is problematic because it is difficult to parse out the various economic benefits of social concerns. Social concerns fall under the purview of CSR. Too often, CSR is judged solely against return-on-investment. Instead of thinking in terms of accounting, we should think in terms of strategy. Social concerns can be used to construct business strategies that fuse social concern into an organization's operations. In turn, this fusion should produce both social and financial gains for constituents and organizations.

Social concerns can drive constituent expectations and serve as a foundation for organizational strategy. Social concerns embody values. Corporations encounter problems when their values are not aligned with their key constituents – an expectation gap occurs. Values for social concerns can be used to construct a business strategy that anticipates future values and avoids expectation gaps.

Moving beyond "just PR" with corporate social responsibility

SourceWatch, a group critical of corporate public relations, actually defines CSR as a public relations specialty. SourceWatch notes the connection between the increased importance of CSR and the growth of specialized CSR groups in the major public relations consulting agencies in Europe and the US. The link between public relations and CSR is not favorable, according to SourceWatch. They fear it reproduces much of the manipulation and purely symbolic actions that plague public relations. In this section we consider the concern over public relations' involvement with CSR and a rationale for the connection.

Linking CSR with public relations: the cons

Many writers, including those who are pro-corporation, question the wisdom of linking CSR with public relations. Some in business feel that CSR is now too important to leave to public relations. When CSR mattered little, it was okay to let public relations run it. But now that CSR is emerging as an essential element of corporate life, it is time for the more valued disciplines, such as marketing, to take control. The question is whether or not public relations practitioners have the knowledge and skills to effectively manage CSR. We shall address this point shortly.

Behind this facade of importance is the taint that still follows public relations. In her position paper that posits CSR should not be linked to public relations, Lisa Roner (2005), an editor for *Ethical Corporation*, argues public relations has too many of its own ethical issues. Her point is that public relations' chequered past will be transferred to CSR programs operated by public relations. She fears guilt by association. To illustrate public relations' ethical problems she notes Hill and Knowlton's role in promoting the Persian Gulf War in 1991 and Fleishman-Hillard overbilling the city of Los Angeles. These are isolated examples and actually have no connection to CSR work for clients. Roner (2005) believes that early CSR communication emphasized production value (style) over substance. In turn, constituents are left wondering if CSR is actually part of a corporation's strategy and practices. CSR communication should emphasize action over words. But do we know that these early CSR communication efforts were a function of public relations involvement or simplistic CSR efforts that offered little substance? CSR communication does need to be more effective and public relations can help achieve that goal.

Linking CSR with public relations: the pros

Effective public relations should be an ideal contributor to CSR efforts. Strategic CSR requires that management understand the social and environmental concerns of its constituents, adjust practices to reflect those concerns, and communicate the organization's CSR actions to constituents. Public relations people should have a strong understanding of constituents; therefore, public relations can be a valuable resource when integrating CSR into organizational policies and practices. Moreover, public relations is one of the vital communication conduits to a variety of constituents including employees, community members, and activists (Heath & Coombs, 2006). Two examples will help to illustrate the potential value of public relations for CSR.

Research suggests that constituents find employees to be credible sources for CSR information. However, employees feel ill-informed about their organization's CSR efforts. If employees do not understand their organization's CSR, their value as a channel for CSR communication is lost (Workers, 2007). Public relations can help organizations to better inform employees about a range of topics, including CSR. Utilizing the employee channel is not only credible with constituents but also avoids issues with spending to promote CSR efforts. Constituents do not believe organizations should spend large amounts of money promoting their CSR efforts – promotional efforts that are high profile and high cost. For instance, constituents greet expensive advertising campaigns about an organization's CSR with suspicion and concern. Why spend so much to promote CSR? Could not that money be spent for other purposes?

Another way for organizations to bolster their CSR messages is through third-party endorsements. An example would be when an organization receives certification from a recognized and credible certifying agency. Certification requires an organization to meet certain standards of behavior. Its compliance with these standards is evaluated by the independent certifying agencies. TransFair USA is the US arm of the international organization that certifies fair trade products such as coffee, tea, cocoa, and honey. Box 13.1 presents a list of its fair trade principles. These principles are then translated into industry-specific criteria TransFair USA uses to certify applicants' products for the fair trade designation and logo.

The certification adds credibility and legitimacy to the organization's CSR. Certification indicates that certain valued practices are being employed and have been verified by an independent organization. An example would be products certified as fair trade and permitted to carry the fair trade logo. Box 13.2

Box 13.1   Fair Trade Principles

TransFair, a US fair trade certification organization, lists the following fair trade principles on its website:

- *Fair price*: the organized farmer groups receive a guaranteed minimum floor price, an additional premium for certified organic products, and are eligible for pre-harvest credit.
- *Fair labor conditions*: forced labor is prohibited and any workers on fair trade farms have freedom of association, safe working conditions, and living wages.
- *Direct trade*: farmers are empowered by eliminating unnecessary middlemen. Importers buy as directly as possible from the fair trade farmers.
- *Democratic and transparent organizations*: the fair trade farmers and farm workers choose how to invest fair trade revenues using a democratic process.
- *Community development*: fair trade premiums are invested in social and business development projects by fair trade farmers and workers. The investments include scholarship programs, quality improvement training, and organic certification.
- *Environmental sustainability*: There is a prohibition against harmful agrochemicals and GMOs. Farming methods are to be environmentally sustainable and serve to protect farmers' health and preserve the ecosystems for future generations. (Fair trade overview, n.d.)

Box 13.2   Legitimacy Procurement Model

Corporations must find ways to support their claims that they are legitimately involved in socially responsible actions and policies – they must build social legitimacy. Corporations do not realize a return on their CSR investments unless constituents are aware of their CSR actions. The legitimacy procurement model uses endorsements from third-party organizations to establish social legitimacy and prove an organization is engaged in CSR.

The drivers for the legitimacy procurement model are the socially responsible actions and policies of a corporation. CSR must be derived from actual behaviors. If the CSR is legitimate, the corporation seeks an endorsement from a third-party organization that is recognized for its commitment to a particular social issue. The Forest Stewardship Council, for instance, is recognized by many as a legitimate voice on issues of sustainable forest management. The endorsement can be as

Box 13.2   (*cont'd*)

formal as certification and use of appropriate logos, such as the Forest Stewardship Council or Fairtrade, or simply public statements of support from the endorser that a corporation can use as part of its communication materials on websites, news releases, blogs, and brochures.

The corporation then promotes the social issue, the third-party endorser, and the endorsement in its promotional messages. Promoting the social issue and the endorser makes more constituents aware of a particular social issue, while the endorsement shows the corporation really cares and is involved with that social concern. Many constituents are trendy followers of social issues. Trendy followers know a little about the social issue but lack detailed knowledge and commitment. However, they are looking for ways to be socially responsible. The endorsement is a signal to these trendy constituents that they can fulfill their social concern desires by forming a relation (e.g., buy products and invest) with the endorsed corporation.

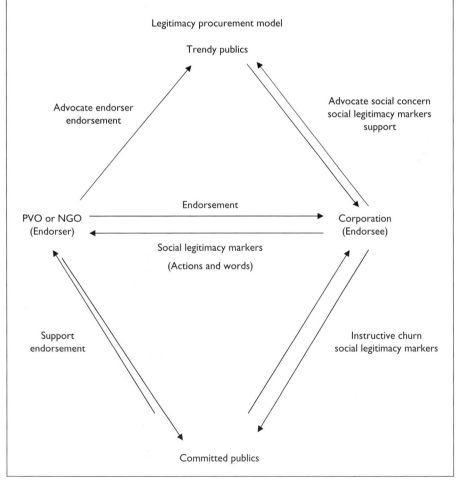

elaborates on the process by explaining the basics of the legitimacy procurement model. The certification endorsement can become a part of any promotional efforts, including low-profile and low-cost efforts such as providing this information to employees and efforts to garner media coverage. Public relations can make valuable contributions to strategic CSR.

We can turn to Grunig's situational theory of publics for insights into constituents and CSR. The theory is based on people's willingness to get involved with and communicate about an issue. Researchers use three variables to assess willingness to communicate: (1) problem recognition – do they see the situation as a problem; (2) constraint recognition – do they see anything blocking their efforts to address the problem; and (3) level of involvement, the personal and emotional relevance of the problem to the constituents. Constituents are most likely to communicate when problem recognition and level of involvement are high and constraint recognition is low.

Situational theory research consistently yields four publics: (1) apathetic, inattentive on most issues; (2) hot-issue, active on issues that involve almost everyone/are widely discussed in the mainstream media; (3) single-issue, are active on one or a small set of issues; and (4) all-issue, are active on all issues (Grunig, 1989c, 2005).

These four publics have a direct bearing on promotional communication for CSR communication. Apathetic publics are not a target because they will not care about social concerns. Hot-issue publics are a target for CSR communication when the social concern is widely known. Widely known social issues will vary by country. Single-issue social concern publics and all-issue publics are targets for CSR communication because they already have a keen interest in whether or not an organization addresses their social concerns. Essentially, two publics emerge from situational theory that inform CSR communication: committed publics (the single-issue and all-issue publics) and trendy publics (the hot-issue publics).

Trendy publics have a moderate level of interest and knowledge about CSR issues. They want to feel better about their actions by having those actions reflect social concerns. For instance, they want to buy products that are eco-friendly or patronize stores that show concern for their workers. Committed publics are difficult to convince because they know a lot about CSR and the social issues and may expect the organization's commitment to match their own level of intensity. Committed publics seek organizations that truly match their values. They are unlikely to establish relations, such as purchasing, with organizations that fail to meet their high expectations. In fact, committed publics may never really embrace and support an organization that is adopting a new social concern. Rather, the organization should use its messages to prevent constituent churn. The goal is to create quiescence among the committed publics so that they do not actively oppose the organization or initiate vocal opposition to the organization or its operations. This can include efforts to partner with the committed publics to improve CSR.

Reflections

The previous section is not a wholesale endorsement of public relations as *the* vehicle for CSR communication and practices. Effective public relations can be a valuable part of strategic CSR. However, superficial CSR practices will result in superficial CSR communication. If an organization simply seeks a few cosmetic changes to exploit constituent interest in CSR, the entire effort becomes a sham. There is no real change or long-term consequences for the corporation or its constituents. Superficial alterations can be used to win support from trendy publics that possess just a passing interest in CSR. The committed publics (activists) should see through the charade and complain. The committed provide a service by adding an additional layer of transparency to the process. Still, management can engineer value from superficial CSR – but at what cost?

Consider the concepts of greenwashing and bluewashing first mentioned in chapter 5. Greenwashing is the more familiar term. Corporations make cosmetic changes to behaviors but drastically revise their communication to reflect a concern for the environment. Bluewashing uses affiliation with United Nations agencies (symbolized by the color blue) in the same way. The connection to the UN is used to establish and to promote CSR even though little if any behaviors might have changed (Hall, 2007; Whose partnership, 2007). The problem is that, at least for greenwashing, the illusion can work. Simply using "green language" is enough to convince a significant segment of constituents that the corporation is green (Hall, 2007). This harkens back to the worst practices of public relations where words substitute for rather than reflect reality. Again, trendy publics have just a passing interest in CSR, so greenwashing can work on them. Committed publics will not be fooled and hopefully will work to expose the CSR illusion.

Public relations can help corporations to identify and promote partnerships with committed publics (typically, activist groups). The idea is to create instructive churn, a situation where changes recommended by activists are used to improve and to benefit a corporation (Coombs, Holladay, & Winch, 2007). The activists tell management their concerns and management determines how to integrate those concerns into corporate strategy and policies. In turn, the partnership with the activists becomes a source of legitimacy and credibility for the CSR efforts. An example of a corporate-activist partnership would be Unilever and Oxfam conducting a five-year study in Indonesia on the effects of multinational corporations (MNCs) on poverty in developing countries where MNCs have local operations. Oxfam was given unprecedented access to Unilever's Indonesian operations and records. Benefits were found in poverty reduction, but it was noted that the benefits were much greater for permanent than for contract workers (Exploring, 2005).

As noted in chapter 5, corporate-activist partnership presents risks for both sides. Activists run the risk of appearing to sell-out or being co-opted by the corporation. Critics may view simply working with a corporation as accepting a corporate view of the world (co-optation). Activists must retain a sense of identity and independence in the partnership. Activists must feel free to continue critiquing the corporation and suggesting additional ideas for change and improvement. Commonly, the activist partners with corporations are characterized as conservative activist groups. Corporations can be criticized as capitulating to activist demands. The corporations are deemed weak and told they will face additional attacks because they gave in on one point (Nichols, 2003). Ideally, public relations seeks to blend the interests of various constituents. Activist-corporate partnerships can be a viable way to manage mutual influence, but it requires corporations to allow for greater constituent influence (Doane, 2005).

Finally, some critics will attack the motives of corporations involved in legitimate CSR efforts. By *legitimate* we mean serious changes that positively affect society, not superficial changes. Are corporations only making the changes to advance business interests? If you read the first part of this chapter you might answer "yes" and be correct. Very few corporations have been built around CSR from the start, what some have called earnest organizations (Doane, 2005). A few names of earnest organizations that come to mind are the Body Shop, Ben & Jerry's, and Patagonia. Each of these organizations was built on principles of social responsibility that consistently guide its business decisions. Interestingly, only Patagonia still stands as a separate entity from a large corporate collective. The Body Shop is part of L'Oreal and Ben & Jerry's is part of Unilever.

Odds are if a corporation has not made CSR part of its founding philosophy, that organization is taking a strategic view of CSR and using it to advance some business interest. But corporations do advance business interests. Even the three icons of CSR noted here turn profits. We should not be so obsessed with *why* corporations engage in true CSR, but whether or not they *do engage* in true CSR. Societal benefits are not changed by *motives*; they are changed by *actions*. Attempts to speculate on the motives of corporate actions are fruitless, as we cannot know what is in the hearts and minds of corporate executives. We should focus on the validity of the CSR, not the possible motives behind it.

A valid concern would be for the beneficiaries of CSR. Even proponents of CSR are skeptical of who benefits from the practice. If you look at how CSR is evaluated, we see the focus on the financial impact on the organization. In most cases no effort is made to understand how CSR benefits the constituents it was supposed to help. Even when stakeholders do benefit it tends to be only the powerful ones, while marginalized stakeholders remain outside of CSR efforts and benefits (Scherer & Palazzo, 2007). One view of public relations is that it should be an advocate for marginalized voices (Holtzhausen & Voto, 2002). Public relations can add the voices of the marginalized to the CSR discussion and push for evaluations that include the constituents, not just financial outcomes for the corporation.

Conclusion

CSR is an important step forward for society. We are witnessing an awakening to the myriad of social concerns corporations face in addition to financial obligations. The face of business is beginning to change. As that face changes, business practices shift in a direction that should lead to the betterment of society. With CSR the world could become a better place. We use the qualifier *could* because CSR is not a panacea for all of society's ills, nor at times even an effective way to address problems. CSR can be style over substance. Small changes are made to enhance a reputation with little concern for how the changes really impact constituents. Other constituents are simply reassured that something is being done. Still, the potential of CSR is there to be tapped. Public relations has a role to play in that process by bringing its expertise to bear on creating strategic CSR. Public relations can help corporations and constituents benefit from CSR. Corporations can leverage the benefits of doing good. Public relations can help to identify the social concerns of constituents and assess whether or not the CSR actions produce tangible outcomes for those the activities are designed to help.

Case Study: Millennium Goals as an Opportunity

The UN Millennium Goals provide a rich source of values that could be used to prevent expectation gaps. Stated another way, the values found in the UN Millennium Goals represent future social concerns for constituents. Table 13.1 provides a short inventory of the goals. Clearly, a wide variety of values can be drawn from the list and used to create CSR business strategies for an organization. Two short cases will illustrate how organizations are already attempting to use the Millennium Goals as business strategy.

Case background

The UN Millennium Goals place primary responsibility for the first seven goals on the developing countries. Rich countries bear the responsibility for the eighth goal of developing a global partnership for development. This includes debt relief, effective aid, and fairer

Table 13.1   UN Millennium Goals

- Eradicate extreme hunger and poverty
- Achieve universal primary education
- Promote gender equity and empower women
- Reduce child mortality
- Promote maternal health
- Combat HIV/AIDS, malaria, and other diseases
- Ensure environmental sustainability
- Develop a global partnership for development

trade. However, the eighth goal is the most important as it will make the other seven possible (Introduction, n.d.). Corporations have a natural fit with the eighth goal through fair trade. Fair trade ensures that producers in developing countries get a fair price for their goods, support such as training to develop their business skills and knowledge, and receive long-term contracts to provide security (Fair trade, n.d.). Fair trade is promoted under the trademark Fairtrade. Fairtrade indicates a product has met the standards for being fair trade. A wide range of products are covered under fair trade, including fresh fruit, coffee, cocoa, chocolate, tea, sugar, herbs, spices, honey, rice, beer, nuts, and sports balls. Marks & Spencer and Starbucks are two corporations recognized as fair trade retailers (Retailers, 2006). Both corporations have integrated fair trade (a manifestation of a Millennium Goal) into their organizational identity and promoted it through their messages.

Marks & Spencer: Look Behind the Label and Plan A

Marks & Spencer is a major retailer in the UK. Its "Look Behind the Label" campaign was designed to address a variety of social concerns that the corporation believes are important to its stakeholders. Look Behind the Label covers such concerns as less fat and salt in food, ethical treatment of workers, recycling, safe use of chemicals, responsible fishing, and Fairtrade products. Fairtrade products connect Marks & Spencer to the Millennium Goals.

Currently, Marks & Spencer uses Fairtrade coffee and teas in its cafés. There are also plans be the first major UK retailer to use Fairtrade cotton (Our coffee, 2006). As its website notes, Fairtrade is one way to combat poverty in developing countries by building relationships with producers there and providing fair prices (Fairtrade, n.d.). The Fairtrade decision was based on market research – listening to customers. Marks & Spencer discovered customers wanted more Fairtrade products. The corporation identified a potential social concern that was emerging among a key constituency group.

In 2006 Marks & Spencer became the first major retailer to use only Fairtrade coffee in its coffee shops (Our coffee, 2006). This is one of a variety of actions Marks & Spencer has taken that reflect a commitment to Fairtrade. The corporation was changing its behavior to reflect the social concern. Marks & Spencer used a variety of channels to promote Fairtrade and to illus-

trate its commitment to Fairtrade. Those channels include corporate advertising, its website, and in-store displays. Marks & Spencer was increasing the value of Fairtrade and demonstrating how it had become part of its organizational identity – it is engaged in values advocacy.

The Marks & Spencer website has a link to the Fairtrade Foundation, a collection of organizations dedicated to increasing awareness of the Fairtrade mark (the symbol that a product is Fairtrade) and to promote the sale of Fairtrade products (About us, n.d.). The Fairtrade Foundation has recognized the work of Marks & Spencer to advance the Fairtrade cause (Retailers, 2006). Having a third party that is actively involved in Fairtrade tied to Marks & Spencer increases the credibility of its claim to being dedicated to Fairtrade. Marks & Spencer has used Fairtrade, an operationalization of one of the Millennium Goals, to foster identification with a segment of its customers. A social concern was used to construct a strategy for attracting stakeholders.

The Look Behind the Label campaign has transitioned into "Plan A." As of autumn 2008, you could still find information about Look Behind the Label on the Marks & Spencer website, but it is under the heading "Our Old Responsibilities." Plan A is an even more ambitious project to address critical social concerns by changing how Marks & Spencer does business. It is called Plan A because there is no Plan B if one is committed to social change. As Marks & Spencer describes it:

Plan A is our five-year, 100-point "eco" plan to tackle some of the biggest challenges facing our business and our world. It will see us working with our customers and our suppliers to combat climate change, reduce waste, safeguard natural resources, trade ethically and build a healthier nation.

We're doing this because it's what you want us to do. It's also the right thing to do. We're calling it Plan A because we believe it's now the only way to do business.

There is no Plan B. (About Plan A, 2007)

Plan A has five focal concerns which it calls the five pillars: climate change, waste, sustainable raw materials, health, and being a Fair Partner. As you can see, it is extending upon concerns developed from Look Behind the Label. With these five concerns come specific goals/commitments from Marks & Spencer to reach by 2012, including becoming carbon neutral, helping improve the lives of those in its supply chain, extending sustainable sourcing, sending no waste to landfills, and helping customers and employees live healthier lifestyles (Five Pillars, 2007). Again, Plan A extends on the commitments made in Look Behind the Label and has the same links to the UN Millennium Goals.

Starbucks: Fairtrade coffee

For many people, the name Starbucks is synonymous with coffee. Starbucks prides itself on building ties with constituents. Its stores are really communities where people gather to drink coffee, read, and use the Internet. Starbucks has also shown a longstanding commitment to social responsibility. In 2000 Fairtrade became a part of that commitment as Starbucks began its commitment to buying and selling Fairtrade. Starbucks identified early on the potential of Fairtrade as a social concern and changed its behavior to reflect that concern. In fact, Starbucks has a policy that if you ask for a cup of Fairtrade coffee it will French press you one if it is not the coffee of the day.

Starbucks promoted the value of Fairtrade and its commitment to Fairtrade coffee through its website, its social responsibility reports, and in-store brochures. Fairtrade has become part of Starbucks' organizational identity. Fairtrade is promoted and Starbucks embodiment of the value is strongly communicated to constituents. The corporation and stakeholders are connected through the values of this Millennium Goal. Starbucks has worked with TransFair USA, a major organization for Fairtrade coffee growers, Oxfam, and the Fairtrade Foundation. Again, these third-party sources help to confirm that Starbucks has a true commitment to Fairtrade.

But all is not perfect in Starbucks' pursuit of Fairtrade coffee. Its own policy of on-demand brewing of Fairtrade coffee has come back to haunt it. Some have criticized Starbucks for not doing enough to promote fair trade, arguing that its purchases of Fairtrade coffee could be much greater than what they are. Two bloggers, one in the US and one in the UK, created the Starbucks Challenge. People were told to go into their local Starbucks and request a cup of Fairtrade coffee. The response to this request is then posted online. The Challenge resulted from people making the request and being told they could not have the Fairtrade coffee; this was a violation of Starbucks' policy. Starbucks has contacted the US blogger in an effort to correct the problem. Names and locations of stores that violated the policy were given to Starbucks. Starbucks has sent two reminder messages to all stores about the policy. The Challenge is still finding Starbucks outlets that will not provide the Fairtrade coffee on demand and Starbucks maintains it is still working to solve the problem (Starbucks Admits, 2005; Starbucks Challenge, 2006). The Starbucks Challenge began as a way to demonstrate constituent demands for Fairtrade coffee.

The Starbucks Challenge reveals the need for a corporation to back its words with actions. Anyone can go to the Starbucks website and find its policy on Fairtrade coffee. But somehow not all stores are getting the message or workers do not want to take the extra time and hassle for hand-pressing a cup of coffee. Whatever the reason, Starbucks has failed at some stores to back their Fairtrade words with actions. To its credit, Starbucks is trying to correct the problem. That Starbucks is even aware of the problem is a testament to the potential power of the Internet to reveal corporate missteps. Corporate actions are becoming increasingly transparent because of the Internet, as people are finding it easier to learn when a company does not support its words with actions.

In October 2008 Starbucks announced it would double its purchases of Fairtrade certified coffee in 2009, making it the largest buyer of Fairtrade certified coffee in the world. Whether the decision resulted from increasing pressure from activists, an eye toward increased profits, or a growing commitment to social responsibility, as outlined in the UN Millennium Goals, Starbucks' move to increase Fairtrade purchases should please constituents concerned with the Fairtrade issue.

Conclusion

We should think of social concerns such as the Millennium Goals in terms of business strategy and not simply accounting. A carefully crafted business strategy that utilizes social concerns is very likely to yield positive results. It may be difficult to parse these positive results into specific numbers and clearly attach dollar figures to each action. But weaving social concerns into the organizational identity prevents expectation gaps that can result in stakeholder churn and negative consequences for an organization. Instead, corporations differentiate themselves from competitors by being leaders in addressing a social concern. Both Marks & Spencer and Starbucks are Fairtrade leaders. In turn, the values that underpin the social concerns provide a foundation for connecting the corporation and its stakeholders – people are given another reason for developing a relationship with the corporation. When viewed as strategy, we can see how social concerns can be built into what a corporation does and serve as a means for promoting a favorable operating environment for the organization.

Case questions

1   Visit the website for the International Fairtrade Labeling Organization (FLO) (www.fairtrade.net/), the organization that certifies that products are fair trade. TransFair USA (www.transfairusa.org/) is the US arm of the FLO. How could these third-party organizations assist corporations who want to establish a good record on their fair trade efforts?

2   Visit Marks & Spencer's website to learn more about Plan A, Look behind the Label, and its fair trade efforts (www.marksandspencer.com/gp/node/n/42966030/275–6449955–4366703). What do you think of Marks & Spencer's Plan A? How is Plan A consistent with ideas about corporate social responsibility? How is Plan A consistent with the UN Millennium Goals? If you were a Marks & Spencer customer, how would you prefer to learn about Plan A efforts and its work with Fairtrade?

3   Starbucks' commitment to double its purchases of Fairtrade coffee seems consistent with its commitment to social responsibility in general. Visit this Starbucks website to learn more about its corporate social responsibility efforts: www.starbucks.com/aboutus/csr.asp. Since 2001 Starbucks has issued corporate social responsibility reports. You can link to these corporate social responsibility reports from this website. What do you think about the information contained in their CSR reports? To what extent does this information influence you to view Starbucks as socially responsible? Would you like to see any additional information in the reports to convince you of its commitment to corporate social responsibility?

Discussion Questions

1 What are key elements of corporate social responsibility? What are the benefits of CSR? For example, how is CSR related to the bottom line? How is it related to corporate reputation?

2 What do we mean when we claim that constituents define CSR by indicating which social concerns are appropriate?

3 How are expectation gaps related to CSR? How are reality gaps related to CSR? How is stakeholder churn related to expectation gaps?

4 Why should CSR be considered a public relations function? What are the arguments against public relations' involvement in CSR?

5 Why are charges of greenwashing (or bluewashing) problematic for organizations? If the charges are inaccurate, what can be done to counter these perceptions?

6 Based on what you learned in this chapter, do you think organizations can engage in CSR efforts without being viewed as having ulterior motives? Explain your response.

7 Identify examples of corporations you perceive to be socially responsible. What sources of information have influenced your judgments? Visit the corporate websites to see if they contain a section devoted to CSR. If so, do their statements about their CSR activities match your perceptions of the organization's activities?

8 Identify examples of corporations you believe to be socially irresponsible. What sources of information have influenced your judgments? Visit the corporate websites to see if they contain a section devoted to CSR. If so, do their statements about their CSR activities match your perceptions of the organization's activities? Have your perceptions of their social irresponsibility affected the way you interact with the organization (e.g., in terms of buying their products, engaging in negative word-of-mouth, etc.)?

Demonstration during the World Trade Organization summit in Seattle, 1999.
PHOTO CHRISTOPHER J. MORRIS/CORBIS

14

Public Relations Goes International

Where were your favorite shoes made? How about the clothes you are wearing now? Think of a car you have ridden in recently. Where were the various parts made? Where was it assembled? When was the last time you visited a website from outside of your home country? These questions serve to illustrate the international flavor to our daily lives. Corporations such as ABN-Amro, L'Oreal, IKEA, Honda. Nokia, and General Electric are but a few of the multitude of transnational corporations that populate our world. Transnational corporations have interests such as production facilities or marketing efforts in more than one country. As this chapter notes, the internationalization of business will continue to grow.

The growth of international business is the fuel for international public relations. Webs of relationships long ago exceeded geographic boundaries. Consider how each time an organization enters a new country it must learn how to deal with "new" versions of old constituents such as the media, communities, employees, and customers. These relationships with "new" constituents are why public relations must now be international. Public relations helps to manage these transnational webs of mutually influential relationships. International public relations is a vast topic and the subject of many books. We have chosen three international topics to illustrate the complexity of public relations as it becomes international: (1) globalization, (2) terrorism, and (3) public diplomacy. Globalization was selected because public relations writings tend to neglect this critical component of the international experience. Terrorism is an international concern that has unfortunate linkages to public relations. Public diplomacy represents the first application of international public relations and retains a vital role in shaping societies around the globe.

Conceptualizing Globalization

Globalization is a complex process that is not easy to define. Marshall McLuhan, a media scholar, first referred to the "global village" in the early 1960s when he speculated on the future of electronic communication technology and its effects on individuals and society. He presaged the future where time and distance would be minimized and people around the world would be connected through electronic media. At the time of McLuhan's death in 1980, the globalization of society was underway. The development of powerful information technologies and the irresistible allure of business opportunities around the world helped to complete McLuhan's vision.

The concept of globalization is not exactly new. Consider how sea and land travel enabled merchants to conduct global trade in spices, tobacco, and precious metals. Following the lead of Bartolomeu Dias, Vasco da Gama was the first to sail from Europe to India. This was an improvement over land trade routes pioneered by the likes of Marco Polo and his journeys on the Silk Road to China. However, globalization in its current form is more widespread and complex. We often assume that "globalization is good for business." However, that is not to say there are no unintended consequences or undesirable outcomes. Some critics of globalization argue that it may be good for business but it also is bad for many individuals, nations, and the planet. Let's look at some issues involved in globalization and then explore the implications of globalization for the practice of public relations.

Globalization generally is used to refer to how our world seems to have "shrunk" due to the widespread availability of communication technologies and the increased ease of conducting business around the world. The development of the Internet and the ability to easily and inexpensively share information including documents, purchase orders, advertising, and work processes meant that business could be accomplished without physical boundaries. The Internet is one technology that makes it possible to function in more geographically dispersed environments where links in supply chains can easily develop. A supply chain is the series of steps that move from raw materials to finished products or services. Additionally, the widespread availability of means of transportation for goods, including air transport and large-scale sea transport, meant that products could be distributed around the world. Hence, an organization's supply chain could be international rather than simply local. Moreover, business people could themselves travel more freely and conduct business around the world when requirements for travel visas and time-consuming border checks to many areas were eliminated.

Liberalization of trade

A significant contributor to the growth of globalization is the liberalization of trade. The growth of *free market capitalism* eliminated trade barriers and reduced the cost of doing business internationally by eliminating many tariffs and taxes that made goods produced overseas very expensive. Prohibitive costs were reduced by the elimination of these extra fees that were required on imports and exports. The ideology of free market capitalism suggests that players should be allowed to compete in this expanded marketplace and those who "do it best" by offering the products and services at the lowest prices will win. The competition is assumed to encourage organizations to do it better, faster, and cheaper than their competitors. With globalization came the growth of large, multinational corporations as mergers enabled companies to reduce costs and compete more effectively. In this Darwinian system those corporations that failed to emerge as dominant players in the marketplace were forced to reposition themselves in more niche markets or leave the playing field altogether.

Some have even credited the growth of free market capitalism and globalization with bringing about changes in political systems, including the spread of democracy to nations that formerly were run in a more autocratic fashion. To be favored trading partners, governments would need to demonstrate stability. Political stability makes trading alliances more predictable and easier to work with. Similarity in systems of government helps. It also means companies may be willing to expand their physical presence in those areas, bringing jobs and opportunities with them. When the possibility of disruptions due to coups, revolts, and other forms of insurgency exists, trade is complicated and corporations are naturally wary of developing agreements. Stable political systems, especially democratic ones, typically are seen as better trading allies. Additionally, countries that support human rights practices that we find more palatable often are seen as preferred trading partners. Embarrassment can ensue when partners are found to be using child labor or sweatshop labor and enacting other coercive practices in the workplace, including requiring workers to work overtime, forcing female workers to take birth control pills, separating workers from their families, and operating factories in ways that resemble prisons.

In North America, the North American Free Trade Agreement (NAFTA) was a major trade agreement designed to reduce the cost of doing business on the continent. In addition to trade agreements such as NAFTA, international organizations were formed to facilitate the global trade process. One of the best-known international organizations charged with overseeing trade is the World Trade Organization (WTO), formed in 1995 and based in Geneva, Switzerland. The WTO has over 150 member nations; non-members may petition to join the organization. The WTO facilitates the liberalization of trade by reducing trade barriers, negotiating trade agreements around the world, and helping to resolve disputes when nations disagree on the rules of trade. The WTO aims to facilitate trade by enhancing the predictability and transparency of trading agreements. However, international organizations such as the WTO and globalization itself are not without critics, as we will explore later in this chapter when we discuss the 1999 protests in Seattle against the WTO's ministerial trade meeting.

The process of globalization also has contributed to a greater awareness of different cultures, including cultural differences and similarities that may increase or complicate our understanding of different people around the world. In addition to exchanging news from around the world, we have exchanged products, services, and ideas, some of which could be seen as controversial and incommensurate due to value implications and clashes. Minimizing real differences in values, ideology, and cultural practices is disrespectful. People are "not all the same," although there may be some fundamental commonalities in values, such as those reflected in the United Nations' Universal Declaration of Human Rights or those human rights advocated by Amnesty International or Global Exchange, two large non-governmental organizations that call for respect for basic human rights.

Implications for public relations

Overall, many assume globalization benefits corporations. With globalization come opportunities as well as threats. Globalization presents a new set of challenges to the practice of public relations. Globalization means the web of stakeholder relationships has grown exponentially and has become more diverse. It also suggests it may be more difficult to understand constituents and their expectations. Public relations becomes increasingly important to building and managing these complex relationships. The following, while not exhaustive, outlines some ways in which the practice of public relations has been influenced by globalization.

Globalization has provided opportunities for expanding the marketplace and the reach of organizations. This means public relations professionals should be knowledgeable about the cultures in which they operate. Practitioners need to develop practices and reputation management strategies that address and respect the values and perspectives of important constituencies. In addition, those constituencies who are not deemed central to their operations also should be understood and listened to. This may mean obvious modifications such as altering business practices in some areas (e.g., McDonald's serves vegetarian options in India where cows are sacred and many people do not eat meat for religious reasons). It also can mean modifying plans to account for cultural and language differences.

For example, it is important for corporations to carefully consider potential product names to ensure those names are not offensive or problematic in other languages. Now it is common practice to conduct Internet-based searches in all languages to explore possible meanings and interpretations of product names. This helps to explain why corporations will "invent" unique names that are not found in other languages. It can avoid the embarrassment or even hostilities that might ensue from the naive selection of product names. Mazda sold the Laputa automobile not realizing the name was Spanish for whore. A curling iron called the Mist-Stick appeared in Germany where mist means dung. And Puffs tissues were sold in Germany even though the name was a slang term for whorehouse (Ricks, 1999).

It is important to understand how the relationships between journalists, public relations practitioners, and the media vary in different countries. In her study of global media relations, Tsetsura (2008) found it is fairly common practice for public relations professionals to pay for media coverage. One in three public relations practitioners and one in five journalists reported it was legitimate for national media in their countries to accept payments for coverage. In only 60 percent of the cases was the material identified as advertising. While this practice would be seen as unethical in the US and elsewhere, it clearly is an acceptable practice in other countries. This difference demonstrates the importance of understanding the norms for doing business in other countries and the ethical questions those norms may raise.

Even when a corporation is not operating in another country, its practices can be scrutinized by others around the world. This highlights the need for public relations practitioners to understand how their organizations are regarded as members of the world community, irrespective of their physical presence in a country. Greater transparency is demanded by constituents who believe they have the right to appraise how organizations, as citizens of the world, are operating and to assess their potential impacts on anything from people to the environment to economic and political systems. For example, organizations may face legitimacy challenges from activist groups that are concerned with issues such as human rights, the effects of trade on indigenous populations, or democratic government. The call for greater transparency in operations has grown with the development of the Internet that provides access to information as well as other like-minded activist groups. (See the discussion in chapter 3 on the need for transparency.) The growth of anti-globalization sentiments in general also has spurred increased scrutiny by those who decry the adverse consequences of international trade.

Reputation management becomes more complex when we consider how an organization's Internet presence means multiple constituencies from around the world can access a single website about the organization or multiple websites devoted to specific countries or regions of the world. The corporate website becomes an increasingly important tool for addressing the interests and concerns of those who seek information about the organization in cyberspace. It also can be an important tool for soliciting feedback from constituencies. However, it becomes difficult to target messages to different constituents groups and solicit feedback when language barriers and other cultural barriers exist. More localized media, however, can be used to target constituents through reputation ads and press releases to local newspapers. In addition, town hall-type meetings can be held to facilitate two-way communication and representatives can attend meetings held by local organizations to hear their concerns.

Multinational organizations become more vulnerable to criticism when they operate in conflicting political, economic, and cultural systems. For example, constituencies in the US and other countries may question the ethics of a US-based corporation operating subsidiaries in countries with oppressive governments, such as China, Nigeria, or Burma/Myanmar. Operating in these countries could be interpreted as tacit support for the regimes because conducting business there benefits their economies and supports the status quo.

The supply chains that organizations depend upon for raw ingredients and materials are increasingly scrutinized. It is common for organizations to secure low-cost ingredients from around the world. Moreover, when organizations contract with suppliers, those suppliers may contract with other suppliers to obtain ingredients, thus increasing the complexity of the supply chain and obscuring original sources of ingredients. Nevertheless, the public expects organizations to have knowledge of and control over their supply chain to prevent inferior and/or dangerous ingredients or materials from being used to create the final products that bear the organization's name. For example, Disney and Mattel, two well-known brands in much of the world, came under fire when it was discovered that many of the toys bearing their names contained paint with dangerous levels of lead. The toys were manufactured in China and the suppliers apparently were unaware of or unconcerned about the use of the dangerous paint. However, stakeholders believed that Disney and Mattel *should* have been aware of what was happening in factories that produced the toys. The toys were recalled. Organizational reputations suffered in the minds of parents who associated the brands with quality products and wholesome fun. Parents never thought to question the safety of those products.

Similarly, problems may arise when companies rely on low-cost ingredients obtained in other countries that are found to be tainted or hazardous. The US Food and Drug Administration (FDA) is charged with ensuring food safety in the US. However, it does not inspect all food or ingredient imports. This means that unhealthy and/or dangerous products can enter the world's food supply. In 2007, 154 brands of pet food manufactured by Diamond Pet Foods were found to contain the dangerous chemical melamine. Melamine has industrial uses and is not approved for use in human or animal food products in the US. The melamine was added to wheat gluten, a pet food ingredient, in facilities in China in order to boost overall protein content. The ingredients were shipped to the US for the final production process. Pet deaths and illnesses were attributed to the melamine.

Melamine problems resurfaced in 2008, this time appearing in milk products originating in China. The problem centered in powdered milk produced by the Sanlu Group. Melamine had been added to the milk product to increase its protein content and value. However, later tests found the melamine appearing in additional dairy products. Early on, four children died in China and over 54,000 became ill from the tainted product. The melamine and milk scare reflects our global society. The European Union banned the importing of Chinese products that contained milk (Sanderson, 2008). UK sweet maker Cadbury issued a recall of China-made chocolates that included China, Taiwan, and Australia (Spencer, 2008). Later, contaminated milk appeared in the US and parts of Europe due to their use as ingredients in candy. Global supply chains for food result in people and pets in various countries being placed at risk by tainted products from one country.

Supply chain concerns also reflect an interest in the way labor is used in the manufacturing process. For example, retail organizations typically outsource their manufacturing of apparel to countries where labor is cheaper. Clothing production cannot be totally mechanized. Human labor is required to operate sewing machines. Developing countries, eager for foreign investments, promise a low-cost, stable, and compliant workforce. These countries also recognize that manufacturing facilities are easy to relocate when lower bids are offered by other countries competing for foreign investments. This creates tremendous pressure to keep labor costs down. Outsourcing manufacturing allows organizations to sell clothing at lower prices but still earn higher profits than they would if the clothing were manufactured in the US. The labor is cheaper because young workers are employed, there are no labor laws or minimal labor laws, no unions, and low wages are paid. However, when abusive practices in these types of sweatshops are revealed, the organizations can suffer negative repercussions. Organizations are expected to be aware of the conditions in which their products are produced. Growing awareness of egregious worker abuses in developing countries has led many consumers to seek "sweat free" apparel and boycott organizations that rely on sweatshop labor.

In some cases individual companies may be targeted as examples of or symbols of general problems, such as the use of sweatshop labor in the manufacturing of apparel (Rosenkrands, 2004). For example, Nike, Disney, and the Gap have been targeted at various points in time. These prominent organizations were held up to be the poster children of organizations that prosper from using abusive sweatshop labor. Protesting against well-known organizations can help to shape public opinion on the issue and influence politicians who are responsible for developing policies to guard against such abuses. Public relations professionals must offer explanations and propose plans that will help curb the abusive practices. For example, the Gap developed a vendor code of conduct in response to criticisms of its use of sweatshop labor. The code demonstrates it is aware of and concerned about the issue and provides grounds for terminating business contracts with vendors that do not conform to the guidelines. Often, these organizations, once they have sought to rectify the situation, will seek third-party verification of their efforts to eliminate the use of sweatshop labor. The third-party verification lends legitimacy to the process of securing a non-exploited, "sweat free" labor force.

Globalization has presented many other opportunities for abuses. Corporate behavior that would not be tolerated in one country may be seen as acceptable in another. For example, in the quest for increased profits some corporations have relocated to countries with minimal environmental restrictions. This means they can pollute without oversight and avoid the inspections and penalties they might face from governmental organizations such as the US Environmental Protection Agency (EPA).

The "Battle for Seattle": activists vs. the WTO

We have been focusing on corporate perspectives on globalization. In addition, activists from around the world have focused on globalization and its effects on society. The majority of activist groups are concerned with the negative effects of globalization and have used public relations to bring attention to its impact on a variety of issues and people. Activist groups may act alone to bring attention to a particular cause or may join with other groups from around the world to form transnational advocacy networks (TANs). Box 14.1 offers additional information about TANs.

Among the best-known public relations actions is the 1999 "Battle for Seattle." The protests associated with the third ministerial meeting of the WTO attracted activists from around the world. The overall purpose of the series of WTO meet-

---

Box 14.1 Transnational Advocacy Networks

Keck & Sikkink's (1998) book, *Activists Beyond Borders*, focuses on transnational advocacy networks (TANs) in which NGOs play a central role. TANs are possible because of globalization. TANs are distinguished by their commitment to working for particular values and causes and their ability to mobilize effective information exchanges. The authors explain: "a transnational advocacy network includes those relevant actors working internationally on an issue, who are bound together by shared values, a common discourse, and dense exchanges of information and services" (p. 2). TANs may include NGOs (both international and domestic), social movements, media, churches, etc. that are motivated by values and exchange information and services.

TANs can be highly effective at framing issues in ways that attract the attention of the general public and of politicians. Their ability to share information among interconnected organizations and with the public and to influence public opinion is critical to their effectiveness. TANs may be associated with a diversity of issues ranging from human rights to women's rights to poverty to AIDs to hunger. The issues they support may be very broad, such as the promotion of democratic practices around the world, or may reflect a more narrow focus, such as the elimination of sexual slavery in a particular country.

Keck and Sikkink observe that TANS are most likely to emerge around issues where (1) channels between domestic groups and their governments are blocked or hampered, or where such channels are ineffective for resolving a conflict, (2) activists or political entrepreneurs believe they can further their mission, and (3) conferences and other forms of Internet contact create opportunities for developing and strengthening networks. Because issues often cannot be resolved at the local level, TANs take their issues to the international court of public opinion where those outside the local government can generate pressure for change. The information management and social construction abilities of TANs are central to this function.

ings was to discuss international trade agreements. Member nations and non-governmental organizations (NGOs) were invited to participate along with nations seeking WTO admittance. The organizers were aware their meetings would attract activist groups concerned with a wide range of issues. President Bill Clinton, who was attending the meeting and who positioned trade as a major component of his foreign policy, said he welcomed demonstrators and looked forward to a "huge debate" (Ford, 1999). He may have gotten more than he bargained for in Seattle.

The Internet facilitated information sharing among activist groups. The protesters represented a wide range of groups reflecting a diversity of concerns, including international trade in general, labor issues (e.g., the US AFL-CIO), the environment, anti-corporate interests, poverty, bio-engineered foods, freedom for Tibet, consumer organizations, women's rights, radical anarchists, etc. Diverse groups formed alliances. They shared information such as where they could stay, where meetings were being held, where representatives from the member nations were staying, locations where protesters should gather, and where workshops for activists were being held. Information needed by protesters to orchestrate their efforts was widely shared among groups and available on the Internet. Additionally, protesters created online protests against the WTO in which cyber-protesters could participate. Many represented activist groups that were well trained by groups such as the Ruckus Society, a grassroots organization seeking to fight globalization. This organization helps to train demonstrators. Protests also erupted in other cities around the world (Zielenziger & Bussey, 1999). Box 14.2 presents the Ruckus Society in its own words. The Internet-based campaign to inform and organize protesters prior to the meeting and to keep them updated as events unfolded was deemed a success (Ford, 1999; Higgins, 1999; May, 1999).

Interestingly, much of the early news coverage seemed to emphasize the street theatre aspect of the protests by describing the "spectacle" of costumed activists dressed as sea turtles, butterflies, trees, bananas, and clowns, or the activists as dancing, drum-banging zealots (e.g., May, 1999; Zielenziger & Bussey, 1999). This type of portrayal of their civil disobedience may overshadow the activists' messages when the demonstrators themselves garner more media attention than the reason for their protests. This is a point first broached in chapter 5's discussion of direct action.

Estimates suggest there were somewhere between 50,000 to 100,00 protesters. Although the majority of the protests were peaceful, some of the protesters turned violent and activists were criticized for their "mob violence." Many media reports emphasized the destructive actions of some protesters. For example, some protesters spray-painted buildings, smashed windows, and looted. Police were out in force, armed with tear gas and rubber pellets which were used against some protesters. The National Guard was called in, some arrests were made, a 7:00 p.m. to 7:30 a.m. curfew was set downtown where the meetings were being held, and a state of emergency was declared on the first day of the WTO meeting.

Box 14.2   Ruckus Society

The following is a description of the Ruckus Society posted on its website.

The Ruckus Society sees itself as a toolbox of experience, training, and skills. We provide instruction on the application of tactical and strategic tools to a growing number of organizations and individuals from around the world in skill shares and trainings that are designed to move a campaign forward. We do this work in strong collaboration with our partner organizations, working together to define and create the training agenda.

Additionally, the Ruckus Society is dedicated to fostering leadership of those most affected by the injustice and oppression we struggle against. Therefore, in all our initiatives, we aim to prioritize the voices and visions of youth, women, people of color, indigenous people and immigrants, poor and working-class people, lesbian, gay, bisexual, gender queer, and transgendered people, and other historically marginalized communities. Ruckus has trained and assisted thousands of activists in the use of non-violent direct action. We either bring activists to us or we go to them.

Ruckus promotes and teaches:

- Implementation of strategic non-violent direct action against unjust institutions and policies.
- Organized strategic development and coherent planning to advance campaign goals.
- The establishment of broad coalitions with common objectives.
- Effective methods of media outreach and Internet/technology activism to inform the general public.
- Respect for all living things and a commitment to the power of diversity. (Ruckus Society, n.d.)

Businesses around the convention center where the meetings were being held closed temporarily. Although some media described the police responses as over-reactions, the depiction of protesters as violent seemed to justify the police actions and overshadow much of the coverage (Higgins, 1999; Paulson & McClure, 1999). People following the media coverage of the WTO protests might be turned off by the reports of destruction of property and attacks on police. When protesters become the story rather than the issues they are concerned about, we may question their success at conveying their messages and persuading the public to embrace their concerns. Their advocacy efforts may have been overshadowed by negative media portrayals. The media frames focused on the protesters' activities and the police responses rather than the messages the protesters wanted to convey. Additionally, the protests seem to have little negative impact on the WTO's reputation.

Nevertheless, the protests associated with the WTO meeting often are heralded as a major success by activist groups. The protesters did protest, but it is unclear if their protests could be credited for the failure of the 135 nations to reach consensus. For example, some suggest the developing nations felt excluded from much of the negotiations and complained that the US and Europe had too much influence. The talks eventually collapsed when delegates said they could not agree on an agenda for future trade talks. Although they tried to reach consensus, it did not happen (Paulson & McClure, 1999). The activists did not play a direct role in the decision making. However, the activist groups may claim success because their protests were covered in the media. Their efforts brought negative attention to the WTO itself and may have created greater awareness of some of their concerns. In that sense the protests may be seen as a public relations success.

The protesters were successful in completely stopping the opening ceremonies of the conference and the first day of talks (Paulson & McClure, 1999). However, the mainstream press often focused on sensationalistic portrayals of protesters' actions rather than providing in-depth examinations of the complex issues underpinning the reasons for the protests. The fact that so many diverse activist groups attended the protests to demonstrate against a wide range of issues may help to explain the media coverage. Many of the groups were not solely "anti-trade" or "anti-globalization." For example, some activist groups acknowledge that globalization will happen and is not inherently evil; but they desire a more measured approach to trade that accounts for the interests of all parties involved. Although many groups were concerned with unfair trading agreements that benefited economic powerhouses at the expense of developing nations, other groups represented issues that might be seen as less directly associated with trade agreements. For example, the general public might be unaware of the impact of trade agreements on environmental policies and labor practices. However, the common threads that bound together the activists was a concern for the power of the WTO in influencing international trade agreements and the disproportionate power of some countries over the others. The complexities of the protesters' concerns and the bases for their arguments against the WTO are difficult for the media to report. It is easier for the media to report the visible actions of protesters, police, and meeting attendees.

Although we have focused on the public relations efforts of the activists thus far, we also can examine the WTO protests in terms of the public relations efforts of the WTO, businesses, and the city of Seattle affected by the protests. They can claim to be victimized by the protesters in order to gain public sympathy. For example, businesses around the convention center were closed and they lost profits for several days. The storefront windows of downtown Starbucks, Nordstroms (a department store), and other businesses were smashed, some spray-painting marred buildings, and some looting occurred. Traffic was disrupted. The police and Seattle citizens reported feeling threatened by protesters. WTO delegates also were intimidated by the protesters. The head of the WTO, Mike Moore, was observed to claim the WTO gets blamed for "everything that has gone wrong in the world in many decades" (May, 1999). The public comments of the WTO delegates defended the work of the WTO, praising the value of international trading agreements, and condemned the protesters for interfering with the business of the WTO. They sought to reinforce the legitimacy and protect the reputation of the WTO.

Reflection on globalization

Globalization is a complex phenomenon that affects the relationships among numerous constituencies. Globalization has expanded the reach and altered the salience of constituents within the web of relationships. Both positive and negative challenges and consequences have emerged from globalization and corporate and non-corporate public relations practitioners are developing ways to operate within this expanded environment.

Overall, the Battle for Seattle provides insights into contested issues associated with globalization in general and international trading agreements in particular. Highly visible meetings and activist actions provide the opportunity to engage in education and advocacy, two important public relations functions.

Terrorism

Terrorism may not be the first, or second, or even any topic that comes to mind with international public relations. However, terrorism is often international because terrorists cross national boundaries and because the terrorists' nation of operation may differ from where they attack, where terrorists seek asylum, or that of the persons the terrorists are trying to intimidate or coerce. Terrorism, unfortunately, has a public relations link through the need for the "publicity" of terrorist acts. This section examines what terrorism is and its connection to public relations.

Defining terrorism

We can agree that violence against people is a terrible and deplorable act and that violence against property is generally criminal. But when we label an act as terrorism, the disagreements begin. Terrorism is a political term imbued with ideology and perspective. A group fights for freedom from an oppressive government. Are they terrorists or freedom fighters? A government uses excessive force to quell opposition. Are they taking the necessary actions to protect citizens from extremism or engaging in state-sponsored terrorism? A group firebombs a facility they believe to be morally wrong. Are they terrorists or heroes for the cause? Your answers to these questions are shaped by your perceptions and ideology. Consider the last example. Conservative groups in the US might tacitly support firebombing of an abortion clinic but decry the same tactic used against a housing development that threatens an environmentally sensitive area. The acts are essentially the same crime – violence against property – but the motivation and political agenda behind them are what shape the reactions.

The US government defines terrorism as "the unlawful use of force and violence against persons or property to intimidate or coerce a government, the civilian population, or any segment thereof, in furtherance of political or social objectives" (28 CFR Section 0.85). *Unlawful* is a key term. When the government oppresses people that is often legal. Consider the 2007 violent suppression of the Buddhist monks in Burma/Myanmar. In 1989 the ruling military junta renamed Burma, Myanmar. Not all countries recognize the name change. Even many citizens still prefer Burma. That is why we use the distinction Burma/Myanmar here. The actions were "legal" in Burma/Myanmar, but most civilized societies saw them as terrorism perpetrated by the government, often called state-sponsored terrorism. Still, the decision about the violence against the Buddhist monks was a matter of perspective, even if you reasonably disagree with the minority view. Are there not times when unlawful actions are necessary to make a point? The entire concept of civil disobedience is premised on violating the law to make a point. Unfair laws are violated to facilitate the social change necessary to correct the problem. Starting with Gandhi in India, through the Civil Rights movement in the US and the Solidarity movement in Poland, civil disobedience has been an agent of important social change. The point is that there are times when laws need to be challenged and even violated. Ultimately, the legality of an action may not be the best criterion to use in assessing if an act is terrorism or not.

Clearly, terrorists are not to be confused with Gandhi. Terrorism has violence as a central defining feature. Non-violent resistance is not terrorism because there is no violence against people and/or property. However, non-violent resistance and terrorism may share the same goals of political or social change. People are much more accepting of non-violent resistance as a change mechanism because "innocent" people or their property are not harmed to make a point or to win change. But people accept some terrorism because of the target. Return to the example of some US conservatives supporting attacks on abortion clinics, including the assassination of physicians, by helping to hide offenders. The violence perpetrated by terrorists is deemed just because the target is not innocent but deserving. But who defines what is just or who is deserving? Once more, political leanings make the identification of terrorism murky. What emerges is a sense that even violence can be acceptable or palatable at times for many people.

Instead of hard rules for defining terrorism we see evaluations based on situations and ideology. The Bush Administration created a "global war on terrorism." But the US government is inconsistent in what it considers terrorism. The terrorist label is as much a function of who agrees or disagrees with US policies as anything else. Terrorism is a value-based label rather than a clearly defined assessment. In essence, people vary in their tolerance of terrorists. Some are evil, some are misguided, and some are taking steps necessary to create change.

Terrorism shares with activism the desire to create change. Extremists in activist groups at times resort to violence. In the US, for instance, environmental extremists are now defined as domestic terrorists under the phrase *ecoterrorism*. The FBI defines ecoterrorism as "the use or threatened use of violence of a criminal nature against innocent victims or property by an environmentally oriented, subnational group for environmental-political reasons, or aimed at an audience beyond the target, often of a symbolic nature" (Jarboe, 2002). Ecoterrorists, on the other hand, see themselves as protectors of the earth, only engaging in crimes to save the planet. This statement from the Animal Liberation Front (ALF) reveals its targets and vow not to harm humans:

Animal Liberation Front Guidelines

1. To liberate animals from places of abuse, i.e., fur farms, laboratories, factory farms, etc. and place them in good homes where they may live out their natural lives free from suffering.
2. To inflict economic damage to those who profit from the misery and exploitation of animals.
3. To reveal the horror and atrocities committed against animals behind locked doors by performing non-violent direct actions and liberations.
4. To take all necessary precautions against hurting any animal, human and non-human.

In the third section it is important to note the ALF does not, in any way, condone violence against any animal, human or non-human. Any action involving violence is by its definition not an ALF action, and any person involved is not an ALF member.

The fourth section must be strictly adhered to. In over 20 years, and thousands of actions, nobody has ever been injured or killed in an ALF action. (ALF, 1991)

Earth First! is another fairly well-known ecoterrorist group that began in the US and has now spread to the United Kingdom. Earth First! utilizes a mix of non-violent and violent methods of *ecodefense*, their term for strategies designed to defend the environment. The violent methods used by ecoterrorists are called *monkeywrenching*. Monkeywrenching tactics can include arson, tree spiking, billboard vandalism, road reclamation, and ecotage (eco-sabotage). Tree spiking is very dangerous and became a federal crime in the US in 1988. Tree spiking involves driving metal rods or other materials into the trunk of a tree. The danger occurs when the tree is cut. If a metal saw blade hits a spike, the blade will break or shatter, posing a danger to loggers felling the tree or people in the sawmills processing FBI tree. Spikes are placed high so that loggers will not hit them and trees are marked so that they will not be harvested. Spiking is designed to significantly reduce the economic value of a tree but also creates the potential for injury. Earth First! renounced tree spiking in 1990, but you can still find references to it on its website.

We are not trying to vilify or to praise ecoterrorism. The extended discussion is another example of the term terrorism being closely tied to ideology. It also raises the point of justification. If a group feels the only alternative left to correct an injustice or end oppression is violence, is it justified? It is an unfortunate situation when people see violence as their only remaining option, but that does happen. Public relations can be used to promote non-violent options to change. By amplifying the voice of the powerless, public relations helps groups to realize alternatives to violence. Hence, public relations can help supply a safety valve that can relieve societal pressure through non-violent change-seeking options.

Terrorism and the media: the link to public relations

Terrorists have objectives; they want to force change in a society. To that end, violence is used to intimidate the government and/or segments of society. Terrorists usually attack targets that are not the actual decision makers. Examples would be attacking public places, transportation venues, and businesses. The attacks on the World Trade Center in New York City and the Underground in London illustrate the use of non-decision making targets. The violent, terrorist act is a form of communication. The terrorists are sending a violent "message" to the people who can create change. The terrorist message has two purposes. The first purpose is to create fear among people. Fear becomes the motivator for societal change. The second purpose is to convey the terrorists' demands or ideas to other people. If you want change, you must tell people what that change is. The Basque terrorist attacks in Spain illustrate the communicative nature of terrorist attacks. The attacks create fear and the need for change – make a change and the attacks will end. The desired change is greater political freedom and autonomy for Basques in Spain. Ideally, the two purposes are clear. However, some attacks are vague, such as the Madrid train bombings in 2004 that killed 192 people. Initially, the Madrid bombings were blamed on the Basque group ETA. Eventually, the bombings were linked to an al-Qaeda-inspired terrorist group. The reason for the confusion was that there was no specific message or immediate claim of responsibility (Canel & Sanders, in press).

Terrorism benefits from news coverage of an event, the publicity generated by a terrorist attack. In most cases, terrorists need public attention to advance their agendas. The exceptions would be terrorists with no clear agenda. Publicity helps to (1) generate fear and (2) present the terrorist's objectives. As discussed in chapter 6 on media relations, the news media are drawn to conflict stories and unusual events. The violent terrorist acts embody both of these characteristics of an attractive news story. In turn, the media coverage helps to make people aware of the attack and to generate fear (Yalovenko, 2005). Research has shown that exposure to media stories of terrorist attacks does create the intended anxiety among people (Slone, 2000). Terrorists want their actions to be visible in the media so as to maximize their fear-inducing effects.

In addition to creating fear, media attention is an opportunity to present the terrorists' demands and articulate their objectives. There is a parallel here to activist groups that engage in extreme direct actions to draw media attention to their concerns. The terrorist attack provides an opportunity for the terrorists to air or to present their demands for change. Terrorists are using violence as a publicity tactic. Again, we are not condoning the use of violence for change, we are just explaining the dynamics of the situation.

If the news media ignored terrorist attacks would that reduce their use? There is no clear answer, but this is a question being debated on a global scale. Countries are wrestling with how the media should responsibly cover terror attacks. Governments must balance freedom of the press with benefits that might be derived from limited media coverage of terrorism. Russia has gone the furthest in this effort with the Ethical Principles of Professional Conduct of Journalists Covering Acts of Terror and Counterterrorist Measures adopted by their Union of Journalists of Russia in October 2001. One problem is that the new media report on terrorism as well. In fact, terrorist organizations have created their own websites for disseminating information. As a result, what the traditional news media do or do not do becomes less relevant. Moreover, how can any news media simply ignore a major terror attack? A greater concern is the nature of the coverage. The news media need to be careful not to become a promotional platform for the terrorists. Framing terrorists as the villains is considered a valuable tool in fighting terrorism (Yalovenko, 2005). However, freedom of press prevents governments from forcing such frames on the news media. But the idea of voluntary codes for responsible coverage of terrorist acts remains a laudable goal.

Reflection on terrorism

We are hesitant to connect terrorism with public relations. Moreover, it is an oversimplification of the problem to claim terrorism is public relations. Commonly, terrorists do seek publicity to further their objectives. Media coverage helps to create fear and to present terrorist demands to a wider audience. However, the use of violence to engender publicity is the worst possible corruption of public relations. Terrorists may use public relations, but public relations should not be equated to terrorism. Such statements do an injustice to the field of public relations and the many women and men who practice it with integrity and honor. But we would be remiss if we did not recognize the role public relations does play in terrorism, especially when we discuss the international aspect of public relations.

Public Diplomacy

Corporations and NGOs are very active in terms of international public relations. However, nations were the first to enter this arena (Kunczik, 1997) and remain active players to this day. Much of what nations execute as international public relations falls under the heading of public diplomacy. This section defines public diplomacy and its relation to public relations, examines the reputation management function that is the centerpiece of public diplomacy, and offers reflections on public diplomacy.

Public diplomacy: definition and connection to public relations

Public diplomacy is often defined as government-to-people and stands in contrast to traditional diplomacy that is viewed as government-to-government (Wang, 2006). Public diplomacy comprises the efforts of governments from one nation to send messages directly to the "people" in another country and is part of *soft power*. Soft power seeks to attract people to a cause or organization rather than by using force or coercion (Nye, 2004). The tactics valued in public diplomacy include cultural exchanges, lobbying, advertising, websites, state visits, and any commonly used public relations tactics. Common objectives include increasing awareness, managing reputations, changing legislation, and altering attitudes (Wang, 2006; Zhang & Cameron, 2003).

Public relations is strongly akin to public diplomacy. Both fields share similar tactics and objectives. Signitzer and Coombs (1992) outlined the connections between the two fields and argued for their convergence. More specifically, public relations was offered as a way to improve the focus and practice of public diplomacy by integrating ideas for executing public relations efforts into public diplomacy. Essentially, public diplomacy would benefit from being treated as public relations.

An excellent illustration of the public diplomacy-public relations connection is the Foreign Agent Registration Act (FARA) in the US. FARA requires all public relations personnel who work for foreign countries to register with the Justice Department. The registration includes the amount of money received, the actions taken, and copies of messages that will be disseminated to more than one constituent. FARA is frequently used as a database for analyzing public diplomacy even though it is a record of public relations actions (e.g., Lee, 2006; Manheim, 1994).

If we select some of the primary objectives of public diplomacy, the connection to public relations emerges again. The four primary objectives of public diplomacy include attracting foreign investment, drawing tourists, maintaining favorable trading policies, and receiving foreign aid. Attracting foreign investment is similar to the investment relations function of public relations. Potential investors must see the economic viability of a nation and view it as politically stable. Each are tasks well suited to public relations. We touched on this point in the earlier discussion of globalization. Similarly, public relations is actively used in the tourism industry. Search online for travel and you will find many nationally sponsored websites designed to attract travelers. (The case study at the end of this chapter examines tourism in more detail.) Trade policies are political concerns and well suited for issues management. Efforts to craft free trade agreements are a perfect example. Finally, foreign aid is often a result of constituents being aware of the need and having a favorable view of a nation. Nations do not receive aid if politicians do not know they exist or dislike the country. Once more, public relations can be used to build awareness and favorable views of a nation.

The media and reputation management

Historically, public diplomacy research has emphasized mass media reputation management. Basically, the focus has been on how the media cover a nation. The reason is that most constituents, even politicians, rely upon the mass media for the bulk of their information about a nation, although the Internet is increasing as a source. Constituents are unlikely to have direct experience with a nation, so they are dependent upon how the mass media present that nation (Lee, 2006; Manheim, 1994; Zhang, 2007; Zhang & Cameron, 2003). Public relations/public diplomacy targets the news media to manage their reputations. The news media have limited resources to collect information and spend precious little of those resources on international concerns. As a result, the news media are extremely susceptible to influence when it comes to coverage of nations (Manheim, 1994). Research supports the argument that international news media coverage is amenable to influence from public relations efforts. Public relations campaigns have altered media coverage of nations both in terms of amount of coverage and whether the coverage is positive or negative (Albritton & Manheim, 1985; Manheim & Albritton, 1984; Zhang & Cameron, 2003).

Manheim (1994) details the process of how to manage a nation's reputation through the news media. His system is based on a two-dimensional grid of visibility (amount of coverage) and valence (the content is favorable or unfavorable about the nation). Figure 14.1 illustrates Manheim's grid. The quadrant dictates what actions a public relations practioner should take to address the nation's reputation. Manheim (1994) refers to this as "context-sensitive sequence of strategic objectives" (p. 134). In Quadrant 1, the objective is to reduce the amount of coverage. When there is intense, negative coverage, it is unrealistic to assume public relations can shift a reputation from negative to positive. Instead, the objective is to reduce the amount of coverage to make a client less visible to constituents. In Quadrant 2, the objective is to transition from negative to positive media coverage. The coverage is minimal so there is an opportunity to shift the nature of the media stories.

In Quadrant 3, the objective is to increase visibility because the coverage is positive. In Quadrant 4 the objective is to reinforce the existing positive, high visibility. Ideally, public relations seeks to move media coverage toward Quadrant 4. In addition, there is an opportunity to inoculate constituents against possible negative information about the nation. The data collected generally support the model "under normal circumstances" (Manheim, 1994, p. 147). For instance, a public relations effort by the nation then known as Southern Rhodesia shifted the visibility from high to low for the negative valence stories. Abnormal conditions can defeat the model because they will attract media attention independent

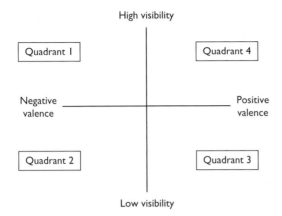

Figure 14.1   Manheim's (1994) dimensions of nation identity

of the public relations effort. Internal violence, humanitarian disasters, or natural disasters are examples of abnormal conditions that will draw negative media attention to a nation.

Refinements to integrating public relations and public diplomacy

Wang (2006) provides three valuable insights into the convergence of public relations and public diplomacy. First, public diplomacy needs to move from simply nations projecting a reputation to nations negotiating meanings and trying to understand the constituents they target. Little attention has been given to public diplomacy research focused on how constituents view a nation or how they arrive at those perceptions. Second, public diplomacy must think beyond one-way communication and mass media, including the effects of the Internet. How are rival sources of information potentially changing the monopolistic power of the traditional news media to shape a nation's reputation? Consider how constituents now retrieve tourism and investment information from online sources. Third, public diplomacy efforts should consider how NGOs and corporations can have an impact on public diplomacy efforts. For instance, how might reports from Amnesty International or Global Witness affect how constituents perceive and interact with nations? We must realize that national governments are not the only agents trying to shape media coverage about a country.

Even within the mass media management of a nation's reputation there is room for improvement. The research generally looks at the reputation as favorable or unfavorable, but not in relation to specific objectives of public diplomacy. Constituents will use different criteria to evaluate a nation depending on the objective. Tourists will be interested in different information than investors. The one similar concern would be political stability, but natural beauty or cultural opportunities hold little interest to an investor unless the investment opportunity involves tourism. The media analysis for a nation's reputation should consider what specific dimensions to locate and to evaluate in the media coverage. It is not just the amount of positive and negative media coverage that matters, but the *focus* of that coverage. Moreover, it is important to include Internet coverage of the country and not just rely on traditional news media.

Reflections on public diplomacy

The early public diplomacy research advocated the use of public relations to simply alter perceptions of nations. This is rather disturbing. The evidence is divorced from reality in these studies. All we know is that publicity efforts were initiated, not that the nations changed any policies or behaviors. For example, Rhodesia and China simply used public relations to change their reputations (Manheim & Albritton, 1984; Zhang & Cameron, 2003). This violates the premise that public relations should be based on substance. As reported in the public diplomacy research, it was simply symbols – words in a public relations campaign – that changed a reputation. This is not an ethical or desirable way to practice public relations. Public diplomacy needs a stronger grounding in substance. Clients should be encouraged, if not required, to take action to resolve the problems drawing negative media coverage before public relations practitioners agree to represent them.

Let us consider a few recent examples of countries trying to polish or perhaps spin their reputations. Columbia has a reputation that conjures up visions of drugs, violence, corruption, kidnappings, and danger to tourists. It is no surprise that representatives from Columbia visited the UK in early 2008 to solicit public relations firms to represent their country. The Columbian representatives sought a public relations firm that would help to overcome the stereotypical view of Columbia and feature a modern, more positive view. The idea is to change how politicians and journalists in the UK view Columbia (Black, 2008). That could be a challenge given the continuing violence and drug problems in the country. At the same time, Columbia fired Burson-Marsteller and hired Johnson, Madigan, Peck, Boland & Stewart to help it secure passage of the US-Columbia Free Trade Agreement.

China sought the international spotlight through its hosting of the 2008 Summer Olympic Games. Hosting an Olympics is considered a viable form of public diplomacy that allows a country to showcase its arrival on the world stage (Manheim, 1994). However, the spotlight is not always kind. Protesters around the globe used the 2008 Olympics as an opportunity to raise questions about China's sale of arms to Darfur, the occupation of Tibet, oppression, and environmental abuses. In the US, Hill & Knowlton was the public relations agency tasked with trying to keep China's reputation more positive than negative. Given China's human rights record, many people might consider China a problem client that is seeking positive coverage without addressing its core troubles. The Olympic torch case study at the end of this chapter provides additional information on public relations problems and the 2008 Olympics.

On the positive side, public relations has helped to increase transparency about the behavior of nations. As with corporations, it is becoming increasingly difficult to hide wrongdoing or other unflattering information such as human rights abuses and other forms of oppression. Burma/Myanmar illustrates the effects of transparency on national reputations and behaviors. Activists used the Internet to make constituents aware of the oppressive actions of the government and show how US businesses, by operating in Burma/Myanmar, were helping to fund the violence. Constituents became aware and this knowledge created arousal as people took action to force US-owned businesses out of Burma/Myanmar. The last US-owned business was PepsiCo. Internet-generated transparency created a negative reputation for Burma/Myanmar and resulted in corporations leaving that country.

As Wang (2006) noted, the Internet could change how national reputations are managed. Activists and ordinary citizens can use the Internet to shine a light in the once dark recesses of national behavior which, hopefully, will create greater accountability with constituents. The potential is there, but the vastness of the Internet means that illustrative information can get lost and nations can keep some of their undesirable behaviors in the dark.

Conclusion

As we noted at the start, the subject of international public relations has filled volumes. This chapter took three slices from this vast topic for discussion. Globalization is a critical issue for international public relations that often is ignored or given short shrift. The debate over globalization will be a powerful force that shapes international business. Public relations should be cognizant of that debate and be a part of it. Terrorism has an unfortunate publicity dimension that ties it to public relations. The link to terrorism can complicate public relations, especially for constituents involved in direct action. Finally, public diplomacy was examined because it was the earliest form and remains an important part of international public relations today. People must be aware that public relations is not limited by national borders. It is important to understand and identify public relations' role in shaping international events.

Case Study: Tourism in the Baltics

People in the US might have a difficult time finding the Baltic region on a map and probably cannot name the three Baltic states. Lithuania and Estonia have begun to develop international public relations efforts to improve name recognition and to attract tourists from the US. Did you know Latvia was the third Baltic state? Maybe not, since Latvia has not invested in these efforts. In January 2008 the Lithuanian government began considering a name change to something that was easier to pronounce in English. This is part of a larger effort to boost its reputation and to attract tourism built around a reputation of "daring." People from outside the area often confuse Lithuania with Latvia, the third Baltic state. The country's name is Lietuva in Lithuanian, and that would not change. Only the English version of the name would change. But why daring? Because Lithuania is a country marked by bravery, including being the last pagan country in Europe and taking a strong stand against the Soviet Union (Marketing Lithuania, 2008).

Estonia found that most of its tourists were from Finland, Russia, Germany, or Sweden, followed by visitors from Norway, Great Britain, and Latvia. The US is considered a developing market. Estonia is pursuing an expansion of the US market as part of its effort to increase revenues from tourism. But it is only part of the effort because the market is relatively small. Its public

relations efforts will include newsletters, travel trips for journalists, and booklets in English. Estonia will feature its medieval heritage and ecological beauty in these messages. One of the slogans is "Nordic with a Twist." As with Lithuania, Estonia is utilizing public relations to help attract tourists, and the money tourists spend.

Case questions

1 How might people in Lithuania react to the proposed marketing name change? Should the Lithuanian government take their attitudes into consideration?
2 What does the phrase "Nordic with a Twist" mean to you? Would this make the country seem appealing to you?

Case Study: 2008 Olympic Torch Controversy

In April 2008 the Olympic torch relay schedule included a stop in Paris, France. The torch relay is supposed to draw crowds cheering on the many people given the honor of carrying the Olympic torch. The event is a celebration of the Olympics and a sharing of the games with other nations. The French visit did not go so well. The crowds included thousands of protesters. The protesters were angry about Chinese policies involving the support of the Sudan during the Darfur humanitarian crisis and continued occupation of Tibet. The main message from the protesters was "Free Tibet." Fighting police and security guards, the French protesters successfully extinguished the torch and frequently forced the torch to be transported in its accompanying van rather than by torchbearers. At one point, 300 pro-Tibet protesters blocked the torch relay path and were dispersed with tear gas. Ultimately, the third leg of the scheduled torch relay in France was cancelled (Paris, 2008). The torch relay was just part of larger efforts that condemned giving China the right to host the Summer Games.

Paris was not the only city where the 2008 Summer Games torch was protested. Similar but smaller events occurred in the US. On one level the Olympic torch relay was a global publicity event. Happy crowds cheering for the torch should make for positive media coverage in each nation on the route, as was the case when the torch visited Brazil. However, the event was not the positive media event the Chinese Olympic organizers had envisioned. Instead, it was frequently a media nightmare of police, protesters, and chaos. China, as others before it, was using the Olympics to feature its entry to the world stage. But the story and public relations role in this drama was just beginning.

Every country rightfully has citizens who are proud of their nation. We often call this a nationalistic spirit. China is no exception. A segment of the Chinese public was offended by the events in France and decided to respond. The Internet and text messaging were the key organizing devices for protests of all things French in China. Over 20 million people signed an online petition to boycott Carrefour and other French establishments. Protesters, often numbering over 1,000, appeared outside French schools and other institutions associated with France. Eventually, the Chinese government interceded by asking people not to boycott but to channel their energies into positive actions (Jacobs & Wang, 2008).

But what of Carrefour? Carrefour, not a sponsor of the Summer Games in Beijing, was placed in a difficult position. China is an important emerging market for the retail chain. Management could ill-afford alienating the Chinese. Public relations was one of the tools Carrefour management employed. This included making public Carrefour's position on the issue. Carrefour Chairman Jose Luis Duran offered support for China and the Olympics through interviews with the Chinese news media. He noted the well-deserved honor Beijing had of hosting the Summer Games and that Carrefour would support the Games. Duran also denied that Carrefour supported Tibetan separatists (Carrefour, 2008). The message was clear: Carrefour was pro-China and pro-Olympics. People should not punish Carrefour because of protesters in their home country. Carrefour did not hold the same hostile view toward Chinese policies nor was it against China hosting the Summer Games. Of course, those in France angry over the Summer Games in China were none too pleased with Mr. Duran's comments. But an organization cannot make all of its constituents happy all of the time.

Two warring activist protests in very different parts of the world drew Carrefour into the debate over China hosting the Olympics. Carrefour had to take a position on the 2008 Summer Games. The case illustrates our interconnected world and how public relations can be complicated by these connections.

Case questions

1 Is it fair to protest sponsors of the Olympics (such as McDonald's, Coca-Cola, and Kodak) when people disagree with the location of the Olympics?
2 How should the French government have responded to the Olympic torch protests?
3 Why would the Chinese government ask their citizens to stop protesting French companies?
4 Do you agree with Carrefour's decision to support China and deny the legitimacy of the Tibetan separatists?
5 How might people in France react to Carrefour's response? Should anticipated reactions by the French have affected Carrefour's response?

Discussion Questions

1 Describe factors associated with globalization. What challenges to public relations are posed by globalization?
2 Globalization means that an organization's webs of constituents include more complex and diverse connections. What public relations challenges are associated with the management of these mutually influential constituency relationships?
3 How does globalization complicate our ethical decision making?
4 How can terrorism be viewed as a form of public relations and activism? Under what circumstances (if any) is terrorism justified as a form of public relations and activism?
5 What is public diplomacy? Describe the four primary objectives of public diplomacy.
6 Visit a government-sponsored tourism website for a country and examine its public relations strategies. Have you seen promotional messages for a country on television or the Internet? If so, what did the messages support (e.g., tourism, investment, image, etc.)? What factors were emphasized in the messages?

Globe.

15

Conclusion
Does Society Need Public Relations?

A consistent position in this book is that we must examine both the good and the bad wrought by public relations being a part of society. We neither chose to demonize nor sanctify public relations, but attempted to shed some light on the practice so we can see all its contours. Much like high definition television reveals the imperfections of celebrities' appearances, an interrogation of public relations exposes its share of problems along with the benefits. As the book draws to an end, we ask the question, "Does society need public relations?" We must ponder whether society would be richer or poorer without PR.

Congregation and Separation

The evolution of society is a progression from small to larger collectives of individuals. Agriculture yields to industry and villages are replaced by cities. Play any of the Sid Meijer's Civilization video games and you can watch this progression on your own computer screen. As people congregate, a sense of community is often replaced by a sense of alienation and anomie. It is ironic that larger numbers of people actually can result in increased isolation. Direct, interpersonal communication channels are supplemented or replaced by mediated channels. Technological innovation further alters these mediated channels by adding more options through the ability to simulate "real" interactions. Consider the progression of the news media from newspapers, to radio, to television, and now the Internet. Meetings are conducted via videoconferencing or through avatars interfacing in cyberspace. Conversations are replaced by text messaging and emails. People can earn a college degree online and then enter the workforce by tele-commuting. They can spend their leisure time in Second Life or some other simulated environment where they interact with other beings in this artificial cyberworld. Human interaction plays a minor role in such lives.

The point is not to condemn progress or to reject technology. Technology has created new forms of congregation as well. Geographically dispersed people can now form communities that provide valuable social and emotional outlets. What we must realize is that in the supposed wired world people can still be isolated and disconnected. One role for public relations is to bridge this separation to end isolation. We believe that public relations is about webs of relationships. Webs are about connections. Public relations, through whatever channels, can be used to expand and to cultivate those webs. Public relations can build connections between people and between people and organizations. An activist group develops organizing materials and places them on its website. People visiting the website download the materials and form their own "chapter." Part of the materials will be public relations materials used to reach other people. Public relations is part of the group-building process that can bring people together over an issue. Similarly, corporations can utilize public relations to reach constituents and engage them in their network of mutually influential relationships.

Whether activist or corporate citizen, public relations helps to build ties and bring people together. Consider how public relations is instrumental in nation building (Taylor, 2000; Taylor & Kent, 2006). Public relations helps to create a sense of shared identity. The various overlapping webs of relationships become the strands with which the fabric of society is woven. However, public relations also can be used to polarize and to divide people. "Ethnic cleansing" is fueled by hatred for others. Hate speech is a cancer that spreads on the Internet. Public relations can be divisive by uniting some people against others. People are separated from enemies while being united with those who share their views. But this is a deceptive form of togetherness. Such unification through division takes a toll on society. The fabric of society is frayed for the benefit of a few.

The Excellence dialectic can help elaborate on how public relations builds connections in society. Constituents utilize public relations to build the web (networks) necessary to establish their power in a relationship. Activists, for instance, recruit others to their cause in order to pressure a corporation into listening to their concerns – increasing their salience for an organization (Coombs, 1998, 2002; Coombs & Holladay, 2007b). Then the constituents and the corporation connect as they dialogue about the constituents' concerns. Public relations can unite constituents around an issue and connect constituents to their opposition.

Contingency theory furthers this argument of public relations as a knitter of social fabric. Contingency theory recognizes conflict as a natural and potentially productive part of public relations. Conflict is not to be avoided but embraced. The recognition of the value of conflict is akin to the shift in sociology from a functionalist view that denigrated conflict to the more positive view articulated by conflict theorists. How people respond to conflict in public relations depends on a set of internal and external factors. Refer to the writings on contingency theory for more details on these variables that determine the stance of the response to conflict (e.g., Cancel et al., 1997). The stance can range from advocacy (persuasion to one's own side) to accommodation (yielding to the demands of the other side) (Cameron, Pang, & Jin, 2008; Reber & Cameron, 2003; Shin et al., 2005). Put another way, does the conflict create a battle over who is right or the willingness to settle differences?

On the one hand, public relations can be used to simply create division and destructive conflict that erodes the fabric of society. On the other hand, it can be used to create conflict designed to improve society and provide a bridge for the positive management of conflict that knits the fabric of society. We believe that public relations is about the web of relationships. Ideally, constituents seek to broaden the web and bring more people into the relationship. Broader webs build greater social capital and generally improve the functioning of society. On the whole, the potential benefits of public relations to building society outweigh the dangers it presents for disrupting society.

On Being Heard

In the ancient Greek world, public speaking was a valued skill. People would need to speak for themselves in legal and political arenas. An early controversy in the Greek writings was over helping people become better speakers. Did some of those offering assistance go too far by, in essence, speaking for the individual by developing the content of their speeches, often with little concern for ethics? Echoes of that ancient debate still resonate today in discussions of public relations.

Free speech is not really about speaking; it is about *hearing*. The marketplace of ideas holds that people should *hear multiple perspectives* so that they can choose the best option. Therefore, people have a right to hear various sides of an issue. In the US this right to hear is a legal justification for corporate public relations to speak on public issues. Public relations facilitates people being heard, whether it be corporations, activist groups, or the government. Public relations firms exist to help those who cannot speak for themselves. Some have likened public relations practitioners to lawyers, perhaps an unfortunate choice. The similarity is that everyone has a right to be represented, even the most vile in society. Hence, public relations agencies can justify representing despised individuals, organizations, corporations, or countries.

While casting public relations' lot with lawyers may be problematic, the fundamental principle is sound. If we believe that everyone has a right to be heard, we have to let everyone speak. Free speech does not apply only to those with whom we agree. If that were true, it would be easy to silence anyone not in the majority. It can be argued that minority voices are marginalized even in societies with free speech, including the US. Public relations is a tool marginalized voices can and have used to be heard in the marketplace of ideas and to move their issues to the public and political agendas. But this means we must tolerate all groups using public relations to have their voices heard. Again, hate groups or other controversial groups can use public relations to spread their ideas. As long as they operate within the law, any groups can practice public relations as a way to be heard. We must take the good with the bad. Freedom means choice and mixing of opinions. We cannot pick and choose who should be heard and who should be silent. That is censorship, not freedom. One price of freedom is the expression of unpopular ideas – but that is a small price to pay to be able to express oneself. We must accept that the price of public relations as a public voice is that it can be used by those we might not wish to be heard.

Consequences for Society

In this book we have noted various ways public relations efforts have impacted society for both good and bad. At this point we would like to highlight a few examples to reinforce public relations' effects on society. These effects are a mix of the positive and the negative. They reflect the great potential of public relations to improve or to degrade society.

Let us start with the obvious bad example, the rise of the Nazi Party in Germany. Adolf Hitler was a believer in the power of public relations and it had a significant function in his Nazi empire. Public relations helped a maniac to engage in some of the worst crimes ever committed against humanity. Public relations built support for the Nazi Party and spread its hateful and destructive ideology. With public support, the world was plunged into war and millions of innocent people were slaughtered.

Public relations was also used as a rallying device by the Allies in World War I and World War II. In the US, public relations experts became part of the war effort to prepare troops for war and the general populace to sacrifice for the war effort. Among the public relations luminaries involved in the US war effort were Edward Bernays, Ivy Lee, and Carl Byoir (Heath & Coombs, 2006). In fact, the war effort was a hot house for advancing the field of public relations, as the ideas spread to the corporate world following both wars. Box 15.1 provides a glimpse into wartime public relations in the US.

Another well-known example of the ill-effects of public relations is Edward Bernays' effort to promote smoking among women. Bernays did not really create the demand among women for smoking, but he did push the trend along (for more details, see chapter 8). Smoking by women has resulted in significant health problems for a growing segment of the population. Promoting a product resulted in health damage for millions and spawned a problem that has spanned generations. The R. J. Reynolds Tobacco Company retains a strong marketing focus on women to this day.

Public relations is a important component of social marketing efforts designed to prevent smoking and to urge people to stop smoking. Around the world a

---

Box 15.1   Four-Minute Men

During World War I, Donald Ryerson created a division of the Committee on Public Information (CPI) known as the Four-Minute Men. This group helped to build support for the war effort by giving short speeches, often during the intermission at movie theatres. Movie going was very popular at this time, with over 10 million people attending movies daily. These volunteers reached every state and territory at the height of the program. The chairman for each state or territory selected and trained the male volunteers. Later, there would be an auxiliary organization of female speakers.

The Four-Minute Men Division would select the topics and distribute materials by means of printed bulletins. The bulletins would contain key points to cover, sample speeches, and even answers to possible questions. The four minutes reflect the amount of time for an intermission at a movie theatre. The Four-Minute Men had over 75,000 speakers, delivered over 755,000 speeches, and had a total audience estimated at over 134 million during an 18-month time frame. This was a great return on a government investment of only $100,000 (Lubbers, 2005). The Four-Minute Men used the public speaking channel to reach the American public as they sought the entertainment of the day. The Four-Minute Men are an excellent example of the strategic use of communication to support organizational objectives.

---

number of organizations oppose smoking and use public relations to convey their message and attempts to change behaviors. The Global Smokefree Partnership is international in scope. Anti-smoking efforts in the UK are supported by the British Heart Foundation, Smokefree, Action on Smoking and Health UK, and the National Health Service. Anti-smoking campaigns in the US are pursued by the American Lung Association, thetruth.com, and the Campaign for Tobacco Free Kids.

These two paradigmatic examples of the negative effects of public relations illustrate the competition of ideas. When one group utilizes public relations for nefarious purposes, other groups seek to counter with their own public relations. Their power may not be equal, but each uses public relations to be heard. Again, freedom of choice has a price. Public relations can be used by groups that will not benefit society. That does not mean we abandon advocacy in public relations or public relations as a whole. Consider how the Coalition of Immokalee Workers used public relations to win concessions from Yum! Brands, McDonald's, and Burger King that improved their working and living conditions. There are numerous examples of when public relations and advocacy are used to improve society. The two case studies at the end of this chapter provide additional examples. Public relations is instrumental in helping people to become aware of and to take action to correct problems. It would be tragic to lose the benefits public relations can offer society because some choose to use public relations for unsavory ends.

People should have a greater understanding of how public relations is used so that they have a greater awareness of its potential influence in their lives.

Toward Public Relations Literacy

In chapter 1 we introduced the concept of public relations literacy. We are not the first to use the term, but we do provide one of the first explications of the concept. The concept of media literacy is receiving increased attention in the mass communication and education literatures. The basic idea is that people should be critical consumers of the mass media because they can have a significant impact on their lives. People should realize that the mass media construct a particular view of reality. That view of reality is subject to manipulation and misrepresentation, hence the need for critical consumption.

We believe that public relations literacy is important as well. In fact, public relations is often noted as a force that distorts and manipulates the media's portrayal of reality. (Refer back to the concerns of public relations critics found in chapter 2.) *Public relations literacy* is the ability to identify, analyze, and evaluate public relations messages. To be public relations literate, a person must be able to identify when public relations is being utilized, be aware public relations does impact society and individuals, have frameworks for analyzing public relations efforts, and apply critical thinking skills to their evaluation. As noted in chapter 1, ideas from chapters 5 through 14 are used to illustrate various ways to build public relations literacy and provide the foundational tools people might employ when critically evaluating public relations actions.

Activists are trying to bring about changes in corporations and/or society. That means they have agendas and ideologies. When evaluating public relations messages from activist groups, examine their backgrounds. What does this activist group stand for? What are their values and goals? What do they have to gain or lose in this situation? Such information is easy to find on websites in the "About Us" sections. Evaluate the sources of the information and understand the biases of the activist group. This would include self-proclaimed watchdog groups. While watchdog groups can be valuable sources of information, it is important to understand their biases when comparing what they say with what the people being watched are saying. Often, you will be confronted with conflicting public relations messages. You are left to decide which ones are more relevant to your life and interests.

Media relations is the most obvious area for public relations literacy because it directly overlaps with media literacy. Media literacy recommends ways to detect when news media content has been developed by public relations. The focal point is video news releases (VNRs). Local news outlets are likely to air VNRs as news stories. Clues that a news story is really a VNR/public relations include visuals the local media would not have been able to capture (such as an exterior shot from another state or country) and when the local newsperson is not shown in the interview (Baran, 2008). When it comes to VNRs, media literacy and public relations are isomorphic.

However, media relations goes beyond VNRs. Research in both the US and UK estimates more than half of all news stories are based on public relations actions. Very favorable articles are the primary objective of media relations. When reading a news story about an organization or corporation, consider if there are any other sources for the story or alternative views. If so, do these sources offer a counter-perspective or agree with the general tenor of the article? If the story lacks balance, a public relations literate person will check additional sources to determine if there is any counter-information about the organization or corporation. Critical evaluation of media relations requires moving beyond the facts at hand to seek additional sources. For instance, does the news story closely resemble a news release from the organization or corporation? What do watchdog groups have to say about the organization or corporation? What does the organization or corporation have to gain from the news story?

New media relations demand even greater critical thinking than traditional media relations because anyone can post information online. Just because a website carries information does not mean it is true or unbiased. Public relations literacy for new media relations is a process of verification. If you find information on an organization's or corporation's website, you know it is biased. Check with watchdog groups or critics to obtain a more balanced perspective on the organization or corporation. If you are reading user generated/social media such as discussion boards, blogs, and an individual's website, investigate the source. Who is posting the information? What biases might they have? Do they have anything to gain in this situation? Read over their descriptions of themselves. If there is no additional information about the creator of the content, be skeptical and search for other sources that can confirm or refute what you have read.

Social marketing is typically pro-social, so we are less critical of its messages. However, as noted in chapter 8, many corporations engage in social marketing as a mechanism for managing issues and reputations. When you see social marketing sponsored by an organization, ask yourself, "What does the organization have to gain from this?" Think about how the social issue is affecting the corporation and what corporate goals the social marketing effort allows them to pursue. Such an evaluation can help to separate pro-social from self-interest concerns.

For non-corporate social marketing, consider whose interests are really being served and why. What other constituencies could benefit but are missing from the social marketing efforts? Why is the social marketing restricted to its current targets? We need to determine if the social benefits of a social marketing effort are being maximized or simply used to help a limited segment of society. A critical consumer could push further to determine what sources were consulted when creating the social marketing effort. Were the target constituents a part of the design process or just targets?

Reputation management is an increasingly important function for corporations and other types of organizations. When you read or see messages designed to build reputations, be skeptical. Is the organization really doing what it says it is doing? Why would the organization want to be associated with these issues or values? Are the changes cosmetic or embedded in who the organization is and what it does? How does the organization embody these issues or values in its actions and policies? What constituents benefit from the reputation-building efforts? Are important faults of the organization being overlooked by shiny reputation messages? Search for other pieces of confirmatory information and additional insights into the behavior of organizations. Watchdog groups, the traditional news media, and online news media are possible sources. However, be sure you are reading actual sources and not stories planted in the news media by the organization or a watchdog group with close ties to the organization.

Issues management is one of the least visible aspects of public relations. The low visibility results from government officials being the primary targets. When you see public relations messages that advocate certain policy options, such as changes in legislation and legal reform, research the issue. Understand what the group advocating the position stands to win or lose with the issue. Who are the sides in the issue? What does each side have to gain or lose? What voices dominate the discussion? What relevant voices are absent from the discussion? Are any of the vocal actors really front groups? How will the proposed outcomes of the issues management effort affect various constituents? Learn both sides of the issue to determine which is most consistent with your perspective and how the issue might impact your life. Also consider the larger ramifications of the issue on society and other constituents. The critical evaluation of issues management requires exploring public relations messages from all sides. Be wary of front groups. Do a search of a group's name to learn more about it. If a group is a known front group, a web search should reveal that information.

Risk management information is plentiful online. Use the resources the government provides. In the US the Environmental Protection Agency (EPA) is just one agency that has detailed information on risks, including background documents and searchable databases. If you live near a chemical facility, use the online resources to educate yourself about that facility and the chemicals it uses. Additional information will make you better prepared to interpret the risk communication messages presented by the organization and participate more effectively in the risk communication process. How much risk information is being provided? Is it the type of risk information constituents really need and want? How does the organization's risk communication compare to the information provided by its critics and watchdogs? How do biases affect the various presentations of risk information you find?

The online environment is ideal for providing health risk information as well. Beware of websites that use health fears to sell products or promote a political agenda. What does the group or organization have to gain or lose from the risk? How can shaping your behavior relative to a risk help or hurt the group or organization? Again, review the website to learn more about the credentials and goals of the sponsors. Utilize credible governmental websites to learn more about health risks. For instance, the World Health Organization has useful information about the Avian Flu. No source is bias free, but government sources are often more detailed and credible for health risk information.

Crisis management should make constituent safety its number one concern, but too often organizations place greater value on protecting reputations than protecting people. Judge for yourself how well or poorly an organization is managing a crisis. Review the media coverage and visit the organization's website to determine what it is saying and doing about a crisis. Does constituent safety seem to be a priority? What action is the organization taking to ensure public safety? If it is taking constituent safety seriously, you will be more comfortable interacting with the organization in the future. If management seems more concerned with protecting its reputation, you should be less likely to interact with that organization. Why become or stay involved with an organization that does not have your best interests in mind? Crisis responses should be examined for the concern shown for victims and substantive efforts to correct the cause of the crisis. How concerned does the organization seem to be with crisis victims? Is this level of concern consistent with the crisis situation? Are substantive efforts being made to identify and to correct the cause of the crisis? Does the crisis response seem to be distracting people from the cause and the need to redress the cause of the crisis? You can refer back to chapter 12 for additional details for the framework you can use for evaluating crisis responses.

CSR is a buzz word in business and buzz words are easy to abuse. CSR efforts should help society and constituents in some way, not just the corporation reputation. Again, we are not denying that corporations should benefit in some way, but true CSR must help society too. How is the CSR effort being assessed? Is a third party involved in the assessment? Does the evaluation of the CSR effort extend beyond corporate benefits? What constituents are benefiting from the CSR efforts? How are they benefiting? Are CSR efforts cosmetic or embedded in corporate policies and practices? Are CSR efforts distracting constituents from important corporate flaws? Again, activists and watchdog groups can provide additional information about CSR efforts. However, determine the biases of these groups as you compare their information to the CSR information from a corporation. What does the activist or watchdog group have to gain from criticizing the CSR efforts?

Finally, public diplomacy, as a form of international public relations, can shape our perceptions of countries. Be skeptical of news media coverage of countries. Why is a country receiving positive coverage? What does a country have to gain from the positive coverage? Why is a country receiving negative media coverage? Does the media coverage reflect what other, credible sources say about the country? Too much positive coverage could be a result of public relations manipulation. No coverage or negative coverage could reflect media biases about international stories or marginalized groups of people. Seek additional information from news sources online, including those from other countries. Also, a variety of websites can be useful, depending upon the topic of interest. For example, Amnesty International is useful if your focus is human rights, but not that useful if you are interested in economic growth or a tourist destination. As always, carefully assess the credibility of online sources.

Public relations literate people could spend a significant part of their lives investigating information. This is actually a form of transparency, as discussed in chapter 3. Obviously, motivation is a factor in applying public relations literacy, just as it is in triggering transparency. People will carefully examine the relevant public relations messages that enter their lives. For instance, you may not be interested in every crisis, but you can follow the crisis management of organizations in your web of relationships or that could potentially be added to your web. Here, motivation is a matter of salience. Public relations literate individuals should have the tools to critically evaluate public relations efforts when they matter to them or they desire to be informed on a topic.

Chapters 5 through 14 illustrate when public relations is used and how its use can affect society. They provide various frames of reference for critically evaluating specific types of public relations efforts. This section has highlighted some of the key ideas that can be used to evaluate various public relations efforts – the groundwork for public relations literacy skills. Notice the heavy reliance on questions people might ask in their evaluation process. Questions are highlighted because public relations literacy is about inquiry. We need to question public relations messages rather than simply grant quiescence to them. A public relations literate individual will be a more critical consumer of public relations messages and be better able to understand what ideas they should support in the marketplace of ideas. In the end, public relations literate individuals are better able to pursue and to protect their own best interests.

Parting Comments

As we conclude this book it is fitting to return to our definition of public relations: *the management of mutually influential relationships within a web of constituency relationships.* Public relations is a complex process encompassing much more than media relations. Moreover, we believe public relations should embrace its dependence on advocacy and power rather than hide from it. Public relations is about managing influence – our attempts to influence others and their attempts to influence us. Public relations efforts attempt to create both small and large-scale changes that help to shape society and our lives. Whether it is the content of news stories, attempts to prevent regulation of pharmaceutical marketing, or efforts to promote seatbelt usage, public relations is one element that influences our lives. Power is a concern as practitioners employ discourse to facilitate change. Greater power results in a stronger voice and an increased likelihood of successful influence. Public relations traffics in mutual influence, but mutual does not mean equal.

In chapter 1 we offered an alternate reality for public relations. We argued that the roots of public relations could be traced to activism and efforts to improve society. Of course, what makes society "better" is a value judgment. Not everyone agrees that a prohibition on alcohol or banning smoking in public areas makes society better. Still, public relations would probably be held in greater esteem if its origins resided in social change rather than media relations and the defense of corporate interests. We cannot rewrite history, but we can acknowledge public relations is much greater than media relations and advocates for more than just corporate interests.

Through examples and case studies we have tried to give voice to activist public relations. This was a conscious attempt to represent the marginalized voices of public relations. On the whole, the public relations work and contributions of activists are overlooked and marginalized in the public relations literature. Recent trends are providing greater attention to activist public relations, but it remains on the periphery of the field. We could have added more activist examples or solely used activist examples, but that would have been too narrow. We demonstrated how activists and corporations influence one another. To appreciate the breadth of public relations we must sample a variety of the actors who partake in the drama.

People might view our efforts here differently. Some may view the text as an attack on public relations, while others may view it as a defense of the practice. We think it is both. One of our goals was to explore the impact of good and bad public relations on society through efforts to manage influence. Our field preaches the virtue of transparency and the sins of spin by emphasizing that public relations practitioners must share the good and the bad with constituents. We tried to follow this advice by offering reflections throughout the text designed to help the reader consider the positive and negative aspects of various public relations practices.

A field benefits from reflection and attempts to understand its own flaws. An over-zealous defense serves to stunt a field's development, not to enhance its growth. Public relations is neither all good nor pure evil, it provides both for society. Ultimately, public relations can provide a valuable means of helping to knit the fabric of society if people choose to utilize it in that way. We hope this volume has helped readers to reflect on the practice of public relations, stimulating their thinking as to how the practice can improve and enhance its positive contributions to society and to recognize when it is being used to the detriment of society. Take care in how you employ public relations and be vigilant and critical of how others may employ it.

Case Study: Girlcott

Abercrombie & Fitch is a well-known trendsetter in the US youth market and pushes the edge with advertising and merchandising. In 2005 a group of around 24 teenage girls from the Women & Girls Foundation of Southwest Pennsylvania decided Abercrombie & Fitch had gone too far with "attitude" t-shirts they felt were degrading to women. The t-shirts had expressions such as

"Who needs brains when you have these?" and "Blondes Are Adored, Brunettes Are Ignored." The young women called for a "Girlcott" of Abercrombie & Fitch and wrote a letter of complaint to management. The first reaction of Abercrombie & Fitch management was to ignore the young women (Kilman, 2005). And then the public relations campaign began.

The young women of the Women & Girls Foundation of Southwest Pennsylvania began emailing friends about the Girlcott and urged their friends to email others. Thus, one strategy was to generate negative word-of-mouth via the Internet. The young women also utilized media relations to generate negative publicity for Abercrombie & Fitch. They announced their Girlcott through a news conference and rally at Chatham College. The national media gravitated quickly to this unusual story. Emma Blackman-Mathis, the 16-year-old co-chair of the group, appeared on *Today*, Fox News, and CNN. Abercrombie & Fitch initially held firm by stating: "Our clothing appeals to a wide variety of customers. These particular t-shirts have been very popular among adult women to whom they are marketed" (Haynes, 2005).

Inside of a week, Abercrombie & Fitch management had negotiated with the Girlcott leaders and arrived at a settlement, announced on November 4, 2005. The text of the news release, issued jointly by Abercrombie & Fitch and the Women & Girls Foundation of Southwest Pennsylvania, can be found below. The agreement resulted in Abercrombie & Fitch agreeing to stop selling several of the offensive t-shirts and to meet with representatives of the Girlcott. A total of 14 of the Girlcott members did visit Abercrombie & Fitch headquarters in New Albany, Ohio. They were invited to offer suggestions for t-shirt messages and were eager to provide input. However, no guarantees were made that the ideas would be used and none have made it to store racks (Rockwell, 2005). The Girlcott is testament to the power of public relations for creating change. A handful of young women can make a major clothier change policies when they launch a public relations campaign that generates sufficient negative publicity and word-of-mouth. It is also evidence that society can benefit from the application of public relations to societal problems.

Abercrombie & Fitch Issues Joint Statement With Women & Girls Foundation of Southwest Pennsylvania, New Albany, Ohio, November 4

Abercrombie & Fitch Statement
Abercrombie & Fitch has reached an amicable agreement with the Women & Girls Foundation of Southwest Pennsylvania under which we will stop selling several t-shirts in our stores.

In recognition that these t-shirts might be found to be objectionable to many young women, who are among our best customers, we contacted Heather Arnet, Executive Director of the Women & Girls Foundation, and offered to discuss the issue with them. We recognize that the shirts in question, while meant to be humorous, might be troubling to some.

We look forward to meeting in person with representatives of the "Girlcott" action in the immediate future. We are pleased with this resolution.

Women & Girls Foundation of Southwest Pennsylvania
The Girlcott we launched this week got the attention of Abercrombie & Fitch. They contacted us and we reached an agreement that satisfies us. Several offensive t-shirts to which we objected are being removed from store shelves.

We look forward to meeting with Abercrombie & Fitch to discuss ways we could collaborate on more empowering messages their products could be sending to their customers.

We appreciate Abercrombie's quick action.

Case questions

1 What public relations tactics were used by members of the Girlcott? Why were they effective?
2 What role did the news media and the Internet play in the Girlcott?
3 Why did Abercrombie & Fitch change its position toward the demands of the Girlcott?

Case Study: PepsiCo and Burma

The world was reminded of human rights abuses in Burma (also known as Myanmar) with the 2007 Buddhist monks' protests and subsequent brutal suppression by the State Law & Order Restoration Council (SLORC) that rules Burma. However, Burma's government has been brutally oppressing its people and violating their human rights for decades. In the 1990s, PepsiCo became one of many multinational corporations to become entangled in the Burma human rights abuse issue.

In the 1980s the SLORC government decided to open Burma to foreign investment. The Burmese economy was weak and the government needed new sources of income. Taxes and other fees paid by the foreign investors would help to support SLORC and keep it in power. Human rights groups encouraged corporations to forsake Burma because the corporations would be supporting the suppression of human rights. This message fell on many deaf ears, as Burma was an attractive market for some corporations, including PepsiCo. In November 1991 PepsiCo opened a bottling plant in Rangoon.

Oddly, PepsiCo had supported the boycott of South Africa that helped to end apartheid (the separation of blacks and whites, along with white domination). But PepsiCo management decided to engage the Burmese government. The engagement principle holds that by working in a country, a corporation can help to create change. PepsiCo's official position was as follows: "Deciding to do business in Burma was one of the toughest decisions. But we believe that trade is a positive factor in changing the world" (Pepsi in Burma, 2003). In over twenty years, the SLORC government had not changed its abusive ways.

PepsiCo and other multinationals in the US soon became the focus of protests for their participation and tacit support of SLORC. The Pepsi Boycott was launched in the US in 1992. The first North American PepsiCo/Burma boycott flyers appeared in early 1993. The flyers explained the situation in Burma by promoting the link between corporations and human rights abuse. The campaign started slowly, as its media relations efforts generated little coverage at first and the boycott message was slowly moving by word-of-mouth. Still, this was an organized public relations campaign designed to pressure PepsiCo to leave Burma by exposing PepsiCo's indirect support of human rights abuses (Cooper, 1997).

In 1995 the Free Burma Coalition (FBC) was founded at the University of Wisconsin. The FBC moved the public relations campaign to the Internet. The Internet was used to raise awareness of the issue and coordinate actions against PepsiCo and other multinationals operating in Burma. The Internet increased the pressure on PepsiCo by making the FBC a more powerful stakeholder (Coombs, 1998). A sign of the shift in power was that PepsiCo management now began discussions with the FBC. Negative media coverage for PepsiCo increased.

The Pepsi Boycott quickly spread to over 100 college campuses where students pressured administrators to end contracts with PepsiCo. PepsiCo lost contracts with the University of California, Berkeley, Stanford University, Colgate, and the highly publicized million dollar contract with Harvard. The cities of Berkeley, San Francisco, Oakland, Santa Monica, Ann Arbor, and Madison also ended business with PepsiCo. PepsiCo was also seeing protests and business losses in the UK, Canada, and Australia (Pepsi in Burma, 2003). The Internet made the FBC an international venture.

PepsiCo began to change its position in 1996 with a partial pullout from Burma. It sold all its direct interests in Burma, but had some indirect investments. The FBC wanted complete divestment from Burma. In May 1997 PepsiCo severed all business connections with Burma. Later that year, the US government banned US companies from making new investments in Burma (Pepsi in Burma, 2003). That law was essentially a ban on Burmese investment because PepsiCo was the last US company to leave Burma.

People can employ public relations to make changes even on a global scale. It was through public relations efforts that the FBC was able to pressure PepsiCo into ending business operations and ties in Burma. Again, public relations proves it can be used to facilitate positive social change.

Case questions

1   How was PepsiCo supporting oppression by staying in Burma?
2   Why would PepsiCo want to stay in Burma even after the initial protests began?
3   How did the Internet generate power for the FBC?
4   Why were college students an effective target for the FBC?
5   Do you think PepsiCo would have remained in Burma if it had not lost contracts with universities? Why or why not?

Discussion Questions

1   What is public relations literacy? Why is it important? What can you do to become more public relations literate?
2   Throughout this book we have argued public relations is a practice that can be used to pursue both good and evil. Based on your own experience with public relations, identify examples to illustrate this idea. Do you believe the practice of public relations can ever be "neutral"? Explain.

3   A theme throughout this book is that corporations and activists practice public relations. How can we determine when corporations and activist groups have "gone too far" in their public relations activities? What standards, if any, can provide the foundation for your assessment?
4   Based on what you have learned from this book, do you believe society needs public relations? Explain your answer.

Appendix 1

US Food & Drug Administration
News Release

FDA Statement

FOR IMMEDIATE RELEASE

Statement

October 28, 2008

Media Inquiries:
Michael Herndon, 301-827-6242

Consumer Inquiries:
888-INFO-FDA

FDA Statement on Release of Bisphenol A (BPA) Subcommittee Report

We appreciate the hard work and long hours the subcommittee has invested in scientific peer review of the FDA's draft safety assessment of the use of BPA in food contact applications. The FDA requested this peer review to provide additional insight into this complex issue. This group of distinguished scientists has devoted their considerable knowledge and experience to this effort.

The subcommittee report to the Science Board raises important questions regarding the draft safety assessment, and the FDA looks forward to the review of the subcommittee's report by the Science Board on Oct. 31.

The FDA agrees that, due to the uncertainties raised in some studies relating to the potential effects of low dose exposure to bisphenol A, additional research would be valuable. The FDA is already moving forward with planned research to address the potential low dose effects of bisphenol A, and we will carefully evaluate the findings of these studies.

Consumers should know that, based on all available evidence, the present consensus among regulatory agencies in the United States, Canada, Europe, and Japan is that current levels of exposure to BPA through food packaging do not pose an immediate health risk to the general population, including infants and babies.

Regarding Canada, the FDA notes that Health Canada's assessment of bisphenol A on newborns and infants up to 18 months of age concludes that exposure levels are below the levels that could cause health effects. Out of an abundance of caution, the Government of Canada is taking steps to restrict the use of BPA.

Parents who, as a precaution, wish to use alternatives for their bottle-fed babies can use glass and other substitutes for polycarbonate plastic bottles; avoid heating formula in polycarbonate plastic bottles; and consult their pediatrician about switching to powdered infant formula.

For a copy of the Subcommittee Report, go to:
http://www.fda.gov/ohrms/dockets/ac/oc08.html#Scienceboard.

Statement of the Acting Surgeon General, Rear Admiral Steven K. Galson, M.D., M.P.H.

"The most important thing parents can do for their babies is ensure that they receive adequate nutrition. While the best source of nutrition for babies is the mother's breast milk, infant formula remains the recommended alternative when breast milk is not an option."

RSS Feed for FDA News Releases
www.fda.gov/bbs/topics/NEWS/2008/NEW01908.html

Appendix 2

US Centers for Disease Control and Prevention News Release

CDC Media Analysis Examines Car Surfing

Injuries and Deaths Reported at Wide Range of Speeds

For Immediate Release: October 16, 2008

Contact: Gail Hayes, CDC Injury Media Center, Phone: (770) 488-4902

Teens are getting injured or killed by riding on the outside of a moving vehicle – an activity known as car surfing, according to a Centers for Disease Control and Prevention (CDC) review of newspaper articles released today in the Morbidity and Mortality Weekly Report. The report also noted that car surfing injuries and deaths were reported at a wide range of vehicle speeds, from as low as 5 mph up to 80 mph.

CDC researchers examined 18 years of news reports from January 1990 to August 2008 using a newspaper article database. The researchers found 99 reported incidents of car surfing, 58 percent of which were fatal.

"While car surfing may be appealing to teens and others, our recommendation is simple – don't do it! Even a vehicle moving at a slow speed can be deadly," said John Halpin, M.D., the study's lead author.

"Parents should talk to their teens about the dangers of car surfing, especially if they feel that 'car surfing' has gained attention and popularity in their community," Halpin said.

Researchers excluded cases of injury related to activities that resemble car surfing, such as ghost riding, an activity that involves a driver exiting, and dancing next to a moving vehicle. They also noted that newspapers may vary in terms of the amount of attention they devote to these stories, or may not report them at all.

- In the news stories reviewed, the average age of those injured or killed was 17.6, with males accounting for 70 percent of the victims.
- The largest number of car surfing injuries and deaths reported in U.S. newspapers occurred in August.
- Most (74 percent) of the news stories involved incidents in the Midwest and the South.
- Three out of four of the news stories reported car surfing deaths were caused by a bump or blow to the head.
- The news stories also suggest that car surfing may be both seasonal and regional in nature.

The media analysis also found that in 29 percent of incidents, a sudden movement or maneuver was mentioned, such as an abrupt turn or sudden braking, which caused the person car surfing to fall off the vehicle. These types of falls can result in serious injuries or death, even at slow speeds.

National Teen Safe Driving Week is Oct. 19 – 25 and information from CDC is at: http://www.cdc.gov/ncipc/duip/spotlite/teendrivers.htm, the National Highway Traffic Safety Administration at http://www.nhtsa.dot.gov, and the Children's Hospital of Philadelphia at http://stokes.chop.edu/programs/injury/our_research/ydri.php.

For a complete copy of the MMWR report, please visit http://www.cdc.gov/mmwr. For more information about CDC's work in injury and violence prevention, please link to: http://www.cdc.gov/injury.

#####

www.cdc.gov/media/pressrel/2008/r081016.htm

Appendix 3

American Veterinary Medical Association Media Alert

MEDIA ALERT

Back

FOR MORE INFORMATION:

Michael San Filippo
Phone: 847-285-6687
Cell: 847-732-6194
email: msanfilippo@avma.org

FOR IMMEDIATE RELEASE

September 14, 2007

Update: AVMA warns of potential new threat to pets

Schaumburg, Ill.

The American Veterinary Medical Association (AVMA) has recently been made aware of several complaints from pet owners and veterinarians that multiple brands of jerky treats manufactured in China have been making pets sick. Symptoms of illness have included vomiting, diarrhea, and lethargy. To our knowledge, no deaths have been reported.

The AVMA posted an alert on its Web site on September 13 to inform its members and the public about what was known. Today, the American College of Veterinary Internal Medicine (ACVIM) issued a statement saying it also has become aware of an unusual number of dogs presenting similar symptoms and abnormal test results associated with consumption of some jerky treats. The ACVIM statement is available at www.acvim.org/ uploadedFiles/Jerky_Treat_Info_September_14.doc.

The Food and Drug Administration (FDA) is currently testing several products to see if a contaminant can be found. So far, they have ruled out melamine, one of the chemicals that led to the massive pet food recall this spring, but have yet to identify anything that might be making pets sick.

While a list of brand/product names of affected treats is not yet available, the AVMA has learned that all complaints have involved jerky treats from China. We recommend that pet owners use their best judgment in this matter.

Suspected cases should be reported to the FDA. To find the number for the FDA district office consumer complaint coordinator in your region, visit www.fda.gov/opacom/backgrounders/complain.html.

The AVMA is monitoring the situation and will provide updated information on our Web site (www.avma.org) as soon as it becomes available. Like all information on our Web site, we will only post information that is credible and has been confirmed.

For more information, contact Michael San Filippo, AVMA media relations assistant, at 847-285-6687 (office), 847-732-6194 (cell), or msanfilippo@avma.org.

####

The AVMA and its more than 75,000 member veterinarians are engaged in a wide variety of activities dedicated to advancing the science and art of animal, human and public health. Visit the AVMA Web site at www.avma.org for more information.

www.avma.org/press/media_alerts/070914_jerky_treats_pf.asp

Appendix 4

US Food & Drug Administration Pitch
Letter Guidance

Pitch Letter

This document also available in Spanish

[YOUR LETTERHEAD]

[Month, date, year]

[NAME OF YOUR AGENCY] LAUNCHES EDUCATIONAL CAMPAIGN WARNING THE HISPANIC COMMUNITY ABOUT RISKS OF EATING RAW OYSTERS

Have you ever eaten a raw oyster? If you or someone you know has, please read the enclosed information - it could save someone's life.

The [Name of Your Agency] is issuing a warning to the Hispanic community [in name of city], about the risks in eating raw oysters contaminated with a bacteria that lives in the waters of the Gulf coast. In the last two years, nine Hispanic men died in the U.S. from eating raw oysters contaminated with the bacteria, *Vibrio vulnificus*.

It is imperative we get the message out to the community about this issue as soon as possible because as the weather gets warmer the amount of bacteria in the water increases. Also, as you know, raw oysters are a favorite food among Hispanics, especially Hispanic males.

A(n) [name of agency] representative will be available for interviews next week on [insert date(s)] to speak to you. Please consider scheduling an interview to discuss this important topic.

Enclosed is the following information:

- Press Release
- *Vibrio vulnificus* Fact Sheet
- Myths about raw oysters
- Cooked oyster recipes
- Feature article

For more information, please contact:

[Contact name]

[Organization]

[Phone]

[Email]

References

A 'humanitarian campaign' to sell bottled water (March 11, 2008). Retrieved March 21, 2008 from www.prwatch.org/node/7082.

About (n.d.). Retrieved December 15, 2007 from www.esrb.org/about/education.jsp.

About Plan A (2007). Retrieved May 20, 2008 from www.plana.marksandspencer.com/index.php?action=PublicAboutDisplay.

About us (n.d.). Retrieved August 11, 2006 from www.fairtrade.org.uk/about_us.htm.

About us Tanning Truth (n.d.). Retrieved October 22, 2008 from www.tanningtruth.com/index.php/about_us/.

ACC calls on FDA to update review of bisphenol A (2008, April 17). Retrieved September 28, 2008 from www.factsonplastic.com/acc-calls-on-fda-to-update-review-of-bisphenol-a/.

Albarracin, D., Johnson, B. T, Fishbein, M., & Muellerleile, P. A. (2001). Theories of reasoned action and planned behavior as models of condom use: A meta-analysis. *Psychological Bulletin, 127,* 142–161.

Albritton, R. B. & Manheim, J. B. (1985). Public relations efforts for the third world: Images in the news. *Journal of Communication, 35,* 43–59.

Alexander, E. (2000, December 6). Students debate effectiveness, accuracy of well-known anti-drug commercial. Retrieved January 13, 2008 from www.cnn.com/fyi/interactive/news/brain/brain.on.drugs.html.

Alinsky, S. (1972). *Rules for radicals: A pragmatic primer for realistic radicals.* New York: Random House.

Alsop, R. J. (2004). *The 18 Immutable laws of corporate reputation: Creating, protecting, and repairing your most valuable asset.* New York: Free Press.

America's most admired companies (2007). Retrieved September 16, 2007 from www.money.cnn.com/magazines/fortune/mostadmired/2007/index.html.

American Farmers for the Advancement and Conservation of Technology (March 11, 2008). Retrieved March 17, 2008 from www.sourcewatch.org/index.php?title=American_Farmers_for_the_Advancement_a.

Amos, A. & Haglund, M. (2000). From social taboo to "torch of freedom": The marketing of cigarettes to women. *Tobacco Control, 9*, 3–8.

Andreasen, A. R. (2003). The life trajectory of social marketing: Some implications. *Marketing Theory, 3*(2), 293–303.

Animal Liberation Front (ALF) (1991). The ALF primer, 1991. Retrieved January 29, 2007 from www.animalliberationfront.com/ALFront/ALFPrime.htm.

Ansoff, H. I. (1980). Strategic issue management. *Strategic Management Journal, 1*(2), 131–148.

Ansolabehere, S., Behr, R., & Iyengar, S. (1993). *The media game: American politics in the age of television.* New York: Macmillian.

Apollonio, D. E. & Bero, L. A. (2007). The creation of industry front groups: The tobacco industry and "get government off our back." *American Journal of Public Health, 97*(3), 419–427.

Arpan, L. M. & Roskos-Ewoldsen, D. R. (2005). Stealing thunder: An analysis of the effects of proactive disclosure of crisis information. *Public Relations Review, 31*(3), 425–433.

Aspen Institute (1992). Report of the national leadership conference on media literacy. Retrieved March 13, 2008 from www.medialit.org/reading_room/article582.html.

Audience segments in a changing news environment: Key news audiences now blend online and traditional sources (2008, August 17). Retrieved September 10, 2008 from www.people-press.org/reports/pdf/444.pdf.

Bagdasarov, Z., Banerjee, S., Greene, K., & Campo, S. (2008). Indoor tanning and problem behavior. *Journal of American College Health, 56*(5), 555–561.

Balmer, J. M. T. & Soenen, G. B. (1995). The acid test of corporate identity management. *Journal of Marketing Management, 15*, 69–92.

Baran, S. J. (2008). *Introduction to mass communication: Media literacy and culture,* 5th edn. Burr Ridge, IL: McGraw Hill.

Barney, J. B. & Stewart, A. C. (2000). Organizational identity as moral philosophy: Competitive implications for diversified corporations. In M. Schultz, M. J. Hatch, & M. H. Larsen (Eds.), *The expressive organization: Linking identity, reputation, and the corporate brand* (pp. 36–50). New York: Oxford University Press.

Barone, M. J., Miyazaki, A. D., & Taylor, K. A. (2000). The influence of cause-related marketing on consumer choice: Does one good turn deserve another? *Academy of Marketing Science Journal, 28*, 248–262.

Barrett, S. M. (2004). Implementation studies: Time for a revival? Personal reflections on 20 years of implementation studies. *Public Administration, 82*, 249–262.

Barstow, D. (2008, April 20). Behind TV analysts, Pentagon's hidden hand. Retrieved May 9, 2008 from www.nytimes.com/2008/04/20/washington/20generals.html?_r=1&oref=slogin.

Barton, L. (2001). *Crisis in Organizations II,* 2nd edn. Cincinnati: College Divisions South-Western.

Basic information (n.d.). Retrieved December 31, 2007 from www.epa.gov/compliance/basics/ejbackground.html.

Baskin, O. & Aronoff, C. (1992). *Public relations: The profession and the practice,* 3rd edn. Dubuque, IA: William C. Brown.

Beder, S. (2002). *Global spin: The corporate assault on environmentalism,* revd. edn. White River Junction, VT: Chelsea Green.

Bennett, W. L. (1975). Political scenarios and the nature of politics. *Philosophy and Rhetoric, 8*, 23–42.

Bennett, W. L. (1988). *News: The politics of illusion.* New York: Longman.

Bennett, W. L. (2004). Communicating global activism: Strengths and vulnerabilities of networked politics. In W. van de Donk, B. D. Loader, P. G. Nixon, & D. Rucht (Eds.), *Cyberprotest: New media, citizens and social movements* (pp. 123–146). New York: Routledge.

Benoit, W. L. (1995). *Accounts, excuses, and apologies: A theory of image restoration.* Albany: State University of New York Press.

Benoit, W. L. & Czerwinski, A. (1997). A critical analysis of USAir's image repair discourse. *Business Communication Quarterly, 60*, 38–57.

Berens, G. & van Riel, C. B. M. (2004). Corporate associations in the academic literature: Three main streams of thought in the reputation measurement literature. *Corporate Reputation Review, 7*(2), 161–178.

Bergstein, B. (2007, January 24). Microsoft offers cash for Wikipedia edit. Retrieved October 30, 2007 from www.boston.com/business/technology/articles/2007/01/24/microsoft_offers_cash_for_wikipedia_edit/.

Best, J. (2005, March 17). The limits of transparency. Retrieved March 30, 2008 from www.iht.com/articles/2005/03/16/opinion/edbest.php.

Bhattacharya, C. B. & Sen, S. (2003). Consumer-company identification: A framework for understanding consumers' relationships with companies. *Journal of Marketing, 67* (4), 76–88.

Bhattacharya, C. B. & Sen, S. (2004). Doing better at doing good: When, why, and how consumers respond to corporate social initiatives. *California Management Review, 47*(1), 9–24.

Black, A. (2008, May 8). Columbia seeks to update its image. Retrieved May 9, 2008 from www.prweek.com/uk/sectors/media/article/807772/front-page-colombia-seeks-update-image/.

Bloggers' code of ethics (2003, April 15). Retrieved October 29, 2008 from www.cyberjournalist.net/news/000215.php.

Blood, R. (2002). *The Weblog handbook: Practical advice on creating and maintaining your blog.* Cambridge: Perseus Publishing.

Boorstin, D. J. (1978). *The image: A guide to pseudo-events in America.* New York: Antheneum.

Borland, J. (2007, August 14). See whose editing Wikipedia. Retrieved October 30, 2007 from www.wired.com/politics/onlinerights/news/2007/08/wiki_tracker.

Bostdorff, D. M. & Vibbert, S. L. (1994). Values advocacy: Enhancing organizational images, deflecting public criticism, and grounding future arguments. *Public Relations Review, 20*, 141–158.

Botan, C. (1993). A human nature approach to image and ethics in international public relations. *Journal of Public Relations Research, 5*(2), 71–82.

Botan, C. (1997). Ethics in strategic communication campaigns: The case for a new approach to public relations. *Journal of Business Communication, 34*, 188–202.

Botan, C. & Hazleton, V. (2006). Public relations in a new age. In C. H. Botan and V. Hazleton (Eds.), *Public relations theory II* (pp. 1–18). Mahwah, NJ: Lawrence Erlbaum Associates.

Botan, C. & Taylor, M. (2004). Public relations state of the field. *Journal of Communication, 54*, 645–661.

Bourdieu, P. (1985). The forms of capital. In J. G. Richardson (Ed.), *Handbook of theory and research for the sociology of education* (pp. 241–258). New York: Greenwood Press.

Bowen, S. A. (2005a). Ethics of public relations. In R. L. Heath (Ed.), *Encyclopedia of public relations*, Vol. 1 (pp. 294–297). Thousand Oaks, CA: Sage.

Bowen, S. A. (2005b). Moral philosophy. In R. L. Heath (Ed.), *Encyclopedia of public relations*, Vol. 2 (pp. 542–545). Thousand Oaks, CA: Sage.

Bowen, S. A. (2005c). Excellence theory. In R. L. Heath (Ed.), *Encyclopedia of public relations*, Vol. 1 (pp. 306–308.). Thousand Oaks, CA: Sage.

Bowers, J. W., Ochs, D. J., & Jensen, R. J. (1993). *The rhetoric of agitation and control*, 2nd edn. Prospect Heights, IL: Waveland Press.

Brandt, A. M. (1996). Recruiting women smokers: The engineering of consent. *Journal of the American Medical Women's Association*, 51 (January/April), 63–66.

Bransford, K. (n.d.). Create a killer online newsroom or be killed by the inferior alternative. Retrieved December 5, 2007 from www.aboutpublicrelations.net/ucbransforda.htm.

Bridges, A. (2006, December 13). Lettuce suspected in Taco Bell E. coli. Retrieved December 14, 2006 from www.news.yahoo.com/s/ap/20061214/ap_on_re_us/e_coli_outbreak_taco_bell_34.

Brinson, S. L. & Benoit, W. L. (1996). Dow Corning's image repair strategies in the breast implant crisis. *Communication Quarterly*, 44, 29–41.

Brown, J. J. & Reingen, P. H. (1987). Social ties and word-of-mouth referral behavior. *Journal of Consumer Research*, 14, 350–62.

Brown, T. J. & Dacin, P. A. (1997). The company and the product: Corporate associations and consumer product responses. *Journal of Marketing*, 61(1), 68–84.

Bulldog Reporter/TEKgroup International (2007). 2007 Journalist survey on media relations practices. Retrieved January 24, 2008 from www.tekgroup.com/article_download.cfm?article_id=170.

Burke, K. (1969). *A rhetoric of motives*. Berkeley: University of California Press.

Business Roundtable's post-8/11 crisis communication toolkit (2002). Retrieved April 24, 2006 from www.brtable.org/pdf/722.pdf.

Cameron, G. T., Cropp, F., & Reber, B. H. (2001). Getting past platitudes: Factors limiting accommodation in public relations. *Journal of Communication Management*, 5(3), 242–261.

Cameron, G. T., Pang, A., & Jin, Y. (2008). Contingency theory: Strategic management of conflict in public relations. In T. L. Hansen-Horn and B. D. Neff (Eds.), *Public relations: From theory to practice* (pp. 134–155). Boston: Pearson.

Campaign to stop killer Coke (2006). Retrieved April 14, 2006, from www.killercoke.org.

Canan, P. & Pring, G. W. (1988). Strategic lawsuits against public participation. *Social Problems*, 35, 506–519.

Cancel, A. E., Cameron, G. T., Sallot, L. M., & Mitrook, M. A. (1997). It depends: A contingency theory of accommodation in public relations. *Journal of Public Relations Research*, 9(1), 31–63.

Canedy, D. (1997, June 12). Novartis is latest rival to accuse Schering-Plough of unfairly attacking its product. Retrieved January 3, 2008 from www.query.nytimes.com/gst/fullpage.html?res=9505E5DE163FF931A25755C0A961958260&sec=&spon=&pagewanted=print.

Canel, M. J. & Sanders, K. S. (in press). Crisis communication and terrorist attacks: Framing a response to the 2004 Madrid bombings and 2005 London bombings. In W. T. Coombs and S. J. Holladay (Eds.), *Handbook of Crisis Communication*. Oxford: Wiley-Blackwell.

Car seat education (n.d.). Retrieved September 29, 2008 from www.sacdhhs.com/article. asp?content=72.

Career: Public relations (n.d.). Retrieved October 20, 2007 from www.princetonreview. com/cte/profiles/dayInLife.asp?careerID=171.

Carlisle, J. (1993). Public relationships: Hill & Knowlton, Robert Gray, and the CIA. Retrieved March 30, 2008 from www.whatreallyhappened.com/RANCHO/LIE/HK/ HK2.html.

Carmeli, A. (2004). The link between organizational elements, perceived external prestige and performance. *Corporate Reputation Review, 6*, 314–331.

Carney, A. & Jorden, A. (1993, August). Prepare for business-related crises. *Public Relations Journal, 49*, 34–35.

Carrefour CEO Denies Backing Dalai Lama (2008, April 19). Retrieved April 28, 2008 from www.forbes.com/commerce/2008/04/19/carrefour-china-duran-face-markets-cx_ pm_0419autofacescan01.html?feed=rss_business_commerce.

Carroll, A. (1999, September). Corporate social responsibility. *Business and Society*, 268–296.

Carroll, C. E. (2004). How the mass media influence perceptions of corporate reputation: Exploring agenda-setting effects within business news coverage. Dissertation, University of Texas, Austin.

Carroll, C. E. & McCombs, M. (2003). Agenda-setting effects of business news on the public's images and opinions about major corporations. *Corporate Reputation Review, 16*, 36–46.

Chang, I. (2007, July 19). Cocktails by Jenn positions its drinks as party accessory. Retrieved November 11, 2008 from www.prweekus.com/Cocktails-by-Jenn-positions-its-drinks-as-party-accessory/article/57379/.

Chase, W. H. (1977). Public issue management: The new science. *Public Relations Journal, 33*(1), 25–26.

Chase, W. H. (1980). Issues and policy. *Public Relations Quarterly, 24*(2), 5–6.

Chase, W. H. (1982, December 1). Issues management conference: A special report. *Corporate Public Issues and Their Management, 7*, 1–2.

Clarkson, M. B. E. (1995). A stakeholder framework for analyzing and evaluating corporate social performance. *Academy of Management Review, 20*, 92–117.

Cobb, R. W. & Elder, C. D. (1972). *Participation in American politics: The dynamics of agenda-building*. Baltimore: Johns Hopkins University Press.

Cobb, R. W., Ross, J., & Ross, M. H. (1976). Agenda building as a comparative political process. *American Political Science Review, 70*, 126–138.

Cocktails by Jenn case study (n.d.). Retrieved November 11, 2008 from www. charlescomm.com/case_histories/cs_cocktails_by_jenn.html.

Cohen, E. & and Falco, M. (2002, January 30). Ad campaign uses humor to fight colon cancer. Retrieved September 29, 2008 from www.archives.cnn.com/2002/HEALTH/ conditions/01/30/polyp.man.ad.

Cohen, J. R. (2002). Legislating apology: The pros and cons. *University of Cincinnati Law Review, 70*, 819–895.

Collins, E., Kearns, K., & Roper, J. (2005). The risks of relying on stakeholder engagement for achievement of sustainability. Retrieved March 20, 2009 from www.mngt.wai-kato.ac.nz/ejrot/Vol9_1/CollinsKearinsRoper.pdf.

Company methodology (2007, May 21). Retrieved September 16, 2007 from www.forbes.com/leadership/2007/05/21/reputation-institute-survey-lead-citizen-cx_sm_0521methodology.html.

Cooke, K., Hefley, M., Warhol, J., & Kelly, J. J. (2007, April 18). An open letter to US Netcom Corporation. Retrieved October 29, 2008 from www.badpitch.blogspot.com/2007/04/open-letter-to-us-netcom-corporation.html.

Coombs, W. T. (1990). A theoretical extension of issue status management: An extension of the four argumentative strategies. Ph.D. dissertation, Purdue University.

Coombs, W. T. (1992). The failure of the task force on food assistance: A case study of the role of legitimacy in issue management. *Journal of Public Relations Research, 4,* 101–122.

Coombs, W. T. (1998). The Internet as potential equalizer: New leverage for confronting social irresponsibility. *Public Relations Review, 24*(3), 289–303.

Coombs, W. T. (1999). *Ongoing crisis communication: Planning, managing, and responding.* Thousand Oaks, CA: Sage.

Coombs, W. T. (2002). Assessing online issue threats: Issue contagions and their effect on issue prioritization. *Journal of Public Affairs, 2*(4), 215–229.

Coombs, W. T. (2004a). A theoretical frame for post-crisis communication: Situational crisis communication theory. In M. J. Martinko (Ed.), *Attribution theory in the organizational sciences: Theoretical and empirical contributions* (pp. 275–296). Greenwich, CT: Information Age Publishing.

Coombs, W. T. (2004b). Impact of past crises on current crisis communications: Insights from situational crisis communication theory. *Journal of Business Communication, 41,* 265–289.

Coombs, W. T. (2005). Objectives. In R. L. Heath (Ed.), *Encyclopedia of public relations* (pp. 583–584). Thousand Oaks, CA: Sage.

Coombs, W. T. (2006). The protective powers of crisis response strategies: Managing reputational assets during a crisis. *Journal of Promotion Management, 12,* 241–259.

Coombs, W. T. (2007a). Attribution theory as a guide for post-crisis communication research. *Public Relations Review, 33,* 135–139.

Coombs, W. T. (2007b). *Ongoing crisis communication: Planning, managing, and responding,* 2nd edn. Los Angeles: Sage.

Coombs, W. T. (2007c). Protecting organization reputations during a crisis: The development and application of situational crisis communication theory. *Corporate Reputation Review, 10*(3), 163–177.

Coombs, W. T. (2008). Competitive intelligence. In W. T. Coombs (Ed.), *PSI Handbook of Business Security,* Vol. 1 (pp. 217–223). Thousand Oaks, CA: Sage.

Coombs, W. T. & Holladay, S. J. (1996). Communication and attributions in a crisis: An experimental study of crisis communication. *Journal of Public Relations Research, 8,* 279–295.

Coombs, W. T. & Holladay, S. J. (2002). Helping crisis managers protect reputational assets: Initial tests of the situational crisis communication theory. *Management Communication Quarterly, 16,* 165–186.

Coombs, W. T. and Holladay, S. J. (2004). Reasoned action in crisis communication: An attribution theory-based approach to crisis management. In D. P. Millar and R. L. Heath

(Eds.), *Responding to crisis: A rhetorical approach to crisis communication* (pp. 95–115). Mahwah, NJ: Lawrence Erlbaum Associates.

Coombs, W. T. & Holladay, S. J. (2005). Exploratory study of stakeholder emotions: Affect and crisis. In N. M. Ashkanasy, W. J. Zerbe, & C. E. J. Hartel (Eds.), *Research on emotion in organizations, Vol. 1: The effect of affect in organizational settings* (pp. 271–288). New York: Elsevier.

Coombs, W. T. & Holladay, S. J. (2006). Privileging stakeholder expectations: A co-creation approach to corporate social responsibility. Paper presented at the annual meeting of EUPRERA, Carlisle, UK.

Coombs, W. T. & Holladay, S. J. (2007a). Consumer empowerment through the web: How Internet contagions can increase stakeholder power. In S. C. Duhe (Ed.), *New media and public relations* (pp. 175–188). New York: Peter Lang.

Coombs, W. T. & Holladay, S. J. (2007b). *It's not just PR: Public relations in society*. Oxford: Wiley-Blackwell.

Coombs, W. T. & Holladay, S. J. (2007c). The negative communication dynamic: Exploring the impact of stakeholder affect on behavioral intention. *Journal of Communication Management, 11*(4), 300–312.

Coombs, W. T., Holladay, S. J., & Winch, M. E. (2007, September). Securing social legitimacy markers: The legitimacy procurement model. Paper presented at the meeting of EUPRERA, Roskilde University, Denmark.

Cooper, R. (1997). A historical look at the Pepsico/Burma boycott. Retrieved March 13, 2008 from www.thirdworldtraveler.com/Boycotts/Hx_PepsiBurmaBoy.html.

Cooperative Bank (n.d.). Our ethical policy. Retrieved November 2, 2007 from www.cooperativebank.co.uk/servlet/Satellite?c=Page&cid=1177569063509&pagename=CB/Page/tplStandard.

Corporate conscience award (2003, October 8). Retrieved March 6, 2006 from www.chiquita.com/chiquita/announcements/releases/pr031008a.asp.

Corporate Leadership Council (2003). Crisis management strategies. Retrieved September 12, 2006, from www.executiveboard.com/EXBD/Images/PDF/Crisis%20Management%20Strategies.pdf#search='corporate%20leadership%20council%20crisis%20management.

Covello, V. T. (2003). Best practices in public health risk and crisis communication. *Journal of Health Communication, 8*, 5–8.

Cowe, R. (2006, September 18). UK supermarkets: Waking up to sustainability marketing. Retrieved September 19, 2006, from www.ethicalcorp.com/content_print.asp?ContentID=4503.

Cox, R. (2006). *Environmental communication and the public sphere*. Thousand Oaks, CA: Sage.

Crable, R. E. & Vibbert, S. L. (1985). Managing issues and influencing public policy. *Public Relations Review, 11*, 3–16.

Criteria (n.d.). Retrieved October 28, 2007 from www.charitywatch.org/criteria.html.

Crossley, N. (2003). Even newer social movements? Anti-corporate protests, capitalist crises and the remoralization of society. *Organization, 10* (2), 287–305.

Davidson, J. (2000). *Project management: 10 minute guide*. Indianapolis: Macmillan.

Davies, G., Chun, R., da Silva, R. V., & Roper, S. (2003). *Corporate reputation and competitiveness*. New York: Routledge.

Dawkins, J. (2004). The public's view of corporate responsibility 2003. Retrieved August 12, 2006 from www.ipsos-mori.com/publications/jld/publics-views-of-corporate-responsibilty.pdf.

Dean, D. H. (2003/2004). Consumer perceptions of corporate donations: Effects of company reputation for social responsibility and types of donation. *Journal of Advertising, 32*(4), 91–102.

Derville, T. (2005). Radical activist tactics: Overturning public relations conceptualizations. *Public Relations Review, 31*(4), 527–533.

Devinney, T., Auger, P., Eckhardt, G., & Birtchnell, T. (2006, Fall). The other CSR. Retrieved February 20, 2007, from www.bcccc.net/index.cfm?fuseaction=page.viewPage&pageID=1467&bcccprintfriendly=1.

Dinar, W. & Miller, D. (2007). *A century of spin: How public relations became the cutting edge of CO.* London: Pluto Press.

Doane, D. (2005). The myth of CSR: The problem with assuming that companies can do well while also doing good is that markets don't really work that way. *Stanford Social Innovative Review.* Retrieved November 1, 2007 from www.ssireview.org/pdf/2005FA_Feature_Doane.pdf.

Doh, J. P. & Guay, T. R. (2006). Corporate social responsibility, public policy, and NGO activism in Europe and the United States: An institutional-stakeholders perspective. *Journal of Management Studies, 43*, 47–73.

Dowling, G. (2002). *Creating corporate reputations: Identity, image, and performance.* New York: Oxford University Press.

Downing, J. R. (2003). American Airlines' use of mediated employee channels after the 9/11 attacks. *Public Relations Review, 30*, 37–48.

Downs, A. (1972). Up and down with ecology: The "issue-attention cycle." *Public Interest, 29*, 39–50.

Dozier, D. & Lauzen, M. (2000). Liberating the intellectual domain from the practice: Public relations activism, and the role of the scholar. *Journal of Public Relations Research, 12*(1), 3–22.

D'Silva, M. U. & Palmgreen, P. (2007). Individual difference and context: Factors mediating recall of anti-drug public service announcements. *Health Communication, 21*(1), 65–71.

Dutta-Bergman, M. J. (2005). Theory and practice in health communication campaigns: A critical interrogation. *Health Communication, 18*(2), 103–122.

Dutton, J. E. & Ashford, S. J. (1993). Selling issues to top management. *Academy of Management Review, 18*(3), 397–428.

Dutton, J. E. & Jackson, S. E. (1987). Categorizing strategic issues: Links to organizational action. *Academy of Management Review, 12*, 76–90.

Dutton, J. E. & Ottensmeyer, E. (1987). Strategic issue management systems: Forms, functions, and contexts. *Academy of Management Review, 12*, 355–365.

Dutton, J. M., Durerich, J. M., & Harquail, C. V. (1994). Organizational images and members identification. *Administrative Science Quarterly, 39*, 239–263.

Edelman Trust Barometer (2007). Retrieved September 17, 2007 from www.edelman.com/trust/2007/trust_final_1_31.pdf.

Edward Bernays, 'Father of Public Relations,' and Leader in Opinion Research Dies at 103 (1995). www.partners.nytimes.com/books/98/08/16/specials/bernays-obit.html.

Elkington, J. (1994). Towards the sustainable corporation: Win-win-win business strategies for sustainable development. *California Management Review, 36*(2), 90–100.

Esrock, S. & Leichty, G. (1999). Corporate world wide web pages: Serving the news media and other publics. *Journalism and Mass Communication Quarterly, 76*(3), 456–467.

Ewen, S. (1996). *PR! A social history of spin*. New York: Basic Books.

Ewen, S. (2000). Public relations campaign. *American Heritage Magazine, 51*(3), www. americanheritage.com/articles/magazine/ah/2000/3/2000_3_77.shtml.

Ewing, R. P. (1980). Issues. *Public Relations Journal, 36*(6), 14–16.

Exploring links between international business and poverty reduction: A case study of Unilever in Indonesia (2005). Retrieved November 5, 2008 from www.oxfam.org.uk/ resources/policy/trade/downloads/unilever.pdf.

Fair trade overview (n.d.). Retrieved November 5, 2008 from www.transfairusa.org/content/about/overview.php.

Fair trade and you (n.d.). Retrieved August 11, 2006 from www.maketradefair.com/en/ index.php?file=25032002111113.htm&cat=4&subcat=1&select=1.

Fairtrade (n.d.). Retrieved August 11, 2006 from www.www2.marksandspencer.com/ thecompany/trustyour_mands/fairtrade.shtml.

Farrelly, J. M. (2006, March 26). Internet news-gathering in US on the rise. Retrieved September 10, 2008 from www.voanews.com/english/archive/2006–03/2006–03–29– voa77.cfm?CFID=126028708&CFTOKEN=68314316.

Federal Bureau of Investigation (2002). Terrorism 2000/2001. Retrieved January 27, 2007 from www.fbi.gov/publications/terror/terror2000_2001.htm.

Fitzpatrick, K. (2006). Baselines for ethical advocacy in the "marketplace of ideas." In K. Fitzpatrick & C. Bronstein (Eds.), *Ethics in public relations: Responsible advocacy* (pp. 1–17). Thousand Oaks, CA: Sage.

Fitzpatrick, K. & Bronstein, C. (2006). *Ethics in public relations: Responsible advocacy*. Thousand Oaks, CA: Sage.

Fitzpatrick, K. R. & Palenchar, M. J. (2006). Disclosing special interests: Constitutional restrictions on front groups. *Journal of Public Relations Research, 18*(3), 203–224.

Fitzpatrick, K. R. & Rubin, M. S. (1995). Public relations vs. legal strategies in organizational crisis decisions. *Public Relations Review, 21*(1), 21–33.

Five Pillars (2007). Retrieved May 20, 2008 from www.plana.marksandspencer.com/index. php?action=PublicPillarDisplay.

Fombrun, C. J. & Shanley, M. (1990). What's in a name? Reputation building and corporate strategy. *Academy of Management Journal, 33*(2), 223–250.

Fombrun, C. J. & van Riel, C. B. M. (2004). *Fame and fortune: How successful companies build winning reputations*. New York: Prentice-Hall/Financial Times.

Ford, P. (1999, November 26). Activists converge on Seattle summit. *Christian Science Monitor*, p. 1.

Foreign Agents Registration Act (FARA) (n.d.). Retrieved April 7, 2008 from www.usdoj. gov/criminal/fara/.

Freeman, R. E. (1984). *Strategic management: A stakeholder approach*. Boston: Pittman.

Frequently Asked Questions (2005). Retrieved November 11, 2007 from www.parentstv. org/PTC/faqs/main.asp.

Friedman, M. (1970). The social responsibility of business is to increase its profits. *New York Times Magazine*, pp. 32–33, 122, 126.

Frito-Lay target of Olestra lawsuit (2006, January 4). Retrieved August 15, 2006 from www. cspinet.org/new/200601041.html.

Frito-Lay to better label chips with olestra (2006, June 1). Retrieved December 19, 2007 from www.msnbc.msn.com/id/13086412/.

Fuchs-Burnett, T. (2002, May/July). Mass public corporate apology. *Dispute Resolution Journal, 57*, 26–32.

Gans, H. J. (1979). *Deciding what's news: A study of the "CBS evening news," "NBC nightly news," Newsweek and Time.* New York: Pantheon Books.

Government Accountability Office (GAO) (2006, August). Report to the subcommittee on transportation, treasury, judiciary, housing and urban development and related agencies, committee on appropriations, US Senate: ONDCP media campaign. Retrieved January 13, 2008 from www.gao.gov/new.items/d06818.pdf.

Gilligan, C. (1977). In a different voice: Women's conceptions of self and morality. *Harvard Educational Review, 47*(4), 481–517.

Gilligan, C. (1982). *In a different voice.* Boston: Harvard University Press.

Goldenberg, E. N. (1975). *Making the papers.* Lexington, MA: Lexington Books/D. C. Heath.

Gower, K. K. (2006). Truth and transparency. In K. Fitzpatrick & C. Bronstein (Eds.), *Ethics in public relations: Responsible advocacy* (pp. 89–106). Thousand Oaks, CA: Sage.

Graber, D. A. (1980). *Mass media and American politics.* Washington, DC: Congressional Quarterly Press.

Graber, D. A. (1982). The impact of media research on public opinion studies. In D. C. Whitney & E. Wartella (Eds.), *Mass communication review yearbook 3* (pp. 555–564). Beverly Hills: Sage.

Grefe, E. A. & Linsky, M. (1995). *The new corporate activism: Harnessing the power of grassroots tactics for your organization.* New York: McGraw-Hill.

Grier, S. & Bryant, C. A. (2005). Social marketing in public health. *Annual Review of Public Health, 26*, 319–339.

Grunig, J. E. (1989a). Publics, audiences, and market segments: Segmentation principles for campaigns. In C. T. Salmon (Ed.), *Information campaigns: Balancing social values and social change* (pp. 199–228). Newbury Park, CA: Sage.

Grunig, J. E. (1989b). Symmetrical presuppositions as a framework for public relations theory. In C. H. Botan & V. T. Hazelton (Eds.), *Public relations theory* (pp. 17–44). Hillsdale, NJ: Lawrence Erlbaum Associates.

Grunig, J. E. (1989c). Sierra Club study shows who become activists. *Public Relations Review, 15*(3), 3–24.

Grunig, J. E. (Ed.) (1992). *Excellence in public relations and communication management.* Hillsdale, NJ: Lawrence Erlbaum Associates.

Grunig, J.E. (2001). Two-way symmetrical public relations: Past, present, and future. In R. L. Heath (Ed.), *Handbook of Public Relations* (11–30). Thousand Oaks, CA: Sage.

Grunig, J. E. (2005). Situational theory of publics. In R. L. Heath (Ed.), *Encyclopedia of public relations*, Vol. 2 (pp. 778–780). Thousand Oaks, CA: Sage.

Grunig, J. E. & Grunig, L. (1992). Models of public relations and communications. In J. E. Grunig (Ed.), *Excellence in public relations and communicative management* (pp. 285–325). Hillsdale, NJ: Lawrence Erlbaum Associates.

Grunig, J. E. & Hunt, T. (1984). *Managing public relations.* New York: Holt, Rinehart & Winston.

Grunig, J. E. & Repper, F. C. (1992). Strategic management, publics, and issues. In J. E. Grunig (Ed.), *Excellence in public relations and communication management* (pp. 117–158). Hillsdale, NJ: Lawrence Erlbaum Associates.

Grunig, L. (1992). Activism: How it limits the effectiveness of organizations and how excellent public relations departments respond. In J. E. Grunig (Ed.), *Excellence in public relations and communication management* (pp. 503–530). Hillsdale, NJ: Lawrence Erlbaum Associates.

Gunter, M. (2006, October 18). Corporate blogging: Wal-Mart's fumbles. Retrieved October 29, 2006 from www.money.cnn.com/2006/10/17/technology/pluggedin_gunther_blog.fortune/index.htm.

Habermas, J. (1974). The public sphere: An encyclopedia article (1964). *New German Critique, 1*(3), 49–55.

Habermas, J. (1989). *The structural transformation of the public sphere: An inquiry into a category of bourgeois society*, trans. T. Burger. Cambridge, MA: MIT Press.

Hager, N. & Burton, B. (1999). *Secrets and lies: The anatomy of an anti-environmental PR campaign*. Nelson, NZ: Craig Potton Publishing.

Hall, E. (2007, May 28). Want UK consumers to label your company 'green'? Just use PR. *Advertising Age, 78*(22), 20.

Hallahan, K. (1999). Seven models of framing: Implications for public relations. *Journal of Public Relations Research, 11*(3), 205–242.

Hallahan, K. (2005). Communication management. In R. L. Heath (Ed.), *Encyclopedia of public relations* (pp. 161–164). Thousand Oaks, CA: Sage.

Hansen-Horn, T. L. & Neff, B. D. (Eds.) (2008). *Public relations: From theory to practice*. Boston: Pearson.

Hardt, H. (2005). Return on investment. In R. L. Heath (Ed.), *Encyclopedia of public relations* (p. 748). Thousand Oaks, CA: Sage.

Hart, S. L. & Sharma, S. (2004). Engaging fringe stakeholders for competitive imagination. *Academy of Management Executive, 18*(1), 7–18.

Hastings, G. & Saren, M. (2003). The critical contribution of social marketing: Theory and application. *Marketing Theory, 3*(3), 305–322.

Hatch, M. J. & Schultz, M. (2000). Scaling the tower of babel: Relational differences between identity, image, and culture in organizations. In M. Schultz, M. J. Hatch, & M. H. Larsen (Eds.), *The expressive organization: Linking identity, reputation, and the corporate brand* (pp. 11–35). New York: Oxford University Press.

Haynes, M. (2005, November 3). Bawdy t-shirts set off 'girlcott' by teens. Retrieved March 13, 2008 from www.post-gazette.com/pg/05307/599884.stm.

Hearit, K. M. (1994). Apologies and public relations crises at Chrysler, Toshiba, and Volvo. *Public Relations Review, 20*, 113–125.

Hearit, K. M. (1995a). "Mistakes were made": Organizations, apologia, and crises of social legitimacy. *Communication Studies, 46*, 1–17.

Hearit, K. M. (1995b). From "we didn't do it" to "it's not our fault": The use of apologia in public relations crises. In W. N. Elwood (Ed.), *Public relations inquiry as rhetorical criticism: Case studies of corporate discourse and social influence*. Westport, CN: Praeger.

Hearit, K. M. (1999). Newsgroups, activist publics, and corporate apologia: The case of Intel and its Pentium chip. *Public Relations Review, 25*(3), 291–308.

Hearit, K. M. (2001). Corporate apologia: When an organization speaks in defense of itself. In R. L. Heath (Ed.), *Handbook of public relations* (pp. 501–511). Thousand Oaks, CA: Sage.

Hearit, K. M. (2006). *Crisis management by apology: Corporate response to allegations of wrongdoing*. Mahwah, NJ: Lawrence Erlbaum Associates.

Heath, R. L. (1988). *Strategic issues management: How organizations influence and respond to public interests and policies*. San Francisco: Jossey-Bass.

Heath, R. L. (1990). Corporate issues management: Theoretical underpinnings and research foundations. In L. A. Grunig & J. E. Grunig (Eds.), *Public relations research annual*, Vol. 2 (pp. 29–66). Hillsdale, NJ: Lawrence Erlbaum Associates.

Heath, R. L. (1994). *Management of corporate communication: From interpersonal contacts to external affairs.* Hillsdale, NJ: Lawrence Erlbaum Associates.

Heath, R. L. (1997). *Strategic issues management: Organizations and public policy challenges.* Thousand Oaks, CA: Sage.

Heath, R. L. (1998). New communication technologies: An issues management point of view. *Public Relations Review, 24,* 273–288.

Heath, R. L. (Ed.) (2005). *Encyclopedia of public relations.* Thousand Oaks, CA: Sage.

Heath, R. L. & Coombs, W. T. (2006). *Today's public relations: An introduction.* Thousand Oaks, CA: Sage.

Heath, R. L. & Nelson, R. A. (1986). *Issues management.* Beverly Hills: Sage.

Herman, D. & Chomsky, N. (1988). *Manufacturing consent: The political economy of the mass media.* New York: Pantheon.

Herr, P. M., Kardes, F. R., & Kim, J. (1991). Effect of word-of-mouth and product attribute information on persuasion: an accessibility-diagnostic perspective. *Journal of Consumer Research, 17,* 452–462.

Higgins, D. (1999, December 2). Virtual marchers spin the web. *Sydney Morning Herald,* p. 12.

Higgins, M. & Tadajewski, M. (2002). Anti-corporate protest as consumer spectacle. *Management Decision, 40,* 363–371.

Hirschman, A. O. (1970). *Exit, voice, and loyalty: Responses to decline in firms, organizations, and states.* Boston: Harvard University Press.

Hofstede, G. (1980). *Culture's consequences.* London: Sage.

Holloway, J. & Pelaez, E. (1998). Introduction to Zapatistas! Reinventing the revolution in Mexico. Retrieved April 30, 2008 from www.korotonomedya.net/chiapas/intro.html.

Holtz, S. (1999). *Public relations on the Net: Winning strategies to inform and influence the media, the investment community, the government, the public, and more!* New York: AMACOM.

Holtzhausen, D. R. & Voto, R. (2002). Resistance from the margins: The postmodern public relations practitioner as organizational activist. *Journal of Public Relations Research, 14,* 57–84.

How chemical industry rewrote history of banned pesticide (1998). Retrieved December 15, 2007 from www.ewg.org/node/8005.

How commercialism has twisted proper sun care (n.d.). Retrieved October 22, 2008 from www.tanningtruth.com/index.php/sun_scare/.

Howard, C. M. & Mathews, W. K. (1985). *On deadline: Managing media relations.* Prospect Heights, IL: Waveland Press.

Husted, B. W. & Salazar, J. D. J. (2006). Taking Friedman seriously: Maximizing profits and social performance. *Journal of Management Studies, 43,* 75–91.

Hutton, J. G., Goodman, M. B., Alexander, J. B., & Genest, C. H. (2001). Reputation management: The new face of corporate public relations? *Public Relations Review, 27,* 247–261.

Important information about Gardasil (n.d.). Retrieved October 24, 2008 from www.gardasil.com/.

Indoor tanning is out (2008). Retrieved October 22, 2008 from www.aad.org/media/psa/index.html.

Introduction (n.d.). Retrieved August 11, 2006 from www.millenniumcampaign.org/site/pp.asp?c=grKVL2NLE&b=186389.

Iyengar, S. & Kinder, D. R. (1981). *News that matters*. Chicago: University of Chicago Press.

Jacobs, A. & Wang, J. (2008, April 20). Indignant Chinese urge anti-west boycott over pro-Tibet stance. *New York Times*, p. A8.

Jaques, T. (2004). Issues definition: The neglected foundation of effective issue management. *Journal of Public Affairs, 4*(2), 191–200.

Jaques, T. (2006). Activist "rules" and the convergence with issue management. *Journal of Communication Management, 10*(4), 407–420.

Jaques, T. (2007). Issue or problem? Managing the difference and averting crisis. *Journal of Business Strategy, 28*(6), 25–28.

Jarboe, J. F. (2002, February 12). The threat of eco-terrorism. Retrieved January 29, 2007 from www.fbi.gov/congress/congress02/jarboe021202.htm.

Jones, B. L. & Chase, W. H. (1979). Managing public policy issues. *Public Relations Review, 5*(2), 3–23.

Jorgensen, B. K. (1996). Components of consumer reaction to company-related mishaps: A structural equation model approach. *Advances in Consumer Research, 23*, 346–351.

Karlberg, M. (1996). Remembering the public in public relations research: From theoretical to operational symmetry. *Journal of Public Relations Research, 8*, 263–278.

Kaufmann, J. B., Kesner, I. F., & Hazen, T. L. (1994, July/August). The myth of full disclosure: A look at organizational communications during crises. *Business Horizons, 37*, 29–39.

Kearns, M. (n.d.). Network-centric advocacy. Retrieved June 23, 2007 from www.activist.blogs.com/networkcentricadvocacypaper.pdf.

Keck, M. E. & Sikkink, K. (1998). *Activists beyond borders: Advocacy networks in international politics*. Ithaca, NY: Cornell University Press.

Kelleher, T. A. (2006). *Public relations online*. Thousand Oaks, CA: Sage.

Kent, M. (in press). What is a public relations "crisis?" Refocusing crisis research. In W. T. Coombs & S. J. Holladay (Eds.), *Handbook of Crisis Communication*. Oxford: Wiley-Blackwell.

Kent, M. L. (2005). Dialogue. In R. L. Heath (Ed.), *Encyclopedia of public relations*, Vol. 1 (pp. 250–251). Thousand Oaks, CA: Sage.

Kent, M. L. & Taylor, M. (1998). Building dialogic relationships through the World Wide Web. *Public Relations Review, 24*, 321–334.

Kent, M. L. & Taylor, M. (2002). Toward a dialogic theory of public relations. *Public Relations Review, 28*, 21–37.

Kent, M. L. & Taylor, M. (2003). Maximizing media relations: A web site checklist. *Public Relations Quarterly, 48*(1), 14–18.

Kersten, A. (2005). Crisis as usual: Organizational dysfunction and public relations. *Public Relations Review, 31*(4), 544–549.

Khermouch, G. & Green, J. (2001, July 30). Buzz marketing: Suddenly this stealth strategy is hot – but it's still fraught with risk. Retrieved October 29, 2008 from www.businessweek.com/magazine/content/01_31/b3743001.htm.

Kilman, C. (2005, November 8). Abercrombie pulls sexist shirts. Retrieved March 13, 2008 from www.tolerance.org/news/article_tol.jsp?id=1330.

Kim, P. H., Ferrin, D. L., Cooper, C. D., & Dirks, K. T. (2004). Removing the shadow of suspicion: The effect of apology versus denial for repairing competence-versus integrity-based trust violations. *Journal of Applied Psychology, 89*, 104–118.

KLM – Fly for Fortune (n.d.). Retrieved October 29, 2008 from www.viraltracker.com/Viral_Cases/Viral_Cases_-_Get_Insights_and_Ideas.html.

Kolb, A. & Pinske, J. (2004). Market strategies for climate change. *European Management Journal, 22*, 304–314.

Konrad, R. (2007, October 3). Sellers warned about recalls on eBay. Retrieved December 19, 2007 from www.cio-today.com/news/Sellers-Warned-About-Recalls-on-eBay/story.xhtml?story_id=123003UFSGII.

Kosicki, G. M. (1993). Problems and opportunities in agenda-setting research. *Journal of Communication, 43*(2), 100–127.

Kotler, P. & Levy, S. J. (1969). Broadening the concept of marketing. *Journal of Marketing, 33*, 10–15.

Kotler, P. & Roberto, E. (1989). *Social marketing: Strategies for changing public behavior.* New York: Free Press.

Kotler, P. & Zaltman, G. (1971). Social marketing: An approach to planned social change. *Journal of Marketing, 35*, 3–12.

Kovacs, R. (2001). Relationship building as integral to British activism: Its impact on accountability in broadcasting. *Public Relations Review, 27*, 421–436.

Kunczik, M. (1997). *Images of nations and international public relations.* Mahwah, NJ: Lawrence Erlbaum Associates.

Lackluster online PR no aid in crisis response (2002). *PR News.* Retrieved April 20, 2006, from www.web.lexis-nexis.com/universe.

Laczniak, R. N., DeCarlo, T. E., & Ramaswami, S. H. (2001). Consumers' responses to negative word-of-mouth communication: An attribution theory perspective. *Journal of Consumer Psychology, 11*, 57–73.

Lang, S., Fewtrell, L., & Bartram, J. (2001). Risk communication. In L. Fewtrell & J. Bartram (Eds.), *Water quality: Guidelines, standards and Health* (pp. 317–332). London: IWA Publishing.

Lauzen, M. M. (1995). Toward a model of environmental scanning. *Journal of Public Relations Research, 7*(3), 187–204.

Lavoie, D. & Lindsay, J. (2007, February 2). Turner CEO apologizes for Boston scare. Retrieved February 2, 2007 from www.news.yahoo.com/s/ap/20070202/ap_on_re_us/suspicious_devices&printer=1;_ylt=AhFQjTf75LWvZxJRG62YD_RH2ocA;_ylu=X3o DMTA3MXN1bHE0BHNlYwN0bWE-.

Leaks: Walmart PowerPoint On "3 Customer" Plan (2007, March 6). Retrieved May 25, 2007 from www.consumerist.com/consumer/top/%0Aleaks-walmart-powerpoint-on-3–customer-plan%0A-241939.php.

Lee, S. (2006). An analysis of other countries' international public relations in the US. *Public Relations Review, 32*, 97–103.

Leiss, W. (1996). Three phases in the evolution of risk communication practice. *American Academy of Political and Social Sciences, 545*, 85–94.

Leventhal, H. (1970). Findings and theory in the study of fear communication. In L. Berkowitz (Ed.), *Advances in experimental social psychology*, Vol. 5 (pp. 119–186). New York: Academic Press.

Lichtenstein, D. R., Drumwright, M. E., & Braig, B. M. (2004). The effect of corporate social responsibility on customer donations to corporate-supported nonprofits. *Journal of Marketing, 68*(10), 16–32.

Linsky, M. (1986). *Impact: How the press affects federal policy making.* New York: W.W. Norton.

Lobe, J. (2007, July 18). 160 top US corporations: Act now on global warming. Retrieved January 4, 2008 from www.commondreams.org/archive/2007/07/18/2616/.

Lohn, M. (2006, December 19). Taco John's CEO aims to blunt damage. Retrieved December 19, 2006 from www.biz.yahoo.com/ap/061219/taco_john_s_e_coli.html?.v=1.

Lubbers, C. A. (2005). Four-minute men. In R. L. Heath (Ed.), *Encyclopedia of public relations*, Vol. 1 (pp. 337–338). Thousand Oaks, CA: Sage.

Lyon, L. & Cameron, G. T. (1999). Fess up or stonewall? An experimental test of prior reputation and response style in the face of negative news coverage. *Web Journal of Mass Communication Research, 1*(4). Retrieved March 15, 2007 from www.scripps.ohiou.edu/wjmcr/vol01/1–4a.htm.

McCall, M. (2007, February 1). Aqua teen terror forces? Retrieved February 1, 2007 from www.buzz.yahoo.com/buzzlog/60487/aqua-teen-terror-force.

McComas, K. & Shanahan, J. (1999). Telling stories about global climate change: Measuring the impact of narratives on issue cycles. *Communication Research, 26*, 30–57.

McCroskey, J. C. (1966). *An introduction in rhetorical communication.* Englewood Cliffs, NJ: Prentice-Hall.

McGongale J. J. & Vella, C. M. (2007, February 7). I spy your company secrets. *Security Management*, pp. 64–70.

McGuire, W. J. (1981). Theoretical foundations of campaigns. In R. E. Rice & W. J. Paisley (Eds.), *Public communication campaigns* (pp. 41–70). Beverly Hills: Sage.

McKie, D. & Galloway, C. (2007). Climate change after denial: Global reach, global responsibilities, and public relations. *Public Relations Review, 33*, 368–376.

McKie, D. & Munshi, D. (2007). *Reconfiguring public relations: Ecology, equity, and enterprise.* New York: Routledge, Taylor & Francis.

McLaren, C. (2000). How tobacco company "anti-smoking" ads appeal to teens. Retrieved September 29, 2008 from www.social-marketing.com/Whatis.html.

Maccoby, N. & Solomon, D. S. (1981). Heart disease prevention: Community studies. In R. E. Rice & W. J. Paisley (Eds.), *Public communication campaigns* (pp. 105–126). Beverly Hills: Sage.

McWilliams, A. & Siegel, D. S. (2001). Corporate social responsibility: A theory of the firm perspective. *Academy of Management Review, 26*, 117–127.

McWilliams, A., Siegel, D. S., & Wright, P. M. (2006). Corporate social responsibility: Strategic implications. *Journal of Management Studies, 43*, 1–18.

Manheim, J. B. (1987). A model of agenda dynamics. In M. L. McLauglin (Ed.), *Communication yearbook 10* (pp. 499–516). New York: Sage.

Manheim, J. B. (1994). *Strategic public diplomacy and American foreign policy: The evolution of influence.* New York: Oxford University Press.

Manheim, J. B. & Albritton, R. B. (1984). Changing national images: International public relations and media agenda setting. *American Political Science Review, 78*, 641–654.

Marconi, J. (2004). *Public relations: The complete guide.* Mason, OH: South-Western.

Marketing Lithuania: How about name change? (2008, January 25). Retrieved January 26, 2008 from www.msnbc.msn.com/id/22841519/?GT1=10755.

Marquez, A. & Fombrun, C. J. (2005). Measuring corporate social responsibility. *Corporate Reputation Review, 7*, 304–308.

Martin, P. & Tate, K. (1997). *Project management memory jogger.* Salem, NH: Goal/QPC.

Martineau, P. (1958). Sharper focus for the corporate image. *Harvard Business Review*, *36*(6), 49–58.

May, P. (1999). In Seattle, activists ready for business. *Philadelphia Inquirer*, p. E13.

Mayer, R. N. (2007). Winning the war of words: The "front group" label in contemporary consumer politics. *Journal of American Culture*, *30*(1), 96–109.

Media Literacy (1997). Resource guide. Retrieved November 3, 2008 from www.media-awareness.ca/english/teachers/media_literacy/key_concept.cfm.

Meijer, M. M. (2004). *Does success breed success? Effects of news and advertising on corporate reputation*. Amsterdam: Aksant Academic Publishers.

Menton, S. & Kahn, B. E. (2003). Corporate sponsorships of philanthropic activities: When do they impact perceptions of sponsor brand? *Journal of Consumer Psychology*, *13*, 316–327.

Merkl, L. K. & Heath, R. L. (2005). Tactics. In R. L. Heath (Ed.), *Encyclopedia of public relations* (pp. 843–846). Thousand Oaks, CA: Sage.

Middleberg, D. (2001). *Winning PR in the wired world: Powerful communications strategies for the noisy digital space*. New York: McGraw-Hill.

Mitchell, R. K., Agle, R. A., & Wood, S. J. (1997). Toward a theory of stakeholder identification and salience: Defining the principle of who and what really counts. *Academy of Management Review*, *22*(4), 853–886.

Mitra, A. (2004). Voices of the marginalized on the Internet: Examples from a website for women of South Asia. *Journal of Communication*, *54*(33), 492–510.

Mizerski, R. W. (1982). An attribution explanation of the disproportionate influence of unfavorable information. *Journal of Consumer Research*, *9*, 301–310.

Moloney, K. (2005). Trust and public relations: Center and edge. *Public Relations Review*, *31*(4), 550–555.

Moloney, K. (2006). *Rethinking public relations*, 2nd edn. London: Routledge.

Monbiot, G. (2002). The greens get eaten. In E. Lubbers (Ed.), *Battling big business: Countering greenwash, infiltration and other forms of corporate bullying* (pp. 53–55). Monroe, ME: Common Courage Press.

Money, K. & Hillenbrand, C. (2006). Using reputation measurement to create value: An analysis and integration of existing measures. *Journal of General Management*, *32*(1), 1–12.

Moss, D. A. (2005). Strategies. In R. L. Heath (Ed.), *Encyclopedia of public relations* (pp. 823–826). Thousand Oaks, CA: Sage.

Moynihan, R. & Cassels, A. (2005). *Selling sickness: How the world's biggest pharmaceutical companies are turning us all into patients*. New York: National Book.

Multihazard design (1997). Retrieved January 1, 2008 from www.fema.gov/library/file?type=publishedFile&file=fema_424_ch3.pdf&fileid=7f60edd0–d653–11db-866c-000bdba87d5b.

Mumby, D. K. (1988). *Communication and power in organizations: Discourse, ideology and domination*. Norwood, NJ: Ablex Publishing.

Nelson, R. A. & Heath, R. L. (1986). A system model for corporate issues management. *Public Relations Quarterly*, *31*, 20–24.

Nichols, N. (2003). Stopping the activists attackers. In S. John & S. Thomson (Eds.), *New activism and the corporate response* (pp. 137–151). New York: Palgrave Macmillan.

Nye, J. S., Jr. (2004). *Soft power: The means to success in world politics*. New York: Public Affairs.

Odden, L. (2007, August 24). How not to pitch a blog. Retrieved October 28, 2007 from www.toprankblog.com/2007/08/how-not-to-pitch-a-blog/.

The odds of dying … (2007, November 7). Retrieved January 20, 2008 from www.nsc.org/lrs/statinfo/odds.htm.

O'Keefe, D. J. (2002). *Persuasion: theory and research*, 2nd edn. Thousand Oaks, CA: Sage.

Oneal, M. (2007, August 7). Toymaker: 3 brands, pails contain lead. Retrieved December 17, 2007 from www.chicagotribune.com/business/chi-fri_leadaug10,0,7269948.story.

Online sexual exploitation (n.d.). Retrieved May 8, 2008 from www.adcouncil.org/default.aspx?id=56.

Our coffee won't leave a bitter taste in your mouth (2006). Retrieved August 11, 2006 from www.www2.marksandspencer.com/thecompany/trustyour_mands/fairtrade.shtml.

Palanchar, M. J. (2005). Risk communication. In R. L. Heath (Ed.), *Encyclopedia of public relations* (pp. 752–755). Thousand Oaks, CA: Sage.

Palanchar, M. J. & Heath, R. L. (2006). Responsible advocacy through strategic risk communication. In K. Fitzpatrick & C. Bronstein (Eds.), *Ethics in public relations: Responsible advocacy* (pp. 131–154). Thousands Oaks, CA: Sage.

Palanchar, M. J. & Heath, R. L. (2007). Strategic risk communication: Adding value to society. *Public Relations Review, 33*(2), 120–129.

Paletz, D. L., & Boiney, J. (1988). Interest groups and public opinion. In J. Anderson (Ed.), *Communication yearbook 11* (pp. 534–546). Newbury Park, CA: Sage.

Paletz, D. L. & Entman, R. M. (1981). *Media power politics*. New York: Free Press.

Paris protests force cancellation of torch relay: Security officials call off final section after huge pro-Tibet demonstrations (2008, May 6). Retrieved June 3, 2008 from www.nbcsports.msnbc.com/id/23978408/.

Parsons, P. J. (2004). *Ethics in public relations: A guide to best practice*. London: Kogan Page.

Patel, A. & Reinsch, L. (2003). Companies can apologize: Corporate apologies and legal liability. *Business Communication Quarterly, 66*, 17–26.

Patten, S., Vollman, A., & Thurston, W. (2000). The utility of the transtheoretical model of behavior change for HIV risk reduction in injection drug users. *Journal of the Association of Nurses in AIDS Care, 11*(1), 57–66.

Paul. A. M. (2008). What's wrong with environmental alarmism? How to mobilize, but not paralyze, the public with fear. Retrieved September 28, 2008 from www.slate.com/id/2197280/?from=rss.

Paulson, M. & McClure, R. (1999, December 4). WTO summit ends in failure. *Seattle Post-Intelligencer*. Available at www.seattlepi.nwsource.com/national/wto04.shtml.

Pespi in Burma: A globalization catastrophe (2003). Retrieved March 13, 2008 from www.icmrindia.org/casestudies/catalogue/Business%20Ethics/BECG026.htm.

Perry, M. & Bodkin, C. D. (2002). Fortune 500 manufacturer web sites: Innovating marketing strategies or cyberbrochures? *Industrial Marketing Management, 21*, 133–144.

Peters, B. G. & Hogwood, B. W. (1985). In search of the issue-attention cycle. *Journal of Politics, 47*, 238–253.

Pew (2004). Older Americans and the internet. Retrieved July 28, 2006 from www.pewinternet.org/pdfs/PIP_Seniors_Online_2004.pdf.

Pfau, M. & Wan, H. (2006). Persuasion: An intrinsic function of public relations. In C. H. Botan & V. Hazleton (Eds.), *Public relations theory II* (pp. 101–136). Mahwah, NJ: Lawrence Erlbaum Associates.

Polyp Man character returns to communicate life-saving message in new PSAs (2003, February 1). Retrieved September 29, 2008 from www.adcouncil.org/newsDetail. aspx?id=116.

PR firm admits it's behind Wal-Mart blog (2006, October 20). Retrieved October 29, 2006 from www.money.cnn.com/2006/10/20/news/companies/walmart_blogs/?postversion= 2006102011.

Pritchard, J. (2007). After 1st recall, train-maker sent tainted toys as bonus gifts. Retrieved December 19, 2007 from www.nctimes.com/articles/2007/10/06/business/news/ 3_53_1110_6_07.txt.

Prochaska, J. O. & Velicer, W. F. (1997). The transtheoretical model of health behavior change. *American Journal of Health Promotion, 12*(1), 38–48.

Propaganda model: An overview (n.d.). Retrieved October 21, 2007 from www.medialens. org/about/overview_of_the_propaganda_model.php.

Proposed Malibu bag ban wrong for environment (2008, May 2007). Retrieved October 3, 2008 from www.americanchemistry.com/s_acc/sec_news_article.asp?SID=1&DID=7 489&CID=206&VID=142&RTID=0&CIDQS=&Taxonomy=&specialSearch=.

Public Relations Society of America (PRSA) (2000). *Member code of ethics.* New York: Public Relations Society of America.

Quainton, D. (2007, January 31). Wikipedia founder issues warning to agencies. Retrieved October 30, 2007 from www.prweek.com/uk/search/article/629946/Wikipedia-founder-issues-warning-agencies/.

Rakow, L. F. (1989). Information and power: Toward a critical theory of information campaigns. In C. T. Salmon (Ed.), *Information campaigns: Balancing social values and social change* (pp. 164–184). Newbury Park, CA: Sage.

Rawlins, B., Paine, K. D., & Kowalsi, P. (2008). Measuring transparency of environmental sustainability reporting through websites of Fortune 50 companies. Paper presented at the annual meeting of the International Public Relations Research Conference, Miami.

Ray, S. J. (1999). *Strategic communication in crisis management: Lessons from the airline industry.* Westport, CT: Quorum Books.

Raymond, D. (2003). Activism: Behind the banners. In S. John & S. Thomson (Eds.), *New activism and the corporate response* (pp. 207–225). New York: Palgrave Macmillan.

RC2 recalls five additional Thomas & Friends wooden railway items (2007, September 27). Retrieved December 19, 2007 from www.rc2corp.com/press/2007/Release_TWR_ recall_0907.pdf.

Reber, B. H. & Berger, B. K. (2005). Framing analysis of activist rhetoric: How the Sierra Club succeeds or fails at creating salient messages. *Public Relations Review, 31,* 185–195.

Reber, B. H. & Cameron, G. T. (2003). Measuring contingencies: Using scales to measure public relations limits to accommodation. *Journalism and Mass Communication Quarterly, 80*(2), 431–446.

Reber, B. H. & Kim, J. K. (2006). How activist groups use websites in media relations: Evaluating online press rooms. *Journal of Public Relations Research, 18*(4), 313–334.

Recall of wooden vehicles and train set components (2007). Retrieved December 19, 2007 from www.recalls.rc2.com/recalls_Wood_0607.html.

Recalled items (2007). Retrieved December 19, 2007 from www.pages.ebay.com/help/ policies/recalled.html.

Redding, P. (2006). Georg Wilhelm Friedrich Hegel. Retrieved from www.plato.stanford.edu/entries/hegel/.

Reinchart, J. (2003). A theoretical exploration of expectational gaps in the corporate issue construct. *Corporate Reputation Review, 6*, 58–69.

Results (n.d.). Retrieved May 8, 2008 from www.adcouncil.org/default.aspx?id=320.

Retailers (2006). Retrieved August 11, 2006 from www.fairtrade.org.uk/suppliers_retailers.htm.

Richins, M. L. (1984). Word of mouth communication as negative information. *Advances in Consumer Research, 11*, 697–702.

Ricks, D. A. (1999). *Blunders in international business.* Oxford: Blackwell Publishing.

Rindova, V. & Fombrun, C. (1999). Constructing competitive advantage: The role of firm-constituent interactions. *Strategic Management Journal, 20*, 691–710.

Rockwell, P. (2005, December 9). The latest on the Abercrombie "girlcott." Retrieved March 13, 2008 from www.salon.com/mwt/broadsheet/2005/12/09/abercrombie/?calendar=200708.

Rokeach, M. (1968). *Beliefs, attitudes, and values.* San Francisco: Jossey-Bass.

Roner, L. (2005, August 24). Corporate responsibility and public relations. Retrieved March 10, 2008 from www.ethicalcorp.com/content.asp?ContentID=3852.

Roper, J. & Toledano, M. (2005). Taking in the view from the edge: Issues management recontextualized. *Public Relations Review, 31*, 479–485.

Rosenkrands, J. (2004). Politicizing homo economicus: Analysis of anti-corporate web-sites. In W. van de Donk, B. D. Loader, P. G. Nixon, & D. Rucht (Eds.), *Cyberprotest: New media, citizens and social movements* (pp. 57–76). New York: Routledge.

Rowan, G. (2005). Managing and avoiding outrage. In E. H. James & L. I. Smith (Eds.), *An executive briefing on crisis leadership* (pp. 61–68). Charlottesville, VA: Darden Business Publishing.

Rowell, A. (2002). Dialogue: Divide and rule. In E. Lubbers (Ed.), *Battling big business: Countering greenwash, infiltration and other forms of corporate bullying* (pp. 33–43). Monroe, ME: Common Courage Press.

Rowley, T. J. (1997). Moving beyond dyadic ties: A network theory of stakeholder influence. *Academy of Management Review, 22*(4), 887–910.

Rowse, A. E. (1992). How to build support for war. Retrieved April 7, 2008 from www.backissues.cjrarchives.org/year/92/5/war.asp.

Ruckus Society (n.d.). History and Mission. Retrieved September 29, 2008 from www.ruckus.org/article.php?list=type&type=24.

Ryan, C. (1991). *Prime time activism: Media strategies for grassroots organizing.* Boston: South End Press.

Salmon, C. T. (1989). Campaigns for social "improvement": An overview of values, rationales, and impacts. In C. T. Salmon (Ed.), *Information campaigns: Balancing social values and social change* (pp. 19–53). Newbury Park, CA: Sage.

Sanderson, H. (2008). EU bans baby food with Chinese milk, recalls grow. Retrieved September 29, 2008 from www.abcnews.go.com/International/wireStory?id=5881376.

Sandman, P. (1998). The other side of risk communication: Alerting people to serious hazards. Retrieved January 1, 2008 from www.psandman.com/handouts/sand34.pdf.

Sandman, P. (2003). Four kinds of risk communication. Retrieved January 1, 2008 from www.psandman.com/col/4kind-1.htm.

Sandman, P. (2006, March). The outrage industries: The role of journalists and activists in risk controversies. Retrieved January 1, 2008 from www.psandman.com/col/outrage.htm.

Scherer, A. G. & Palazzo, G. (2007). Towards a political conception of corporate responsibility: Business and society seen from a Habermasian perspective. *Academy of Management Review, 32*, 1096–1120.

Schlosser, A. E. (2005). Source perceptions and the persuasiveness of Internet word-of-mouth. *Advances in Consumer Research, 30*, 202–203.

Schnietz, K. E. & Epstein, M. J. (2005). Exploring the financial value of a reputation for corporate social responsibility during a crisis. *Corporate Reputation Review, 7*, 327–345.

Search engine reputation management resource site and blog launched (2006). Retrieved October 28, 2007 from www.prweb.com/releases/2006/1/prweb331388.htm.

Sellnow, T. L., Ulmer, R. R., & Snider, M. (1998). The compatibility of corrective action in organizational crisis communication. *Communication Quarterly, 46*, 60–74.

Set 'em up in style: Cocktails by Jenn (2006). Retrieved November 11, 2008 from www.findarticles.com/p/articles/mi_m1272/is_/ai_n27059622.

Sethi, S. P. (1979). A conceptual framework for environmental analysis of social issues and evaluation of business response patterns. *Academy of Management Review, 41*, 63–74.

Sethi, S. P. (1987). *Handbook of advocacy advertising: Concepts, strategies and applications.* Cambridge, MA: Ballinger.

Shin, J. H., Cameron, G. T., & Cropp, F. (2006). Occam's razor in the contingency theory: A national survey on 86 contingent variables. *Public Relations Review, 32*, 282–286.

Shin, L., Cheng, I., Jin, Y., & Cameron, G. T. (2005). Going head to head: Content analysis of high profile conflicts played out in the press. *Public Relations Review, 31*(3), 399–406.

Sigal. L. V. (1973). *Reporters and officials.* Lexington, MA: D. C. Heath.

Signitzer, B. H. & Coombs, T. (1992). Public relations and public diplomacy: Conceptual convergence. *Public Relations Review, 18*(2), 137–147.

Silverblatt, A. (2001). *Media literacy*, 2nd edn. Westport, CT: Praeger.

Simmons, D. (2003). Use of the staged event in successful community activism. *Public Relations Quarterly*, Spring, 35–39.

Simola, S. (2003). Ethics of justice and care in corporate crisis management. *Journal of Business Ethics, 46*, 351–361.

Simola, S. (2005). Concepts of care in organizational crisis prevention. *Journal of Business Ethics, 62*, 341–353.

Simon, H. (1959). Theories of decision making in economics and behavioral science. *American Economic Review*, 253–283.

Siomkos, G. J. & Kurzbard, G. (1994). The hidden crisis in product harm crisis management. *European Journal of Marketing, 28*(2), 30–41.

Skelton, R. & Miller, V. (n.d.). The environmental justice movement. Retrieved December 31, 2007 from www.nrdc.org/ej/history/hej.asp.

Slone, M. (2000). Responses to media coverage of terrorism. *Journal of Conflict Resolution, 44*(4): 508–523.

Smith, M. E. & Ferguson, D. P. (2001). Activism. In R. L. Heath (Ed.), *Handbook of Public Relations* (pp. 291–300). Thousand Oaks, CA: Sage.

Smith, M. F. (2005). Activism. In R. L. Heath (Ed.), *Encyclopedia of public relations* (pp. 5–9). Thousand Oaks, CA: Sage.

Socrates (2007). Retrieved September 16, 2007 from www.kld.com/research/socrates/index.html.

Solomon, D. S. (1981). A social marketing perspective on campaigns. In R. E. Rice & W. J. Paisley (Eds.), *Public communication campaigns* (pp. 281–292). Beverly Hills: Sage.

Sour gas (2008). Retrieved September 28, 2008 from www.centreforenergy.ca/silos/ong/ongEnvironment/usOilAndGasIndEnvAir04.asp.

Spencer, R. (2008, September 29). China milk scandal: Cadbury recalls dairy milk bars. Retrieved November 10, 2008 from www.telegraph.co.uk/news/worldnews/asia/china/3102123/China-milk-scandal-Cadbury-recalls-Dairy-Milk-bars.html.

Spicer, C. H. (1993). Images of public relations in the print media. *Journal of Public Relations Research, 5*, 47–61.

Spin Master recalls aqua dots (2007, November 7). Retrieved December 19, 2007 from www.cpsc.gov/cpscpub/prerel/prhtml08/08074.html.

Stacks, D. W. (2002). *Primer of public relations research.* New York: Guilford Press.

Starbucks admits "break down" in customer service (2005). Retrieved August 11, 2006 from www.greenlagirl.com/2005/10/15/starbucks-admits-break-down-in-customer-service/.

Starbucks Challenge 3.0: Demand an answer! (2006). Retrieved August 11, 2006 from www.greenlagirl.com/2005/12/03/starbucks-challenge-30–demand-an-answer-2/.

Stauber, J. & Rampton, S. (1995). *Toxic sludge is good for you! Lies, damn lies and the public relations industry.* Monroe, ME: Common Courage Press.

Stoker, K. (2005). Utilitarianism. In R. L. Heath (Ed.), *Encyclopedia of public relations,* Vol. 2 (pp. 883–885). Thousand Oaks, CA: Sage.

Strategic communications planning (n.d.). Retrieved May 15, 2008 from www.spinproject.org/article.php?id=113.

Stratospheric ozone (2007, September 13). Retrieved January 8, 2008 from www.epa.gov/ozone/.

Sturges, D. L. (1994). Communicating through crisis: A strategy for organizational survival. *Management Communication Quarterly, 7*, 297–316.

Sunday Times "best companies to work for" (2007). Retrieved September 17, 2007 from www.bestcompanies.co.uk//Overview.aspx.

Sustainability reporting framework (n.d.). Retrieved March 15, 2008 from www.global-reporting.org/ReportingFramework/ReportingFrameworkDownloads/.

Taco Bell responds to FDA and CDC (2006, December 13). Retrieved December 14, 2006 from www.tacobell.com.

Tate, C. (1999). *Cigarette wars: The triumph of the "little white slaver."* New York: Oxford University Press.

Taylor, M. (2000). Toward a public relations approach to nation building. *Journal of Public Relations Research, 12*(2), 1–14.

Taylor, M. & Kent, M. L. (2006). Public relations theory and practice in nation building. In C. H. Botan & V. Hazleton (Eds.), *Public relations theory II* (pp. 341–357). Mahwah, NJ: Lawrence Erlbaum Associates.

Taylor, M. & Kent, M. L. (2007). Taxonomy of mediated crisis responses. *Public Relations Review, 33*(2), 140–146.

Taylor, M., Kent, M. L., & White, W. J. (2001). How activist organizations are using the Internet to build relationships. *Public Relations Review, 27*, 263–284.

Taylor, M. & Perry, D. C. (2005). Diffusion of traditional and new media tactics in crisis communication. *Public Relations Review, 31*(2), 209–217.

Taylor, M., Vasquez, G. M., & Doorley, J. (2003). Merck and AIDS activists: Engagement as a framework for extending issues management. *Public Relations Review, 29*, 257–270.

Thomas, C. (2003). Cyberactivism and the corporations: New strategies for new media. In S. John & S. Thomson (Eds.), *New activism and the corporate response* (pp. 115–135). New York: Palgrave Macmillan.

Transparency (n.d.). Retrieved March 3, 2008 from www.financialdictionary.thefreedictionary.com/transparency.

Transparent (n.d.). Retrieved March 4, 2008 from www.merriam-webster.com/dictionary/transparent.

Treadwell, D. & Treadwell, J. B. (2005). *Public relations writing: Principles and practice*, 2nd edn. Thousand Oaks, CA: Sage.

The trust index (2009). Retrieved March 19, 2009 from www.greatplacetowork.com/best/trust-index.php.

Tsetsura, K. (2008). An exploratory study of media relations practices. Retrieved February 20, 2008 from www.instituteforpr.org/research_single/an_exploratory_study_of_global_media_relations_practices/.

Tuchman, G. (1981). The missing dimensions: News media and the management of social change. In E. Katz & T. Szecsko (Eds.), *Mass media and social change* (pp. 63–82). Beverly Hills, CA: Sage.

Tucker, L. & Melewar, T. C. (2005). Corporate reputation and crisis management: The threat and manageability of anti-corporatism. *Corporate Reputation Review, 7,* 377–387.

Twardy, S. A. (1994). Attorneys and public relations professionals must work hand-in-hand when responding to an environmental investigation. *Public Relations Quarterly, 39*(2), 15–16.

Tye, L. (1998). *The father of spin: Edward Bernays and the birth of public relations.* New York: Crown Publishers.

Tyler, L. (1997). Liability means never being able to say you're sorry: Corporate guilt, legal constraints, and defensiveness in corporate communication. *Management Communication Quarterly, 11*(1), 51–73.

Ulmer, R. R., Sellnow, T. L., & Seeger, M. W. (2006). *Effective crisis communication: Moving from crisis to opportunity.* Thousand Oaks, CA: Sage.

US Chemical Safety and Hazard Investigation Board (2007, March 20). Investigation report: Refinery explosion and fire. Retrieved April 2, 2008 from www.csb.gov/completed_investigations/docs/CSBFinalReportBP.pdf.

US Department of Health and Human Services (2002). *Communicating in a crisis: Risk communication guidelines for public officials.* Washington, DC: Department of Health and Human Services.

van de Donk, W., Loader, B. D., Nixon, P. G., & Rucht, D. (2004). *Cyberprotest: New media, citizens and social movements.* New York: Routledge.

Vogel, D. (1989). *Fluctuating fortune: The political power of business in America.* New York: Basic Books.

Wang, J. (2006). Managing national reputation and international relations in the global era: Public diplomacy revisited. *Public Relations Review, 32,* 91–96.

Wartick, S. L. (1992). The relationship between intense media exposure and change in corporate reputation. *Business and Society, 31,* 33–42.

Watts, E. K. (2001). Voice and voicelessness in rhetorical studies. *Quarterly Journal of Speech, 87,* 179–196.

Weick, K. E. (1979). *The social psychology of organizing*, 2nd edn. Reading, MA: Addison-Wesley.

Weiner, B. (2006). *Social motivation, justice, and the moral emotions: An attributional approach.* Mahwah, NJ: Lawrence Erlbaum Associates.

Weinreich, N. K. (n.d.). What is social marketing? Retrieved January 13, 2008 from www.social-marketing.com/Whatis.html.

Werder, K. P. (2006). Responding to activism: An experimental analysis of public relations strategy influence on attributes of publics. *Journal of Public Relations Research, 18,* 335–356.

Werther, W. B., Jr. & Chandler, D. (2006). *Strategic corporate social responsibility: Stakeholders in a global environment.* Thousand Oaks, CA: Sage.

What is a SLAPP? (n.d.). Retrieved December 15, 2007 from www.slapps.org/faq.htm.

What we have here is environmental injustice at both ends of the spectrum (n.d.). Retrieved December 31, 2007 from www.gather.com/viewArticle.jsp?articleId=281474976939534.

What we're doing (n.d.). Retrieved February 4, 2008 from www.plana.marksandspencer.com/we-are-doing.

Whose partnership for whose development? Corporate accountability in the UN system beyond the global compact (2007). Retrieved May 9, 2008 from www.globalpolicy.org/reform/business/2007/0801whosepartnership.pdf.

Wiebe, G. D. (1952). Merchandising commodities and citizenship on television. *Public Opinion Quarterly, 15,* 679–691.

Williams, A. B. (2008, April 28). Burger King VP puts self on grill. Retrieved May 2, 2008 from www.news-press.com/apps/pbcs.dll/article?AID=/20080704/NEWS01/80705023/1014.

Wilner, F. N. (2008, March 31). Lobbying loopholes and antitrust. Retrieved October 3, 2008 from www.trafficworld.com/newssection/columns.asp?id=45762.

Wilson, J. (2002). The sponsorship scam. In E. Lubbers (Ed.), *Battling big business: Countering greenwash, infiltration and other forms of corporate bullying* (pp. 44–52). Monroe, ME: Common Courage Press.

Witte, K., Meyer, G., & Martell, D. (2001). *Effective health risk messages: A step-by-step guide.* Thousand Oaks, CA: Sage.

WOMMA (n.d.). WOMMA is … word of mouth marketing. Retrieved December 5, 2007 from www.womma.com/about/.

Wood, A. F. & Smith, M. J. (2001). *Online communication: Linking technology, identity, and culture.* Mahwah, NJ: Lawrence Erlbaum Associates.

Workers satisfied with company's responsibility are more engaged and positive, study shows (2007, May 2). Retrieved May 10, 2008 from www.sirota.com/pressrelease/5-CSR_Release_050207.pdf.

Yalovenko, A. (2005). Can the media help to fight terrorism? *International Affairs, 51*(5), 96–101.

Young, J. H. (1981). The long struggle for the 1906 law. Retrieved October 1, 2008 from www.cfsan.fda.gov/ lrd/history2.html.

Zhang, J. (2007). Beyond anti-terrorism: Metaphors as message strategy of post-September-11 US public diplomacy. *Public Relations Review, 33,* 31–39.

Zhang, J. & Cameron, G. T. (2003). China's agenda building and image polishing in the US: Assessing an international public relations campaign. *Public Relations Review, 29,* 13–28.

Zielenziger, M. & Bussey, J. (1999, December 1). Protests paralyze Seattle. *Philadelphia Inquirer,* p. A1.

Zinn, H. (2005). *A people's history of the United States: 1492 to present.* New York: Harper-Perennial Modern Classics.

Zoch, L. M. & Molleda, J. C. (2006). Building a theoretical model of media relations using framing, information subsidies, and agenda-building. In C. H. Botan & V. Hazleton (Eds.), *Public relations theory II* (pp. 279–309). Mahwah, NJ: Lawrence Erlbaum Associates.

Zuckerman, M. (1979). Sensation seeking: Beyond the optimal level of arousal. Hillsdale, NJ: Lawrence Erlbaum Associates.

Index